THE BATTLE FOR BOND

The Genesis of Cinema's Greatest Hero

ROBERT SELLERS

First published in 2007 by
Tomahawk Press
PO Box 1236
Sheffield S11 7XU
England

www.tomahawkpress.com

© Robert Sellers 2007

The right of Robert Sellers to be identified as the author of this work is hereby asserted in accordance with the Copyright, Designs and Patents Act 1988.

All rights reserved. No part of this publication may be reproduced or transmitted in any form or by any means, electronic or mechanical, including photocopy, recording, or other information retrieval system, without permission in writing from the publisher.

ISBN-10: 0-9531926-3-6
ISBN-13: 978-0-9531926-3-2

Edited by Bruce Sachs

Designed by Steve Kirkham – Tree Frog Communication 01245 445377

Printed in the EU by Gutenberg Press Limited

Picture Credits
All photographs used in this book are owned by private individuals. If we have inadvertently published a photograph without credit, please contact the publishers so that the omission can be corrected in the next printing.

A catalogue record for this book is available from the British Library.

ACKNOWLEDGMENTS

I wish to thank all those who kindly gave of their time to be interviewed for this book:

SIR KEN ADAM
VIC ARMSTRONG
RICOU BROWNING
EARL CAMERON
BARBARA CARRERA
DICK CLEMENT
LEN DEIGHTON
GUY HAMILTON
RICHARD JENKINS
IRVIN KERSHNER
JORDAN KLEIN
GEORGE LEECH
LUCIANA PALUZZI
MOLLIE PETERS
PAMELA SALEM
JEREMY VAUGHAN
SYLVAN WHITTINGHAM MASON
NIKKI VAN DER ZYL

Special thanks must go to Sylvan Whittingham Mason. Without her sterling support and efforts, this book wouldn't exist. Thanks also for the use of documents and photographs from the Whittingham family archive. For more information visit Sylvan's website – www.sylvanmason.com.

My thanks also go to Raymond Benson for supplying a terrific foreword and also to my publisher and editor, Bruce Sachs of Tomahawk Press. Special thanks too to our designer, Steve Kirkham for work beyond the call of duty. I'd also like to thank Len Deighton and Graham Rye for agreeing to endorse my book and for their very kind and encouraging words.

And lastly thanks to my family, who however hard they try to understand my passion for all things Bond, fail miserably, but continue to support me anyway.

FOREWORD
BY RAYMOND BENSON

Over twenty-five years ago I embarked on a personal labour of love that resulted in a book entitled *The James Bond Bedside Companion*. It took me roughly three years to complete and was first published in the United States in 1984. An updated second edition was published in both America and the United Kingdom in 1988. I'm very flattered when Bond fans have come up to me over the years to tell me that the *Bedside Companion* is their Bond "Bible". Little did I know back then that I would one day be asked by Ian Fleming's literary business, Glidrose Publications Ltd. (now called Ian Fleming Publications Ltd.), to write original continuation 007 novels.

While much of my fascination and interest in Fleming's creation began for me in 1964, when I first saw the film *Goldfinger*, most of my knowledge and expertise in the character was garnered during my exhaustive research forays for the *Bedside Companion* between 1981 and 1983. It was over these years that I began a correspondence – and ultimately a friendship – with several of Ian Fleming's closest friends and family members. Among these were two people closely associated with the subject of Robert Sellers' book, i.e., the tortured history of *Thunderball*. I'm speaking of Ivar Bryce and Ernest Cuneo, two of the key players in the original conception of the "Thunderball Film Project" of 1959-1960.

I first met Ernest Cuneo in Washington D.C. in the spring of 1982. I had found him through his publisher (Cuneo was a terrific author of several non-fiction works, including a biography of New York City Mayor Fiorello LaGuardia, for whom Cuneo worked during the 1930s). Cuneo graciously met with me over dinner and we began a warm camaraderie that lasted until his death in 1988. Cuneo, as this book will reveal, came up with the original two-page "outline" that was the catalyst for the *Thunderball* story. This occurred one weekend in May 1959, when Ian Fleming, Ivar Bryce, filmmaker Kevin McClory, and Cuneo met at Black Hole Hollow Farm, Bryce's country estate in upper New York State. Fleming later paid tribute to Cuneo for the original outline by dedicating his 1961 novel *Thunderball* "To Ernest Cuneo-Muse."

Cuneo and I got along so well that he agreed to write the Introduction to the *Bedside Companion*, a gesture for which I am eternally grateful.

I met Ivar Bryce at his fabulous mansion Moyns Park, near Birdbrook, in England during the summer of 1982. Bryce was perhaps Fleming's closest friend, having met when they were children. Throughout Fleming's life, the author shared wild adventures with Bryce (Fleming's wife always considered Bryce to be a bad influence on her husband!). Bryce, an eternal playboy and man of the world, lived a life that some might say was an inspiration for James Bond. He served in British Intelligence during the war (Cuneo also did so for the Americans), was a risk-taker and gambler, and a ladies' man. He was also one of the gentlest and kindest men I've ever met.

Both Cuneo and Bryce shared with me some of their recollections of the *Thunderball* case, much of which appeared in my *Bedside Companion*. Even so, it was evident that the case was complicated and convoluted—it would take more than two people to make sense out of it.

That same year I also had the pleasure of meeting Kevin McClory, who was busy working on the rogue *Thunderball* remake, *Never Say Never Again*. McClory was very generous and kind, and he and I met at least three times when he was passing through New York. He gave me *his* version of the story, which I also attempted to spell out in the *Bedside Companion*. Needless to say, some of the tales conflicted with what I had previously learned.

Many years later, in 1998, I was called upon by MGM to help them in the court case that McClory had launched against the studio (and the EON Productions' Bond films). I was made privy to all the various scripts, outlines, and notes by Fleming, Cuneo, McClory, and Jack Whittingham, and asked to write a couple of reports reflecting my thoughts on the case. Nothing I wrote was used; in the end, MGM must have thought everything I had to say was just as conflicting as it was in the early 80s when I was writing the *Bedside Companion*.

In other words, the truth was elusive.

Robert Sellers has done a monumental job breaking through the complexities of the *Thunderball* case. Wisely, he has left it up to the reader to make up his or her mind as to what really happened. What he does do is provide an entertaining and thought provoking treatise on how projects in Hollywood can go terribly awry … or wonderfully successful … depending on how one looks at it!

Raymond Benson
Autumn 2006

Between 1996 and 2002 Raymond Benson wrote six original James Bond 007 novels, three film novelisations, and three short stories—all published worldwide. THE JAMES BOND BEDSIDE COMPANION was published in 1984 and was nominated for an Edgar. As "David Michaels" Raymond was the author of the NY Times best-sellers TOM CLANCY'S SPLINTER CELL and TOM CLANCY'S SPLINTER CELL – OPERATION BARRACUDA. Raymond's recent original thrillers are FACE BLIND, EVIL HOURS, and SWEETIE'S DIAMONDS. www.raymondbenson.com

INTRODUCTION

"Every so often, the law shakes off its cobwebs to produce a story far too improbable even for the silver screen – too fabulous even for the world of 007. This is one of those occasions, for the case before us has it all."
A US judge's 2001 summing up of Kevin McClory's 40-year dispute over the parentage and ownership of the movie James Bond.

Cinema history might have been very different had the first James Bond film not been *Dr. No* starring Sean Connery, but instead *Thunderball* directed by Alfred Hitchcock and starring Richard Burton as agent 007. It sounds preposterous and unbelievable, but it almost happened.

The story is the most fascinating, certainly the most controversial, in the entire history of James Bond. It began way back in 1958 when maverick Irish producer Kevin McClory collaborated with 007 creator Ian Fleming and screenwriter Jack Whittingham on a film script that was eventually entitled *Thunderball*. Had the project gone ahead it would have been the first ever James Bond movie, a full four years before the series actually began in 1962. But it was never made and when the audacious enterprise fizzled out Fleming used the screenplay as the basis for his new Bond novel without seeking permission. Feeling betrayed McClory and Whittingham sued for plagiarism resulting in one of the biggest media trials of the 20th century, the outcome of which was to change the screen fate of 007 forever and put the man who created James Bond into an early grave.

McClory walked away from the court case armed with the means to make his own Bond movie independently of the established Sean Connery series, something any producer in the world would've sold his granny for. Instead he decided to join forces with the official Bond team of Albert R. Broccoli and Harry Saltzman, making *Thunderball* a one-off joint production. Hitting screens in 1965 *Thunderball* became the most financially successful Bond movie ever made. In America alone an incredible 58 million people went to see it. No other Bond film has ever matched its popularity.

McClory also retained the option to remake *Thunderball*, resulting in 1983's *Never Say Never Again*, notable for the return of Sean Connery to the Bond role after a 12-year absence. But a calamitous shooting schedule almost destroyed the film, with Connery comparing the production to working in a toilet and afterwards lamenting the fact he never killed the producer. No one knew if he was joking or not.

Determined now to launch his own 007 film series in direct competition with the formidable Albert R. Broccoli, McClory faced numerous legal battles. Most audacious of all were his claims that because *Thunderball* was the first ever Bond screenplay, it influenced every subsequent 007 movie, meaning McClory had personally played a significant role in the creation of the cinematic James Bond. Had this been substantiated in court it would have turned the movie-making world of 007 upside down, even threatened its very existence. Just how close McClory came to achieving his ambition is only part of the fascinating true story behind *Thunderball*.

AUTHOR'S NOTE

Thunderball isn't just the best Bond movie ever made; it's my favourite film of all time! Sad I know, but there you go. For me it epitomises all the best elements of the Bond series – exotic locations, casinos, violent action, sultry women, epic set pieces, sharp witty dialogue, outlandish gadgets and Connery's on peak form as Bond.

Not surprisingly I've always wanted to write a book on *Thunderball* but the journalist in me wanted something more than just an obvious "making of." Then one day I found it. While surfing the net I came across a site run by Sylvan Whittingham Mason, the daughter of Jack Whittingham, who wrote the first complete James Bond screenplay – *Thunderball*. I phoned her hoping she might wish to talk about her famous father. As I was later to happily discover Sylvan is one of the most generous people I've ever met and was only too willing to help all she could. That offer would lead to one of the most significant discoveries in Bond history.

Sylvan had already told me that she had all of her father's private documents, including the three draft versions he'd completed of the *Thunderball* screenplay, but there was more, much more. When I arrived at Sylvan's house, lying on the floor of her lounge were several brown cardboard boxes bound by red ribbon which she'd brought in just for the occasion from safe storage elsewhere. Inside were all the documents relating to the infamous 1963 *Thunderball* court case. These were the actual papers used by the prosecution in the trial and had remained unopened since then. McClory's key lawyer Peter Carter-Ruck had taken charge of them and just before his death passed them on to Sylvan's safe keeping. Now here we were opening them for the first time in over 40 years. What secrets would they reveal? What treasures would be uncovered?

Most of what you are about to read derives from what we found in those stained from age boxes. Inside were hundreds of private letters written by the main protagonists in the *Thunderball* story – Fleming, McClory, Bryce and others. There was Fleming's court statement and also McClory's which ran for almost a hundred pages. There were Fleming's two attempts at a Bond screenplay, written before Jack Whittingham took over the writing reins and so much else besides, all revealing hitherto unknown truths about this most controversial slice of Bond history.

And if that wasn't enough, we uncovered seven pre-production drawings executed in 1959, the first realisations of what a Bond film could look like three years before *Dr. No*. Bond fans never even knew of the existence of these drawings, let alone seen them before. All seven are reproduced in this book for the first time ever.

CAST OF CHARACTERS

PRINCIPAL PLAYERS

IAN FLEMING
Author of the James Bond novels.

KEVIN McCLORY
Flamboyant and resourceful Irish filmmaker and the first person to sense the cinematic potential of 007 forming Xanadu Productions in order to bring the character to the screen.

IVAR BRYCE
Life-long friend of Ian Fleming; financier and philanthropist, and partner with Kevin McClory in Xanadu film productions.

JACK WHITTINGHAM
Successful and experienced screenwriter hired by Kevin McClory to write the first James Bond movie script.

ERNEST CUNEO
American lawyer and writer and former adviser to Franklin D. Roosevelt; one of Ian Fleming's closest American friends and confidantes.

PETER CARTER-RUCK
Britain's top libel lawyer with a fearsome reputation and unrivalled client list. Hired by Kevin McClory to handle his prosecution of Ian Fleming for plagiarism.

SYLVAN WHITTINGHAM MASON
Daughter of Jack Whittingham.

LEIGH AMAN
Former Royal Marine and experienced film production supervisor brought onto the Bond project by Kevin McClory.

LAURENCE EVANS
Ian Fleming's agent.

CHAPTER 1
THE IRISH MAVERICK

Ever since James Bond's literary birth in 1953 with *Casino Royale*, Ian Fleming dreamed of transferring his hero's adventures to the silver screen. But each effort met with rejection and disappointment. It had started all so promisingly. In 1954 a deal was made (worth $1,000) with the American television network CBS to adapt *Casino Royale*, with Barry Nelson as 007. Peter Lorre starred as the screen's first Bond baddie, Le Chiffre. Fleming wasn't watching the live one-hour broadcast on the night of 21 October, which was just as well. Not only was it a bastardisation of his novel, but an utter bastardisation of the character of James Bond, reducing him to the persona of an American gumshoe private detective instead of the suave gentleman spy readers adored. At one point in the proceedings he's mentioned by his nickname of "card sense Jimmy Bond!"

A year later Britain's premier movie company, Rank, snapped up the film rights to the third 007 novel *Moonraker*, only to do nothing with it. Britain's top movie mogul Sir Alexander Korda had been so captivated by *Live and Let Die*, Fleming's follow-up to *Casino Royale*, that he'd called it one of the most exciting books he had ever come across and intended showing it to Carol Reed and David Lean for their opinions. Nothing came of Korda's interest or that of Stanley Meyer, the Hollywood producer of the hit TV series *Dragnet*. He wanted on option on both *Moonraker* and *Live and Let Die* but Fleming was asking too much money and the deal collapsed.

In 1956 producer and multi-millionaire Henry Morgenthau III approached Fleming with the idea of doing an adventure television series for NBC, provisionally titled *Commander Jamaica*, featuring a character by the name of James Gunn. Fleming set about writing a pilot episode that revolved around a gang of criminals on an island fortress sending Cape Canaveral missiles off course. Sound familiar? When the project inevitably fell apart Fleming used elements of the plot for his sixth Bond novel *Dr. No*.

By 1958 it must have seemed to Fleming that neither the British or American film and TV industries were interested in the potential of James Bond. However, a man called Ivar Bryce was about to change all that.

Bryce had been a lifelong friend of Fleming's. The two had first encountered each other as children on holiday in Cornwall. Bryce was walking along a beach when he spied, "four strong, handsome, black-haired, blue-eyed boys" building sandcastles. Invited to join in Bryce quickly singled out Fleming as the leader of the group. The year was 1917 and Fleming was just nine years old. The pair renewed their friendship at Eton, although Bryce was a few years older, finding that they shared common laddish interests such as playing truant and meeting girls. Both men were uncommonly attractive. Fleming sported the kind of matinee idol looks of an Ivor Novello, while Bryce's part Aztec-Indian origins endowed him with more exotic features. The writer Cyril Connolly was so taken by the pair that he commented, "It would be hard to imagine two more distinguished-looking young men; a Greco-Roman Apollo and a twelfth dynasty pharaoh."

It wasn't just good looks that the two men shared. Both came from similar stock, the upper echelon of the class system, which in the 1920s dominated every avenue of British life. Fleming's father worked for a prestigious banking firm, had considerable private wealth and counted Winston Churchill amongst his circle of friends. Bryce's family fortune derived from trading in guano, or bird shit, which was widely used as a natural fertiliser. Fleming's sense of adventure and living life to the fullest also found resonance within Bryce. Fleming's greatest fear was succumbing to boredom and throughout the years the two friends frequently went on holiday together or indulged in numerous escapades. They were always sending letters or cables to each other suggesting some new outlandish enterprise; every invitation closing with the warning, "Fail Not". So close were the two men that Bryce once said of Fleming, "There was very little in my life he did not know or share."

In 1952 Fleming married the former wife of Lord Rothermere, Ann Charteris, a coldly beautiful and strong-willed woman he'd first met during the war. When she became pregnant it was seen as the gentlemanly thing to do that at 43 Fleming, the confirmed bachelor, really ought to tie the knot. Terrified at the prospect of marriage and of having to provide for a child Fleming decided to try his luck as a novelist. The result was *Casino Royale*. Fleming intended dedicating the book to Ann but she objected strongly. "You do not dedicate a book like this to *anyone*," she said. Ann largely disapproved of her husband's creation, an opinion that only marginally decreased as the series of books met with success. For a man who was always seeking his wife's approval this was devastating. Ann always felt that Fleming should concentrate more on "serious" journalism with the Sunday Times, for which he'd worked for many years and continued to work almost up until his death.

Fleming and Ann honeymooned in Nassau and Bryce met them at the airport. Ann took an instant dislike to Bryce, considering him a bad influence on her husband. For the rest of the decade Fleming often spent his summers at Bryce's home in Vermont, but Ann never accompanied him on these trips. In one revealing letter in 1955 to Lord Beaverbrook, the famed proprietor of the Daily Express, Ann wrote of Bryce: "It's a pity Ian's so fond of crooks, particularly as Bryce is an unsuccessful one."

British born but an American resident, Bryce was a financier and philanthropist. Always on the lookout for new avenues to invest in, the movie bug had recently overtaken him after making the acquaintance of Kevin McClory, a young Irish filmmaker. McClory was a born adventurer too. Before making it in movies he'd already, according to early press reports, driven across the Sahara in a land-Rover in 12 days, tried prospecting for tin in French Equatorial Africa and been a crocodile hunter in the Belgian Congo, selling the skins for £5 each.

It was his flamboyant personality and zest for life that made McClory popular amongst the elite of British high society, and devilishly attractive to the most glamourous women in Hollywood. Such was his reputation with the ladies that while working on *Around the World in 80 Days* the other lads in the crew used to call him "around the girls in 80 ways". McClory even introduced Elizabeth Taylor to film entrepreneur Mike Todd, with whom she was later married until his untimely death in a plane crash in 1958. He was also romantically linked with Shirley MacLaine. "Kevin used to phone me from all over the world," MacLaine later recalled. "In winter, in New York, he would suddenly say, 'let's go

Chapter 1: THE IRISH MAVERICK

to Bermuda and do some skin-diving,' and he would take off within the hour. How well I remember those phone calls. Of course, he always reversed the charges."

McClory certainly heralded from fine artistic stock. He was descended from Alice McClory, grandmother of the Bronte sisters, and his parents were both actors on the Irish stage. Born in 1926 in Dublin, at school McClory didn't fit in due to crippling dyslexia, although the illness had one advantage, enabling him later to, "see and write visually for films." Drawn to a world of high adventure McClory joined the Merchant Navy upon leaving school in the early days of World War Two. On 21 February 1943 his ship was torpedoed in the North Atlantic and along with other surviving crewmembers managed to scramble into the captain's lifeboat. For 14 freezing and terrible days they drifted, with McClory assisting in the burial at sea of eight of his shipmates. Picked up off the coast of Ireland having travelled 700 miles, McClory was emaciated and suffering from severe shock and exposure. The sole of his boot had burst with the pressure of his swollen, frostbitten feet. Spending nine months in hospital, having completely lost his speech, the incident left McClory with a permanent nervous stammer, but also a new reverence for life.

Unable because of his stammer to find work as an actor, which had been his ambition, McClory was still resolute upon a career in films. His break arrived in 1946 when he gate-crashed his way into a £4-a-week job at Shepperton Studios as a boom operator, and fetching tea for the directors. Determined to get to the top McClory worked on classics like *Anna Karenina* and *Cockleshell Heroes* (produced, incidentally, by Albert R. Broccoli). He also developed a close friendship with legendary director John Huston when he worked on *The African Queen* (1951), going on elephant hunts together. Like everyone else on the crew McClory suffered from diarrhoea on location in the Bush. It was so bad that usually three or four people were waiting at any one time to use the portable toilet. One day McClory rushed out with his pants down round his ankles yelling, 'Black Mamba! Black Mamba!' He'd been sitting there when he looked up and saw the reptile moving above his head. The crew watched in silence as it slid under the toilet door and into the long grass. The Black Mamba is one of the few really aggressive snakes and highly poisonous. They're also known to move in pairs. As Huston later recalled, "From that moment all symptoms of diarrhoea in camp disappeared."

McClory subsequently worked for Huston on *Moulin Rouge* (1952) but really endeared himself to the director on *Moby Dick* (1956). Filming was hugely dangerous as it took place in the real ocean with a massive working model of a whale constructed out of metal, wood and latex, which was secured by a cable on the seabed. One day the cable broke and the model began drifting away. Huston knew it couldn't be replaced at this late stage and without it he didn't have a picture. Grabbing a bottle of scotch he climbed into the giant prop and shouted, 'lose this whale and you lose me.' As the crew looked on in amazement McClory and one of the assistant directors jumped into the roaring ocean and repeatedly dived under in an effort to secure the line. All the time the big waves were raising the whale out of the water and slamming it down again. "These men were risking their lives," Huston later wrote in his memoirs. "As tons of whale could come down, wham! But they did it, saved the whale, saved the picture, saved me!"

In the course of *Moby Dick*'s production McClory met Mike Todd, who appointed him director of foreign locations on his pet project *Around the World in 80 Days* (1956). Forming a small unit McClory spent five months location hopping 44,000 miles around the world, risking imprisonment in order to get the shots Todd wanted in his film. Shooting in Paris outside the Ritz hotel, the police co-operated by blocking off the road from traffic but 65 cars were still parked there, all locked, and would obviously look out of place in a period picture. No problem, McClory organised them to be towed away, breaking some of the locks with jammies. Unfortunately one of the cars belonged to the French Minister of Justice who kicked McClory and his unit out of Paris. But the Irishman sneaked back in again to surreptitiously film Phileas Fogg's balloon going past Notre Dame. As the police arrived in two black Marias, sirens wailing, McClory rushed out of the church's back door with the can of film and jumped in a waiting car to take him to the airport. In Bangkok a scene of a boat sailing down the river was ruined because of a busy trolley track in the background. Officials wouldn't help so McClory got his assistant to literally hurl himself in front of the oncoming tram to make it stop long enough to get the shot. The poor man was arrested for attempted suicide and McClory had to bail him out of jail. Once finished on *80 Days* McClory joined Todd in Hollywood and helped out in post-production, earning himself an associate producer credit.

One of McClory's closest friends during the late 50s and 60s was Jeremy Vaughan, who also knew Fleming well, as his neighbour in Jamaica. "Kevin was a smooth operator, an attractive character, but not a particularly pleasant one, certainly compared to his brother, Desmond, who was one of the kindest people you could ever meet. If a friend were in trouble, Desmond would always be there. Kevin would just tell you to piss off, if you weren't any good to him. He's been very cruel to a number of people over the years who thought they were his friends. The overdriving thing with Kevin was that he just wanted to be a celebrity, he wanted to be famous, he wanted to be 'look at me, I'm Kevin McClory'. He probably had some semi-professional technical interest in making a film, but he really wanted the glamour. He wanted to be amongst the people that he thought he should be amongst."

McClory was also a keen practical joker. He even formed a club of other like-minded rabble-raisers and jesters that included Errol Flynn and Trevor Howard. Early one morning in Hollywood as a big night-club was turning out, McClory drove up in an open car wearing a ghastly horror mask he'd borrowed from a studio. All the departing partygoers suddenly shrieked with fright and stampeded inside again. This was pretty typical of McClory's adolescent sense of humour, as was the fact that he had a detective friend in New York called Kelly whom he got to arrest people as a joke. Sylvan Mason, daughter of Jack Whittingham, recalls another McClory pastime: "He would see someone he knew in a restaurant and, on the basis that you don't normally look at who is serving you, would borrow a uniform and pretend to be the waiter at that table and spill things everywhere till they actually looked at him and realised who it was."

Jeremy Vaughan remembers one jape in particular: "In 1961 I owned a horse that won the Grand National and some time after that Kevin and I hatched this plot. He and his wife, Bobo, were going to give a birthday party to John Schlesinger, not the film director, but a South African who was a multi-zillionaire. And the gift to John Schlesinger from all three of us was what we thought was the one thing a super rich man would never have, and that was a gold casket full of horse shit."

Another gag was at the expense of Peter Carter-Ruck, McClory's lawyer on the *Thunderball* case. Ruck visited McClory in the Bahamas, bringing with him some important film contracts and was picked up at the airport. What he didn't know was that McClory was driving an amphibious car and without warning he violently swung the steering wheel and they careered off the road and into the sea. Splashing its way across the harbour, the car duly arrived at Paradise Island. "It was a little wet, with waves coming over the windscreen, forcing me to protect the contracts from the water." Ruck later wrote.

Exhausted after his strenuous efforts on *Around the World in 80 Days* McClory took a holiday in the Bahamas, his first ever visit there. Almost immediately he fell in love with the islands and walking along the beach one morning a thought gripped him. "My God, if you took a wide screen camera underwater it would be fantastic." The immense clarity of the Bahamian waters and the colour of it bedazzled him. No one had made a major underwater picture since Disney's *20,000 Leagues Under the Sea* back in 1954 and movie equipment had advanced greatly since then. No more so than wide screen techniques, introduced by leading studios in a bid to attract audiences away from television and back into cinemas. McClory's friend Mike Todd had pioneered his own wide screen process, Todd-AO, used on blockbusters like his own *80 Days*, plus *Oklahoma* and later *Cleopatra*.

Seized by the commercial and entertainment value of marrying an underwater adventure movie with the Todd-AO process McClory contacted John Steinbeck, the American author of *The Grapes of Wrath*, in December 1957 about the possibility of collaborating on a script about treasure hunters

Chapter 1: THE IRISH MAVERICK

Xanadu Productions letterhead.

in modern-day Bahamas. Steinbeck had worked in Hollywood but his interest in films, as he described in a letter to McClory in December 1957 had, "diminished to the vanishing point because of the lack of creative originality among picture makers." But Steinbeck was strongly drawn to McClory's proposal and after several meetings with the Irishman his enthusiasm increased. "Such a film," he wrote, "would be a work of art as well as being financially attractive, which is another way of saying that one hell of a lot of people would pay to see it." Though a short treatment was written, the project faded away.

Back in the States McClory bumped into Mike Todd, exuberant after the box office success of *Around the World in 80 Days*, which had also managed to pick up that year's Best Picture Oscar. Todd invited McClory to come and work for him again, but by then the Irishman was keen to strike out on his own and explained his plan to make the ultimate underwater picture. Todd liked the idea, but then McClory started talking about another script he was working on, this one based on a short story by American writer Leon Ware about a boy who runs away from home to live on the San Francisco Bridge. McClory wanted to switch locations to London and use Tower Bridge and a Cockney child. 'It'll have a lot of appeal and human interest.' He said. Todd wasn't convinced. "Kevin, make the underwater picture". Puzzled, McClory asked why. "Well, I know you Kevin and if you make this bridge film you'll go to festivals and win a lot of awards. But remember, you can't eat awards."

Ignoring Todd's advice (which turned out to be highly prophetic) McClory went ahead with his script for *The Boy and the Bridge* and it was his search for backers that led him to Ivar Bryce's door. The pair first met in January 1958 when McClory was out in the Bahamas working on the Steinbeck/treasure hunter project. Bryce revealed to him his interest in the movie business and that if he should have any suitable projects to get in touch with him in New York. Bryce certainly had money to spare, owning homes in Vermont, New York, London, and Nassau. Best of all was Moyn's Park, a country mansion in Essex with several hundred acres of park and woodland where Bryce and his wife Josephine could indulge in their passion for breeding horses and entertaining their friends in suitably ostentatious fashion.

Marie-Josephine Hartford was Bryce's third wife and part of her attraction undoubtedly was the fact that she was the granddaughter of George Huntington Hartford, founder of the huge American A&P supermarket chain and thus independently wealthy. They'd first met during a voyage on the *Queen Elizabeth*, during which Lord Beaverbrook had pointed out Bryce to some friends and said, "here's the wickedest man in Europe."

Knowing full well how difficult it was going to be to obtain finance for such a slender story as *The Boy and the Bridge* McClory sought out Bryce during a trip to New York in April. Bryce liked the idea, liked McClory's fun loving enthusiasm even more, and agreed to back it. Together they formed a business partnership, Xanadu Productions, named after Bryce's beach house in Nassau. On the terms of a contract dated 6 May 1958 Bryce agreed to provide the necessary finance and McClory agreed to act as the film's producer/director and assume the day to day management duties of the business, being paid expenses and a salary. He was also authorised to withdraw monies from the partnership bank accounts. Any net profits would be divided equally between them.

The day after signing the agreement McClory sailed back to England and rented a small town house in London at 7 Belgrave Place, converting the downstairs rooms into an office for Xanadu and living in a two bedroom apartment upstairs. He then set up the necessary machinery and organisation for producing *The Boy and the Bridge*. In collaboration with his brother Desmond and Geoffrey Orme, veteran screenwriter of several 1940s Old Mother Riley comedies, McClory wrote the script and hired key crew personnel. Notable amongst those was Leigh Aman, whom he'd first met on the set of *The African Queen*. Aman had a long pedigree in the British Film Industry, working first for Alexander Korda on films like *The Private Life of Henry VIII* (1933) then for Ealing and latterly John Huston. Aman had also been a Major in the Royal Marines during the War and took a leading part in the D-Day landings. His skill and experience as a production supervisor was to lend crucial support to the fledgling McClory, who'd never made a picture of his own before.

The Boy and the Bridge, which began shooting in August 1958 under McClory's direction, was to be a real baptism of fire for himself and Bryce. But the filmmaking experience for both men proved creatively stimulating and personally rewarding, despite a strain on their relationship when the picture went over budget. McClory's High Society connections also allowed things to run smoother than they might otherwise have done. The British Foreign Office personally stepped in and helped McClory "borrow" Tower Bridge for two months of filming and Princess Margaret was only too happy to attend the film's premiere in Mayfair. Although inexperienced as a producer/director to an absurd degree and practically unknown throughout the industry McClory at 35, acted as if he was already at the top and revelled in a luxurious bachelor's lifestyle that included his own manservant and a 120-mph sports car. In Hollywood he had his very own Cadillac.

Bryce was so enthused about the box office chances of *The Boy and the Bridge* after seeing a rough cut that he suggested to McClory that they should continue their movie making partnership. "There are so many pictures screaming to be made." He said in a letter to the Irishman dated 7 December 1958. During a reading spree McClory had come across one fascinating true story, which no doubt appealed to his adventurous spirit, that of Dr John Williamson who in 1943 discovered a vast diamond mine in Tanzania. Bryce meanwhile was toying with adapting Paul Gallico's new novel, *Flowers for Mrs Harris*. "The most touching and appealing story ever penned," he wrote. It concerned a London charlady who won the football pools and travelled to Paris in order to achieve her dream of buying a Christian Dior dress. Much more commercial was his idea to film the true story of one of the FBI's most notorious criminals. Upon capture he was held in a special detention fortress in New York but bragged to FBI boss J. Edgar Hoover that it was childishly insecure. "I can show you seven ways I could escape today, if I decided to." And he did just that. Recaptured, Hoover offered him the chance to choose which prison he wanted to spend his life sentence in if he designed an escape proof establishment for New York. Next day the criminal produced an impeccable engineer's blueprint, which the FBI built and maintained for years. 'Which prison shall it be?' Hoover asked. "Alcatraz", the man replied. "But that's the toughest of all", said Hoover. "I know", the man replied. "But all my friends are there."

One gets the feeling from Bryce's 7 December letter to McClory that he was immensely enjoying the buzz of being a part of the film world. Enmeshed as he was in the high finance world of tax experts, lawyers and bankers from morning to night Bryce couldn't help but find that all, "terribly dull in comparison to our enterprise, which will have an impact on countless inhabitants of this mortal world."

His mind now full of "grandiose ideas" and dreaming of "future peaks to climb" Bryce had clearly decided that *Boy and the Bridge*, far from being a one-off production, should be the launch pad for a whole slew of films from Xanadu, under the aegis of himself and McClory. He had acquired a

Chapter 1: THE IRISH MAVERICK

> KEMSLEY HOUSE,
> LONDON. W.C.1.
>
> 29th April, 1959.
>
> Dear Kevin,
>
> Here are some specimen episodes and I also enclose a short story, "Risico", which is an expansion of "Red Heroin".
>
> On the other hand, I would have thought that either "Diamonds Are Forever" or "Live and Let Die" would make good films, although there have been various offers for both these books, neither of them has been sold.
>
> For instance, "Diamonds are Forever" could be trimmed to a more straightforward narrative by cutting out the Saratoga chapters and taking Bond straight from New York to Las Vegas. Tiffany Case would make a good and unusual heroine and the location shots would not be difficult.
>
> The trouble about writing something specially for a film is that I haven't got a single idea in my head, whereas if you were to decide on one of my books, such as "Diamonds Are Forever", I could probably embellish it with extra gimmickry.
>
> Please keep the material I am sending you strictly to yourself and, if Ivar wants to read it, I would prefer him to do it in your office rather than to have these things floating around down at Moynes.
>
> I also enclose some editorial notes I had written for C.B.S. and which you may also find of interest.
>
> Yours ever,
>
> Ian.
>
> Kevin McClory Esq,
> 7 Belgrave Place,
> London, S.W.1.

Fleming's letter to McClory offering suggestions as to which of his Bond novels would make the best debut 007 film.

McClory's letter to Fleming confirming his interest in making a James Bond film.

> 11th May, 1959
>
> Ian Fleming Esq,
> 16 Victoria Square,
> London, S.W.1.
>
> Dear Ian,
>
> This is to confirm our conversation at the conference attended by Mr. Ivar Bryce and myself.
>
> Our Company, Xanadu Productions, have decided that we would like to go ahead with our plans to make a full length motion picture feature, based on the character created by you, "JAMES BOND"
>
> We are at present exploring the wonderful and secretive world of Bond, and hope to be able in the very near future to make a choice of the novel we should like to film.
>
> I have unfortunately had to enter hospital for a couple of weeks, but will be in touch with you just as soon as I am "allowed out".
>
> Sincerely,
>
> KEVIN McCLORY
>
> KM/bm.

certainty equal to that of McClory about what could be achieved by their debut feature. "Fame for you, a warm reflected glow for me, and some lovely real money to jingle in our pockets and throw carelessly back into further and grander exploits." Among those grander exploits Bryce had in mind a film about James Bond.

"Have you read any of the Bond books?" Bryce asked McClory out of the blue one day. The Irishman shook his head. "Then why don't you read them and tell me what you think?" In January 1959 McClory purchased copies of *Moonraker*, *Live and Let Die*, *Diamonds Are Forever* and *Casino Royale*. He didn't just read these books; he analysed and digested them. "I enjoyed them but didn't think they were particularly visual", McClory later recalled. "That each and every one of them would have to be rewritten for the screen – written in a visual sense." These views were later borne out, as most of the Bond films have indeed been major adaptations of the original source material. McClory also believed that much of Fleming's works were "steeped in sadism," which if transferred to the screen would be unpalatable to mainstream audiences, especially the young. But in James Bond 007, McClory knew that Fleming had conceived the most visually exciting character that if put into a cinematic formula using strong box office ingredients could be highly successful. "He leapt out of every page he was in," said McClory. "And clearly could be a great fantasy figure for film audiences of all sexes and ages."

It wasn't long before McClory was craving a meeting with Fleming, and Bryce dutifully obliged. Fleming obviously responded positively to their encounter, despite McClory's criticism of his work, because he sent the producer some specimen material, including a new Bond short story *Risico*, later published in the anthology *For Your Eyes Only*. In the covering letter, dated 29 April, Fleming argued, "I would have thought that either *Diamonds Are Forever* or *Live and Let Die* would make good films." Alluding to McClory's belief that his books would have to be rewritten for the cinema Fleming revealingly confessed. "The trouble about writing something specially for a film is that I haven't got a single idea in my head, whereas if you were to decide on one of my books, such as *Diamonds Are Forever*, I could probably embellish it with extra gimmickry."

On 7 May McClory and Bryce met with Fleming at Claridges and declared Xanadu's intention to bring Bond to the cinema screen for the first time. Fleming was happy to agree to them using the character of James Bond but asked McClory to send him an official letter on the company's notepaper confirming their interest. Despite being suddenly struck down from a duodenal ulcer, which McClory blamed on the intense amount of work involved on *Boy and the Bridge*, the Irishman wrote to Fleming from his hospital bed on 11 May to confirm. "Xanadu Productions have decided that we would like to go ahead with our plans to make a full length motion picture feature based on the character created by you, James Bond. We are at present exploring the wonderful and secretive world of Bond, and hope to be able in the very near future to make a choice of the novel we should like to film."

Where producers and studios had failed to recognise the filmmaking potential in 007, it had taken a relatively inexperienced Irish filmmaker to see what should have been staring more seasoned pros in the face. But what no one could possibly have realised at the time was that cinema history had just been made. The seeds had also been sown for 40 years of lawsuits, court cases, injunctions, betrayals, deaths and broken lives.

CHAPTER 2
THE FIRST JAMES BOND MOVIE PLOT

Fleming was obviously flattered that someone in the film business was finally taking a serious interest in his character and he wrote to McClory the day after receiving his offer. "After seeing your work on *The Boy and the Bridge*, there is no one who I would prefer to produce James Bond for the screen. I think you would have fun doing it and a great success." Then about to go on holiday to Venice, Fleming stated his hope: that by his return to London, "You and Ivar will have made up your minds on your choice of a James Bond story."

But McClory's approach to Bond was radical. Ditching the idea of filming one of the existing novels, he was now convinced that the only way to go was to create a totally new Bond scenario, out of which would emerge an original screenplay geared entirely to the tastes and requirements of a modern film audience. McClory suggested that Bond was a character that would perfectly fit in with his own desire to make an underwater picture amidst the opulent setting of the Bahamas. In the late 50s the Bahamas was an unreachable paradise for most people, a world of millionaires, private yachts, palm trees and beautiful women; a playboy's haven ideal for someone like Bond. Nor had a Bahamian location been truly exploited before by movies. McClory positively bristled with the creative possibilities of merging the two elements together. Bond and the Bahamas - it simply couldn't miss.

This was agreed and the search was on for a story using James Bond, underwater locations and the Bahamas. McClory later claimed that he was also responsible for throwing into the creative mix the notion of an atom bomb and influenced by the recently released film *Al Capone*, his belief that the Mafia would be a useful ingredient too.

As news of the Bond project filtered out a new figure was added to the team, that of American lawyer and writer Ernest Cuneo. A former legal adviser to Franklin D. Roosevelt, both a well-respected and cultivated man, Cuneo had known Fleming since World War Two when the author was with British Naval Intelligence and Cuneo worked for General William Donovan, head of the OSS (Office of Strategic Services) – the forerunner of the CIA. In 1941 Fleming visited Sir William Stephenson, the man called "Intrepid", who had been picked by Churchill to be the Prime Minister's personal representative in the United States. In Stephenson's office on the 36th floor of the RCA building in Rockefeller Centre Fleming first met Cuneo, the man who would become probably his closest American friend.

After the war Fleming saw Cuneo whenever he was in the States. One memorable trip occurred in 1954. Fleming had never seen the Midwest or California so the pair took off by train to Chicago. Cuneo always liked to describe how the train was already pulling into Albany before Fleming had finished instructing the steward how to mix the perfect martini. In Chicago Fleming wanted to see the location of the St. Valentine's Day Massacre and annoyed Cuneo by describing it as "America's greatest shrine". The two men travelled on to Los Angeles, where Fleming insisted on paying a call to the LAPD and then flew to Las Vegas, where Cuneo proposed a casino crawl, with a difference. Starting at the Sands they bet one dollar on a game of blackjack. When they won their stake back, two glasses of champagne were ordered, drunk, and then it was off to the next joint where the same pattern was followed. In this way both men could claim to have beaten every casino in Las Vegas. Fleming used much of the material from his cross county trip in his novel *Diamonds Are Forever*. He even named a character in the book, a Las Vegas cab driver, Ernest Cuneo.

As Bryce's solicitor in the States, Cuneo had represented his interests in *Boy and the Bridge* and now flew into London to bring his highly charged legal brain to bear on Bond. Buoyed by the news that *The Boy and the Bridge* had been selected as Britain's sole representative at the Venice Film Festival, vying for honours alongside works from Ingmar Bergman and Akira Kurosawa ("A thousand congratulations," Fleming wrote McClory upon hearing the news. "This is a feather in your cap as tall as the Eiffel Tower!"), a meeting between the four main protagonists took place at Moyn's Park, Bryce's sumptuous UK residence. Here ideas bounced around for a possible scenario for the Bond project which tied-in with McClory's idea of some kind of underwater adventure: A notion that particularly appealed to Fleming, himself a keen scuba diver and personal friend of acclaimed oceanographer Jacques Cousteau.

During the meeting Cuneo carefully jotted down a rough plot based on the group's ideas. After returning to Washington he sent a memo to Bryce, dated 28 May 1959, detailing his idea. This was in turn handed to McClory, who later claimed that Bryce told him: "I do not know whether it is any good but have a look at it. It seems to use most of your ideas and so we might like it." McClory then sent a copy to Fleming.

Given that Cuneo's memo stands today as the first ever story outline for a James Bond movie, it was sent by the author with a cautious covering note: "Enclosed was written at night, mere improvisation hence far from author's pride, possible author's mortification. Haven't even re-read it."

It seems, given McClory's connection with *Around the World in 80 Days*, that Mike Todd's film heavily influenced how Cuneo approached the Bond film plot. He wrote, "Assume that part of the essential formula for *80 Days* was a fast moving plot, suspense, variety of scene, excellent photography and big name stars in bit parts." As Cuneo also understood it, what Xanadu needed was a movie that would qualify under the British Eady Plan. Set up after the war the Eady Plan was a government sponsored protectionist subsidy for home-produced films. If the Bond picture qualified a significant portion of its costs would be underwritten by the much put upon British tax payer. But to qualify, Cuneo observed, the cast and crew had to be at least 75% British.

The story also needed to take place in the Bahamas, where Xanadu was hoping to establish its permanent home. As early as February 1959 McClory and Bryce had broached the idea of setting up a studio in the Bahamas and making films on the island. The ambitious plan was to convert an old aircraft hangar at Oakes Field into two sound stages, which would employ some 100 English, American and qualified local technicians. McClory took Bryce to the prospective site on at least one occasion, walking over the roof of the hangar and showing him how it could be soundproofed to meet their purpose. Setting up base in the Bahamas made sound commercial sense. As part of the British Commonwealth it was within Eady subsidy boundaries, and as a Bahamian corporation any

Chapter 2: THE FIRST JAMES BOND MOVIE PLOT

```
              KEMSLEY HOUSE, LONDON, W.C.1.


                                  12th May 1959.



      Dear Kevin,


           Many thanks for your letter of May 11th and I hope
      that by the time I get back from Venice, on the 1st of
      June, you will be quite well again and that you and Ivar
      will have made up your minds on your choice of a James
      Bond story.

           After seeing your work on "The Boy And The Bridge"
      there is no-one who I would prefer to produce James Bond
      for the screen.  I think you would have fun doing it and
      a great success.


                           Yours ever,

                              Ian


      Kevin McClory Esq.,
      7, Belgrave Place,
      S.W.1.
```

Fleming's reply to McClory including the critical remark – 'There is no one who I would prefer to produce James Bond for the screen.'

profits the Bond picture earned in America would not be US taxable. Astutely, Cuneo also suggested that shares could be sold in the Bond picture, "assuring Xanadu Bahamas promoters a profit before it started shooting."

Cuneo set down: "Now, combining all of the latter, following is a basic plot, capable of great flexibility, but containing all elements, as outlined, financial and artistic. Offhand, a myriad of similar plots could be generated, but the following is illustrative."

In Cuneo's story an enemy agent has infiltrated the United Service Organisation (performers who travel the world giving morale boosting shows to Allied forces), with the intention of detonating an atomic bomb on an American base. Bond and his CIA buddy Felix Leiter are assigned to the case. Going undercover as a British entertainer Bond seeks the theatrical advice of Noel Coward and Laurence Olivier who work out a suitable routine for him.

Bond identifies the spy and follows him to the Bahamas where he quickly discovers that an East European power have a fleet of trawlers all equipped with watertight underwater hulls. Atomic bombs are to be delivered to them by enemy submarines, so the whole transfer operation can be conducted unseen. Before the bombs can be planted, Bond leads a unit of scuba commandos into a daring underwater battle with the baddies, while above the waves an evening of celebrations are taking place on the island with a huge concert featuring the likes of Frank Sinatra. Bond naturally emerges victorious. (*For a longer version of this script see Appendix 1*).

>   Washington.
>
>   May 28, 1959.
>
>
> Dear Ivar,
>
>   Enclosed was written at night, mere improvisation
>   hence far from authors pride, possible authors
>   mortification. Haven't even re-read it.
>
>
>   ......Ernest Cuneo.

Ernest Cuneo's memo to Bryce that introduces the first ever James Bond movie story line.

Cuneo included in his outline the hope that the American government would be willing to cooperate by allowing a British camera crew to film at certain US installations, perhaps even aboard their new aircraft carrier, The Independence. He also suggested that the plot could be engineered to take place throughout the British Commonwealth, everywhere from Hong Kong to Gibraltar, to comply with the Eady Plan. As for the star cameos Cuneo reasoned that many entertainers holidayed or worked in Miami during high season and could be flown over to Nassau, "for half an hour, cost very low. Kevin knows how 47 stars were bought into *80 Days* for peanuts."

The response to Cuneo's story outline was swift and positive. Fleming called it "first class" with "just the right degree of fantasy" and "a wonderful basis to work on." He was right. The stepping stones had been laid for Bond's historic move to screen stardom.

CHAPTER 3
ENTER SPECTRE

Despite Fleming's glowing appreciation of Cuneo's work, he saw problems with it too, like the lack of a heroine for his hero to dally romantically with. Cuneo had suggested one of the female entertainers could turn out to be CIA. "Love interest easy to insert," he wrote, offhandedly.

In a fascinating memorandum dated 15 June, Fleming suggested instead a new character, a beautiful double agent under M's control that assists the enemy spy. Her name – Fatima Blush. It's from her that Bond learns details of the spy plot. In the underwater finale Fatima would be on the enemy side and Fleming wrote: "Her appearance in tight-fitting black rubber suiting will make the audiences swoon." As the battle progresses the spy finds Fatima sabotaging his aqualung and realises that she's a double agent. In the ensuing fight Bond kills him just as he is turning off the valve in Fatima's oxygen tanks. "The curtain goes down as Bond and Fatima kiss through their snorkels," Fleming envisaged, adding, "My imagination has slightly run riot over this last scene but you see the point." Perhaps too much. At the trial McClory stated that he thought Fleming's idea of hero and heroine kissing through their snorkels "infantile." Indeed when the passage was described in court there were bursts of laughter.

After this memo neither the name nor the character of Fatima Blush reappeared in any of the subsequent treatments or screenplays relating to *Thunderball*, nor in the novel or the 1965 film. Fleming too never reused it. But it was too good a name to ignore and McClory resurrected it for the black widow SPECTRE assassin played by Barbara Carrera in *Never Say Never Again*, thus becoming one of the few bona-fide Fleming contributions in the film.

In his memo Fleming next turned his attention to Cuneo's proposed use of guest stars: "I am all for the light relief of the actors," he said. "But this should be kept very separate from the main espionage plot, which must be kept serious and entirely credible." Fleming was adamant that if the film was to work, its use of atom bombs needed to be expertly researched and presented accurately. "This story needs to be solidly tethered to the earth with technical and factual background or we shall be dangerously on the verge of farce."

By far Fleming's biggest criticism was with Cuneo's use of Communists as the principal villains. "It might be very unwise," he wrote, "to point directly at Russia as the enemy. Since the film will take about two years to produce, and peace might conceivably break out in the meantime, this should be avoided." So what to put in their place? Fleming's suggestion turned out to be the most significant contribution to the entire *Thunderball* story-line, and one of the most important for the future of the Bond legend – the creation of super villains SPECTRE.

An international terrorist group that's run with all the corporate efficiency of Microsoft or Shell, SPECTRE became Bond's recurring foe in the film series and in subsequent novels. As laid out in Fleming's memo SPECTRE, short for Special Executive for Terrorism, Revolution and Espionage (later modified to, the Special Executive for Counterintelligence, Terrorism, Revenge and Extortion), was: "An immensely powerful, privately-owned organisation manned by ex-members of Smersh, The Gestapo, the Mafia and the Black Tong of Peking." Its ruse, Fleming suggested, was "placing these bombs in NATO bases with the objective of then blackmailing the Western powers for $100 million or else."

Their headquarters, Fleming reasoned, might be "some large and well-guarded chateau in Normandy and we must be given a real idea of the hidden powers of both SPECTRE and the Secret Service." To this end Fleming confirmed that he had received full Foreign Office clearance for depicting the British Secret Service "as I have done in my books and nothing in the Cuneo story would appear to be a breach of security."

Like all great ideas more than one person has claimed responsibility for coming up with SPECTRE. McClory later argued that using some form of international terrorist group was his suggestion. The Bond books, he felt, were too obsessed with the "red menace" and it would work much better if the enemy agents weren't aligned to any specific government or political doctrine, but a private force. Both Cuneo and Bryce believed McClory came up with SPECTRE. But the Irishman's court statement only reveals that it was his idea to replace the Russians with the Mafia. No mention was made of SPECTRE. Significantly, various newspaper journalists covering the trial reported that it was agreed in court that SPECTRE "was an invention of Mr Fleming."

As for the origin of the word SPECTRE, as any well-read Fleming fan will know, the author had long been fascinated with this particular word. In the novel *Diamonds Are Forever* the villain has his own bogus western town called Spectreville. While in *From Russia with Love* the decoder Bond steals was named the Spektor, changed in the film version to Lektor.

Overall Cuneo's plot found favour with Fleming, though to the public at large the idea of holding the world to ransom with an atomic bomb must have sounded utterly preposterous circa 1959. Indeed Kingsley Amis, a Fleming advocate, called *Thunderball* one of the most implausible of all of the Bond books. Even in 1965, when the film was released, the scenario was a little far-fetched. But in recent years, notably in this post-September 11th world, the idea has become all too realistic and alarming, making *Thunderball* more relevant today than ever before, and politically the most far-sighted of the Bond series.

Upon receiving Fleming's comments on the Cuneo outline McClory's first inclination was to screw it up and throw it in the bin. "It appeared on reading Fleming's comments," he later wrote. "That we were very much in danger (if we followed his suggestions) of creating another far-fetched plot seeped in sex and sadism which might be excellent for a novel but would not be suitable for transfer visually to the screen by Xanadu." McClory now firmly believed that Fleming's earlier confession about not having a single idea in his head when it came to writing specifically for movies was correct so far as a James Bond screenplay was concerned.

CHAPTER 4
THE DEAL IS DONE

Early in July 1959 much was beginning to happen in the world of James Bond. As Fleming described it to Bryce, "Conflicting bids for and interests in part or whole of the James Bond sausage have been coming thick and fast." American television executive Hubbell Robinson had made a firm bid of $10,000 for a 90-minute TV version of *From Russia with Love*, and also wanted an option on a television series with a maximum of 44 episodes. "for a fat fee," wrote Fleming. Another American producer had offered a similar proposal, plus movie rights. And there was an offer of £20,000 and 15% of the profits on a British TV series. In desperation Fleming appointed MCA as his agents for all film, television and dramatic rights. In charge of those was the highly influential Laurence Evans, who also represented Alec Guinness and Ingrid Bergman. "So I'm in good company," boasted Fleming.

Fleming accepted the *From Russia with Love* bid (although the programme would never be made), but was deliberately stalling on everything else, only too acutely aware of Xanadu's Bond film proposal. In a letter to Bryce, dated 2 July, he urged his friend to hurry up and make a definite offer or he would be forced to accept the other bids. "Xanadu will of course get a most favoured treatment if and when they express a firm interest." Influenced no doubt by the powerful MCA, Fleming was out to get the best possible deal. If the *From Russia with Love* TV spectacular and Xanadu's Bond film were successes all past and future Bond material would acquire a greatly enhanced value. "And I am urged by MCA not to mortgage the future, except at a worthwhile price." Fleming then tempered his greed by saying, "I fear I must think of all these considerations since James Bond is my entire stock-in trade and I have not got the energy to create a new character."

Fleming was happy to act as creative consultant on the film, even write a draft script, providing he be paid a fee ("as you would have to pay any other writer for good material"), as well as a percentage of the gross profits. "I think that you should be clear in your mind how far you really want to go with this James Bond project and what terms Xanadu is prepared to lay on the line." Then it would only be a question of putting the proposal to MCA. "And I shall naturally press them to accept any reasonable offer. But I cannot afford to put the whole James Bond copyright in escrow in exchange for shares in a non-existent company."

Then came the crunch: "My own recommendation is that you have made one successful film, perhaps too expensively. You should now make a second successful film watching the costs a bit more carefully. This film should be a James Bond film and thus be likely of success under Kevin's brilliant direction." Fleming had been deeply impressed with *The Boy and the Bridge* when he saw it at a private screening at Shepperton Studios and wrote to McClory telling him so: "*The Boy and the Bridge* is a small masterpiece for which you can be said to be solely responsible."

Put simply, Fleming was offering Xanadu first refusal on the character of James Bond for movie exploitation. "And in him you have potentially a very valuable property if you can sign him up for several years." McClory was only too well aware of this. Why else were he and Bryce so intent on acquiring not just any old rights to make a Bond film, but the rights to make the *first* Bond film?

Having acquired those rights, there was no reason, suggested Fleming, why the Bond character couldn't then be sub-leased, first to Hubbell Robinson's TV *From Russia with Love*, then back to Xanadu for the feature film or later to a television series. Another ingenious Fleming proposal was that the same thing could apply in lesser degree to various subsidiary characters like M, Felix Leiter etc.

One gets the impression reading this letter that Fleming was desperate for Bryce to buy into Bond; to have someone he knew and respected owning the film copyright to his character rather than some faceless conglomerate or Hollywood cowboy producer. The concluding paragraph strikes a particularly friendly note: "Sorry to send you all this food for thought but the whole thing is getting a bit too big for me and, before MCA finally devours me, I thought I ought to give you a last clear think." He then added a PS: "If anything isn't clear to you in this letter, it isn't clear to me."

Fleming's letter did the trick and within days Bryce got in touch to make a firm offer - Xanadu wanted to go ahead with the Bond film. As payment Bryce agreed to send Fleming a cheque for $50,000, which the author would then use to take shares of equivalent nominal value in Xanadu. "I am really over-joyed that everything is now settled in this splendid and expeditious fashion." Fleming's reply to Bryce on 8 July was by way of being his letter of agreement – a contract if you will "which should be quite enough between us." Then came the legal bit: "In exchange for $50,000 worth of shares in the new company, I give you the right to make the first full length James Bond feature film. I will write a full suggested treatment which can be altered as you wish and I will provide editorial and advisory services whenever they can be helpful."

Within 24 hours of giving Bryce the green light to put 007 on the movie screen, Fleming was having second thoughts and wrote to Laurence Evans at MCA for advice: "Bryce is a very old personal friend and the rather airy suggestion at the moment is that remuneration should be in the form of shares in Xanadu, a company he has already formed but now being reformed in Nassau with a capital of $3 million. This is an awkward business due to the friendship element. Much will hang on the degree of success of *The Boy and the Bridge*."

Later that same day, Fleming changed his mind yet again and phoned Evans to tell him the deal with Bryce was done and that he would no longer be seeking his representation in the matter. But Evans was evidently uneasy about the status of Xanadu and his client's interest in it and wrote to Fleming on 17 July offering to have an unofficial look at the proposed terms. "I am not concerned so much with your ultimate remuneration from this project as with the certainty or otherwise of the film being made." Clearly Evans was anxious about the viability of Xanadu mounting a Bond film and with the pending American TV version of *From Russia with Love* was sure there would be renewed interest in Bond film rights. "It would be a great pity if our hands were tied by arrangements which were not clearly defined and suitably rewarding."

Evans was right; Xanadu's involvement had effectively put on hold other potentially more lucrative film proposals. But this didn't seem to worry Fleming, although the idea of a Bond TV series was still of interest to him. Even then, he was in no great hurry to conclude such a deal until the *From Russia with Love* special had aired and Xanadu's Bond film was in production, "since a television series would get off to a much better start if it were to follow these two productions," he told Evans.

Evans was concerned too about the strong personal tie between his client and Bryce and, using Fleming's own words, the "rather airy suggestion" that his remuneration should be in the form of shares in Xanadu. "This again makes me wonder if I might not be able to advise you to your advantage without creating personal difficulties for you. Perhaps you will think this over."

The advice was taken on board, but since Bryce was upset over the prospect of having to deal with his old friend through an agent. Fleming decided to proceed with the Xanadu deal without consulting Evans, for the time being. Personally he was satisfied with both the price paid and the share holdings, along with the plans Bryce had drawn up. All Fleming had to do now was finish, in his words. "a provisional script."

(FROM IAN FLEMING TO BRYCE)

2nd July 1959

I am ploughing on dutifully but painfully with a rough James Bond script which I hope to have in draft form by the end of the month.

Meanwhile, conflicting bids for and interests in part or whole of the James Bond sausage have been coming thick and fast and, in desperation, I have had to appoint M.C.A. as my agents for all film, television and dramatic rights. Their Mr. Laurence Evans, who knows Kevin, is the particular chap concerned here.

The point was that Hubbell Robinson telephoned again from New York yesterday and has made a firm bid of $10,000 for a 90-minute spectacular on television of "From Russia, With Love" but he also wanted an option on a television series, minimum 12 maximum 44 episodes, at a fat fee.

Through M.C.A. I have accepted the bid for "From Russia, With Love", subject to contract, but I have reserved the rights on all other Bond material.

A big independent producer, the Seven Arts Productions, Inc., have telephoned and written asking for much the same thing, plus movie rights, and I have written stalling them.

Meanwhile, Maurice Winnick stands on the sidelines with a provisional offer of £20,000 down and around a 15% of the profits on a television series. I continue to stall him.

All this brings me to Xanadu and they will of course get a most favoured treatment if and when they express a firm interest in the television properties but, in discussing the problem with M.C.A., they say whoever the company is, whether friend or foe, who acquires the James Bond copyright they should make a down payment for the basic copyright plus a percentage of the gross on any films or television series they may make.

Further, they point out that, with the appearance of Hubbell Robinson's spectacular, which is for the Ford Motor Company, and the subsequent appearance, if you decide to make it, of Kevin's Bond film, all past and future Bond material will acquire a greatly enhanced value and I am urged by M.C.A. not to mortgage the future, except at a worthwhile price.

They also place great weight on the time factor and they are concerned that whoever I ultimately trade with will have to go through the normal contract routine of laying down a timed programme of production. They say that otherwise, whether in the case of Xanadu or any other company, the producer might be knocked down by a taxi or the financial backer (save the mark) might be and I should be in the position of waiting for a never-never percentage of a never-never gross.

I fear I must think of all these considerations since James Bond is my entire stock-in-trade and I have not got the energy to create a new character.

Fleming writes to Bryce that he is, "ploughing on dutifully but painfully with a rough James Bond script.

CHAPTER 5
IAN FLEMING'S 'LOST' BOND SCREENPLAY

After careful consideration of Ernest Cuneo's suggested story, Fleming sat down to write a film treatment based around it using his own and McClory's ideas. But it didn't come easily to the author as it did one of his books. As he said in a letter to Bryce at the beginning of July, "I am ploughing on dutifully but painfully with a rough James Bond script."

It was completed by the close of July 1959. What's immediately noticeable about it is that either Fleming himself or his filmmaking partners were less than enthusiastic by the momentous introduction of SPECTRE, as here the Mafia has replaced them as chief villains. The story begins with Bond at a shooting range. Called in to see M, Bond learns that a Mafia gang, led by a huge bear of a man named Henrico Largo, are planning to raid a new rocket site in Shoeburyness, stocked with American missiles. Bond makes his way to a nightclub owned by Largo to check him out. There he meets Dominique (Domino) Smith, a member of Scotland Yard working incognito as a cigarette girl.

Disguised as a burglar alarm repairman, Bond enters Largo's private quarters, only to be captured. Domino rescues Bond but too late to stop the robbery. Largo and his men make off with a bomb to the Bahamas where they and other Mafia big shots hole up in a hotel. Already their demands have been made, a payment of £100 million in gold within 14 days or a vital western defence installation will be destroyed.

Bond is ordered to Nassau to begin investigations along with Domino. Once there, he meets Felix Leiter and together they agree to keep Largo's yacht *The Virginia* under surveillance. Bond makes an underwater recce of the yacht and is ambushed by a sentry but manages to escape.

Largo is suspicious of seeing Domino on the island and submits her to intense interrogation in his hotel room. Bond enters in the nick of time and saves her. A grateful Domino submits that evening to 007's carnal desires. The next day Bond and Felix, acting like tourists, water ski near *The Virginia* and spy Mafia frogmen entering the underwater hatch in the ship's hull. Bond persuades Domino to take a Geiger counter aboard to see if the bomb is there. Needless to say she's caught and tortured with a lighted cigarette.

Cover of Ian Fleming's draft treatment for a James Bond screenplay.

Meanwhile a US submarine has been trailing the yacht and as the Mafia set out to plant the bomb Bond, Leiter and their frogman army surprise them. A pitched battle ensues culminating in Domino killing Largo with a CO_2 spear. The battle won, Bond and Domino swim alone to a shallow alcove. Taking off their masks Bond kisses Domino strongly on the mouth. The credits roll. (*For a longer version of this script see Appendix 2*)

In an accompanying letter Fleming spelled out his hopes for the script: "My concern has been only

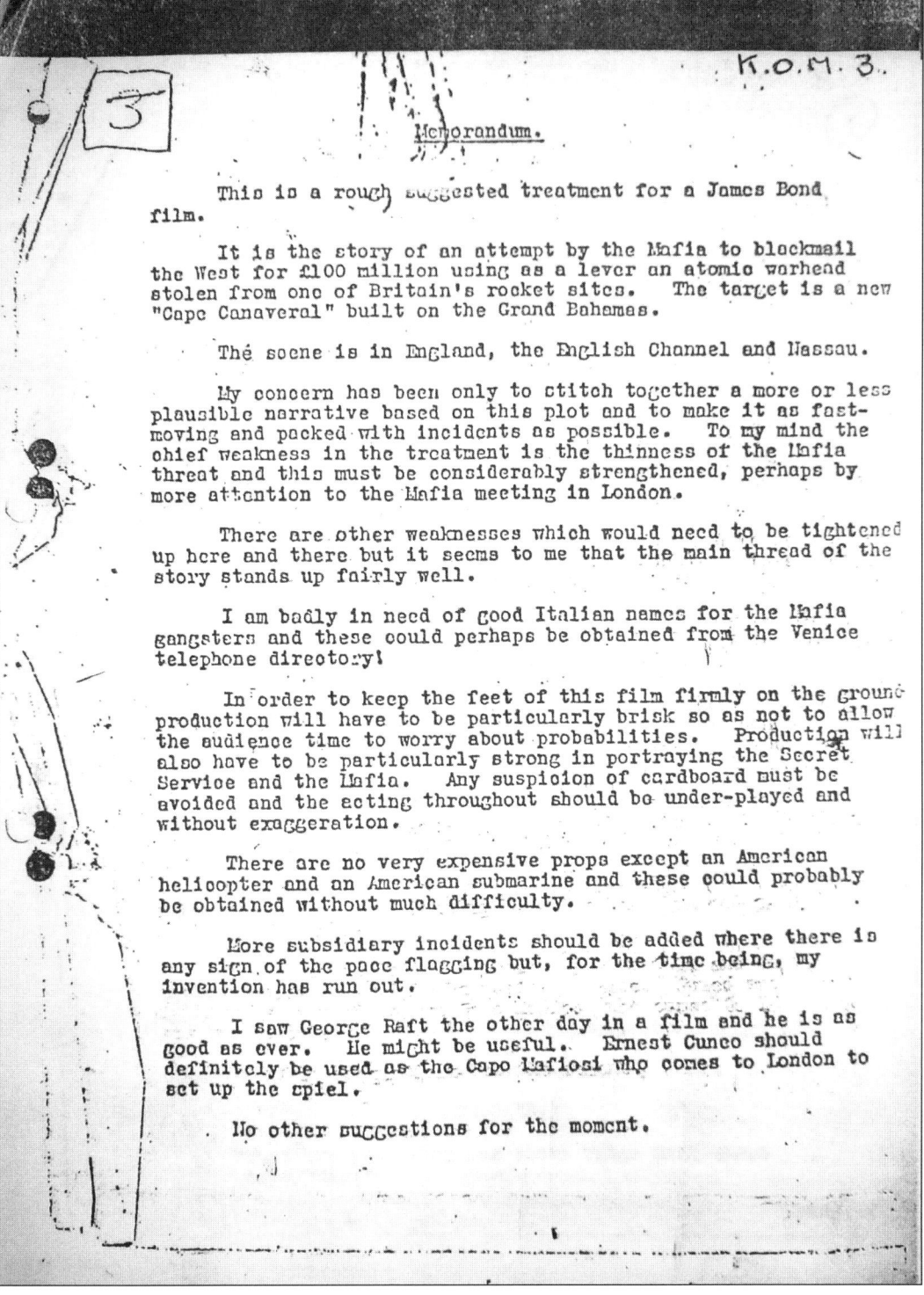

Fleming's covering letter detailing his hopes and personal critique of his intended James Bond screenplay.

to stitch together a more or less plausible narrative based on this plot and to make it as fast-moving and packed with incidents as possible." But he was well aware of its shortcomings, chiefly: "the thinness of the Mafia threat. This must be considerably strengthened. There are other weaknesses which would need to be tightened up here and there but it seems to me that the main thread of the story stands up fairly well." He was also badly in need of good Italian names for the Mafia characters. "These could perhaps be obtained from the Venice telephone directory!" it's cheekily suggested. In the end Fleming wrote off to a journalist colleague in Rome who provided him with a mixture of names of minor thugs picked from the crime pages of a Naples newspaper.

Fleming was also astute enough to realise that in order to keep the feet of this film on the ground the on-screen action needed to be particularly brisk "so as not to allow the audience time to worry about probabilities. Production will also have to be strong in portraying the Secret Service and the Mafia. Any suspicion of cardboard must be avoided and the acting throughout should be under-played and without exaggeration."

There were other suggestions too. Seeing a film recently starring George Raft prompted Fleming to muse that, "he is as good as ever. He might be useful." Was Fleming suggesting that the veteran Hollywood star, famous for his gangster roles, play Largo? Ironically Raft would appear briefly in 1967's 007 spoof *Casino Royale*.

Then most revealingly of all, Fleming wrote of his script, "More subsidiary incidents should be added where there is any sign of the pace flagging but, for the time being, my invention has run out."

At such an early stage of the story's evolution it's amazing just how much of what Fleming would eventually recycle in his *Thunderball* novel is already present in this his first film treatment – a stolen atom bomb, Largo and Domino, her taking a Geiger counter aboard the yacht, underwater battles. Many of the elements of the future cinematic Bond are in place too. His humour is more pronounced than the character was ever allowed in the novels, and his signature introduction, amongst the most famous pieces of dialogue in movie history, is spoken here for the first time: "My name is Bond, James Bond." But overall the treatment looks a bit rushed, as if Fleming didn't take the enterprise all that seriously. Certainly there isn't the same care and attention to background detail and characterisation which he brought to his novels. And there's a strong reason for that. To be brutally honest Fleming was hopeless as a screenwriter. The treatment tends to read more like a short story than a film script. Its biggest flaw is that far too much of the action isn't shown, but given to characters like M to describe in bum-numbingly long passages of dialogue. If this film was ever going to fly, 007's very own creator was going to have to take a back seat and allow someone else to come in and take over the reins. But who?

CHAPTER 6
LOOKING FOR A WRITER

To be fair on Fleming's rather ropey efforts at a film treatment, writing for movies is a totally different skill to writing fiction. Few authors have successfully traversed the two mediums. He was also a total innocent when it came to the film business, knowing next to nothing about its machinations, in one letter confessing, "The whole film world is a bit of a jungle to me."

So McClory took it upon himself to hire a screenwriter, satisfied that Fleming, while an established and experienced novelist, would be quite unable to produce a satisfactory film script. The man he chose was Paul Dehn whose first screenplay, *Seven Days to Noon*, back in 1950, had earned him an Oscar. At first Dehn was interested and met with Fleming, but that enthusiasm ultimately dissipated and he turned the assignment down, much to Fleming's disappointment as he expressed in a letter to Bryce dated 11 August: "Alas, Dehn can't take the job on for two excellent reasons. Firstly, he wrote a film script called something like 'Seven Hours to Midnight' (Fleming almost got it right), in which London was held up by an atomic bomb. And, secondly, he says that he is really only interested in the development of character in murderers etc, and this bang, bang, kiss, kiss stuff is not for him. On the other hand, he greatly likes the treatment and thinks it will be a terrific success." Just five years later Dehn, with Richard Maibaum, would write arguably the greatest Bond script of all – *Goldfinger*.

Despite passing on the project Dehn made some constructive suggestions, notably that the film start in slam bang fashion with the actual theft of the atomic warhead. Then Bond would make his introduction. Dehn also suggested Fleming contact screenwriter Janet Green, responsible for a recent well received police thriller entitled *Sapphire*. Although approached to write the Bond film, Miss Green proved unavailable.

Fleming noted that Dehn's two previous films as screenwriter, *On Such a Night* (1956) and *Orders to Kill* (1958) were directed by Anthony Asquith. Why not, Fleming asked Bryce, bring in Asquith as co-producer/director on the Bond? "It would have to be put very delicately to Kevin, but it does seem to me that there might be something in it as Puffin (Asquith's nickname) is immensely experienced, is now off the drink and has a great sense of style." This letter was the first instance of Fleming cooling to the idea of McClory as sole creative force on the Bond film. He even went on to suggest that Asquith handle the London sequences on the film and McClory the Nassau ones. "I leave this rather prickly thought with you," Fleming added, diplomatically.

It seems that the question of McClory's shortcomings stayed with Fleming as the following day he had lunch with Laurence Evans and asked his opinion on the matter. Evans didn't mince his words. Of course he thought McClory had talent and potential, but his first stab at movies with *The Boy and the Bridge* had not really come off, if the first batch of negative reviews were to be believed. Fleming wrote to Bryce on 12 August about Evans' misgivings: "What he is alarmed about is that, while we may all want big stars to feature in the Bond film, he thinks it very possible that people of the calibre we have been discussing may not wish to be produced and directed by a young man with only one film to his name and a film that has not found favour with the critics. He advises more or less on the lines of what I suggested in my last letter – that Kevin should be number 2 to a bigger man; say Asquith or Hitchcock for instance."

McClory later believed this letter showed, "the first seeds of distrust being planted in Bryce's mind by Fleming suggesting that I might not necessarily have the experience and should take second place to someone else." This was in direct contradiction to a Fleming letter of just four months previous when he'd told McClory, "There is no one who I would prefer to produce James Bond for the screen."

Laurence Evans was on the verge of leaving for Hollywood on a business trip and told Fleming that the Bond property was arousing great interest there. Why not, he suggested, have Xanadu team up with a big studio to make the film? The idea certainly appealed to Fleming, but not to Bryce, who'd endured recent sour dealings with American movie executives. "One in particular is so ghastly that I really cannot remain in his vicinity," he wrote Fleming. "This is what I want to avoid in the movie business. Life is too short to have to spend it with people it is disagreeable to be with." Bryce also made the point that a co-production with a big Hollywood studio would almost certainly disqualify Xanadu from benefiting from the Eady Plan.

Despite the grave concerns of Evans and Fleming, Bryce still had confidence in McClory and backed him up at a meeting in a London restaurant towards the end of July, just after the British release of *Boy and the Bridge*. McClory claimed that he told Bryce that in view of the less than favourable reviews their film had received, it was anyone's guess as to whether it would be a commercial success or not. McClory later wrote, "I told Bryce that as we had originally agreed to make one motion picture but had now got ourselves involved in the second I would like to give him the opportunity of withdrawing at this stage before we incurred any more expenditure. He insisted that we should continue." We only have McClory's word about this exchange. Although Fleming was present at that dinner, this conversation with Bryce occurred when the author was momentarily away from the table. Convenient?

Not only did Bryce wish to continue his partnership with McClory, he saw him as vital to Xanadu's ambitions, telling him so in a letter dated 14 September: "I see you particularly as the Master Impresario – the collector of the stars and other big wigs, colour processes and so on, as well as the producer and final authority on everything to do with making the picture." But more than most Bryce was acutely aware of McClory's erratic and difficult to handle personality. "Kevin is, unfortunately, someone who is impossible to control," he wrote Fleming on 25 August.

One of McClory's character traits that could easily run riot was his attitude to money, perfectly illustrated by the *Boy and the Bridge*'s debut at the Venice Film Festival in late August. "I have got a problem with Kevin and his passion for festivals, which cost a great deal and, I believe, bring in nothing," wrote Bryce to Fleming. Revelling in the business side of filmmaking, Bryce was less enamoured with the publicity end and hardly looking forward to 60 foreign journalists invading his yacht for lunch, followed by a cruise, then a press conference and finally a banquet for Italian officials. "I feel as if I was going to have a severe abdominal operation," he moaned. "And poor Jo (Bryce's wife); all the sort of people she detests even more than I do."

Chapter 6: LOOKING FOR A WRITER

Worse, McClory had committed *Boy and the Bridge* to the Cork Film Festival later in the year. "More, I don't know how many thousand dollars wasted," continued Bryce's rant. "And, though I should think we might well get an award, I cannot feel that it matters much either way. So I am going to speak to him very seriously about our whole program, and financial outlook. Given his head he would make us the laughing stock of movie-dom I fear."

Prior to the Venice Film Festival McClory had hired Stephen Grimes, John Huston's art director, to paint a number of scenes based on Fleming's treatment; Bond driving his trusted Bentley, Bond with Domino on the beach and several underwater tableau. These are utterly fascinating as they depict the first imaginings of what a James Bond movie could look like. Bryce was impressed too, referring them to Fleming as "Dreams, in my opinion. Wonderfully evocative and clear and attractive." They were put on display during the festival for viewing by attending journalists. In later years Stephen Grimes graduated from art director to full blown production designer working on such films as *Ryan's Daughter*, *Out of Africa* and, ironically, *Never Say Never Again*.

Besides personally escorting *Boy and the Bridge* around the festival circuit McClory also made a habit of popping into public screenings to gauge audience reaction. In one cinema he was surprised to see a large number of old age pensioners "when previously a lot I'm told have stopped going to the cinema because of the sex and violence," he wrote Bryce. "They found they were generally frightened out of their wits by horror pictures and at their age probably have very little time for sex."

While in Venice, McClory told Bryce that he would require additional funds soon as pre-production on the Bond film had begun in earnest and all monies were at present being paid for by payments deposited in the *Boy and the Bridge* bank account. Bryce promised that on his return to London he would give the Xanadu office a cheque for $10,000. McClory also hadn't been paid a salary now for several months. He'd first raised this issue with Bryce way back in February after having agreed to defer his salary when work on *Boy and the Bridge* went over schedule. However, since they were now continuing to make films, McClory, understandably, wished to go back on salary. He'd only been claiming expenses. Bryce agreed to this and as an interim measure lent McClory $15,000 that was to be repayable in due course from the activities of the partnership. McClory later claimed that Bryce lent him the money in order that he continued with Xanadu and not take film employment elsewhere.

But by August McClory was still not receiving a salary and raised the subject again in Venice. Bryce asked if McClory could carry on a little longer just claiming expenses because he was working out the details of the formation of the new Nassau-based Xanadu, which involved bringing in several shareholders. These new investors were Charles Wacker III, Bryce's rich friend from Chicago; Sir Francis Peake, an old Etonian baronet who now resided in the Bahamas; and Jean de la Bruyere, a young Canadian businessman.

As far as the Bond film was concerned Bryce still wanted McClory to be "the producer and final authority on everything," and also asked that a proper budget be worked out as soon as possible. Bryce put in writing the intermediate arrangement to pay McClory expenses during his pre-production duties but no salary until the new company was formed. As their relationship was still a friendly one McClory had no reason to doubt at that stage that Bryce would end up not paying him anything for his services on the Bond film.

With Paul Dehn having ruled himself out of the running to bring 007 to the nation's screens, another scriptwriter was sought. Bryce suggested to Fleming an ex-Cornish naval officer by the name of William Fairchild. Among his screenwriting credits were *The Gift Horse* (1952), starring Trevor Howard, Richard Attenborough and a certain Bernard Lee, and *The Malta Story* (1953) with Alec Guinness. Most significantly Fairchild had just written and directed *The Silent Enemy*, about the wartime exploits of naval frogmen in the Mediterranean, a picture that employed numerous undersea gadgets and underwater photography. "He might be the answer." Bryce told Fleming, and when Fairchild met with the author they got on extremely well and seemed keen to work together.

Early in September McClory saw Fleming in France, where the author was on holiday with Ann and their son, Caspar. Numerous matters were discussed, most importantly McClory's views on Fleming's treatment. McClory liked it but harboured misgivings, not least the idea of Mafia men disguised as US officers sneaking into a US base and just grabbing a bomb willy-nilly. That was straining reality. "Boy's own stuff," he mocked. As for the elaborate smuggling out of the bomb by means of a helicopter and thence to a waiting ship, it was "completely unrealistic and impracticable and obviously would have no chance of success."

McClory, who thought the bomb theft "the hardest-to-believe part of the story," brought to Fleming's attention a recent news report from The Daily Mail about a Victor Valiant Bomber that had disappeared under mysterious circumstances from Britain while on a training flight. So why not have the bomb heist occur in the air McClory suggested, by having a Mafia agent secreted on board, eliminate the crew and take over the plane. It was a wild idea and probably the first ever conceived cinematic hijack.

Fleming was not convinced, it just wasn't feasible; or was it? McClory thought if the film featured a carefully planned operation it wouldn't be difficult to persuade an audience of the credibility and possibility of a military aircraft being taken over in the air, and the sequence itself be made very exciting visually. But the problem remained of what to do with the aircraft once the baddies have captured it. The solution, as McClory saw it, was to force the plane to one of the outer islands in the Bahamas where there was no radar shield and belly land it in shallow water where it would be scuttled within minutes. "Thereby, shortly after the take over there would be no trace of the aircraft." McClory visualised that the pilot could wear breathing apparatus in order to escape the submerged plane and that the Mafia boss would have a yacht in the vicinity so that the bombs could be quickly recovered. Fleming still resisted changing the story but after a long discussion agreed to re-write the sequence to incorporate the new idea. One of *Thunderball*'s most realistic and impressive moments had been realised. Fleming had admitted, reluctantly, that McClory's idea was better suited for the cinema than his own. "He was also aware," McClory wrote later, "because of my attitude, that I would not be interested in the way that he had previously intended to develop the story, as his plot was much more appropriate to a novel, of which the reader can be induced to believe what cannot be put over credibly on the screen."

Following Bryce's promise that he would soon be arranging finance for the film, McClory re-engaged Leigh Aman to act as his production supervisor and general manager. Aman quickly began interviewing cameramen, editors, sound chiefs and other technicians with a view to obtaining their services for Bond. Underwater filming experts and divers were also sought out. McClory next arranged a meeting with William Fairchild and was impressed by his writing credits and by the man himself, but awaited Fleming's return to London before making any decision. Screening Fairchild's *Silent Enemy* McClory was amazed how similar some of the scenes were to those in the Bond script, especially in regard to an aircraft lying on the seabed. In *Silent Enemy* frogmen enter a crashed plane to recover a briefcase containing important documents. In the Bond story, it's to remove an atomic warhead. McClory ran several underwater pictures for research and gathered photographic material. Some stills of particular interest showed underwater chariots similar to those used by the Italians during the war for raids on Allied shipping in Gibraltar from concealed openings in the hull of a merchant vessel based in Spain. These were sent to Bryce and it wasn't just coincidence that underwater chariots were later used in the Fleming story.

A few days later McClory was observing underwater camera tests around the south coast of England. Such tests led to him investing in scuba diving lessons at his local swimming pool. McClory's enthusiasm for the Bond project was infectious in most of the letters he was writing at this time. About a trip to Weymouth at the end of September, for example, he wrote, "I am spending the weekend dreaming up new and exciting sequences for James Bond in my newly acquired aqua-lung."

McClory carried out other research too, writing to the US Government Printing Office detailing that he was making a film and was interested in publications about the workings of an atomic bomb. A list was duly sent to him which Fleming particularly made good use of. One wonders in today's climate just how far he'd get with such a request.

There was also positive news regarding a possible distribution deal with Columbia pictures. Mike Frankovich, the studio's head honcho in Europe, was enthusiastic about the Bond project and told McClory that with the right star and director Columbia would certainly be interested. British Lion Films also got in touch. "If you have not already finalised your distribution arrangements, we would be most interested in having an opportunity to participate." McClory too was making enquires at Shepperton as a possible studio home for the Bond film. "I must say that now I am back in London I think the project is most exciting," McClory wrote. "Certainly everyone I have spoken to about it thinks it will be great box office."

You will have to come here
in Nov. without a doubt.
I may be able to come to
London in October.   Sept 18th 1959.

                                             161 East 74th Street.

Have written this on 2 sheets of paper in my clumsy haste.

Dear Boy,

    I hear that you liked Bill Fairchild, otherwise have
heard little of events in the old world, since arriving here.
I have however seen the best film of my life: "North by
Northwest" Hitchcock, M.G.M. Cary Grant (as Bond) and Eva
Marie Saint (as Solitaire). It played to a packed audience on
the Q.M. and is in its 2nd month of doing ditto at the Radio
City Music Hall. While critics say "this implausible tale", it
is in fact, the most terrific Bond-style thriller - almost
plagiarising - and, superb. You must manage to see it somehow.

    There are differences, the man is a civilian dragged in
in error, the girl is the agent, M is a CRAGGY, horn-rimmed CIA
professor   but all are wonderful and the conversation and
relationship between Bond and girl are in your very best manner,
and a smasheroo.

    It is exactly the picture we are trying to make, in my
opinion and, though I suppose it cost millions, will no doubt
make double-millions. i.e. Hitchcock would be worth it, if
we could get him.

    I airmailed a book to you today which is a rare and
priceless museum piece, and without which I cannot imagine how
you have ever written a line of dialogue!

    My chief preoccupation at the moment is to workout
the shareholding position of the various members of the future
Xanadu. My original ideas about Kevin having an equal share
are outdated now. As there will be other people's money to
consider, we cannot give him a large share for no money, without
prejudicing their interests. In your case you put on 2 tangible
assets each worth $50,000. Your story, and 50,000 cash. So
there is no problem -- you obviously get 100,000 worth of shares.
But for the others it is more complicated. It would be most
valuable to me if you could let me have your ideas on this
subject.

    Stakes are as follows:

You 100,000
Frances 50,000 in cash and his services in Bahamas, and
the T.V. Contract
Marley services perhaps probably no share.
Me however much cash will be needed, up to my <u>limit.</u>
Plus putting the thing together.

Charlie Cash probably up to 100,000 ability to get
further capital.

Bryce writes to Fleming raving about Hitchcock's 'North by Northwest' and brings up the thorny issue of shares in Xanadu.

- 2 -

? Jean de la Bruyere Cash ? up to 100,000 business advise.

Kevin   His services, producer, and being my original partner.

Star   ?

Director?

Other participants ?

Financial backers of the picture are going to require
millions, which seems probable.

Bank or Distributing Co, or Hollywood Co. ?

Left in treasury for contingency ?

    The whole thing must be given a lot of careful thought,
if we are not to give away 110% -

    Do give me your ideas.

    As usual am in a hurry - the car is waiting to start
for the farm. There have been early frosts, and the leaves
are apparently wonderful.

                      Love,

                        Ivar.

For someone with no talent for writing, I have seldom re-read
a worse letter! Please excuse.

CHAPTER 7
HITCHCOCK FOR BOND

With the box office firmly in mind, Bryce had been mulling over Fleming's idea of bringing in an industry big gun to help out the inexperienced McClory. Sailing on the Queen Mary back to New York Bryce saw Alfred Hitchcock's latest *North by Northwest* with a packed audience and was so impressed that he wrote to Fleming about the experience on 18 September: "It's the most terrific Bond-style thriller – almost plagiarising – and superb. You must manage to see it somehow. There are differences, the man is a civilian dragged in in error, the girl is the agent, M is a craggy CIA professor, but all are wonderful and the conversation and relationship between Bond and girl are in your very best manner, and a smasheroo. It is exactly the picture we are trying to make." Bryce then made the inspired suggestion of grabbing Hitchcock to direct the Bond movie. "Hitchcock would be worth it, if we could get him."

It was becoming increasingly obvious that a top director was needed for the film if it was going to attract not just marquee value actors but big American distributors, not least because McClory had singularly failed to land *The Boy and the Bridge* with a wide release in the States. For a while William Fairchild was considered to direct the film, as well as write it. But Fleming had found his film *Silent Enemy*, "rather uninspired. I'm inclined to think that Kevin could do a much better and more imaginative job as director than Fairchild, but Hitchcock would be the best of all."

Then Fairchild's "hidden 'secret'" was uncovered. "Unfortunately," Leigh Aman wrote to Bryce 21 September, "It has since emerged through conversations with members of the unit who worked with Bill on *Silent Enemy*, that he only went underwater once – and that the experience was accompanied by considerable neurosis. Kevin is very shaken by this news, and in my opinion reasonably so since Fairchild gave no hint of his underwater fears at our meeting and it is, of course, a vitally important part of the film."

Though regarded as a businesslike director, quick and practical, Fairchild had blown his chance, but Xanadu knew that the number of directors prepared to work underwater was limited, either by their age, their prejudice or their insurance policies. Briefly one of Leigh Aman's past associates was considered – Guy Hamilton. Then most famous for directing *The Colditz Story* (1954), Hamilton would go on to become, after Terence Young, the most significant of all Bond directors. He helmed the classic *Goldfinger*, Connery's last official Bond *Diamonds Are Forever* and Roger Moore's first two outings as 007 – *Live and Let Die* and *The Man With the Golden Gun*. Hamilton would also be one of Broccoli and Saltzman's early candidates to direct *Dr. No*.

Having opened in "error" private correspondence between Fleming and Bryce, McClory now knew that his colleagues no longer wanted him to direct the Bond film, though he still desperately wanted to. Little wonder then that Aman revealed to Bryce that "Kevin is ill humoured at the moment" and "needs some tactful handling." Obviously the desire to bring in an outside director was making McClory feel dangerously excluded. "Having been virtually sole production boss of *Boy and the Bridge*," wrote Aman. "He resents any competitive authority – mine, or anybody else's."

McClory could perhaps sense the creative hold he exercised over the project slowly ebbing away from him and this intensely ambitious man wasn't going to give in without a struggle. "It was Kevin's burning ambition to make these movies," says Jeremy Vaughan. "But I don't think he gave a damn who he walked over and what he did in order to get there. Kevin had a project in life and that project was Kevin McClory. Whether it was women, or money, or making movies, or whatever, if that's what I have to do for the Kevin McClory project. Everything had a purpose."

```
Sent 22/9/59                                        AMBLER
LT

ERIC AMBLER  10640 TARANTA WAY  LOS ANGELES 24  CAL.

        PROHITCH STOP  HAVE WRITTEN BOND MOVIE TREATMENT FEATURING
MAFIA STOLEN ATOMIC BOMBER BLACKMAIL OF ENGLAND CULMINATING NASSAU
WITH EXTENSIVE UNDERWATER DRAMATICS STOP  THIS FOR MY FRIEND
IVAR BRYCES XANADU FILMS LIMITED WHICH RECENTLY COMPLETED BOY AND
BRIDGE ENGLANDS CHOICE FOR VENICE FESTIVAL BUT BLASTED BY CRITICS
AND FLOP  AT CURZON THOUGH NOW XXXXX   DOING EXCELLENTLY ON
PRERELEASE RANK CIRCUIT STOP  PRODUCER KEVIN MCCLORY STOP  WOULD
HITCHCOCK BE INTERESTED IN DIRECTING THIS FIRST BOND FILM IN
ASSOCIATION WITH XANADU QUERY PLENTIFUL FINANCE AVAILABLE STOP
THIS PURELY OLD BOY WAVE ENQUIRY WITHOUT INVOLVEMENT BUT THINK WE
MIGHT ALL HAVE A WINNER PARTICULARLY IF YOU WERE CONCEIVABLY
INTERESTED IN SCRIPTING
                    REGARDEST IAN FLEMING
                        KEMNEWS LONDON
```

Fleming's telegram to Eric Ambler regarding the availability of Alfred Hitchcock to direct the first 007 movie.

Chapter 7: HITCHCOCK FOR BOND

Fleming quickly came around to the notion of Hitchcock as their director. "Personally I feel this would be by far the best solution for all of us." He even suggested it to McClory at a meeting and the Irishman responded positively, so long as he stayed on as producer. "I know Hitchcock slightly," Fleming wrote Bryce 23 September. "And he has always been interested in the Bond saga." Fleming decided to send a cable to the director through a mutual friend, the acclaimed crime novelist Eric Ambler. It read: "Have written Bond movie treatment featuring Mafia stolen atomic bomber blackmail of England culminating Nassau with extensive underwater dramatics. This for my friend Ivar Bryce's Xanadu films. Would Hitchcock be interested in directing this first Bond film in association with Xanadu? Plentiful finance available. Think we might all have a winner particularly if you were conceivably interested in scripting. Regards Ian Fleming."

Fleming realised that with Hitchcock aboard it might mean smaller profits for Xanadu's investors, because it would almost certainly mean getting into partnership with the legendary director's own production company. But then Xanadu would have a solid team of experts behind them. "And the prestige value would be colossal," he wrote Bryce. "My own feelings about doing it all ourselves are that we are a terribly amateurish crew playing around with your money. I don't like either of these feelings. To be allied with a friendly, if very businesslike, group like Hitchcock's would, I believe, be healthier for all of us. Moreover, Kevin would be kept in his place, which I think very important." For the first time Fleming had revealed his true feelings about McClory. "I can't make up my own mind about Kevin. I don't particularly like him personally, because I have never particularly liked Irish blarney, but I have considerable respect for his abilities and he is really putting his back into this film."

This was but one of numerous private letters between Fleming and Bryce that McClory swore he never saw or knew anything about and upon later discovery believed to be conspiratorial against him, as the letters discussed partnership matters with which he was principally concerned. For example, discussing with Fleming possible new investors into Xanadu, Bryce wrote, "I have not asked anyone's opinion, such as Kevin." A strange stance, seeing that McClory was Bryce's partner in Xanadu. Maybe it was his own paranoia working on overdrive, but McClory came to believe that these communications, which it was morally and legally wrong to have withheld from him, denoted a stronger business relationship between Fleming and Bryce. They also indicated that both men were considering forming their own partnership in connection with the Bond film, one quite separate and to the exclusion of McClory. Indeed Bryce's letter to Fleming on 22 August implied that such a partnership already existed. Here Bryce talked of "our joint venture" and "as partners in this new venture." Whereas in letters to McClory, Bryce described Fleming as no more than a shareholder. What was the truth?

These "private" letters also demonstrated the influence that Fleming was exerting on Bryce. McClory firmly believed that it was Fleming's desire to remove him from the project's hierarchy and downgrade him to mere employee status. Nowhere was this better demonstrated than in Fleming's attitude to how the new company, Xanadu Productions (Bahamas) Ltd, was being set up; in particular how Bryce was working out the shareholding positions of the various members. It was Fleming's considered opinion that McClory was not entitled to any shares whatsoever. At first McClory was included, despite investing nothing, but with new investors coming in Bryce, perhaps influenced by Fleming, had dramatically altered this view. "My original ideas about Kevin having an equal share are outdated now," he wrote to Fleming 18 September. "As there will be other people's money to consider, we cannot give him a large share for no money, without prejudicing their interests." McClory was kept completely in the dark about these discussions.

There is further evidence in another Bryce letter to Fleming, this one 3 October, which McClory was again not privy to: "I think the solution to Kevin's stockholding in the company is to give him none, or perhaps just a few shares." McClory's name appeared last on a list of proposed shareholders with a dividend of 5%. "Which even then was clearly considered dubious by my partner Bryce," McClory stated later at the trial, when he finally got to read all this correspondence, "because the figure is followed by a question mark." Curiously Bryce signed this letter 'Ivar Krueger' the name of an infamous financial crook, which he'd playfully adopted as a pseudonym.

The main bankroller behind Xanadu was still very much Bryce. However much cash the company needed, up to a certain limit, he was prepared to invest. One document shows he had put up $500,000 and was looking to be the largest stockholder with at least 40% of the shares. Fleming had also put in two tangible assets each worth $50,000, his Bond treatment and $50,000 cash. Other backers, which consisted largely of business associates, had put in $50,000 apiece: Charles Wacker III, Sir Francis

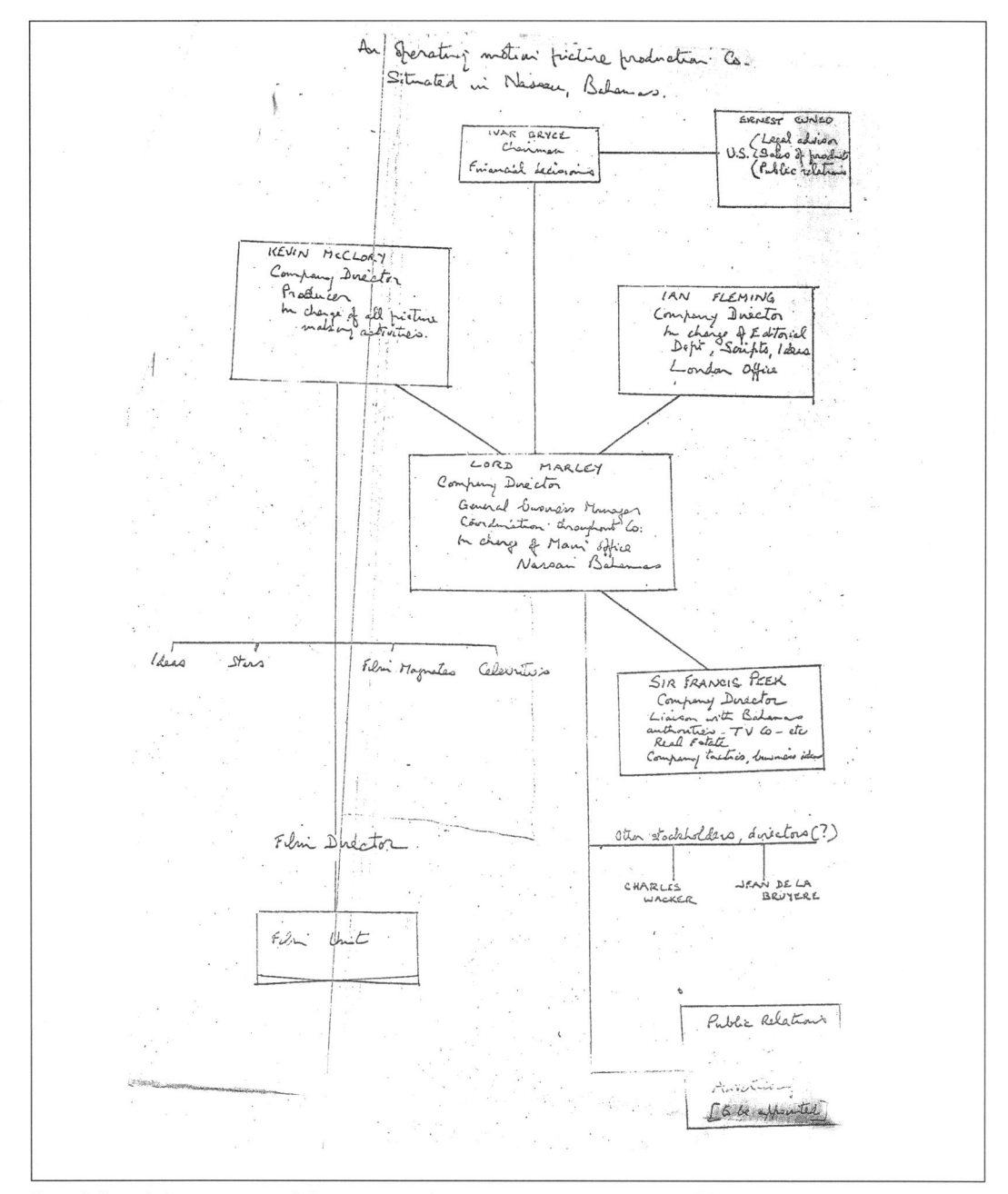

Rough hand drawn copy of the proposed management structure of Xanadu productions.

Chapter 7: HITCHCOCK FOR BOND

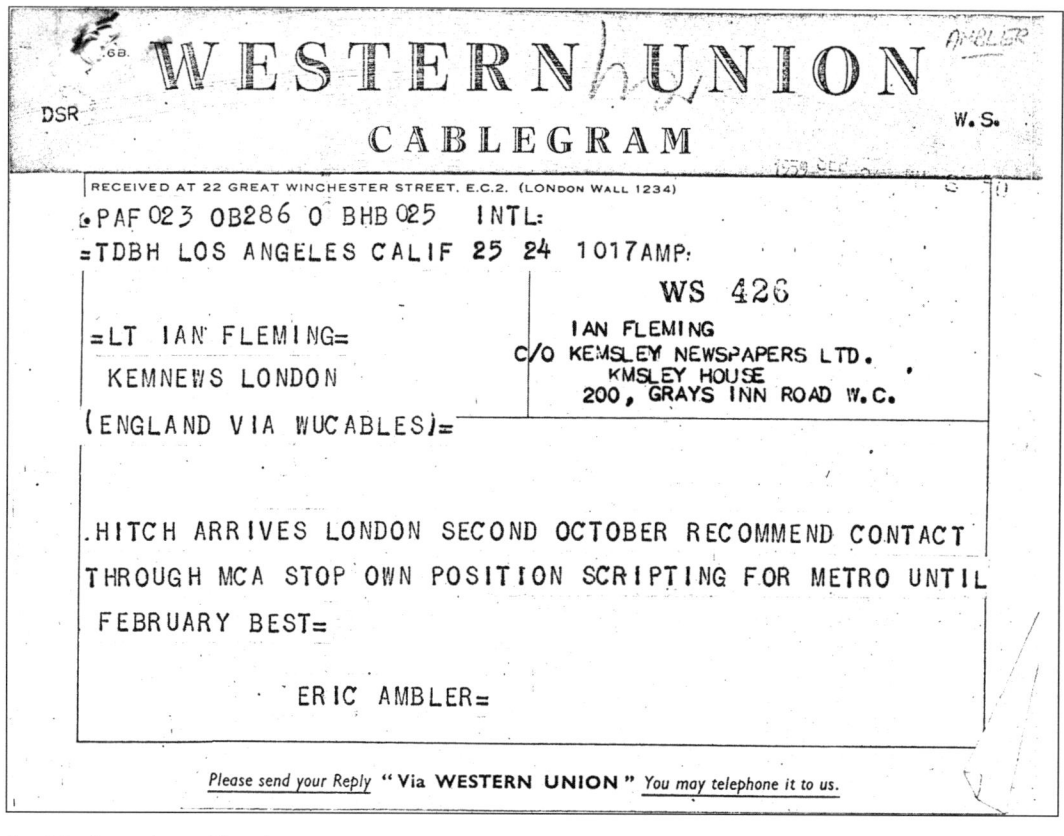

```
WESTERN UNION
CABLEGRAM

RECEIVED AT 22 GREAT WINCHESTER STREET, E.C.2. (LONDON WALL 1234)

PAF 023 OB286 O BHB 025  INTL:
=TDBH LOS ANGELES CALIF 25 24 1017AMP:

                                    WS 426
=LT IAN FLEMING=           IAN FLEMING
                           C/O KEMSLEY NEWSPAPERS LTD.
  KEMNEWS LONDON               KMSLEY HOUSE
                           200, GRAYS INN ROAD W.C.
(ENGLAND VIA WUCABLES)=


HITCH ARRIVES LONDON SECOND OCTOBER RECOMMEND CONTACT
THROUGH MCA STOP OWN POSITION SCRIPTING FOR METRO UNTIL
FEBRUARY BEST=

           ERIC AMBLER=
```

Ambler's reply to Fleming.

Peake and Jean de la Bruyere. McClory had invested no money, his stake in the company was termed by Bryce as: "His services, producer and being my original partner." McClory took this as an admission by Bryce of his rank at the time, although it was obvious to him that by using the word "original partner" Bryce intended to persuade him to sign over his assets in Bond at some stage.

In the end Xanadu Productions (Bahamas) Ltd was never formed, although a structure and job titles in the company hierarchy were drawn up. Ivar Bryce was to be chairman and responsible for financial decisions. Ernest Cuneo was to have been the company's legal advisor and public relations man in the States. Company director in charge of the editorial department, scripts and ideas was Fleming, based out of the London office. McClory too was a company director; his job title was producer, in charge of all filmmaking activities. Leigh Aman was general business manager, to be in charge of the main office in Nassau. Sir Francis Peake was another company director. He was to liaise with the Bahamian authorities and be responsible for business tactics and ideas.

A couple of days after sending his cable to Eric Ambler about Hitchcock, Fleming received a reply: "Hitch arrives London second October recommend contact through MCA. Own position scripting for Metro until February. Best — Eric Ambler." The news was met with glee by Bryce who cabled Fleming with the words, "Let us pray for Hitchcock."

THUNDERBALL

THE PRINCE AND THE PAUPER

DESTINATION BETA SOM

THE BIRTHDAY PRESENT

EXPLOITATION FOLDER

SACRIFICE

THE GIRL ON THE BEACH

LUCKY JIM

PURPLE SIX

THE BIRTHDAY PRESENT

I BELIEVE IN YOU

POOL OF LONDON

WEST OF ZANZIBAR

CAGE OF GOLD

Jack Whittingham's personal collection of screenplays.

CHAPTER 8
ENTER JACK WHITTINGHAM

While waiting for Hitchcock's arrival in the capital and with Fairchild out of the picture, Leigh Aman telephoned an old colleague of his, the screenwriter Jack Whittingham, telling him that McClory wanted to get in touch. Whittingham then ranked amongst the top ten screenwriters in the country, renowned for his work for Ealing Studios on films like *The Divided Heart* (1954) and the drama *Mandy* (1952). Whittingham worked as a journalist before leaving Fleet Street to become a screenwriter for Alexander Korda. Whittingham wrote 14 feature films between 1937-1948 for, amongst other studios, London Films and RKO, while also managing to serve his country during the war in the Royal Artillery. In 1948 Whittingham joined Ealing Studios where his credits included *Hunted* (1952) with Dirk Bogarde and the action adventure *West of Zanzibar* (1954).

Like Fleming and Bryce, Whittingham came from the world of privilege and high education. He was born in 1910 to well off parents, William and Henrietta, the owners of a thriving family wool business with factories around the world. The family lived in great comfort at Stonefall Hall, Harrogate, Yorkshire; there were servants at home and holidays abroad and Jack, along with his three brothers and one sister were all dispatched to private boarding school.

Jack's blonde, blue-eyed choirboy looks left him open at boarding school to the unwelcome attention of older boys. Fagging and beatings with a cane were supposed to turn you into a man and later bullying and ostracism took place when someone discovered that Jack's mother, Henrietta, had once worked in a shop (horror of horrors) before she married his father. This was the kind of narrow-minded bigotry that the upper classes excelled in during this period. In spite of all this Jack did extremely well at school. He gained some popularity due to his cricket skills, but mostly because of his writing ability which shone through from an early age. In fact, quite a profit was to be made, he discovered, by writing essays for other boys in addition to his own.

Jack went on to study law at Oxford University, where he also played football, becoming goalie for the Oxford team at one time. On leaving university he was sent abroad to learn French at Grenoble. Very little time was actually spent learning French in the traditional way and Jack spent a good deal of time in places he was not meant to be. It was during this period that Jack met Betty Offield, the Wrigley chewing gum heiress, to whom he became briefly engaged.

The outbreak of World War Two landed the Whittingham brothers in the thick of the action. Eldest brother Neville saw fierce fighting in France; hurricane pilot Derek, the youngest, fought valiantly against all odds in defence of Malta in the battle of Britain; and army officer Jack was sent to defend Iceland which never was, in fact, invaded. So whilst waiting for "something to happen" Jack busied himself by writing a local newspaper for the men. He also grew a moustache, as all the officers were ordered to do because they looked so young.

Alcohol also became a way of life for the bored men in Iceland and Jack was not the only one to occasionally pass out on parade from a major hangover. Women, too, were in ample supply. A boatload of nurses and other working women were once sent out to boost the men's moral. The plainest women that could be found were chosen and yet, within three months most of them were engaged.

Thanks to his experience in journalism (prior to the war Jack worked for The Morning Post and The Daily Express and also his work for Korda), Jack got a job in the team at Ealing Studios, beginning his run of top screenplays that would eventually bring him to the attention of McClory.

When McClory was finally introduced to Whittingham he came away impressed, telling Bryce in a letter dated 25 September: "I gave him Ian's first rough treatment, which he is extremely enthusiastic about. He also came back with some highly interesting and intelligent and constructive story points." Quickly Whittingham was introduced to Fleming and it was a huge success. The two got on so well that McClory cabled Bryce with the positive news on 28 September: "Excellent meeting Ian and Whittingham. Ian would like Whittingham start work immediately. Meeting his agent Monday. Regards Kevin." It looked like the exhaustive search for the perfect screenwriter for the Bond story was finally at an end. Fleming wrote to Bryce on 1 October in glowing praise of the new writer: "Whittingham, whom I think I told you I greatly liked, is fiddling about most creatively with the story."

Interestingly, before meeting with Whittingham McClory saw Carl Foreman, the American writer of *High Noon* who had fled to England in 1952 after refusing to testify before the House Un-American Activities Committee at the height of the Hollywood Communist witch-hunts. Blacklisted at home,

```
                    (SEPTEMBER 28TH 1959).


        ES210 UWS633   XK318 LONDON 29 28 1950


        JOHN F C BRYCE BRYCELO NEW YORK


        BRIGHTON 721 AVERAGE STOP EXCELLENT MEETING IAN
        AND WHITTINGHAM STOP IAN WOULD LIKE WHITTINGHAM START
        WORK IMMEDIATELY MEETING HIS AGENT MONDAY REGARDS.

        KEVIN


        COLL 721
```

McClory's telegram to Bryce confirming the hiring of Whittingham to write the James Bond screenplay.

Chapter 8: ENTER JACK WHITTINGHAM

```
                    (TO BRYCE FROM FLEMING)

                                          1st October 1959


        It was very nice to get your brisk cable and workmanlike
letter of September 27th.

        I have not changed my habitat and this will not happen
until after Christmas. I do hope you enjoyed Mrs. Neville's
company.

        Regarding Charlie's ideas and passing them on through
our co-ordinator, I would be rather inclined to keep the co-
ordinator out of these rather personal matters until your
company is formed. I already sense that, having appeared as a
director on your family tree, he may be getting a little bit
over excited and, as I have mentioned, I'm not quite certain
that he is directorial timbre.

        I think that J.B. would be a useful colleague because he
will be the only one of us who is a really practical businessman
and I feel he might give you some excellent advice as to how to
set up Xanadu, but I think you should put it to him that we
would all make an effort to meet at least four times a year and
gain the benefit of his advice as otherwise he will merely be
an absentee landlord which is never very much good.

        So far as Jules Stein is concerned, I had no idea you knew
him. I suppose you realise that he is the top man in the dreaded
M.C.A. Anyway, if you can get him in, we're certainly off to
the races as he carries immense influence in the States and also
commands the services of practically every worthwhile star,
director, writer, etc.

        For that reason I would be very doubtful that you
would be able to persuade him to come in. Presumably in his
business he would wish to keep his hands free. But any help
or encouragement you can get from him would be invaluable to all
of us - not least because, as well as me, he controls Hitchcock!

        I'm in the process of arranging to meet Hitchcock early
next week through our common agent, M.C.A., and I will cable you
anything interesting.

        Meanwhile, Whittingham, whom I think I told you I greatly
liked, is fiddling about most creatively with the story. This
doesn't involve us and, if Hitchcock will play, of course we
shall have to be guided by his recommendations, but I'm much
impressed by Whittingham and he has some excellent ideas which
cut out a lot of the muck at the beginning of my story.

        Naturally when I have had my talk with Hitchcock and if
it's successful, I shall immediately arrange a further meeting
between him and Kevin. Personally I pray that the Hitchcock
thing will come off. I'm sure it will solve all our problems
and be a gigantic boost for the project.

        I bought some more steel shares today on the certain
prospect of a Conservative victory at the polls!

        The New Yorker, reviewing "Goldfinger", refers to my works
as steak tartare, which is quite neat.

J.F.C. Bryce Esq.,
161 East 74th Street,
New York City, U.S.A.
```

Fleming's letter to Bryce in which the author compliments the work carried out on the Bond script by Whittingham.

Foreman went on to co-write *The Bridge on the River Kwai* and produce *The Guns of Navarone*. Although not interested in direct involvement in the Bond film, Foreman told McClory that since the film appeared to be aimed at the American market, Xanadu should utilise the services of an American writer. "Foreman thinks the potential box office on our story is a sure," McClory wrote Bryce. Although in the end it would be an English and not an American writer Xanadu chose in Jack

Whittingham, when Broccoli and Saltzman came on the scene they would unconsciously take Foreman's advice by employing New York born screenwriter Richard Maibaum, who would pen an amazing 13 Bond films in total.

It had been agreed that Whittingham should start work immediately provided it didn't interfere with the chances of obtaining Hitchcock, who might well come in with his own set of writers. So this work by Whittingham was provisional, as no firm offer had yet been made for his services. "But I'm much impressed," Fleming continued in his letter to Bryce. "And he has some excellent ideas which cut out a lot of the muck at the beginning of my story." But behind the fulsome praise Fleming's sights were still very much trained on Hitchcock, whom he was arranging to meet through their common agent, MCA. "Personally I pray that the Hitchcock thing will come off. I'm sure it will solve all our problems and be a gigantic boost for the project."

Fleming comes over very bullish in this letter, even mentioning the fact that he's bought some more steel shares that day "on the certain prospect of a Conservative victory at the polls!" A week later Harold Macmillan did indeed win for the Tories a historic third successive term in office. He also quotes from The New Yorker review of the recently published *Goldfinger* novel that referred to his works as steak tartare, "which is quite neat."

With the Bond books having already been turned down by every studio for being too violent, sadistic and unbelievable, it was Whittingham's job to adapt Fleming's treatment into a workable script and present the character of Bond in a way that would find favour with a late fifties cinema audience. But tastes were already changing. Earlier in the decade the likes of Trevor Howard, Jack Hawkins and John Mills spent seemingly years parading with binoculars on ships' bridges as World War Two was re-enacted every week at the local Odeon or ABC. Ealing comedies also ruled the roost, until finally giving way in 1958 to the first of the Carry On films. But a sea change was occurring. A new breed of performer was invading British film, their regional accents unsmothered by the classical diction of the Rank Charm School or the Old Vic theatre; the likes of Albert Finney, Richard Burton, Richard Harris and Alan Bates. Backed up by more socially conscious writers and directors it led to a "new wave" in British filmmaking and the age of the angry young man and kitchen sink dramas. Could James Bond succeed in such a climate?

Conscious of the Mafia overtones in the Bond story Whittingham set about reading books on the subject, including a biography on the notorious gangster Lucky Luciano, as well as re-reading Fleming's novel *Live and Let Die*. Whittingham also sat through a private screening of *Silent Enemy* and wrote to McClory, "I can well imagine what a huge uplift colour and wide screen would make."

With his trained eye Whittingham immediately saw the deficiencies in Fleming's treatment and after reading it formed the opinion that the author had very little idea of writing for the screen. "In my view Fleming's film treatment was terribly bad, was tripe, and completely inappropriate for film development." Whittingham had very firm notions of the differences between a screenwriter and an author of books. "The illustration that he liked to give was of a middle aged man wearing a hat getting into a lift with his wife," says Sylvan Mason, Jack Whittingham's daughter. "The lift stops on the third floor and an attractive young woman gets in and the man removes his hat. A whole field of things has been said, but not a word has been spoken; that's writing for film. Daddy used to say, you are writing for an average mentality of 12 years old, and using the least possible dialogue. Film is visual, you can tell an awful lot by just visuals. You don't need streams of dialogue explaining things. And that was the difference. Fleming was a wonderful writer in his written descriptions, but that didn't work on film."

Whittingham produced notes on Fleming's treatment, plus some early story ideas, and sent them to McClory and in turn Fleming. Whittingham certainly didn't hide his criticism of Fleming's efforts. He found far too much of the story told in dialogue. It needed more visual zip to carry it along. Bond was practically never in danger until the end and Domino far too easily outsmarted the gang, such as in a scene where she steals a wet suit to escape, basically making monkeys of them. Whittingham wanted the Mafia to be far more of a menace. Whittingham considered countless scenes either repetitious, lacking content or not

Chapter 8: ENTER JACK WHITTINGHAM

progressing the story forward. As for the characters, they were all stock two-dimensional types. With the world facing nuclear terrorism, Whittingham was incredulous that, "it can all be left in the hands of two agents and a girl to solve, while everyone else stands by." He was also adamant that the theft of the bomb "*must* precede Bond's entry into the story." The shooting gallery intro, which was, "melodramatic without being in any way progressive to the plot," didn't work for him either; nor did the entire sequence at Largo's night-club. "It creaks and gets nowhere." He was also less than enamoured of Fleming's handicapping of Bond with corny voice-overs, like in a bad private eye movie, and found the whole bomb transfer sequence unbelievable and far too complicated. "It's all too facile."

Perhaps in response, Fleming quickly re-wrote the film's introduction, enhancing it considerably by having the bomb theft occur right at the start. The film was now to open not with Bond at the target range but on the rotating blades of a helicopter. The credits flash one by one across them. No music, only the harsh note of the motor. When the titles end the camera withdraws to show a US Air Force helicopter flying down the final reaches of the Thames at dawn towards Shoeburyness rocket station. Switch to the interior and three men in military uniform sit tensely at the controls. "Wipe that sweat off your face, Carlo," says the leader. "And, whatever happens, both of you, keep your hands away from your guns and don't look so damned scared. If you make like in the rehearsals, we'll be all right."

Only after the robbery do we fade to the previous opening sequence of Bond at the shooting range. Since the bomb hi-jack has already occurred and Fleming has dropped the entire night club section we discover how Scotland Yard were keeping tabs on the Mafia gang through a flashback. Undercover police are all over Soho, in a laundry van with cine cameras, as a window cleaner with a hidden microphone. A black Chevrolet saloon draws up outside a cafe and three men (the ones in the helicopter) get out. A woman disguised as a prostitute lifts her vanity case and powders her nose. She observes the men enter the building. It's Domino. The café meeting was bugged and the authorities overheard vague references about a big operation netting £100 million. Photographs taken of the men sent to the FBI and Interpol identified them as top Mafia hoodlums. They were about to be pulled in on suspicion when the bomb was stolen.

This whole new opening segues neatly into the Air Ministry's search for the missing bomb. "It seems to me this new intro," wrote Fleming, "will get rid of several improbabilities, introduce Domino Smith in a more dramatic form (she meets Bond later at Scotland Yard), avoids the messy and rather old fashioned night club scene and cuts out a lot of walking up and down passages and lengthy dialogue."

Whittingham continued to work on Fleming's treatment and made other suggestions that were to radically alter the story, throwing up some fascinating new characters and plot developments. He ditched the police character of Domino Smith altogether, replacing her with a, "fiery, young sex animal" called Sophia who is Largo's mistress. Whittingham described her relationship with him thus: "Largo, who is flint-hard and utterly unscrupulous, has one weakness common to many ageing men. He wants to possess a young woman in the same way as he owns real property or his yacht. Sophia will take his money; she will favour him when it suits her, but she is not his. This is her power over him."

Also introduced is Jo Petachi, the American pilot who ends up hijacking the bomber. It's fun to speculate on the origin of the name Petachi and whether Whittingham took it from Claretta Petacci, mistress of the Italian dictator Mussolini. The new character did not find favour with Ernest Cuneo who warned Whittingham, in the strongest terms, that the American public would never accept that an American soldier could possibly double-cross his men, kill them and hi-jack a plane. As a result of Cuneo's objection Whittingham changed Petachi from a plain American serviceman to a NATO observer.

Whittingham also invented a totally new opening to the film, which is wonderfully sadistic. Martelli, an Italian informant, arrives aboard Largo's yacht. Handed $10,000 he tells Largo that a man named Petachi is now flying routine NATO patrols in bombers armed with A-bombs, stationed in Britain. Martelli gives details of Petachi's living relatives in Sicily and is confident the airman can be made to do as he is told. The implication being that if Petachi refuses the job his Italian relatives will be wiped out.

Largo thanks Martelli for his invaluable help, then asks whether he is quite sure that he covered his tracks and wasn't followed to the yacht. Martelli assures him, and by doing so writes his own death warrant. Largo shoots Martelli in the back. Leaving his henchmen to dispose of the body, Largo casually returns to a game of backgammon with Sophia, who is completely unaware of what has just happened, even using the saved $10,000 as the stake in a new game. The rules are simple, if Sophia wins she gets the "blood" money, if she loses Largo has his wicked way with her!

Whittingham then harrowingly describes the ultimate fate of Martelli: "Except for his pants, Martelli's body has been stripped. Blood still wells from the wound, and smears his body. They put it into the underwater compartment. Martelli's body floats away from the hull of the yacht and down. Camera pans as two or three sharks move inquisitively towards it. We then see the surface of the sea bubbling from the thrashing bodies of the sharks." It's obvious from this highly descriptive and visually exciting passage that Whittingham was the man for the Bond job.

Soon, other important ideas and elements were being incorporated into the script. At a meeting Whittingham attended with Fleming, McClory raised the notion of having the Mafia steal not one but two bombs. This way the first could be detonated if the government failed to hand over the money, thus raising the stakes even higher. Whittingham immediately saw that this was essential for the plot, but Fleming at first rejected the idea entirely. It took some time to convince him that the idea was necessary to the story.

Whittingham also took up McClory's idea of the aerial theft of the bombs, having agreed with the Irishman that Fleming's robbery sequence at Shoeburyness wasn't credible "even to a half wit." Having Petachi shoot the crew dead and then grapple with the controls to steer the plane off-course would, if properly developed, "be extremely tense and exciting." He also suggested a short "documentary, authentic" scene of the reaction at the Air Ministry that the atom bomber is out of radio contact. Then Whittingham went on to describe how he saw the bomber's crash-landing in the Bahamas. "Not an island in sight, not a ship – only a yacht – Largo's. Then, out from the horizon comes the bomber. Largo and co watching from the deck of the yacht. Inside the bomber, the macabre spectacle of Petachi at the controls, and behind him the corpses of the crew. The bomber crashes on the sea near the yacht. Petachi climbs free and starts swimming towards the yacht. As he swims nearer, he is shot in the water. The bomber slowly sinks."

Whittingham also suggested underwater shots of the bomb being removed from the plane and taken aboard the yacht. Apart from the shooting in the water of Petachi this entire sequence, written at this point only roughly by Whittingham, played unaltered in the 1965 film.

Whittingham next suggested that Bond make his first appearance at a huge conference with M and other big brass where it is revealed that the bomber was traced by radar to some spot in the West Atlantic, and then lost. The authorities also have no clue as to the perpetrators. He then toyed with a possible meeting of Mafia characters in Palermo, Sicily, and their intention to blackmail the western powers. "I suggest a greedy quarrel about the sum to be demanded." Whittingham wrote. "Possibly an argument about what they should threaten to destroy with the A-bomb. Then in London we learn the contents of the blackmailing letter from Palermo, and the demand for $100 million in gold. The conclusion is now obvious: this is Mafia."

One crucial element introduced here by Whittingham takes place during Bond's later discovery of the sunken bomber. Again Whittingham's skill as a screenwriter comes to the fore, introducing the haunting image of Bond negotiating his way through sharks trying to get into the cockpit and at the corpses. Then he finds, "something on the sea bed near the bomber (perhaps a ring or a wrist watch?) which identifies Petachi." This helps Bond convince Sophia that Petachi, who is her brother, has been double-crossed and murdered by Largo: "Thus Sophia moves into Bond's camp."

Fleming read with interest Whittingham's notes and confessed to him that he was not versed in the medium of screenwriting and had never worked on a film screenplay before. "From then onwards," Whittingham later wrote. "Fleming was persuaded almost entirely by the ideas put forward by myself and McClory, and he dropped his first story."

CHAPTER 9
FLEMING'S SECOND BOND SCRIPT

At last the news Fleming had been waiting for arrived. Hitchcock had voiced interest in the Bond project. Fleming immediately wrote to Bryce on 7 October: "Hitchcock is in search of a vehicle, particularly for James Stewart but, whether our story would suit Stewart or not, he is definitely interested and wants to see it." Stewart was a regular star for Hitchcock who'd used him already in four movies, notably *Rear Window* (1954) and *Vertigo* (1958). Hitchcock was then in Paris but due back in London in a few days with the intention of reading the script. "Of course James Stewart is the toppest of stars," Fleming continued. "And personally I wouldn't at all mind him as Bond if he can slightly anglicise his accent. If we got him and Hitchcock we really would be off to the races. Cross all your fingers."

In contrast to Fleming's bursting enthusiasm for Hitchcock, Bryce had blown cold on the idea. "If he did take it," Bryce immediately wrote back, "he would take the whole thing over, lock, stock and barrel, and we should all be no more than 'angels' investing our money in someone else's enterprise – a thing I wouldn't be willing to do, myself. Hitchcock is, of course, the greatest. Let us see what he suggests, but from all I can learn here it will involve the freezing out of our group both financially and personally. Also I shudder at lackadaisical Stewart portraying dynamic Bond."

Bryce in this letter also made clear his preference for Fleming to continue to exert a governing hand over the script. "I personally think it essential for you to spend as much time as is humanely possible during the scriptwriting period on working on it yourself, probably with Whittingham as your number two." And that for this work Fleming should be on a fat salary from the company: "I've no idea what, but anything you like."

About to leave London for Berlin, Fleming hastily did a re-write of his treatment, embodying everybody's fresh suggestions, and sent a copy to Laurence Evans to pass on to Hitchcock. "It will reach you without me having time to look it over for mistakes, but no doubt it will be sufficient to give Hitchcock an idea of what we have in mind. I hope he likes it." Upon receipt Evans phoned his client full of praise, which Fleming then reported to Bryce: "He thinks the story is one of the most exciting he has ever read and he has been on the job for 30 years, so he ought to know. He really was overwhelmingly excited about it and I'm greatly encouraged."

Fleming's trip to Berlin was part of a newspaper assignment and he seemed to be thoroughly enjoying himself. "Spent Sunday afternoon fratting with Russian soldiers in East Berlin," he reported back to Bryce. "And Monday evening watching two almost naked women wrestling in mud in Hamburg. One must try and stay in the swim, you know."

In his second treatment Fleming adopted Whittingham's new opening sequence of the Mafia informant being killed and fed to the sharks word for word, but changed Sophia back to Domino, although she remains Largo's mistress. In M's office, 007 is told that the Mafia is in possession of an atomic warhead stolen from a Valiant bomber which was last reported heading out towards the Bahamas. If the bomb isn't recovered within six days they've no alternative but to pay up. M orders 007 to Nassau.

Disguised as delegates at a garment convention, the Mafia leaders are arousing no suspicions. But Bond and Felix Leiter charter a small plane and find the hidden Valiant, surrounded by sharks. Bond discovers the corpses of the crew and Petachi, but the bombs are missing. Vitally Fleming doesn't include Whittingham's idea of having Bond find the important evidence of Largo's treachery (Petachi's watch or ring) which he can use to more effectively confront Domino.

Bond tells Leiter that his suspicions are focused on Largo's yacht. "These garment people look innocent enough, but they are, after all, Italians," he says, with all the tact of Alf Garnett. Bond meets Domino at the casino where she talks about Petachi, no longer her brother but her lover. Bond realises this is the man whose body he found only a few hours before.

Later that night Bond carries out an underwater search of Largo's yacht and discovers the secret hatchway. He now realises that the convention delegates are Mafia. The next morning, as Largo's frogmen retrieve the bomb from its hiding place, Felix Leiter approaches the yacht in a speedboat, acting the tourist. Taking no chances, Largo machine guns Leiter to death.

With time running out Bond tells Domino that Largo murdered her boyfriend. Anxious for revenge Domino agrees to help. With a Geiger counter, Domino discovers the bombs are on board and signals to the shore. But she is spotted and locked in her room as the yacht sets sail to plant the bomb.

Coldly deducing that Leiter must be dead, having failed to return; Bond boards a submarine and sets out after Largo's yacht, chasing it through the night. As dawn breaks the sub creeps up slowly behind the boat as it moors near a rocket installation. As before a detachment of US frogmen, led by Bond, defeat the Mafia underwater team in a frenzied battle. Fleming's description reads almost like the finished film version: "A great pitched battle ensues with CO_2 guns and knives. There are many individual fights. In one an oxygen pipe is cut, in another a glass mask is shattered, in another a man rips a small octopus off a coral-head and slams it across the neck and mask of his opponent. Everywhere there is foam and blood, flying harpoons and glittering knives. The surface of the sea is a turmoil amidst which bodies float head downwards."

Domino again saves Bond's life by killing Largo with a harpoon and the bomb is safely recovered. Back in Sicily the Capo Mafiosi hears his plan has failed and commits suicide. (*For a longer version of this script see Appendix 3*)

This new treatment is a vast improvement over Fleming's first. There are flashes of genuine brilliance, but even with virtually the entire story structure in place there's something oddly flat and uninvolving about it. It can only lead one to speculate that Fleming didn't give the screenplay Bond the same respect he reserved for his literary counterpart (understandably one supposes), offering up scenarios and situations below the level of his novel writing. Fleming himself was generally pleased with it, noting on the script's last page, "My only comments on this treatment are that there are too many sharks and that we don't see quite enough of Domino. The briefing sequence in M's office is rather too long, but something of the sort will be necessary."

Chapter 9: FLEMING'S SECOND BOND SCRIPT

Fleming included in this draft some editorial notes prepared for CBS when there was talk in 1957 of making a 007 television series. Although not connected to *Thunderball*, they give a fascinating insight into how Fleming wanted Bond and the world he lived in to be presented on screen; which was no doubt the reason he included it here for McClory and Bryce to absorb. On his hero Fleming wrote, "James Bond is a blunt instrument wielded by a government department. He is quiet, hard, ruthless, sardonic, fatalistic. Audiences will tend to dislike him until they get to know him and then they will appreciate that he is their idea of an efficient agent."

Dealing with atmosphere Fleming wrote, "To my mind the greatest danger to be avoided in this series is too much stage Englishness." So monocles, moustaches, bowler hats, Bobbies on the beat and other, "Limey gimmicks" were out. Neither did Fleming want use of blatant English slang and a minimum of public school ties and accents. And the Secret Service was to be presented as a tough, modern organisation. "Above all, they should not slap each other on the back or call each other 'old boy.'" Fleming believed the failure of English thriller writers and the film presentation of their works had always been a lack of sophistication and toughness and a desire to gain the sympathy of the audience "by the use of what I can best describe as English hamminess."

McClory responded positively to Fleming's second treatment: "Very exciting," he called it in a letter dated 16 October. "Although a great deal of work has to be done on it, and I am not as yet convinced that we have the full story, but I think this will come in the next few script conferences."

Bryce was likewise impressed, though in a letter dated 17 October made these criticisms to Fleming: "Be careful not to take Domino off the screen for too long. Also, is it necessary to bump off poor Felix? You will need him again you know – a problem you have already had once. I should like to do *Live and Let Die* one day." Bryce also mentioned Ernest Cuneo's positive reaction. "Although he is worried by all Italian names of Mafia villains, and fears resentment in Italian minority here, but I cannot go along with that." Nor did Fleming pay much credence to Cuneo's suggestion that using the Mafia would infuriate America's Italian population. "Don't agree with Ernie about the Italian names," Fleming wrote back. "The Mafia is a villainous organisation and if the Italians don't like it, they ought to suppress it."

In his letter Bryce also referred to a recent news incident of an American bomber that collided with a tanker plane and crashed. It was carrying two A-bombs, which did not explode. "Of interest for your script?" Is Bryce suggesting that this would be a more realistic way of bringing the aircraft down, of getting the villains to orchestrate a mid-air collision that would look to the authorities like an accident? If it was, it was never followed up in any of the subsequent scripts.

The man who found most at fault in Fleming's second treatment was Jack Whittingham, and again he offered some useful notes and comments soon after reading it. He wanted the audience to learn much earlier that Domino had a boyfriend in the US Air Force and that Largo had him shot, not for any operational reason but merely to eradicate his love rival. As for all the Sicilian Mafiosi going to the Bahamas, surely that would give the whole game away to the western powers. Largo really needed only specialists around him - skin divers, atomic engineers etc. Once the bomb is lost and the Mafia make their demands Whittingham suggested a quick montage of scenes at 10 Downing Street, the Air Ministry, the American embassy and finally a combined meeting of all concerned agencies. This would save having to put over all the information in an endless dialogue scene between Bond and M. Fleming's concept that the whole world was relying totally on Bond just didn't wash with Whittingham either. The British secret service should be a mere cog in a larger global intelligence operation and Nassau only one of numerous suspected areas. "This would put Bond in proper perspective as a brilliant agent, but only one of a team of agents, and not God."

Prior to the Mafia hotel conference, Whittingham suggested a montage of planes landing at Nassau bringing in "a lot of flashy Italians." But not from the Palermo gang – only new faces. "Among the arrivals should be Bond in the role of a wide-eyed tourist bent on having one hell of a good holiday. If that could be in his character?" At the hotel, Bond should nose around the garment convention and there perhaps meet Domino for the first time where she talks about Petachi, the yacht and Largo. As for having the police search the yacht, as Fleming had them do, Whittingham was dead against it. "Surely it would send Largo running a thousand miles. He would know they were on to him. Does Bond want that? Worse still, it would identify Bond and Leiter as detectives."

Whittingham had problems with the climax too. By the script's final third, bomb or no bomb, there was now sufficient evidence for the official spotlight to be full on Largo and Nassau. In that case, would the yacht be allowed to sail off to sea to pick up the bomb? Perhaps – if Bond wanted to catch the gang red-handed. But would Largo, by now maybe suspicious that the heat was on, return to Nassau with the deadly cargo? If he does, why on earth is he then allowed to merely sail off again and get to within miles of the target? Whittingham came up with a plausible reason. Bond, who knows now that the bomb is aboard, dare not risk a battle royal in Nassau harbour in case the bomb explodes and causes mass devastation, so wants to get the yacht far out to sea before attacking it. To engineer this Domino is made to confess to Largo that Bond is an agent and hot on his trail. Largo sets sail immediately and Bond follows. But Largo is no fool and has sabotaged Bond's pursuit vehicle, so the yacht gets a clear start and reaches its target before Bond and his aqua team arrive for battle, now via plane.

After seeing Whittingham's ideas for new scenes and plot developments, McClory became even more certain they'd got their man, writing to Bryce on 9 October. "I do feel sure that the sooner we can give a definite go ahead to Jack Whittingham the better, as he is a most sought after writer in England, and will obviously not be idle for long." Indeed, Whittingham was far from idle. He'd already started work on a full length James Bond script of his own.

CHAPTER 10
MONEY PROBLEMS

McClory had been enjoying a long weekend at the Irish home of director John Huston when inevitably, the subject of the Bond movie came up. "He thinks it's a box office certainty, and made some very interesting and useful suggestions," McClory wrote Bryce. Another guest who was an associate of Hitchcock's, upon learning that McClory was keen to hire him, warned that the master of suspense came with a very heavy price tag. The example he gave was the last deal Hitchcock made with Paramount. Hitchcock and James Stewart divided 75% of the profits between them, leaving just 25% for the studio, who financed the picture 100%. Not put off, McClory echoed Fleming's efforts to get Hitchcock, writing to Bryce. "I think Hitchcock would be the ideal man to direct James Bond and certainly worth pursuing."

With the script progressing in London, Bryce contacted Jean de la Bruyere to go on a fact-finding visit to New York to meet various personalities in different branches of the film industry, and to interrogate leading distributors, bankers and theatre owners. Fleming certainly approved of Bruyere's involvement calling him "a useful colleague because he will be the only one of us who is a really practical businessman."

The mission was a great success and its results digested by Xanadu's leading players. Bruyere learned that both Cinerama and Todd-AO, the two widescreen processes McClory wanted to film in, ensured large profits, but entailed huge investment too. Both necessarily involved complicated financial arrangements with banks, distributors etc, and all exercising supervision over the filmmaking process. Finance anyway was unobtainable for all but the major established producers. With 40% of their audience being children, the first rule in Cinerama and Todd-AO was for films to be family orientated, which ruled out action thrillers. "My own feeling is that Ian Fleming's story would never become (I hope) a family picture and thus would not be eligible for Todd-AO or Cinerama," Bruyere reported.

With Todd A-O and Cinerama now ruled out, everyone still agreed that the Bond film, with its underwater action, needed to be made in colour and in widescreen. Next Bruyere looked at costing the picture on the basis of using CinemaScope. The average budget for a feature film in CinemaScope was then $500,000-$600,000. With around $800,000 in cash at its disposal Xanadu could encompass that without hocking its whole existence, and if necessary also borrow some $250,000 from Bank of America. But as Bruyere wrote, Bond was anything but average: "Our picture of James Bond will not be a cheap picture due to the underwater photography required, which I understand is quite expensive. Further, a great deal of travelling expenses will be involved and presumably a great deal of expensive machinery like submarines, yachts, helicopters etc will have to be rented." As a consequence of the premium cost involved, Bruyere concluded that CinemaScope was another luxury Xanadu simply couldn't afford.

Plus there was the thorny matter of star actors and a star director. Did Xanadu want big names as insurance and where did they want them, in the cast or the director or both? "How much money can we allocate for each and stay within the maximum decided budget?" Bruyere asked in his report. In the back of his mind was the expensive Hitchcock. Bruyere had talked to people who knew how Hitchcock operated, which was that his own company would take the majority of the venture into its own name. "And so possibly we might lose the control." This was voicing fears earlier expressed by Bryce. "And we would thus lose the advantages that we seek in going into this business." Bruyere's answer was simple, dump Hitchcock and look for a director with comparable talents but cheaper wage demands, all of which would leave Xanadu with the creative upper hand. Bruyere's investigations had revealed that Hitchcock's fee would be around $400,000 minimum, half Xanadu's budget! Surely the money would be better spent on star names, which in any case were much more of a draw to the public.

Fleming's attitude to the possibility of Hitchcock railroading the Bond project was simple; it was a policy of wait and see. As he wrote, "I don't think there is any harm in seeing what he has to say, which I dare say will be nothing. Naturally we wouldn't want to be gobbled up by him but, on the other hand, even if he had a small piece and came in as co-director or something of the sort, the prestige value would be enormous."

Bruyere's report also tantalisingly revealed that Xanadu was seriously considering making not just one Bond film, but maybe two. The problem it faced was over lack of funds. Roughly they had $1m capital, for an approximate $800,000 budget. If Xanadu wanted to make two pictures there was no way they could do it for $400,000 each, unless both were done on the cheap and in black and white. If they went ahead on their own with the first film on an $800,000 budget, no money would be forthcoming for any potential follow-up until profits started trickling back, which could take eight months. If Bryce and McClory considered this too long a period to wait, then a suitable partner was needed to help bankroll both pictures, a big studio like Columbia, who could go as much as 50% in partnership. The advantages to such an arrangement would be, of course, the extra cash, but also Xanadu would have access to expensive studio facilities, equipment and experienced technicians. But Bruyere warned they'd lose some of their control, as a studio would insist on re-writes, their own choice of actors and a finished product that more or less was in accordance with their general principles. Of course with a big studio behind the fledgling Bond film there was a higher guarantee of success, and Bruyere felt such co-operation would give Xanadu valuable experience.

All the time in his report Bruyere stressed his concern over the money, urging Bryce that it was essential for the company to get a very thorough study made on the cost involved for the film. If the cost, as he believed, was above Xanadu's financial possibilities he suggested the film's epic scenario be changed so it met with their tentative capital and target figure. Then the script could be written and a final budget done. In conclusion, Bruyere recommended, "We should assume the fact that we have one million dollars as total available monies and make a tentative picture and budget of $800,000. We should spend money on one excellent actor, if possible American, who would take the character of James Bond. This American actor would help tremendously the marketing of this film in the US. We could make a long term deal with him with options for using him in future films."

After digesting Bruyere's report Bryce made some observations of his own, emphasising the importance of arranging distribution before shooting began. The danger of making a film without it was

Chapter 10: MONEY PROBLEMS

that the potential distributor turns it down, with all the others almost certainly following suit, in order to buy your now worthless picture for a song at some later date. Bryce learnt that 80% of pictures made by Columbia, then the only studio showing interest in the Bond project, lost money. However, the other 20% paid for everything. A notable recent case being *Bridge on the River Kwai*. Perceptively Bryce also emphasised the need, especially for the kind of picture they were making, to own the TV rights, which was an important insurance against loss. In conclusion, Bryce noted, "From our point of view – Nassau company (meaning Xanadu), $600,000 budget, Bond script, Kevin's talent, seem to assure a profit of 10-25%, with better than average chance of a multi-million winner."

With the financial aspects of the production under such serious discussion, once again Fleming raised doubts over McClory. Not his inexperience this time, but whether he would be able to keep proper rein on the budget. He wrote Bryce 14 October: "There's a great difference between the sort of Bobo Commando (meaning McClory) that has been running hitherto and the hard working, professional units like the Boulting Brothers and such like who get down to work on tight schedules and simply have to stick to their budget. I think such a unit might be got together under Kevin, but I regard it as absolutely essential that you should sit over his head and be prepared to command the team."

For some time now Fleming had grown concerned about his friend ploughing money into a film whose script hadn't even been written yet, and that he really ought to take a tougher stance. "You will have to be a fairly firm hand on top of the whole thing and not just a horn of plenty paying the bills."

Again, McClory saw this kind of intervention as Fleming "obviously using his influence upon Bryce, my co-partner, gradually to edge me out of the projected company and the partnership."

But Bryce himself was now voicing grave concerns over McClory, principally his inability to keep him informed about financial matters like the box office performance of *Boy and the Bridge*. "I am driven mad by the impossibility of getting any facts out of Kevin," went one letter of complaint to Fleming. "Would that Kevin was more reliable and businesslike. I should so much prefer to know the worst, but truth, than good news that I cannot quite believe. I simply sit here 3000 miles away, and grind my teeth."

The fact that everything McClory said had to be taken with a pinch of salt was an irredeemable flaw in his character make up. But thanks to his Irish charm and handsome demeanour he seemed to be able to persuade people to do his bidding and got his way on most things. "He had the natural chat of a con man," says Jeremy Vaughan. "But the bottom line was he was not a particularly pleasant fellow. You couldn't believe a word out of his mouth, really. That was all part of the con-man type chatter."

Despite growing reservations about McClory, Fleming now clearly accepted Whittingham as the best choice for scriptwriter, but in a letter to Bryce revealed that his own work commitments were starting to get in the way: "As to my help over the script, it will of course be forthcoming in full measure but simply must take second place to the rest of my rather complicated life. In any case, Whittingham will have to be number one on the script, because he is a script writer and I am not, and this is a professional job on which total concentration is necessary."

Xanadu had also just announced its intention to start production on the Bond film in January and February of 1960, but Fleming didn't agree. Worried about the weather in the Bahamas he feared the crew could end up standing about idle waiting for clear blue skies and thought Bryce should reconsider going in March. "Then, back to London with you and everyone else when we can do the London bits in more or less peace and comfort." But Fleming warned Bryce that he himself wouldn't always be around in person. "For a thousand reasons I cannot be more than your shadow chief of staff. Ann is terrified by the prospect of me being constantly away on the film and imagines heaven knows what, but at any rate she imagines it all, and I'm having much trouble with her on this account."

Bryce's response to Fleming's revelation that he might not be on hand for the shooting arrived on 21 October. "The time you are essential is obviously during preparation of the script. Even if Whittingham writes every word, you really must be within reach for overall decisions. I think once that is over, you needn't be there at all, except for fun. I personally think the Nassau shooting should be from mid-April to June, when the weather is much the most reliable, and when Nassau costs of living are quarter of 'season' costs."

Whittingham, too, was expecting to work closely with Fleming and was more than surprised when he instead grabbed a portable typewriter, visas and a round-the-world suit with concealed money pockets and hopped on a BOAC Comet bound for Hong Kong to begin a five-week tour round the world. The Sunday Times wanted Fleming to write a series entitled "The Six Wicked Cities" - observations on places like Las Vegas, Tokyo and Los Angeles. Fleming confessed to being the world's worst sightseer and that he had "often advocated the provision of roller-skates at the doors of museums and art galleries." But his editor argued that such a trip would be a perfect opportunity to pick up material for future Bond stories. Indeed Fleming's Tokyo visit, his first, led to an enthusiasm for Japan and his decision to later use it as the location for *You Only Live Twice*.

Still it took a lot of persuasion to get Fleming on the plane. In a letter to Bryce he complained that the paper had "blarneyed and cajoled" him into taking the assignment. "There are many reasons why I simply have to do this chore, which I can assure you is none of my willing." Still, Fleming was determined to make the best of it and even planned to come back through America, meeting Bryce, McClory and Whittingham in New York around November 20 before flying with them to Nassau for script writing, legal and financial discussions. "A week of concentrated work there should get everything more or less set." He wrote. Then back to London with Whittingham, "where he and I would work on the script during December getting it into more or less final form. Meanwhile Kevin would be getting on with casting, etc." Fleming then hoped, by the close of the year, to fly to Jamaica for two months with Ann and his son Casper.

Just then news reached Fleming that Hitchcock was no longer coming to London, having instead attended the Paris premiere of *North by Northwest* before leaving for America. "He has got the story with him and Evans will try and get some sort of verdict out of him," Fleming wrote Bryce. "On the other hand, Evans confirms that we should be very much in danger of being swallowed up by Hitchcock, who might want to buy the whole thing up, giving you, and perhaps me, shares in the project." This was an enticing prospect since it would surely have made both Bryce and Fleming a tidy sum, but at the same time left Xanadu and everyone else abandoned in the wings, not least McClory who claimed not to have known about this correspondence until years later. Here was Fleming, apparently with the co-ordination of Bryce, envisaging the possibility of carrying out a secret transaction with Hitchcock that would make both of them, in Fleming's words, "a certain fortune." There was no reference whatsoever to McClory, proof, he felt that they deliberately intended to "cut me out completely from any such deal." It was a further demonstration of how relations between the three men had deteriorated in such a relatively short space of time, perhaps irretrievably.

CHAPTER 11
THE SEARCH FOR JAMES BOND

As pre-production continued, news about the proposed James Bond film began appearing in the showbiz and gossip pages of the tabloid press. At society functions, McClory rarely let an opportunity pass by without mentioning it to reporters, happily acting upon Fleming's written advice to him that "I would much prefer for you to be the sole mouthpiece on the project."

Thanks to such publicity, for the first time speculation amongst the general public began about who should play the famous spy. People wrote to newspapers with their own candidates such as Stanley Baker, Patrick McGoohan, Michael Craig, Richard Todd, Peter O'Toole and George Baker, plus Hollywood idols William Holden, James Garner and Montgomery Clift. Bizarrely even Donald Sinden and Peter Cushing were mentioned as possible 007s.

Earlier, during Fleming's meetings with Paul Dehn, the subject of who to cast as Bond had arisen. In his letter of 11 August to Bryce, Fleming announced, "Both Dehn and I think that Richard Burton would be by far the best James Bond!" It's a fascinating suggestion, and possibly the first recorded statement by Fleming about who should play his hero. Year's later Fleming would champion David Niven as Bond, a very traditional English actor and a million miles away from the wild Celtic image and brooding manner of Burton. But what a Bond a pre-*Cleopatra*/pre-Elizabeth Taylor Burton would have been!

Interestingly at this time the makers of the proposed American TV version of *From Russia with Love* had already cast James Mason as Bond. "So if the worst comes to the worst, we might have to settle for him," Fleming wrote Bryce, sounding not entirely won over by the idea. But he must have later warmed to it as Christopher Lee, who was Fleming's cousin, informed this author that Fleming told him that Mason was his preferred choice as Bond.

McClory at this point favoured Trevor Howard and met the actor at least twice to discuss it, in July and October 1959. Fleming disagreed saying that Howard, at 43, was too old and that someone in his early 30s was required. Fleming now suggested Peter Finch. When reminded by McClory that Finch was actually only a year younger than Howard Fleming wrote back, "I would be happier if the part could be given to a young unknown actor, with established stars playing the other roles." A prescient point, for a virtually unknown young actor would eventually win the role of Bond, 32 year old Sean Connery.

As production of the film loomed ever closer, Trevor Howard was still being talked about as a possible Bond, but another new fascinating name entered the frame, that of Dirk Bogarde. In 1959 Bogarde was the top box office draw in Britain, so unsurprisingly was very much in demand. "Dirk Bogarde is probably committed for our dates of location," Leigh Aman wrote McClory that November. "He might, however, be free. His fee is £30,000."

Also, according to McClory, fellow Irishman Richard Harris was interviewed for the Bond role in November 1959. Harris was just embarking upon what was to become a highly successful film career. Also, in New York McClory had dinner with Ingemar Johannsen, then the boxing Heavyweight Champion of the world. "He is looking for an acting career," McClory wrote Bryce. "And, my golly, he would make a wonderful James Bond. Unfortunately, I don't think we can do anything about his Swedish accent – if only we could dub the voice."

Incredibly McClory's London production office was overwhelmed by letters from ex soldiers and out of work actors asking for an audition to show that they were the only person in the world capable of playing Bond. Wives, too, sent letters describing the various attributes of their husband and why they should cast him in the role. Best of all Xanadu's secretary wrote to McClory: "A Mr. Arthur Tarry (accountant) telephoned. Will you be wanting him for James Bond?"

Fleming too was pestered with potential Bond wannabes who sent their photographs to him. One in particular was interesting enough for him to pass it on to McClory, with the proviso. "His acting record seems good, but of course he may be only four feet six inches with a cockney accent and quite out of the question."

Even Laurence Evans got in on the act. But his suggestion was sheer lunacy. He advocated that a man be found whose real name was James Bond and he be groomed for the part. Then, so Evans logic went, wherever he went in the world he would be known as James Bond and become a valuable property for Xanadu. "I think this is an impossible but amusing idea," Fleming wrote Bryce. "But I do think the idea of creating our own James Bond from an unknown and for Xanadu to sign him up for ten years and have a very valuable human property on their hands to act in Bond television series etc, is an excellent one." Not long after Evan's absurd suggestion Bryce actually received three letters applying for the role of James Bond, sent by real James Bonds!

Directors too sent in their CVs, notably Charles Frend, director of classics like *The Cruel Sea* and *Scott of the Antarctic*, then looking for a project to make in association with another stalwart of the British film industry,

Proposed list of characters for the 007 film.

Chapter 11: THE SEARCH FOR JAMES BOND

Michael Balcon. Later on Christopher Mann Ltd, an agency who also represented Jack Whittingham, wrote to Leigh Aman with a list of directors on their books that were available for the Bond film including Charles Crichton, Basil Dearden, Joe Losey and Ronald Neame.

Apart from who should play Bond, little mention was ever made to general casting ideas. Although Whittingham did later reveal that he wrote the character of Largo with Burl Ives in mind because of a letter from Fleming suggesting the American singer/actor should play the part. Fleming was also keen for his friend Ernest Cuneo to play the Capo Mafiosi because, as he wrote, "He has a more fabulous gangster face than has ever been seen on the films." Whittingham also disclosed that McClory was frequently in touch with ex-girlfriend Shirley MacLaine about the Bond project. Was McClory thinking of casting her as the first ever Bond girl? Whittingham recalled one dinner he attended with the acclaimed actress in New York where the Bond film was discussed.

For some time McClory had been concerned that Whittingham, though at work on the script, was still not under contract to Xanadu. "It is most important that we employ Jack Whittingham at the earliest possible moment, he urged Bryce. Finally on 20 October Bryce gave the go-ahead, with one slight reservation. For the first time in the life of the project Bryce felt that this was almost the point of no return. "Like deciding to give a party and then actually putting the first invitation in the post," he explained to Fleming. "Not that I am faltering in any way. Still it is a milestone."

Negotiations with Whittingham's agent progressed smoothly, with the hope he'd agree to write the script for £5000, the equivalent of about £150/200,000 today. "This, for a writer of his experience, is less than he normally takes," McClory wrote Bryce. "And I think we should make an immediate decision on this, as I do know that Walt Disney want very much to put him under contract."

Although agreeing with McClory that Whittingham should now be signed up forthwith, Bryce's patience with his partner was close to breaking point. He urged Fleming to consider replacing Leigh Aman (McClory's man) with Jean de la Bruyere, who in his opinion would be tougher on McClory over the finances. "After watching the money stream through Kevin's fingers for 18 months, it would be life saving to have Jean. Leigh, whom I like, is not good enough for our key business manager post, unfortunately – Jean is the man." Fleming agreed and hoped the Canadian could make Xanadu's 'summit' meetings in New York and Nassau in November. "As it seems to me he has exactly the brain we all lack and badly need for this project."

What rankled the most with Bryce was McClory's passion for touring *The Boy and the Bridge* around the European film festival circuit, all at great cost (in Venice, McClory chartered a luxury yacht to live on), but with little effect on the box office. "I'm afraid the very thought of festivals infuriates me," he wrote McClory on 22 October. "We simply cannot go on spending money faster than it is coming in. Unless we stop spending, and start collecting some of the proceeds, it is obvious that not only shall I never get back my $400,000, but neither of us will ever have any profits to divide."

Generally McClory was pretty free and easy with money, his own as well as other people's. When he travelled, it tended to be first class; and when he was entertaining clients or friends this was done in only the very finest restaurants and clubs. For McClory, like many who attain his kind of wealth, money wasn't merely a means to material possession; it brought power and influence. Self-conscious of his humble beginnings in Ireland and lack of social breeding, when someone said of him, "He has no background," McClory took from his pocket a gigantic roll of five-pound notes. He rubbed his chin with them and grinned, "That's background."

While this growing rift widened between Xanadu's principal players, Fleming remained as positive as ever about the Bond picture. "I'm personally of the opinion that we have a financial winner in this film," he wrote excitedly to Bryce on 23 October. "Whether done in colour or monochrome, so long as we have a couple of good stars, though Jean de la Bruyere should remember that Bond must be an Englishman." This of course refers to Bruyere's earlier suggestion that an American actor be chosen. This flies in the face of Fleming's previous suggestion of the Welsh-born Burton and his acceptance of James Stewart donning a tuxedo. Nor was Fleming much interested in going into partnership with

Columbia, or indeed anyone else, but keeping the Bond film solely as a Xanadu production, keeping it, as he says, "in the family." So confident was he that they had the right team "with Kevin as producer, X as director, Whittingham as script writer and you as general organiser, assisted as much as possible by me, I don't see why the vehicle shouldn't roll."

It's evident in this letter that Fleming was confident of the film going ahead and had started focusing on the expensive props his story called for, principally an American bomber and submarine. Fleming suggested to Bryce that Cuneo and his governmental contacts might be of help; perhaps a $10,000 donation to a Naval and airforce charity might fix it. "The crash and sinking in shallow water would presumably be a matter of good dummies, plus the actual remains of a crashed aircraft of one sort or another as, by the time it got to the bottom of the sea, it would look more or less unrecognisable as a Valiant." At this stage the bomber in question was to be a Valiant, not a Villiers Vindicator as in the book, or a Vulcan as used later in the film.

In this long letter to Bryce, Fleming mentions a script polish on his second treatment, incorporating work done with Whittingham: "Have sent this off to my typist in the country who charges peanuts and she will make ten copies, which can be used for casting purposes etc. I'm having a final meeting with Whittingham soon to iron out any major problems. He will then have plenty to do during November and could perhaps join us in Nassau around November 25 and stay there for two or three weeks getting on with the local stuff."

Fleming also revealed to Bryce that he'd finally seen *North by Northwest* and liked it. "But the trouble is that the old master of suspense, having got us on the edge of our chairs, then makes us dissolve in screams of laughter and, while the mixture is delightful, he really does throw away the most wonderful plot. We need a few touches of comedy but, unless we treat this story with an absolutely straight face and with a desperate sense of urgency, the film will collapse. Personally I'm for keeping the jokes to the minimum and getting people really sweating." Strange then that the approach Broccoli and Saltzman later took with the Bond films was the complete opposite in radically heightening the humour element.

As for Hitchcock personally, Fleming had heard nothing, but this was more likely to mean, he'd been told, that the director was interested rather than not, otherwise he'd have quickly responded in the negative. "However, I see no point in hanging about anymore and we must press on." In the end, Hitchcock passed on the Bond project, turning his back on big budget movies for his next production, a small black and white film that changed cinema forever, one that might never have been made if Hitch had said yes to 007 – *Psycho*.

CHAPTER 12
THE FIRST JAMES BOND SCREENPLAY

Since its inception, the 007 project had simply been known as "James Bond." No suitable title had yet been found. Jean de la Bruyere's suggestion it be called "The Right to Kill" (which Bryce liked) caused Fleming to hurriedly think of an alternative and he wrote to Bryce on 26 October. "Regarding name for the film, I suggest 'James Bond of the Secret Service.' He is well enough known now to bring the customers in and titles like 'The Right to Kill' are all too common."

Despite the amount of work Whittingham had already contributed, it wasn't until 7 December that an agreement was finally drawn up and signed between himself and McClory, on behalf of Xanadu. His usual fee of £6,000 reduced to £5,000 on the understanding that this would be the first of a hopeful series of Bond screenplays. Significantly, Whittingham assigned the copyright in the script over to McClory. A clause in the contract also stated that all material written could be used for subsequent motion pictures. This was a normal contract between producer and writer, but it would later have severe repercussions for Whittingham.

Using Fleming's second treatment as a base and incorporating McClory's ideas and his own, Whittingham sat down to write what he termed a "First Draft Continuity Treatment." This would be the first of three scripts Whittingham would produce; full of different and contrasting material and offering fascinating markers in the evolution of what ultimately became the film *Thunderball*. He sent it out for perusal on 10 November 1959 with the temporary title "James Bond of the Secret Service." In a letter to McClory Whittingham stressed that the material "must only be regarded as a very uncouth, exploratory kick-off. It has the potential for some good scenes, but it also has some glaring weaknesses." This, Whittingham attributed to the time factor in having to produce the script before McClory left for New York and a meeting with Fleming.

The opening third is much as before. In the Mafia meeting in Sicily Whittingham stressed the point that the audience should not see the Capo Mafiosi's face. One wonders if this is where the idea came from not to reveal arch villain Blofeld's identity early on in the official series. Whittingham also ups the stakes in the Mafia's demands. Failure to pay will result in the first bomb being exploded in an area of strategic importance. If the ransom is still not forthcoming the second bomb will be detonated in a major city.

Arriving in Nassau, Bond dines with Felix Leiter in a night-club. Leiter sees Largo and recognises him as one Spider Spinelli, a Brooklyn racketeer with a bulging FBI file. His presence in Nassau is too much of a coincidence so Bond decides to inveigle his way into the affections of Largo's girlfriend Domino.

Bond and Leiter find the sunken bomber and at a remote beach, 007 breaks the news to Domino that Petachi (back to being her brother) is dead, using as proof the identity disc he took from his corpse. "Her Sicilian blood boils for revenge," writes Whittingham. Domino agrees to help Leiter break into Xanadu, Largo's beach house, but they are ambushed and thrown into a swamp: "Leiter sinks rapidly until his head disappears. Domino, who is sinking more slowly, screams with terror." With Leiter dead, Largo orders Domino to be taken prisoner.

On the yacht that night Largo is greeted by the recently arrived Capo Mafiosi, here called Cuneo. Nearby on a police launch, Bond hears works being carried out on the yacht's underwater doors, which have jammed, and investigates. He sees a dozen frogmen swim out, some manning underwater sleds. Largo and Cuneo see Bond's air bubbles and throw grenades into the water. Bond staggers ashore and is at once seized by Mafia thugs, knocked over the head and thrown into the swamp near Leiter's body.

With Bond safely out of the way Largo picks up the hidden bombs and sails to the target area. But Bond is alive, saved by the breathing tube of his aqualung. From the deck of the yacht Largo and Cuneo see a plane heading straight for them. Bond and a team of scuba paratroopers jump out, slashing their parachutes free as they hit the water. They submerge and defeat the Mafia frogmen.

Meanwhile Domino has escaped from her room and set the second atom bomb to explode in three minutes. Largo and Cuneo attempt to escape in the yacht but Domino confronts them and accuses Largo of murdering her brother. "I hope you rot in hell!" Largo just laughs and draws a gun. But Domino doesn't care; she's beyond any further hurt. Boom! The screen is enveloped in a mushroom cloud. The end. What a great climax, the kind of Bond girl self-sacrifice that May Day later executed in *A View to a Kill*. And, with the possible exception of Bond's dead wife over the rolling credits of *On Her Majesty's Secret Service*, would have been the most downbeat ending to any 007 film. (*For a longer version of this script see Appendix 4*)

In early November McClory left for New York. The main thing on his mind at the time was money. It had run out. The partnership account was empty and McClory, so he later claimed, was having to make payments out of his own personal account to cover expenditure for pre-production on the Bond film as Bryce had failed to give Xanadu's London office the promised cheque of $10,000.

On 13 November McClory, together with Bryce, opened a new account at The Chase Manhattan Bank on Madison Avenue expressly for the James Bond film. The next month a similar account was opened at London's Knightsbridge branch of the National Provincial Bank. In the presence of the bank's officer, both men signed a partnership document and Bryce paid into "Xanadu Productions: James Bond Account" the sum of $15,000. Chequebooks were also made out in the name of "Xanadu Productions: James Bond Account." This was McClory's idea to keep the accounting of *Boy and the Bridge* and Bond as separate entities.

Being in a bank was as good a place as any, McClory thought, to broach the subject of his salary and the fact that he was still not receiving one, only expenses. "Don't worry about it," Bryce said. "I'm getting everything worked out."

During his New York stay, McClory found time to introduce Bryce, along with new arrivals Fleming and Whittingham, to Charles Joseph Kelly, a New York City policeman with personal knowledge of the Mafia, not least from run-ins with hoodlum bosses like the infamous Frank Costello. Kelly took the group on a visit to police headquarters and various locations where famous crimes took place and neighbourhoods and restaurants where underworld characters associated and frequented. He also recommended some books on the Mafia, so in writing and preparing the script they'd have the necessary knowledge to present the Mafia sequences accurately.

Chapter 12: THE FIRST JAMES BOND SCREENPLAY

Proof that a bank account was created by Xanadu expressly for the Bond film, something Bryce bizarrely later contested.

Cover of Whittingham's first draft Bond script. Note the numerous titles.

An original cheque slip from the Xanadu James Bond US account.

Script conferences were also held in McClory's hotel suite. At one point Fleming stood up and said he wanted a few words in private with Whittingham. They went into the bedroom and there Fleming revealed his anxiety about a project that had begun relatively simply but was now in danger of getting completely out of hand. The plans for expensive stars and lavish underwater filming were beginning to frighten him. He was worried too that Bryce could suffer irreparable financial damage and it would all be his fault. James Bond, in his view, was big enough now to carry a film without the use of star names and expensive visuals. Whittingham could say nothing to allay Fleming's fears, making the point that he was merely a writer, not a film producer.

After his New York trip, Whittingham accompanied by Leigh Aman, went to the Bahamas for a location reconnaissance. McClory would soon join them. Neither Bryce nor Fleming made the trip, something Aman found particularly surprising since a lot of the filming was planned to take place around Bryce's private waterfront property called Xanadu. As a result Aman later recalled that there was "an atmosphere of tension" during the trip. McClory flew to Nassau in the company of Ernest Cuneo. As McClory later recalled, it was a strange journey. In-between bouts of heavy drinking Cuneo told McClory that he'd had trouble in the past with Bryce over money matters and implied that Bryce could create problems. McClory said that he must be mistaken. In retrospect he believed Cuneo was trying to draw him out to making some negative statement against Bryce. McClory also believed that Cuneo was attempting to create discord between Leigh Aman and himself, as well as making certain remarks to Whittingham calculated to undermine McClory's authority and Whittingham's confidence in him.

Together the men covered the entire island by land, air and sea and suitable location sites were noted by Aman. Part of his report read: "Already suitable locations have been found for the sunken bomber (area between Clifton Pier and Lyford Cay) and the underwater fight (partly around a wreck off Athol Island and partly beneath the Clifton Pier structure)." For the 1965 film the bomber prop would indeed be sunk for filming purposes off Clifton Pier, while the underwater battle climax was filmed there too.

The discovery of a wreck off Athol Island was greeted enthusiastically by Whittingham who had been devising a way to make the underwater battle even more spectacular. Now the Mafia could conceal the A-bomb in the wreck before setting it off and the battle itself take place in and around the sunken vessel with divers swimming through funnels, into the wheelhouse etc. "It would give a wonderful perspective and a sense of geography and surprise, which a simple sea bed could never provide," he wrote.

A marine laboratory on the nearby island of Bimini was also visited. In a series of large fish pens built into the sea were kept shark, barracuda, swordfish etc. "Invaluable for fish-close-ups" goes the report, though the quoted price for filming there was steep at £100 per day. On land it was hoped to use Bryce's beach house Xanadu and the surrounding grounds (which included a mangrove swamp) as much as possible. Chosen as the most suitable place for Bond's first meeting with Domino was the British Colonial Hotel. "This has a bar, patio, pool and jetty together with a background of the harbour and plenty of movement of shipping," wrote Aman. Not only would the 1965 production extensively use the British Colonial Hotel but also *Never Say Never Again*. Its sea front bar is where Bond meets Fatima Blush while sipping his "still dry" vodka martini. The bar was even renamed afterwards in the film's honour. To stand-in for the missile base that is Largo's target, Aman suggested using the Clifton Pier Power House and oil tanks. "with the addition of some mock-up rockets."

Besides location spotting Aman was also in charge of the more nitty gritty task of costing local services and goods, everything from accommodation, vehicle hire, catering facilities, immigration and custom details, a unit nurse and building and electrical supplies. Everything was listed and budgeted in meticulous detail, proof of just how far into pre-production the Bond film was progressing. Aman finished his report with the summation: "It will have been observed that Nassau is a very expensive island. If it is to be assumed that the film is to be made here, as opposed to some other Caribbean

Chapter 12: THE FIRST JAMES BOND SCREENPLAY

Documentation relating to the James Bond bank account held in Britain.

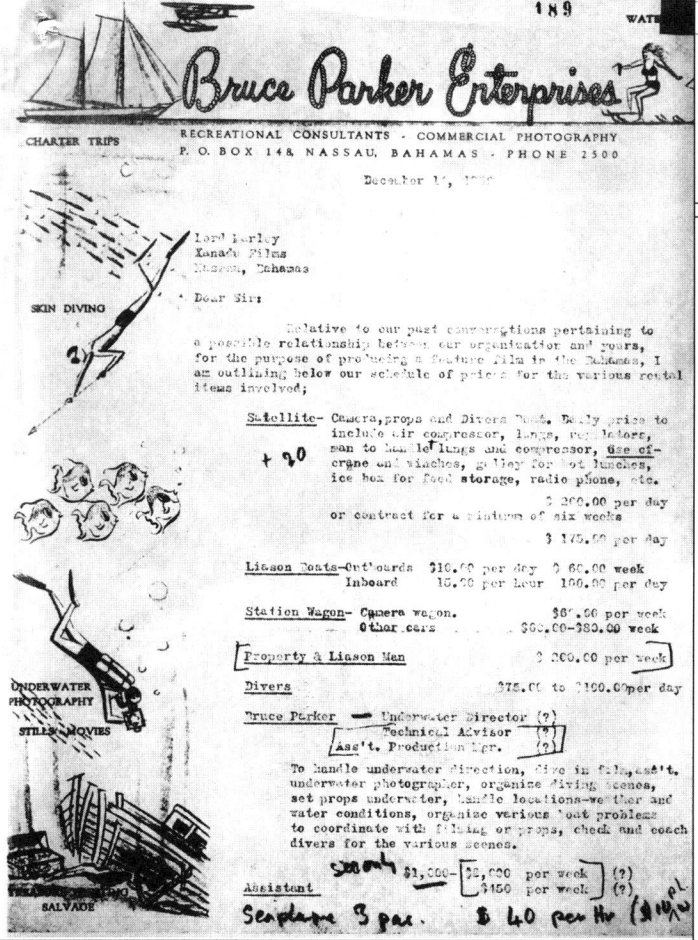

Underwater filming estimate from a local Nassau diving firm.

area, the expense must be accepted. However, the pictorial and production value of these locations are immense and therefore, in spite of the expense, it would be worth doing as much shooting as possible on location using every aspect the island has to offer."

Whittingham certainly found the time he spent in the Bahamas creatively beneficial and the experience aided him greatly in his approach to the Bond screenplay. He wrote his thoughts about the trip on 14 December, shortly before returning to London: "For the requirements of our story, New Providence, Bahamas, is an ideal location. I think the story has developed very considerably as a result of talks with Fleming and others in New York, and this thorough reconnaissance of the Bahamas from a writer's point of view has been invaluable. One takes mental photographs and learns geography instead of having to try and imagine it all. My script is full of notes of new developments which have sprung from being here and from discussions. All I need now is to return to the peace of my own study and write the first draft screen play."

That undertaking would make history as the first complete James Bond theatrical screenplay ever written. It's a fascinating document and holding it in one's hands one can't help feeling – what might have been.

Before the main action Whittingham includes a bizarre short prologue given by the former US President Harry Truman about the nuclear peril. Another new and drastic change is that of the heroine herself. Whittingham never liked the name Domino, so here she's called Gaby and her personality is totally different. Without question one of the most disagreeable of all the Bond women, Gaby is out to get what she can, no matter the consequences to others.

The script opens with the murder of the informant Martelli and the rather perverse notion that Largo is turned on by the thought of his body being ripped apart by sharks because he immediately demands sex from Gaby, paying for it with the money retrieved from Martelli's corpse.

Bond arrives in Nassau just as Largo's fake convention is getting underway. At a bar he meets Gaby. "She looks him up and down, quite unashamedly, and appears to like what she sees," writes Whittingham. The next day they go deep-sea fishing together and Bond tries to press her about Largo and his enormous yacht, the Sorrento.

Jealous and suspicious of Bond, Largo orders a botched assassination attempt. At police HQ Felix Leiter informs Bond that Washington has identified Largo as a high ranking Mafia man. "Hell! This is interesting," says Bond.

During an aerial search, Bond and Leiter find the submerged plane, minus bombs. "We see the corpses of the crew, swollen and bizarre." At the casino, Bond beats Largo at baccarat and steals Gaby from under his nose. They drive to a secluded beach where Largo and his henchman Janni fail in another assassination bid. "Why did they want to kill us?" Gaby asks. Bond explains the whole story and wins her over. Meanwhile Leiter is caught nosing around Xanadu and taken prisoner aboard the Sorrento. Then Bond himself is apprehended and left to die in a swamp.

Largo's divers pick up the bombs from an underwater cave and set sail for Miami. A naval gunboat spots them and follows only to be destroyed by a limpet mine. Meanwhile Largo tells Gaby that Bond is dead. She is distraught, but when he divulges the huge ransom demand her mood changes. "What's my share?" She asks. Largo, sensing her mercenary streak, agrees to keep her on side.

Bond summons up the energy to pull himself out of the swamp, escaping the predatory gaze of hundreds of crabs encircling him. The Sorrento closes in on Miami and the divers unload their deadly cargo. Bond, along with some Royal Marines, parachute out of a plane into the sea, ready for battle.

On board the Sorrento, Largo double-crosses Gaby and loads the second bomb into his private plane, which is shot into the air by a catapult mechanism. Unknown to him, however, Gaby is hiding inside and wiring the bomb to explode. Bond finds an injured Felix Leiter and they look up to see the plane, no more than a speck now in the sky, suddenly explode in a blinding flash. (*For a longer version of this script see Appendix 5*)

CHAPTER 13
DISASTER STRIKES

Despite the effectiveness of Whittingham's first stab at the Bond screenplay things were about to turn decidedly sour. Although it had won awards at some festivals, *The Boy and the Bridge* had flopped badly in the UK. The prognosis for the vital American and international market was even worse. Nobody would touch it. Columbia had released it in Britain and had first option to open it stateside. They were no longer interested. After private screenings, RKO made no offer, Paramount rejected it, MGM made no bid, nor did Fox. The film was even exhibited to Mr Walt Disney, who later declined on the basis of "low commerciality." *The Boy and the Bridge* was dead in the water.

Fearing its poor box office showing was going to hit him hard financially, Bryce was now having grave thoughts about the Bond project. On 18 December he wrote a letter to McClory that must have sent the Irishman's spirits crashing. Bryce had decided that he no longer wished to proceed any further with Bond. Already his personal outlay on the film's pre-production was considerable, and set to rise. With the hoped for cash bonanza from *Boy and the Bridge* non-existent, the 007 project's only chance of redemption was through financial backing from outside sources.

What was being advocated was a total re-examination of the situation. Bryce would only continue financing Bond until 15 February 1960 when the completed script was set for delivery. Then he would give his final decision. "It is apparent that our best chance of going forward is in a splendid script by Whittingham," wrote Bryce. "Which would have the effect of conveying enthusiasm to both Ian Fleming and prospective backers, because their persuasion is absolutely necessary for further progress." Bryce saw Whittingham's script as "a keystone" to anything that may be able to be done with the project in the future.

In no way did Bryce regret the money he had lost thus far but merely wished "to lose as little more as possible. Neither my interest nor my enthusiasm are diminished in any way. However, I think that a mere glance at the large cash depletion already sustained by me fully explains why I can't afford to continue as heretofore."

Bryce dropped another little bombshell in his letter: that Fleming had consented to the use of his character James Bond upon two conditions, namely the formation of a film production company and the actual making of the film itself. Xanadu was set up for the sole purpose of producing *Boy and the Bridge* while its Bahamian counterpart, which was to handle the Bond film, had still not been formed. Cameras hadn't started rolling yet either. Both conditions therefore had failed according to Bryce, thus invalidating the earlier agreement. "It is clear," he wrote, "that any production of the Whittingham script would be subject to the consent, approval and re-negotiations with Ian Fleming. The Whittingham script will not be marketable, nor could I even exhibit it for possible financing without a completely new arrangement with Ian Fleming."

When rumours reached Fleming that Bryce was having second thoughts he wrote to his old friend on 29 December: "Having heard nothing from you for so long, I presume you are not dead," he began. "I have no idea what your plans are for the whole project, but the frost-bitten right toe which I suffered at my delicious Thanksgiving weekend is pulsating that you may have gone a bit cold on the whole business. If so, I shall perfectly understand. The idea of a $3 million budget with Kevin at the helm dismays me, although I'm sure he could *help* to make a James Bond film that would please us both and bring in the cash customers. But I'm in the dark about all this and it may be that the jelly has jelled since I last saw you."

At the start of the project, Fleming had led McClory to believe that he was the only person whom he would like to produce the Bond film, and realised too that it was going to be a very costly enterprise. Now he seemed to be using the very size of the project to undermine McClory's authority as producer and suggesting to Bryce that he be merely an assistant of some kind who could "help" with the picture. Also if Fleming's sums were correct the intended budget was now $3 million, an astronomical sum, and three times the eventual budget of 1962s *Dr. No*. Little wonder that Bryce was stepping back from the prospect of having to foot most of that bill himself. "Showbiz is a ghastly biz," Fleming concluded his letter. "And the last thing I want is for you to lose your pin-striped trousers in its grisly maw, however much fun you may have in the process. Nor do I want the first James Bond film to be botched, but the first consideration is primary. If you decide to skip the whole thing, don't forget that you have, or should have, a good saleable property in the script, so all is not completely lost." In other words, if Bryce wasn't going to make the film, maybe they could find somebody else that would. But where did that leave McClory?

Most of all it left the vexed question of who exactly owned the Bond film project. McClory made it clear that as a partner in Xanadu he believed he owned a share in it and was unwilling to let it go. On 15 December Cuneo had tried to point the way by penning a formal assignment of his own rights and all his interests in the original Bond story idea to Bryce for the token sum of $1. Cuneo never had any desire to get into the movie business; he'd simply helped out as a friend. But McClory was not willing to be pressured into following suit. "I believe very strongly that the Bond picture should be made and I know that it could and will be, if produced as we at present envisage it, a very strong box office picture." He said in a letter to Bryce on 14 January 1960. McClory was equally determined that the Bond film be made under the Xanadu banner, his preferred option, or, in the case of Bryce backing out, going on alone. Early enquiries had led McClory to believe he could get 70% financing from a major distribution company in return for 50% of the profits, meaning that Xanadu would own half of the profits for 30% of the cost of production. A great deal, if it was true; or was McClory perhaps egging the pudding to keep Bryce sweet. This of course was all dependent on Bryce's willingness to go ahead with the project after 15 February, when McClory had guaranteed the screenplay would be ready. An amazing feat since Whittingham had only started it just after Christmas.

Bryce's hesitancy also caused practicable problems in regard to crewing the picture. Technicians had already been hired but with fluctuating production dates; first it was to go ahead in April or May 1960, then June, with up to ten weeks on location in the Bahamas, and now no clear starting date at all, some took up offers elsewhere and left. "I do feel that in order to make it possible for me to make the picture this year," wrote McClory to his partner, "we should make a decision as speedily as possible (after you have had an opportunity to go over the script) as to whether you wish to continue or not."

Chapter 13: DISASTER STRIKES

"THUNDERBALL"
~~LONGITUDE-78-WEST~~

The title *Thunderball* is born.

```
THUNDERBALL i.e. operation T.
A JAMES BOND ADVENTURE


"THUNDERBALL"
LONGITUDE-78-WEST


Dear Ian
    Despatching this with haste from the
Airport - I hope Ivar warned  u about the
title (but it is only a work.   one!) -
Already we have many changes    make in this
- and hope you can meet me here next week
to discuss them.

                Regards,

                Kevin.
```

The film was also no longer to be called "James Bond of the Secret Service." McClory had registered the new titles of "Longitude 78 West" and "Latitude 25" (both derived from the map references of the last known position of the missing bomber) with the British Film Producer's Association. Another title Whittingham had toyed with was "Bond in the Bahamas." McClory was the first to admit these titles, "would appear meaningless to the average individual" but thought them nevertheless intriguing and compared them with other films like *49th Parallel* and, of course, *North By Northwest*; no doubt the main influence.

Fleming however, didn't like either title and would cross out "Longitude 78 West" and place THUNDERBALL on the script cover page. He then proceeded to go through the screenplay adding references that Bond's assignment be known as "Operation Thunderball." The word Thunderball, Fleming later revealed, had stuck in his mind ever since he'd heard it used to describe an American atomic test in the Pacific. Shrewdly McClory took steps to have this name registered as the title of a proposed new film. Registration was finally effected in August 1960. The purpose of this registration was for McClory to obtain priority over any other film producer who might wish to use the same title.

In complete contrast to his downbeat letter to McClory, Bryce was nothing but upbeat about the situation when he wrote to Whittingham on 15 January 1960, giving not the slightest indication of his severe reservations over the Bond project. At the time Bryce was relaxing in his holiday home in Nassau. "Xanadu only needs the presence of Mr Largo to fulfil its destiny," he wrote, "and broods of young sharks in the creek are flexing their muscles in preparation for their screen tests." In spite of calling a halt to McClory's pre-production activities Bryce seemed very anxious to get his hands on Whittingham's script as soon as possible. "I imagine you are toiling in your toil room over stubborn passages, and cursing the day you ever heard of Bond." He asked to be cabled the moment it was finished and for three copies to be sent to him in Nassau and the rest to Cuneo in New York. The date had changed too. Bryce now wanted it as near 1st February, "as you can possibly, possibly make it. What a desperately exciting moment!"

Whittingham telephoned McClory about Bryce's request as he thought it rather odd since he had been engaged by McClory, so naturally could only hand the script over to him. McClory was also interested in the way Bryce had phrased his request: "Please cable me which day I can expect MY script in MY hand here." (Author's use of capitals). Up to this time all references to the Bond script and project had been "our" script and "our" project.

Four days later, Whittingham informed Bryce of the progress he was making on the screenplay: "The characters are coming to life, and the story certainly gallops. I am enjoying it immensely, and that's usually a good sign." But Whittingham was keen to emphasise to Bryce that this was only a first draft script written in a few weeks, without the time for rewrites, and was to be regarded just as raw material to work on before chiselling the finished product. "So please don't judge it as anything else but that, or you will be doing me and the subject an injustice." He also ruled out the possibility of the script being ready by 1 February, as had been rashly promised by McClory. "But I very much hope that you will be reading it by about Feb 17."

Whittingham had been working very much in tandem with McClory on the script, frequently travelling up to London for long discussions with the Irishman, mapping out scenes and ideas, and then returning home to labour alone before his typewriter. He used to write in his study facing the garden. As children, Sylvan Whittingham and her brother Jonathan learned to tiptoe around the house or retreat to the furthest corners of the garden when their father was working. Whittingham's routine would involve getting up quite late, enjoying a leisurely breakfast and then disappearing into his "cave" around 10.00 am. His first drink of the day often started around eleven. After lunch he would work for a while and then take a nap during the afternoon. Apart from a break for supper he would then work steadily until very late at night. "As a writer he was plagued by the need to come up with fresh ideas and it took a huge toll," recalls Jonathan. "He would consume a lot of alcohol and smoke like a chimney. He kept a pet budgerigar from time to time that lived in a cage next to his desk. However they were always free to fly around at will. He had one called Charlie. Charlie would sit and snooze propped up against Jack's neck. Jack would sit at his desk waiting for his "muse", a glass of gin in his left hand and the never-ending cigarette in the other. Every so often Charlie would wake up and take a stroll down Jack's arm to the well of gin at the end, take a sip and then make his weary way back and resume dozing. This would be repeated on a few more occasions until Charlie could barely make his way back up the arm. Then he would very quietly whisper or coo into Jack's ear. Then Jack would begin to write."

During meals, Jack would share with his family news on how the Bond script was going and about McClory, with whom he had endless long conversations on the telephone. "But Kevin didn't do any of the actual physical writing," confirms Sylvan. "It was Dad who had the grind of writing the script."

While enjoying his close working relationship with McClory, Whittingham was finding Fleming harder to tie down, complaining to Bryce that "We are both working in the dark so far as Ian Fleming is concerned – and Bond is very much his personal creation. I know that he will be very helpful at this much more detailed stage, and it would encourage us enormously if we felt we were all still pulling on the same rope." Things had certainly changed since October when Bryce insisted in a letter to Fleming that he "spend as much time as is humanly possible during the scriptwriting period."

So where was Fleming, if he wasn't on hand helping the scriptwriter? The answer was Jamaica and his annual pilgrimage to write his latest Bond novel. Fleming fell in love with Jamaica in 1944 when he attended a special intelligence conference in Kingston. Bryce already owned property there and Fleming asked him to help in his search for a plot of seafront land to build his dream winter retreat. In March 1945 Fleming began construction on Goldeneye, named after a wartime operation he'd masterminded. It was a three-bedroom house designed by Fleming himself, something he was immensely proud of. He'd spend every January and February there until his death in 1964.

Fleming left London on 3 January telling Bryce that if he were needed for meetings, and if Xanadu were prepared to pay his fare "I shall be delighted to come up with my usual keen eye and brain." McClory too had spoken with Fleming prior to his leaving and had been assured that the author would be available for a conference in Nassau after delivery of the new script, to discuss alterations prior to Whittingham beginning work on the final shooting script. McClory also knew that Fleming was working on a new Bond novel. What McClory later claimed he didn't know was that Fleming's new novel was based on Whittingham's film script and the author had no intention of sharing credit.

CHAPTER 14
FLEMING, THE PLAGIARIST

At his beachfront home Goldeneye, Fleming found himself unenthused and bereft of ideas as he faced the task of coming up with another Bond adventure – his ninth. Was it writer's block or the author's growing restlessness with his own creation? He even considered killing Bond off in this latest book, instead opting to postpone the execution. Writing to William Plomer, an old friend from his days with Naval Intelligence who always proof-read and pre-edited the 007 books, Fleming complained that he was "Terribly stuck with James Bond. What was easy at 40 is very difficult at 50. I used to believe – sufficiently – in Bonds and blondes and bombs. Now the keys creak as I type and I fear the zest may have gone. Part of the trouble is having a wife and child. They knock the ruthlessness out of one. I shall definitely kill off Bond with my next book – better a poor bang than a rich whimper!"

Fleming had already revealed to Plomer that he'd, "really run out of puff" after *Goldfinger*, published in 1959, which he intended to be "the last full-length folio on Bond. Though I may be able to think up some episodes for him in the future, I shall never be able to give him 70,000 words again." When a proposed CBS Bond TV series ran aground Fleming lost little time in adapting "Risico", "From a View to a Kill" and "For Your Eyes Only" directly from the television outlines he'd already prepared. Adding two more tales he produced a collection of short stories entitled *For Your Eyes Only* that his publishers agreed to bring out in 1960 in lieu of that year's full-length Bond. But in 1961 they wanted a proper novel. And that was the problem. So, hard up for ideas Fleming simply took the basic story from the *Thunderball* scripts and turned it into his next novel. He sought neither Whittingham nor McClory's permission, nor did he intend to acknowledge them in any way. Fleming didn't even bother to change the title. Why let a good idea go to waste, he must have thought, an idea he himself had helped create and which, after all, was based on his own creation – 007.

But Fleming would suffer from bouts of miserable self-doubt about the *Thunderball* novel. How much, one wonders, was this creative block or inner guilt about where the ideas had come from? When he returned to London, Fleming would inform William Plomer that he'd just completed a, "giant Bond." But having "got thoroughly bored with it after a bit," he'd not been able to re-read the manuscript and it would need "drastic re-writing." When his concerns about the book refused to go away Michael Howard, of publishers Jonathan Cape, felt obliged to write to him: "I suppose it is because you present such an urbane and sturdy front to the world that one tends to forget the quivering sensibilities of the artist which lie behind it. But they must account for those acute pangs of doubt and dissatisfaction about this new James Bond adventure which you have repeatedly expressed to William and me, for which neither of us can see any real justification. Quite the reverse."

Fleming actually never hid the fact he adopted some of Whittingham/McClory's ideas, like the airborne hijack of the bomb, but claimed he added many more of his own, such as an ingenious new introductory sequence at a health farm based on one he frequented in real life. When he couldn't think of what to call his fictional health club, friend Peter Quennell suggested Shrublands, after the name of his parent's home. McClory and Whittingham later argued that these scenes, particularly those revolving around the health farm, were deliberately introduced by Fleming to obfuscate the joint origins of the novel. Whittingham later wrote, "After reading the novel I formed the opinion that Fleming was aware that there might be an action for infringement of copyright and that in writing his novel he was bending over backwards to avoid a legal action by adding details and irrelevancies to the plot."

The most notable new element in the *Thunderball* novel was the re-introduction of SPECTRE. Fleming ditched the Mafia and brought back these criminals from his early screen treatment to become arguably the greatest villainous organisation in literature and film. Fleming also replaced the Capo Mafioso with a far more malevolent embodiment of evil – Ernst Stavro Blofeld.

While the SPECTRE idea had emerged from earlier script conferences, the *Thunderball* novel is the first written documentation of the famous Blofeld character. Claims have been made that Blofeld was created much earlier and not solely by the hands of Fleming, but no proof exists to back this up. And so it looks likely that Blofeld was first conceived for this novel. The unusual surname was "borrowed" by Fleming from a fellow member of his gentleman's club Boodles; a Norfolk farmer called Tom Blofeld.

Fleming also, understandably, changed the villain's headquarters from Sicily to Paris, housing SPECTRE at the Boulevard Haussmann, a business street near the opera house. Fleming contacted a journalist colleague based in Paris for background material on the businesses and residents there. Along with the information Fleming also got the following advice: "I don't know what you are planning, but I should think James Bond would be lynched if he set foot in Paris after his insufferable and idiotic reflections on pages 14 to 18 of his last adventures." The journalist was referring to the 1960 anthology *For Your Eyes Only* and the opening story *From a View To a Kill* in which a woman described her irritation at Frenchmen pinching her backside on the Metro.

As for Largo, now with the Christian name Emilio, he became a much more elegant figure in the novel, less of the thuggish brute of the scripts. Here his villainy is on an almost operatic scale. His cover is also more solid, claiming to be the leader of a treasure hunt, which calls for security precautions and justifies his well-equipped yacht, now finally given the name Disco Volante.

Also in the book, Domino turns into one of Fleming's great heroines, coming to life in a way she never did in any of the screenplays. Fleming brilliantly offsets her beauty, as he had done with Honeychile Rider's broken nose in *Dr. No*, by making one leg an inch shorter than the other resulting in a slight limp. We also learn that Domino's parents are dead and she is very obviously Largo's kept woman. Fleming gives her the Italian surname of Vitali (from the word "vita" meaning life), but later reveals this to be a stage name, as her real surname is Petacchi (one more 'c' than Whittingham's Petachi).

Fleming also keeps Petacchi as Domino's brother, whom she adores. But she is totally unaware of his recruitment to SPECTRE. It's a nice plot line, but a bit illogical. Of all the people in the world Largo's bit on the side just happens to be the sister of the hijack pilot; and Largo doesn't know! Fleming was a past master at writing over poor plotting, his characters and scenarios so richly drawn that one rarely questioned the discrepancies, just as the later films were so fast and well crafted one didn't start questioning them until the journey home from the cinema. But this one is a bit hard to take.

Chapter 14: FLEMING, THE PLAGIARIST

In resume, the book's plot is as follows: Bond is chastised about his monthly medical report that shows if he continues smoking and drinking to excess his health will deteriorate; which found a mirror in Fleming's own life. M orders Bond to Shrublands, a local health clinic where he meets masseur Patricia and the mysterious Count Lippe who sports a tattooed Tong sign on his wrist. Lippe tries to eliminate Bond by sabotaging his traction machine. As revenge, Bond increases the heat on Lippe's electric Turkish bath.

In Paris, a special meeting of SPECTRE is taking place, presided over by Blofeld.

Previous business is conducted, during which one man is electrocuted for raping a kidnap victim. Blofeld reveals Plan Omega - the stealing of two atomic bombs. Lippe is in charge of the first stage of the operation, Shrublands being close to the NATO airbase and Petacchi. Lippe is then eliminated over his botched assassination attempt on Bond. The plane hi-jack follows the pattern already established, but unlike Whittingham's script where Petacchi has his air intake tube cut and drowns, Fleming dispatches him above the waves with a stiletto in the throat. The bombs are then hidden in an underwater cave.

Bond arrives in Nassau and meets Felix Leiter. Both are suspicious about Largo and his yacht full of treasure hunters. Bond meets Domino at the casino and begins his seduction of her. Bond finds the submerged bomber and removes Petacchi's identity disc and watch, which he uses to convince Domino that Largo is a murderer. She agrees to help determine if the bombs are aboard the Disco Volante, but is caught by Largo using a Geiger counter and submitted to torture. Bond has been trailing the yacht in a submarine and with an aqua team successfully ambushes Largo and his SPECTRE frogmen as they attempt to plant the bomb. Domino shoots Largo with a CO_2 gun. With the bombs recovered, SPECTRE's hideout in Paris is raided, but Blofeld has already fled. The book finishes with Bond and Domino recuperating together in hospital.

Whether Fleming deliberately intended to plagiarise the work done by Whittingham and McClory is debatable. Sitting in front of his desk at Goldeneye, obligated and under pressure from his publisher to come up with the next installment of 007, Fleming felt safe in the knowledge that this wasn't the first time he'd used a discarded TV or film script as the basis for a novel. "Commander Jamaica," the abandoned 1956 NBC series, for example, was remounted as *Dr. No*. Yet this time the work was not wholly his.

A degree of arrogance was involved too. All his life Fleming had been in the habit of getting his own way without too much concern for the feelings of people with whom he failed to get on. McClory had certainly fallen into that category. But who knows what Fleming was really thinking? One clue is in the fact that he dedicated the *Thunderball* novel thus: 'To Ernest Cuneo Muse.' If the intention of the inscription to Cuneo was to give the world the impression that the inspiration of the story came from him, it backfired badly. McClory and Whittingham were incensed that having given no acknowledgement of their contribution Fleming should expressly thank Cuneo, whose input did not compare with theirs and whose short film synopsis of May 1959 the *Thunderball* novel, in their view "Derived no or at most an insignificant quantity of material or ideas."

Fleming was also guilty of an element of naivete about the ways of the entertainment world. Perhaps he felt that being the elder statesman gave him superiority over the young and brash McClory and that he could simply get away with it. "I suppose Fleming also felt that because my father had been paid for his screenplay that he would just leave it there," says Sylvan Mason. "And he felt much the same about McClory. And it was a mistake because Kevin wouldn't just disappear." Fleming had totally misjudged McClory and the consequences were to be monumental.

196. continued.

BOND (returning with his drink)
Because he's our only link with the
bombs. In any case, someone else
would take over. We're not only
fighting Largo - it's the Mafia.
Palermo!

LEITER
And we've still no sure proof that it's
Largo. He'd just be showing our hands.

BOND (as if thinking aloud)
He's got one weak spot....It must be
a very weak spot or he wouldn't have tried
to slaughter me.

He takes a long drink from his highball.

BOND (to the Police Commissioner)
You're keeping tabs on him now,
aren't you?

POLICE COMMISSIONER
Yes.

BOND
Is he still on the yacht?

POLICE COMMISSIONER
No, he came ashore at 11.45 with the
girl and most of the guests. He's
now at the casino.

DISSOLVE:

IAN TO RE-WRITE Scene

197. INT. CASINO. NASSAU. NIGHT.

CAMERA starts with a CLOSE SHOT on LARGO. He is sitting at
the green baise bacarrat table. In front of him are a pile
of high denomination chips worth about 30,000 dollars.' He is
the banker, so the shoe is in front of him. He deals four
cards face down from the shoe. Two for his opponent, two for
himself.

CAMERA PULLS BACK to show the CROUPIER with his flat wooden
spatula, and half a dozen other PLAYERS, some of whom we
recognise as delegates to the convention. Behind LARGO,
JANNI is standing, and a few yards to his right GABY is
watching.

LARGO's OPPONENT carefully looks at his cards, then taps them
with a finger to signify that he does not want a third.

LARGO turns his two cards face up. He has a six and a two.

124.

506. UNDERWATER SHOT. THE CAVE. NIGHT.

Once inside, the DIVERS and the Chariot are in less troubled
water. The ocean bed is very uneven, and broken by irregular
rock formations, giving the appearance of valleys and small
mountain ranges. The rock is covered in places by sea fans
and a reddish brown weed, which waves to and fro with the
surging of the water. As the DIVERS swim on they find
themselves beneath a shaft which is open to the night sky, and
here it is lighter. The shaft is quite round, about 15 feet
in diameter. It is in this shaft, just above water level,
that the two atom bombs have been hidden. The DIVERS swim
up to the surface and start to lower the bombs on to the chariot.
While they are doing this, we should cut away to shots of
crayfish, poking their heads out of rugged holes, hundreds of
fish of all species, the beady eyes of the dreaded Moray eels,
even a small octopus. We could possibly show a large Manta
Ray, and a Swordfish. (shot at Bimini).

The DIVERS have now loaded the bombs on to the chariot. They
start back towards the entrance to the cave. The view from
the shaft along the tunnel towards the entrance is sinister and
eerie.

507. UNDERWATER SHOT. ENTRANCE TO CAVE. NIGHT.

At the entrance, they encounter the same struggle with the
ebbing and flowing of the water. The Chariot is nearly
overturned or dashed against the jagged rocks. ONE OF THE
DIVERS loses his weight belt and precipitates upwards,
ANOTHER is dashed against the rocks, and his aqualung torn
away from him. Finally, they reach the safety of the open
sea, and swim on out of sight.

Spn Fish — MANTA-RAY.

508. EXT. THE GUNBOAT. NIGHT.

Without lights, and looking like a grey ghost, she is
anchored in Old Port Bay, some half mile east of the yacht.

509. INT. RADAR ROOM. YACHT. NIGHT.

The outline of the gunboat on the radar screen.

Script pages from Whittingham's final draft of *Thunderball*. Note on one page somebody has written that Fleming was to re-write the now classic Nassau casino scene.

CHAPTER 15
SHOWDOWN IN NASSAU

Like Bryce, McClory was only too aware that Whittingham's script had become the keystone to the whole Bond project either stalling or going forward; the fact that it was in his possession and not Bryces' increased its significance as a possible future bargaining tool. Sensing this was the case, McClory planned not to have it sent out to Bryce and Cuneo as originally planned, but to personally bring it with him on his upcoming Nassau visit. Writing to Fleming on 21 January, McClory hoped the author would, "be able to tear yourself away from your novel, (to attend the Nassau meeting) in order to examine the script closely and give us your views on it before Jack writes the final script."

But Bryce expressed reservations over McClory's suggestion of a script conference in Nassau. He would only sanction one provided such a journey would be at McClory's own expense, and not paid for by Xanadu. He wrote, "I hope to have several people come here as soon as I have the script. Ian, David Niven and so on." Had Niven now entered the frame as a possible James Bond?

McClory's enthusiasm over "the great box office potential" of 007 remained undiminished, as did his desire to start shooting that summer of 1960. He also hoped that a decision as to whether Bryce wished personally to continue with the project could be reached within two or three days of his arrival in Nassau. Along with the script McClory intended to have with him a new comprehensive and slimmed down budget. "I do hope that the enthusiasm on your side of the ocean is still as great as it is here," McClory said in a letter to Fleming. "We only have one object at the moment, and that is to get down to work and get the show on the road."

As Whittingham was putting the finishing touches to his draft script, completely unaware that at the same time Fleming was adopting his ideas for a book, Ernest Cuneo got in touch, first by letter, then by telephone. On both occasions Cuneo pressed Whittingham to send the script as soon as it was finished direct to himself and Bryce, bypassing McClory altogether. Nor did they want McClory to now come to Nassau. Instead Fleming would be consulted and if developments were such that a conference was necessary then and only then would it go ahead. The question of having to re-negotiate with Fleming over the right to use Bond in any prospective movie was also raised. Or to, as Cuneo put it: "Develop a new plan with Ian." What new plan? Was the foundation being laid to attempt to wrestle Whittingham and his work away from McClory's sphere of influence and leave the producer out in the cold on his own? In his letter to Whittingham, Cuneo made it abundantly clear how they regarded the screenwriter: "One of the principal assets of the proposed new venture is that Ivar and I are agreed – and I believe Fleming also – that you are a first class craftsman and a lot of other first class things which make it a great pleasure to work with you." This was buttering up of an exceptional kind.

When Cuneo phoned Whittingham a few days after the letter, his opening remark was peculiar to say the least: "Have you been paid yet?" This surprised Whittingham who replied, "Of course I have." Cuneo then made a vague reference to Xanadu's financial accounts not being in order, to which Whittingham replied that it was none of his business, he was only personally concerned with the writing and not the financial set-up. "Although, having worked on it, and believing in it, I hope very much that eventually the film will be made," he wrote later to Cuneo. "And that is an understatement." The phone conversation then moved to the subject of McClory himself and Cuneo said that although he was "a good chap" he was "a bad businessman." He then requested that McClory not be told of their conversation but Whittingham refused and did indeed divulge it.

Whatever was going on, Whittingham's loyalty (however ultimately misguided it turned out to be) was to McClory first and foremost. When told of the details of the phone call it was obvious to McClory that Cuneo had tried to undermine his responsibility and authority as producer. But McClory did agree with Cuneo over one point: by not drawing up a proper agreement with Bryce before embarking upon the Bond film he could indeed be called a bad businessman, "In carrying a friendship too far."

Though McClory could still rely on Whittingham as an ally, whatever loyalty the Bryce camp had invested in the Irishman was now all but eroded. Past reservations about his relative film inexperience and profligacy had been superseded by Bryce's inability to get straight answers out of him about Xanadu's financial situation. Their partnership agreement had stipulated that McClory be responsible for the financial records. Bryce claimed that his office had been unable to get any *Boy and the Bridge* accounts from McClory and no certified accountant's figures for anything since the beginning of their joint endeavour nearly two years before. "Our partnership agreement stipulates they should get monthly statements," Bryce had pressed McClory.

If Bryce were to continue with the Bond film, for tax and common sense reasons, his current financial structure had to be ascertained with accuracy. As Cuneo told Whittingham, "Ivar does not wish to retire from the situation, nor can he afford to plunge blindly forward." However, repeated requests to provide the figures had failed and patience with McClory had finally snapped. On 28 January Cuneo sent the most caustic letter to McClory one could hope to devise: "I find it more absurd than painful to again call to your attention the imperative necessity of an immediate certified accounting for all moneys entrusted to you by Ivar." Bryce's insistence on wanting to know where all his money had gone, Cuneo wrote, with a heavy dose of sarcasm, wasn't only born out of natural curiosity, "but rooted in some tax laws unfeelingly passed by both the British Parliament and the Congress of the United States, which make these otherwise private affairs matters of governmental concern. In short, the interested governments want the figures, and having at their disposal various constables, marshals and sheriffs, to say nothing of armies, navies, marines and missiles, they have the means of getting them."

So not only was it Bryce's wish, and also his right, to see certified accounts, but it was the law of the land. "And like the rest of us, you must obey," wrote Cuneo. "So, Kevin, be a good boy. Finish up your homework, do your arithmetic, and send in your copybook, even if perchance you've blotted it a bit."

It was being made very plain that Bryce had to see the figures before he would even contemplate seeing McClory in Nassau. He had to know financially where he stood, or as Cuneo put it, "How the hell can you go anywhere when you don't know where you are?" Bryce couldn't even estimate his losses, much less put out another cent, until he knew the facts. "Please, then, the accounting at once," Cuneo urged.

Chapter 15: SHOWDOWN IN NASSAU

Far from viewing such correspondence as mere requests, McClory became convinced that it was all a deliberate ploy and that pressure was being heaped upon him with the direct intention of demoralising his spirits. "This was beginning to work," he wrote.

McClory's reply to Cuneo's letter, which he described as "rather terse," was swift. It was all a misunderstanding, he wrote to Bryce on 2 February. At all times, from the beginning of their partnership, full and faithful records had been kept in the London offices of B. Davis & Co, chartered accountants, and that these books were always open to inspection, as per their partnership agreement. "And yet at no time during these two years have your accountants, either in New York or London, approached B. Davis & Co." McClory was therefore more than surprised to hear that they were having difficulty getting the accounts. As far as he was concerned he'd done all that was required of him.

Focusing upon the pressing matter of the script, McClory reported that they were on, "the last lap, and it is continuing to develop into a more powerful story every day." Again the point was emphasised that it was only a draft script. "And it is most important for us all that Jack and I are able to spend a few days with Ian before finalisation. As Ian has only been able to be together with us on about four short occasions since we started writing the story."

On 3 February 1960 Jack Whittingham completed his first draft script. It had run much longer than he had ever anticipated, 100 pages of foolscap (or one hour forty minutes screen time) was now nearer 140 pages. In order to finish on time, he'd been forced to work seven days a week and never left the house, save for discussions with McClory. "I tell you this," Whittingham wrote on that day to Cuneo, "because I want you to agree that screenplays are not written over the weekend on the back of a post-card! And also to reassure you that I really have done my damndest." All that was needed now was a few days of slight alterations and time to run off the desired number of copies and then pass it on to McClory.

On 4 February McClory read the final sequences of the script and expressed his enthusiasm. So pleased was Whittingham with McClory's response that he wrote him a glowing letter: "I would like to say that without your very active help, your many contributions, and your unfailing encouragement, it could never have been written." Whittingham also wrote to Bryce, appealing to be sent a cable with his thoughts upon reading the script, "Unless of course you hate it!"

With the script finished, Cuneo continued to pile on the pressure, calling McClory on 5 February demanding six copies of the screenplay for tax purposes. When McClory asked what the tax people wanted to read six copies of the script for, Cuneo could give no answer. Throughout the conversation, much to McClory's chagrin, Cuneo kept insisting that the script belonged to Bryce. In letters of the period Cuneo had taken to describing the impending draft as, "Ivar's script." He did, however, claim not to contest McClory's right to produce the film, crucially adding, "at the moment." What McClory wanted to know from Cuneo was why, despite writing numerous times recently to Bryce and Fleming, had he received scarcely a reply. Was McClory fearful that he was being deliberately ignored? McClory also confronted Cuneo about his remarks over the accounts not being in order and that not only were they untrue but libellous. Cuneo wasn't worried, saying he was the best libel lawyer in New York. McClory said he doubted that and there were a fair number of sound libel lawyers in London too. McClory put the phone down incensed and wrote later, "It was quite obvious throughout this telephone conversation Cuneo knew he had behaved in an unethical and unbusiness-like manner, and was completely unable to substantiate any of the veiled, mysterious insinuations he was making." McClory was also worried that Cuneo had talked in this manner to Bryce, Fleming and others and if so it was, "extremely damaging" to the Irishman's reputation.

Still angry, McClory wrote to Bryce about what he termed the "extraordinary conversation" with Cuneo. "I cannot tell you how much these conversations, and the letters that were sent without my knowledge to Whittingham, have affected us here." More than ever it was still his intention to bring the completed draft script personally to Nassau.

McClory landed in Nassau on 19 February (armed with three copies of the script) only to discover that Fleming had been there for a few days but left 24 hours earlier, despite having been informed of the Irishman's imminent arrival. "I am absolutely convinced that this was by design." McClory wrote later. At customs, which in 1960 comprised of one shed, Patrick Broome, Bryce's secretary, met McClory. He had a large envelope and said McClory must hand him the script immediately as a pilot was standing by to fly it to Fleming in Jamaica. This he did.

During meetings with Bryce, McClory was, in his words, "absolutely amazed" to hear the suggestion put forward that the Bond picture should be set up by some other company, not Xanadu, and that McClory should work on it only as associate producer or associate director. McClory gathered the strong impression that Bryce wanted to make the film in association with Fleming and relegate him in the creative pecking order. This was in direct conflict with their earlier verbal agreement that McClory could produce the picture on his own if Bryce wished to withdraw. "It now appears that he was falling in with Fleming's earlier suggestions to dispose of the script." McClory wrote.

Bryce also suggested that Jules Stein, the head of MCA, should be approached in regard to making Bond. McClory regarded MCA with trepidation, believing they'd probably want to provide their own producer, director and stars. "I did not think this was desirable as I did not wish to lose control of the making of the film on which I had spent so much time and energy and with which I was so fully versed," he wrote later. At the time McClory had no idea that Bryce and Fleming had already discussed ways and means of making the Bond film with MCA.

Bryce cabled Fleming on 22 February concerning his talks with McClory. The Irishman never saw this correspondence until the later trial and upon reading it could only conclude that what Bryce referred to as "obstinate misconceptions" was his desire to stick to the original agreement to produce the Bond film. "Although it was becoming obvious that both Bryce and Fleming were trying to deprive me of this position."

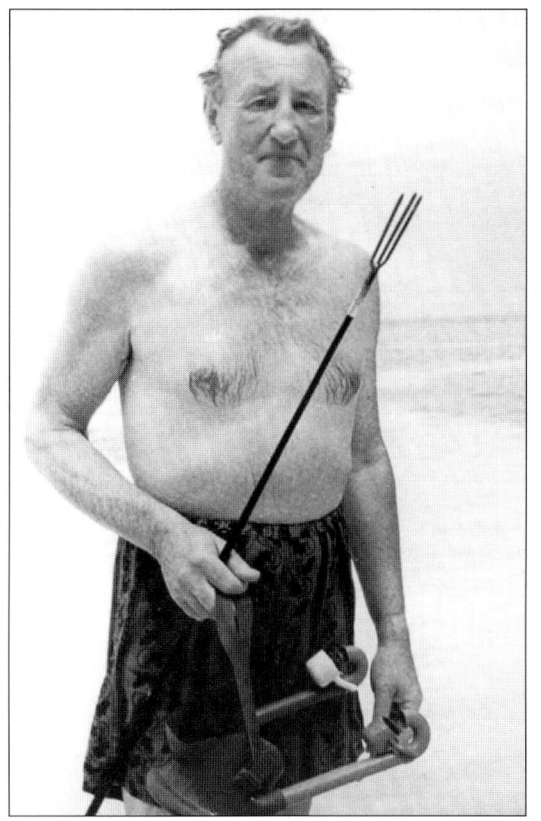

Above Left: Ian Fleming in *Thunderball* mode. Above Right: Kevin McClory – the Irish charmer. Below: Xanadu's inaugural feature – *The Boy and the Bridge*.

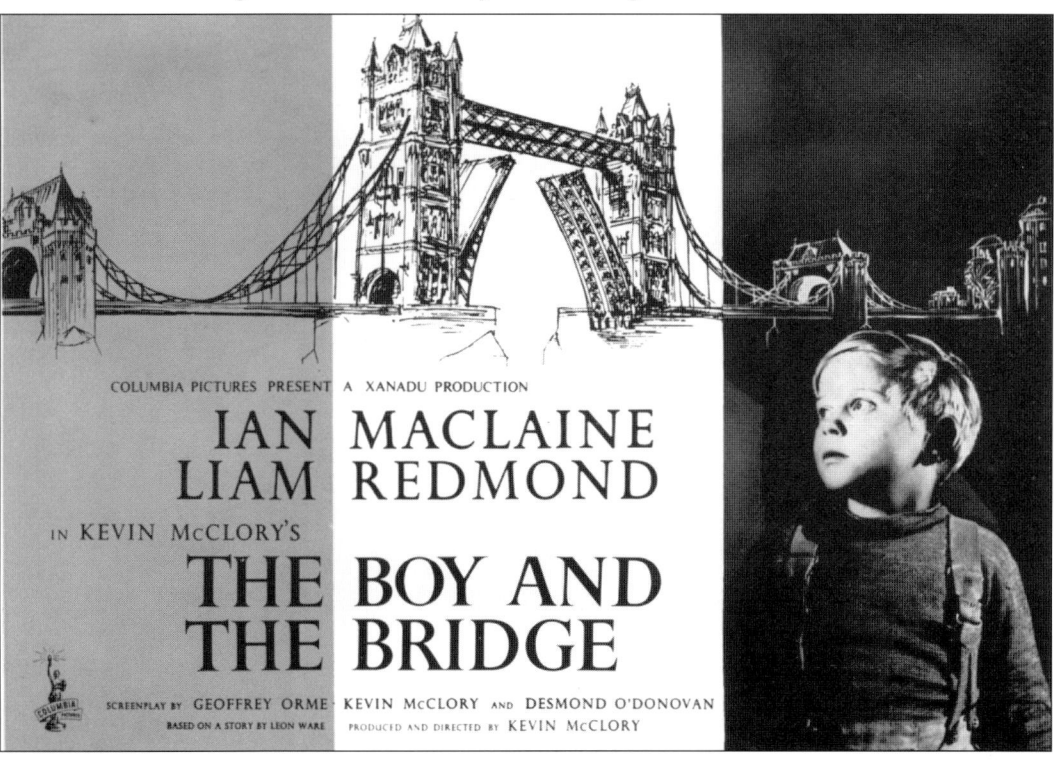

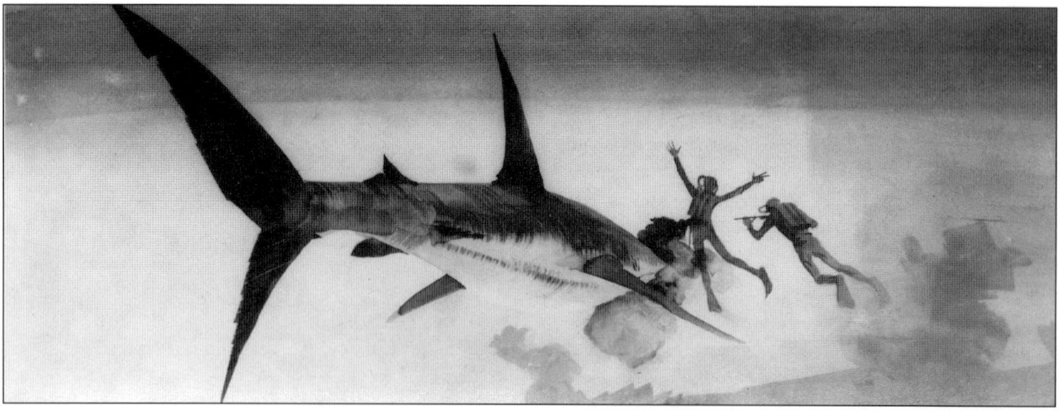
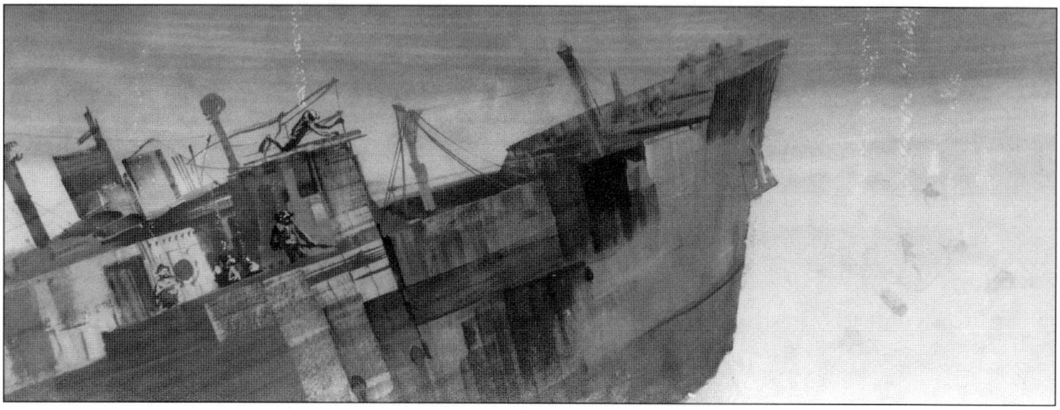
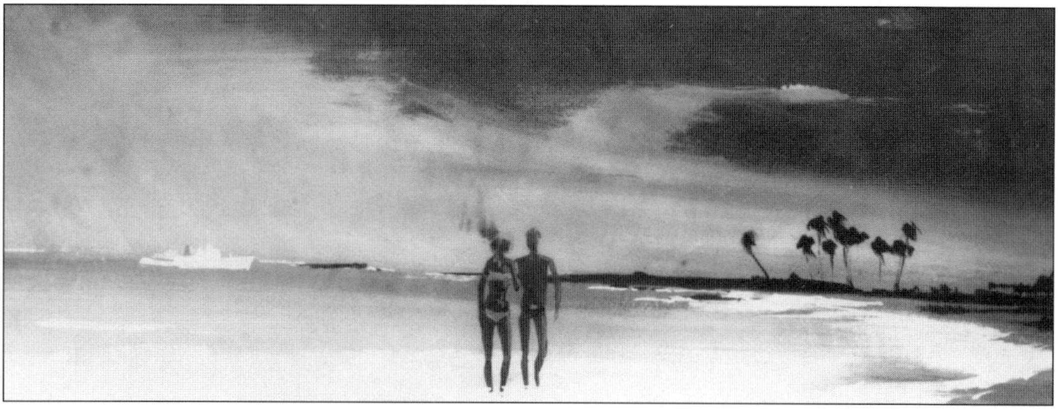
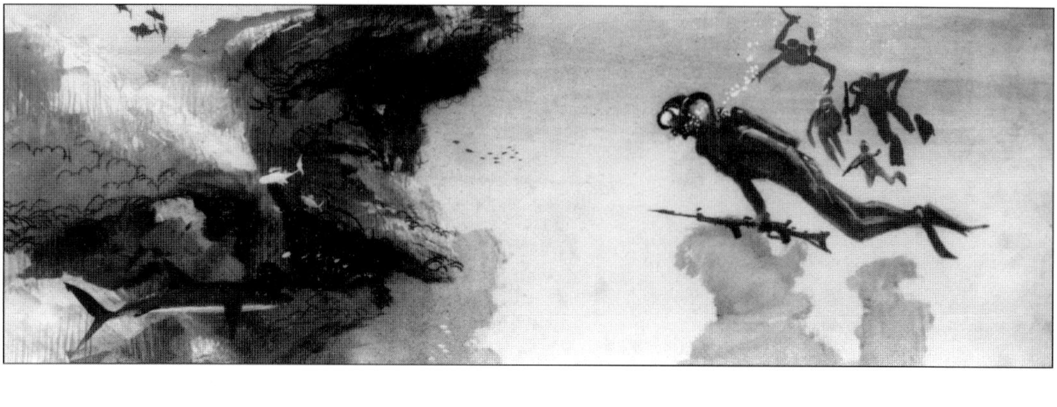

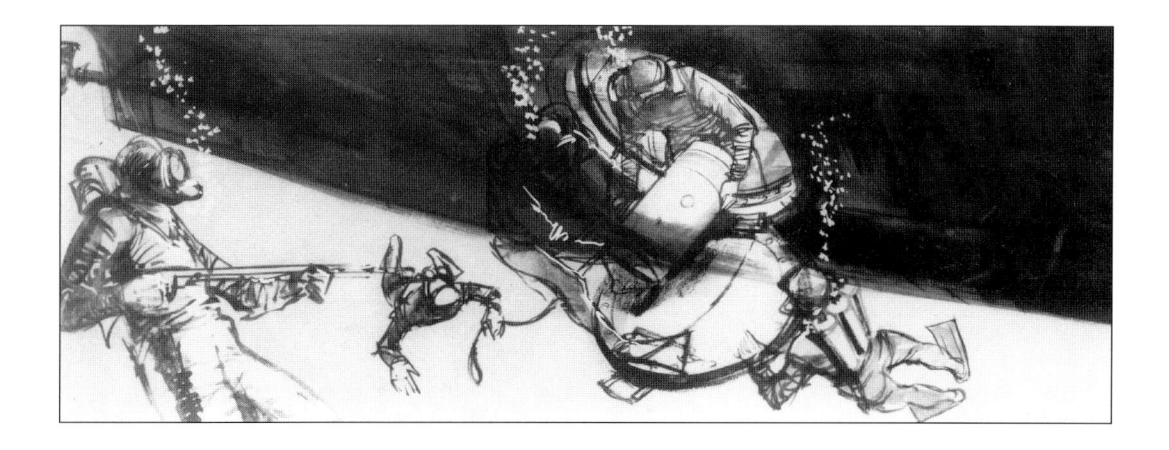

McClory commissioned this series of drawings by John Huston's art director Stephen Grimes in a bid to raise interest in the proposed 007 project at the 1959 Venice Film Festival. These represented the first imaginings of what a Bond film could look like and are reproduced here publicly for the first time.

KEVIN McCLORY

He first made his appearance in British film studios only a dozen years ago as an apprentice.
A protege of the great American director John Huston, he worked on African Queen, Moulin Rouge and Beat the Devil. Huston elevated him to the post of Assistant Director when he began Moby Dick.
The late Michael Todd visited the Moby Dick location in Wales and the result was his hiring the young man as an Assistant Director for his picture Around the World in 80 Days which was then in preparation.
By the time the picture was finished nearly three years later Kevin McClory had become Michael Todd's Associate Producer. The Boy and the Bridge is his first film.
He produced and directed it,
and collaborated in the writing of the screenplay.

IVAR BRYCE

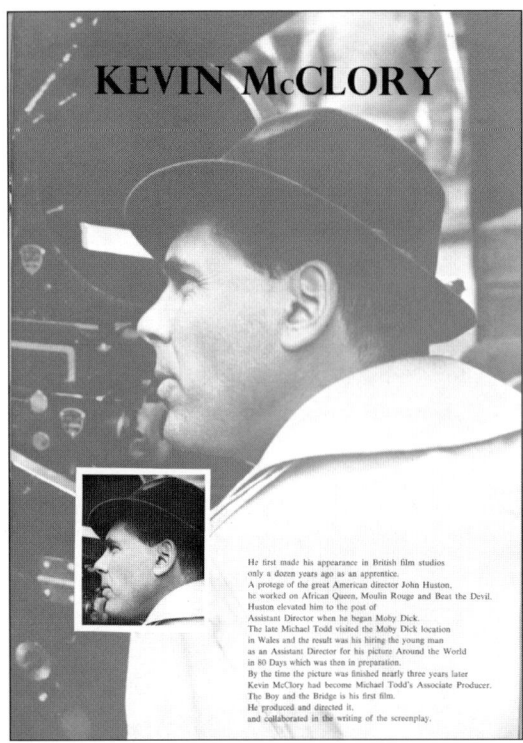

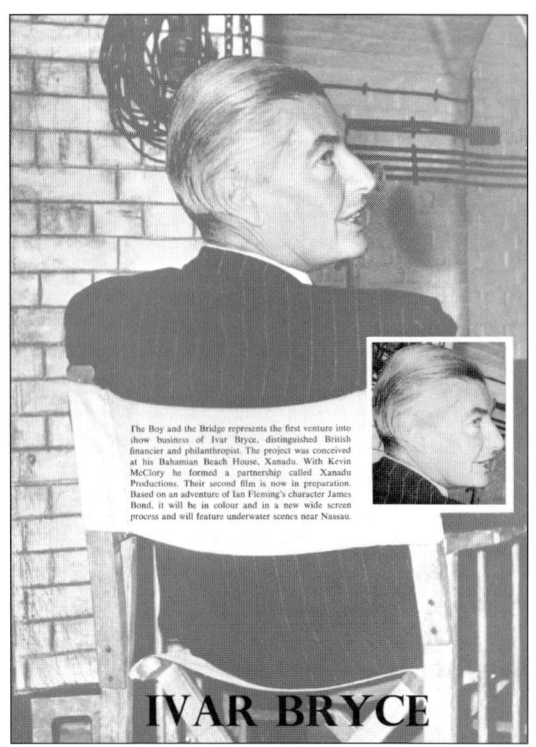

The Boy and the Bridge represents the first venture into show business of Ivar Bryce, distinguished British financier and philanthropist. The project was conceived at his Bahamian Beach House, Xanadu. With Kevin McClory he formed a partnership called Xanadu Productions. Their second film is now in preparation. Based on an adventure of Ian Fleming's character James Bond, it will be in colour and in a new wide screen process and will feature underwater scenes near Nassau.

Above Left: McClory's biography in the *Boy and the Bridge's* premiere brochure.
Above Right: Ivar Bryce's biography in the same publication. Note that reference is made to a James Bond film as the company's next film production.

Left: Fleming at the desk of his London office in Pall Mall. Above: Hitchcock ultimately turned down the opportunity to direct 007's screen debut, opting instead to make *Psycho*.

Above Left: Screenwriter Jack Whittingham in uniform performing his WW2 duties in Iceland.
Above Right: 1950s studio portrait of Whittingham.

Above: Whittingham with director Basil Dearden and Sir Michael Balcon at Ealing Studios.

Whittingham arriving in style at Ealing – 1954.

Above Left: Whittingham and Tony Britton share a joke on the set of *The Birthday Present*.

Left: Director Charles Crichton, producer Julian Wintle and Whittingham on the set of *Hunted*.

Above: Richard Burton was Fleming and the filmmaker's first choice to play Bond.

Above: McClory playfully had his friends arrested during a visit to New York. L to R, Lieutenant Kelly of the New York police, Kevin McClory, Jack Whittingham and Leigh Aman.

Above: The house in Surrey where Whittingham wrote his Bond screenplay.

Right: Whittingham and his wife Margot celebrate a night out at a suitably glamorous film function.

Above: Whittingham's personal copy of the completed *Thunderball* screenplay.

Above Right: Fleming's Jamaican house Goldeneye where his acrimonious confrontation with McClory took place.

Below: Bond producers Harry Saltzman and Albert R. Broccoli.

Right: American Richard Maibaum was Broccoli and Saltzman's preferred choice to write the screenplay to *Thunderball* and subsequent Bond films.

THUNDERBALL

by

IAN FLEMING

Entire story obviously the property of XANADU PARTNERSHIP

JONATHAN CAPE
THIRTY BEDFORD SQUARE
LONDON

Peter Carter-Ruck, the renowned libel lawyer, whose meticulous approach to the 1963 *Thunderball* court case resulted in McClory's victory.

The use of the Group sprang from my original thought that mafia etc. not highly successful Box Office material

(4)

5

S.P.E.C.T.R.E.

THE Boulevard Haussmann, in the VIIIth and IXth Arrondissements, stretches from the Rue du Faubourg St Honoré to the Opéra. It is very long and very dull, but it is perhaps the solidest street in the whole of Paris. Not the richest — the Avenue d'Iéna has that distinction — but rich people are not necessarily solid people and too many of the landlords and tenants in the Avenue d'Iéna have names ending in 'escu', 'ovitch', 'ski', and 'stein', and these are sometimes not the endings of respectable names. Moreover, the Avenue d'Iéna is almost entirely residential. The occasional discreet brass plate giving the name of a holding company in Liechtenstein or in the Bahamas or the Canton de Vaud in Switzerland are there for tax purposes only — the cover names for private family fortunes seeking alleviation from the punitive burden of the Revenue, or, more briefly, tax-dodging. The Boulevard Haussmann is not like that. The massive, turn-of-the-century, bastard Second Empire buildings in heavily ornamented brick and stucco are the 'sièges', the seats, of important businesses. Here are the head offices of the *gros industriels* from Lille, Lyons, Bordeaux, Clermont Ferrand, the 'locaux' of the *grosses légumes*, the 'big vegetables' in cotton, artificial silk, coal, wine, steel, and shipping. If, among them, there are some fly-by-nights concealing a lack of serious capital — *des fonds sérieux* — behind a good address, it would only be fair to admit that such men of paper exist also behind the even solider frontages of Lombard and Wall Streets.

46

MULTIPLE REQUIEM

tionary group who wanted to call attention to its existence and aims by a dramatic piece of self-advertisement. Petacchi closed his ears to this specious tale. He didn't mind in the least who wanted the plane so long as he was paid.) In exchange, Petacchi would receive one million dollars, a new passport in any name and nationality he chose, and immediate onward passage from the point of delivery to Rio de Janeiro. Many details were discussed and perfected, and when, at eight o'clock in the evening of that June 2nd, the Vindicator screamed off down the runway and out over St Alban's Head, Petacchi was tense but confident.

For the training flights, a couple of ordinary civil aircraft seats had been fixed inside the roomy fuselage just back of the large cockpit, and Petacchi sat quietly for a whole hour and watched the five men at work at the crowded dials and instruments. When it came to his turn to fly the plane he was quite satisfied that he could dispense with all five of them. Once he had set George, there would be nothing to do but stay awake and make certain from time to time that he was keeping exactly at 32,000 feet, just above the transatlantic air-channel. There would be a tricky moment when he turned off the East–West channel on to the North–South for the Bahamas, but this had all been worked out for him and every move he would have to make was written down in the notebook in his breast pocket. The landing was going to need very steady nerves, but for one million dollars the steady nerves would be summoned.

For the tenth time Petacchi consulted the Rolex. Now! He verified and tested the oxygen mask in the bulkhead beside him and laid it down ready. Next he took the little red-ringed cylinder out of his pocket and remembered exactly how many turns to give the release valve. Then he put it back in his pocket and went through into the cockpit.

'Hullo, Seppy. Enjoying the flight?' The pilot liked the Italian. They had gone out together on one or two majestic thrashes in Bournemouth.

91

THIS ONLY APPEARS IN WHITTINGHAM SCRIPT PAGE 17.

Top: Jack Whittingham's personal copy of the *Thunderball* novel, used in the case. Here on the front page McClory lays claim to the story. Bottom Left: On this page McClory, it appears, lays claim to the invention of SPECTRE. Bottom Right: In order to win the case McClory's legal team trawled through the *Thunderball* novel highlighting passages taken from Whittingham's various scripts.

Top Left: Whittingham and McClory leave London's High Court on the opening day of the *Thunderball* trial. Behind them is Whittingham's secretary Ann and McClory's wife, Bobo.
Bottom Left: Whittingham escorting Bobo and Ann from the High Court.
Top Right: Victory! McClory leaves the High Court having won the film rights to *Thunderball*. His life would never be the same again – for better and for worse. Bottom Right: Losers! Bryce and Fleming leave court. Their expressions tell their own story.

Lawrence of Arabia himself, Peter O'Toole celebrates with the winning team.

Drawing of Jack Whittingham by cartoonist Maz (Alfred Mazure).

A proud father with his daughter Sylvan in Capri 1961.

Friends who feared the *Thunderball* case would exacerbate Fleming's fragile health were proven right when he died later in the year of a heart attack.

Above: The big guns arrive in the Bahamas to start shooting *Thunderball*.

Below: Connery checks through customs at Nassau airport. Note McClory behind him.

Terence Young, who directed *Dr. No* and *From Russia with Love*, helmed his last Bond movie with *Thunderball*.

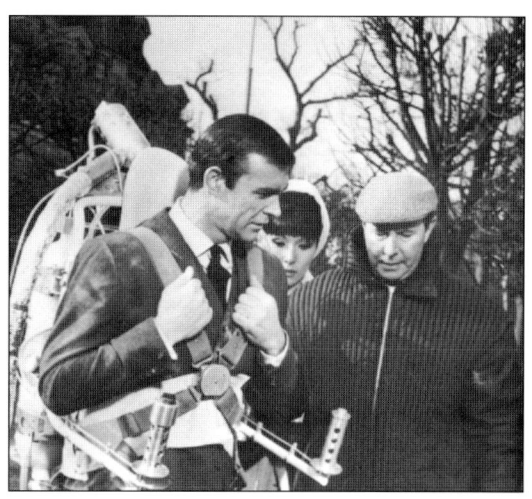

Connery and Young filming the legendary jet pack pre-credit sequence.

McClory, Young, Connery and Ken Adam discuss a script point in-between shooting the chateau fight pre-credit sequence.

Claudine Auger as Domino.

Left: Never seen before publicity image of Luciana Paluzzi. *(Photograph courtesy Luciana Paluzzi Solomon)*

Above: Connery re-lives his Mr Universe days.

Below: Young and McClory relax on one of the boats hired for the film. The marking '007' can just be seen.

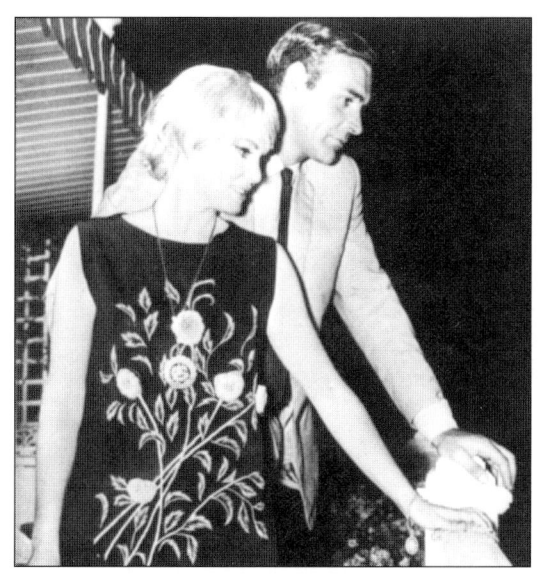

Top Left: Connery with wife Diane Cilento watches the Junkanoo parade.

Above: A day in the life of James Bond. Connery gets to grips with the world's press.

Above Right: Young, Luciana Paluzzi and Connery relax between set-ups.

Right: Martine Beswick enjoys the sun and surf.

Left: **Cubby Broccoli and Claudine Auger** on set.

Below: **McClory** perhaps taking his producer's duties too far.

CHAPTER 16
SHOWDOWN AT GOLDENEYE

Aware that McClory intended to see Fleming next in Jamaica, Bryce offered to make the trip with him. Yet on two occasions Bryce came up with some excuse as to why he couldn't go. McClory felt he was stalling and decided to fly out alone. The following cable was sent to Fleming on 1 March: "Whittingham contract necessitate my having conference regarding screenplay earliest arriving Montego Bay tonight. – Kevin McClory." Despite leaving an address on the island where he could be contacted McClory did not hear from Fleming for three days, although he later discovered that the author was in communication with Bryce during that time, cabling his friend as to what his position was in regard to McClory. Bryce's cable reply to Fleming arrived 3 March: "Kevin has no ownership script. No further financial expectations. However we back him for high position with Stein or other production." This, in spite of the fact that Bryce knew McClory was against going with MCA, which was evidenced by these words of Bryce's cable: "Kevin against Stein help." McClory was also disturbed that despite being partners, Bryce had ended his cable to Fleming with "I will back *your* decision."

Eventually, Fleming contacted McClory and invited him out to Goldeneye for what would be a stormy meeting. First Fleming admitted that he hadn't yet read the script, which astonished McClory. The Irishman was then, in his words "absolutely dumbfounded" when Fleming asked what qualifications he thought he had to produce the first Bond movie. "What do you mean by that?" McClory asked. Fleming replied, 'Well, what have you done, old boy?' McClory reminded him of his experiences and Fleming's own letter in which he said, "There is no one I would prefer to produce James Bond on screen." Fleming replied, "Yes. But this story of ours is a big production now." McClory hit back: "Yes, it has grown into something big through my work."

Fleming then asked, "Do you think someone else with more experience should do it?" McClory stood firm. "No. This is my baby. I worked on it. I helped create it. I have produced it so far and I have the right to produce it." He also reminded Fleming that no one else had been prepared to bring Bond to the cinema screen and that he had turned down numerous big movie offers to stay on the 007 project. "It was quite obvious," McClory later wrote, "that an attempt was being made to wrest this story from me. I believed Fleming to be the prime motivator, and Bryce probably just going along with him."

At the trial, Fleming's lawyers hotly contested this account of McClory's showdown with the author. Sir Andrew Clark, Fleming's QC, remarked, "My evidence will be that 99 per cent of the conversation never took place or that it was totally different; and that Mr McClory must have dreamt it." Whatever the truth, McClory received sterling support from Whittingham: "Just a little private note to congratulate you most humbly on what must have been a real tough battle with the giants."

It was also at this meeting that McClory first learnt that Fleming was writing a novel based on the screenplay. McClory was not unduly concerned or opposed to the idea, being under the impression that Xanadu would have a share in any such enterprise.

Things were now moving quickly. Fleming flew to New York with Whittingham's script to show MCA and Jules Stein. Bryce also wrote to the agent, on 7 March, referring to the project as being co-owned by Fleming and himself. Fleming too, in person, implied that the property was his alone or his and Bryce's and that MCA would therefore be free to negotiate. No mention was made of McClory's own rights, just his wish to produce the film. "Both Ian and I think he would do a wonderful job under the supervision of a major company," wrote Bryce. "And not as with *The Boy and the Bridge* having to do everything himself. But that is beside the point at the moment." What Bryce really wanted to know from Stein was whether MCA would be interested in representing himself and Fleming in the marketing of the Bond property and if the project could go further with American as opposed to British capital.

McClory claimed that he was completely unaware of Fleming's trip to see Stein or Bryce's letter to the agent. Bryce later said that he wrote to Stein at the express request of McClory in the interests of obtaining finance for the film. This was denied, and McClory could only deduce from both events that it was now of secondary importance to Bryce whether he ended up as producer or not and that all he was interested in was Fleming's private interests and his own, "and not in mine, his partner." McClory also believed that Bryce and Fleming had "decided on a course of action of which I was not informed."

CHAPTER 17
SIX MONTHS TO SAVE BOND

Leaving Fleming in Jamaica, McClory returned to Nassau where he found Bryce making numerous excuses to avoid talking about the project with him. When he finally learnt much later of the dealings going on behind his back with MCA, McClory realised that Bryce had been deliberately stalling, maybe because he was "awaiting instructions or information from MCA or from Fleming in New York." Finally a meeting was arranged during which McClory raised the issue that he be allowed to continue to make the Bond picture himself for Xanadu, as Bryce had earlier agreed. It was argued that a reasonable time period be allowed for such an undertaking. McClory said he would require a minimum of one year but Bryce said that although they had exclusive rights to make the first 007 movie, he didn't think they could keep the character of James Bond tied up for much more than six months. So McClory had until the end of October 1960 to find finance and set up the picture himself. Failing that, the rights reverted back to Bryce who would then be free to exploit the film script in any way he wished. It was a gamble, but McClory had no other choice.

At the meeting, other important matters were discussed; namely what financial reward Bryce should receive if McClory succeeded in setting up the film. Conversely, what payment and allocation of profits McClory ought to get for his services should Bryce end up producing the film without him. Also discussed was what role McClory should take were the picture made by another company. Both men agreed to draw up a memorandum of intent and it was signed in each other's presence on 17 March 1960. A proper legal agreement was then to be produced by their respective lawyers and signed at a later date. In fact no such agreement was ever drawn up, the significance of which would prove vital at the trial.

The response to Whittingham's script was positive. According to an internal MCA memo from their film division it was "an excellent first draft screenplay out of which may be produced an excellent commercial motion picture." With respect to casting, the memo read, "Mr. Fleming mentioned David Niven. Another thought would be to set it up with Fox and attempt to obtain the services of Stephen Boyd. Along this same line of thinking the combination of Peter Finch and Warner Bros. would also make sense." At his meeting with MCA Fleming also asked for comments about how best to strengthen the story for the American market. The solution MCA came up with was having the CIA and Felix Leiter brought into the case much earlier and to broaden his role. "This to be done in order to attract the best American name actor possible," went the memo.

But when Fleming saw Jules Stein personally, the agent was less than enthusiastic and didn't mince his words either. Putting pen to paper on 14 March Fleming described to Bryce the outcome of the meeting with equal bluntness. "Jules was chiefly concerned with keeping you out of the movie business, as who isn't?" he started. "He commented that Kevin, so far as America was concerned, would be no asset to the property, which he said on his information, should be a $750,000 budget." During his showdown at Goldeneye with Fleming, McClory was still of the opinion that *Thunderball* be a top budget picture and used a figure close to $3m, which he indicated would be financed without difficulty. When told this by Fleming, Stein was less than convinced. But one must commend McClory here. However financially impractical it was at the time, at least he was thinking BIG when everyone else was largely hedging their bets.

Stein, continued Fleming, thought the script "very marketable, but very British. He thought David Niven would be a good draw but didn't think Burl Ives would be any great help marketwise." Indeed the whole thing was better off being looked at by MCA's London office since, in Stein's view, Bond was largely a British property of secondary American interest and should therefore be handled with UK finance. Which all goes to prove that people in the film business really don't know what they're talking about! Here was the head, indeed the founder, of MCA, probably the biggest agency in the world, saying that Bond wouldn't appeal to the American public. The Bond films went on to smash every box office record in the States. So much for professional advice!

It was all rather dispiriting, "but truthful sounding talk," said Fleming. "I think it is better to have had some straight talk from Jules rather than a lot of show biz waffle." But what to do now? Fleming was against hawking the script all over town, but returning it to Bryce and awaiting his decision on the next step. He wrote to his friend, "I have no doubt that we could sell the finished script to Rank for instance, and at a guess we might get $25,000, and then wash our hands of the whole business. Alternatively, you could perhaps give Kevin a month or some appropriate period to finance and go ahead as he wishes to do." Fleming at this time was totally unaware that Bryce had already personally guaranteed McClory six months to find backers.

In conclusion, Fleming claimed not to have strong feelings either way. "MCA are clearly not very excited, though their Hollywood or London offices, who are much closer to the film world, would probably be more enthusiastic. The important thing is that neither you nor I personally should continue to get tangled up as amateurs in this professional problem, which is time wasting for all of us." Whatever course Bryce decided to adopt, Fleming reassured him that MCA would see to it that both of them would make the maximum revenue out of any sale of the script. "That will free our hands for playing golf."

McClory claimed that neither Bryce nor Fleming informed him that they were showing the script to MCA and that he was kept in the dark about the discussions that went on. When he finally read this Fleming letter, McClory was particularly incensed by his attitude; that the author, presumably with the acquiescence of Bryce, envisaged MCA representing the two of them for the sole purpose of getting the biggest price for the script. There was no mention of any remuneration or share for McClory, although he was Bryce's partner, a fact well known to Fleming. "It is obvious that Fleming, although well aware that he is not the author or even the instigator of the story, has absolutely no scruples about selling me out and freeing his hand to play golf," McClory wrote later.

From the start, McClory had considered any approach to MCA totally hostile because it would prejudice his own efforts in setting up the film elsewhere. Besides it had been agreed that the screenplay be distributed only to Bryce, McClory, Whittingham and Fleming as it was still not the finished version. Thus McClory did not wish it to be seen by anyone else. When Fleming and Bryce's dealings over the film with MCA, carried out behind the back of McClory, were finally revealed, the

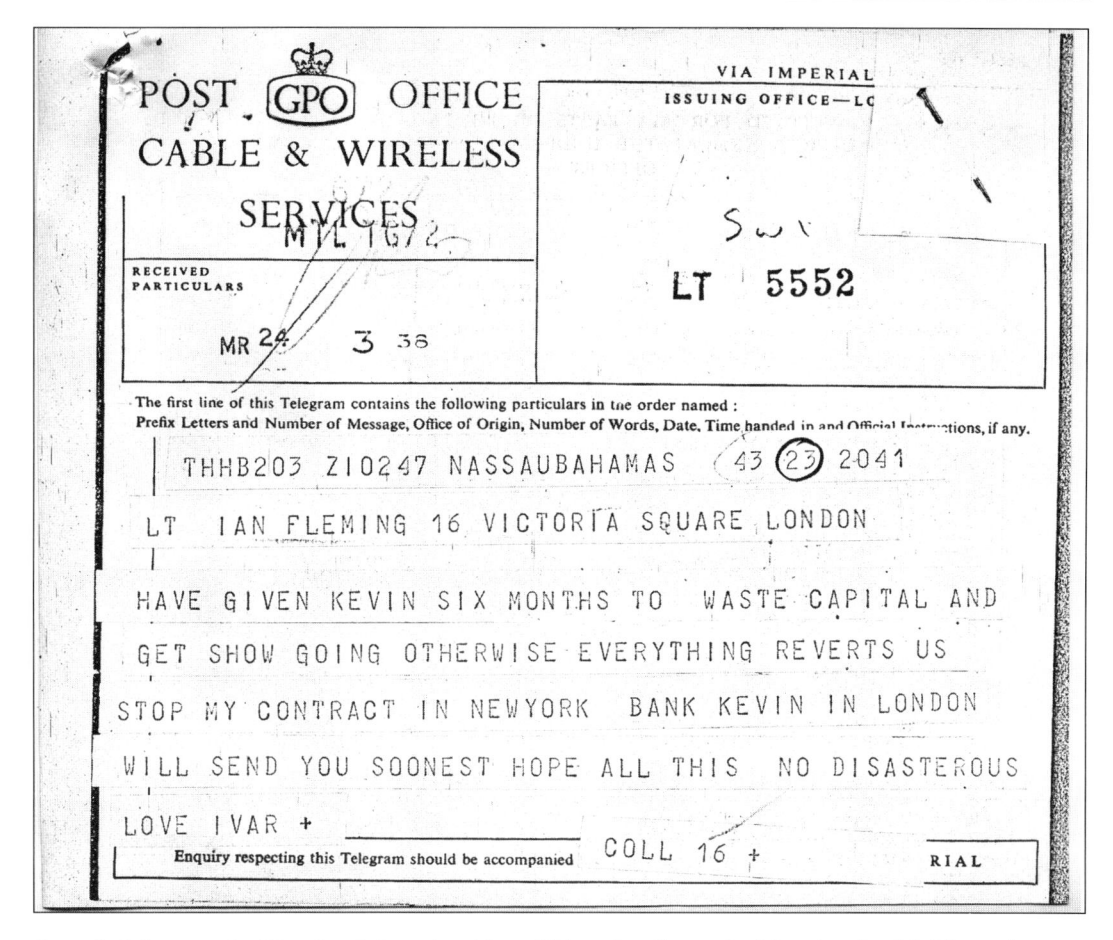

Chapter 17: SIX MONTHS TO SAVE BOND

```
POST OFFICE GPO
CABLE & WIRELESS SERVICES

VIA IMPERIAL
ISSUING OFFICE—LO
LT  5552

RECEIVED PARTICULARS
MR 24  3 38

THHB203 Z10247 NASSAUBAHAMAS  43 23 2041
LT  IAN FLEMING 16 VICTORIA SQUARE LONDON
HAVE GIVEN KEVIN SIX MONTHS TO WASTE CAPITAL AND
GET SHOW GOING OTHERWISE EVERYTHING REVERTS US
STOP MY CONTRACT IN NEWYORK  BANK KEVIN IN LONDON
WILL SEND YOU SOONEST HOPE ALL THIS NO DISASTEROUS
LOVE IVAR +
                                    COLL 16 +         RIAL
```

Bryce's telegram to Fleming informing him of his calamitous decision to give McClory six months to pursue *Thunderball* on his own.

Irishman could only come to one conclusion: "That neither wished me to make this picture and they intended to set it up in some way themselves through MCA."

Back in London on 22 March, Fleming decided to take Stein's advice and approach MCA's London branch. His agent there, Laurence Evans, was keen on the project but suggested that before taking things further he needed clarification about ownership of the script and wanted to see a copy of Bryce's original partnership contract with McClory. Fleming rushed off a cable to Bryce in Nassau: "Think getting Bond film locomotive back on rails, to our mutual advantage. Briskly airmail your original Xanadu contract with Kevin, also obtain from Kevin copy Xanadu's contract with Whittingham, without disclosing objective, which highly germane. Pray scramble. Love. Ian." Fleming intended passing these on to Evans as soon as they arrived. "And then we can marshal our forces."

In asking for these contracts Fleming showed clear evidence of breach of confidence and conspiracy between himself and Bryce to hand to third parties confidential partnership documents without disclosing the reason to McClory, and also against his express wishes. All this with a view of doing a deal with MCA at a time when, under an agreement between Bryce and McClory, the Irishman was to be permitted a clear field to set up the film on his own.

Fleming was in for a shock when Bryce cabled his reply on 23 March. "Have given Kevin six months to waste capital and get show going otherwise everything reverts to us. My contract in New York bank.

Will send you soonest. Hope all this not disastrous." It was, and Fleming knew it, writing to Evans the next day, "This of course is not very good news and it looks as if we are stuck, at any rate, for six months." Fleming's disappointment over his friend's action was also evident in a letter he wrote to MCA in New York on 12 April in which he said, "Bryce had buckled at the knees" in giving McClory the six months.

Again, McClory saw all this as evidence that Bryce and Fleming were in cohorts against him. Bryce's attitude towards his partner, his want of good faith, was shown by that cable reply to Fleming of 23 March in which appeared his cynical interpretation of the arrangement he had earlier made with McClory: "Hope all this not disastrous." This implied that he and Fleming did have plans and the six months might hold them up. Fleming's subsequent letter to Evans in which he considered that they were "stuck for six months" also indicated a future intention to make the film with MCA. It's also clear that Fleming regarded himself as legally unable to do anything for the six-month period and was therefore only too well aware of the rights that McClory owned in the scripts. Still, he desperately needed those Xanadu contracts off Bryce, as did Evans, in order to peruse the situation. And despite Bryce's agreement with McClory and promise that he would not act in anyway that might jeopardise the Irishman's chances of raising finance, he went ahead with their dispatch in order to aid Fleming in his secret dealings with MCA.

Fleming next wrote to Robert Fenn at MCA, who was now personally handling his affairs in this increasingly complicated matter, to see if anything could be salvaged. Fenn in turn passed it over to Philip McNair at the company's legal department and a résumé of the situation was produced. McNair's belief was that Bryce's rights in the Bond film property, and therefore McClory's rights, rested on the letter of 8 July 1959 from Fleming. Although technically not a legal document, it seemed clear to McNair that the original deal was that Bryce should have the right to make the first Bond movie and as payment Fleming was to be allotted $50,000 worth of shares in a new company set up to make the film. "I believe that this company has never been formed," wrote McNair. "And if Mr Fleming wishes now to terminate the arrangements, it should be possible to argue that since the company was not formed, he has not been allotted his shares and that the consideration for the grant of the right to make the James Bond film has totally failed." It must be an implied term of any agreement that it should be carried out within a reasonable time and nine months (July 1959 to now, April 1960) was, in McNairs view "an inordinate time within which to form a company."

The spanner in the works, however, was Bryce's rash decision to give McClory a clear field for six months to set up the film on his own. Thus, if Fleming were to terminate the rights of Bryce, McClory could in turn sue Bryce for breach of contract. "In these circumstances," concluded McNair, "it looks as though Mr Fleming is stuck for six months until McClory's rights have expired, unless he is prepared to terminate Mr Bryce's rights and thereby leave Mr Bryce 'holding the baby.'" As a friend this was something Fleming was simply not prepared to do.

Fenn had lunch with Bryce towards the end of April and advised him that the situation had become so complex and labyrinthine that it was imperative all arrangements between the three parties (Bryce, Fleming and McClory) be put on a more business-like footing. To this end Fenn recommended Bryce to Laurence Harbottle, an experienced lawyer in dealing with film work, to look after his interests. McNair would do the same for Fleming. MCA were worried that virtually no documentation existed to support any of the terms so far agreed. If McClory was to set up a definite deal by October there had to be documents of title between Fleming and Bryce and Bryce and McClory to satisfy whoever was to put up the finance for the film.

There was now a bizarre turn of events. In April, a Mr Kisch, a partner of Arthur Anderson and Co, Bryce's New York accountants, sent a secret memo to James Lamb, Bryce's London accountant. It stated that the rights to produce a James Bond film were acquired from Fleming by Bryce personally, not by the Xanadu partnership, and that therefore the partnership books should not show it as an asset of the company. The memo went on to say that it was possible that McClory might contend that the partnership owned the rights to the Bond film rather than Bryce personally. If this was the case then extreme caution was to be exercised in any discussion regarding the matter with Rosser-James, one of the partners in B. Davis and Co, chartered accountants to Xanadu. It appeared from these instructions that there was a deliberate intention to keep information from Rosser-James, with presumably the connivance of Bryce. This was highly significant in what was to happen next when the Xanadu accounts were, according to McClory, deliberately altered on the instructions of Bryce to marry the facts with this contention.

As of May 1960 the partnership accounts did indeed contain specific reference to the James Bond film as being part of Xanadu. Looking through the books at the London office of B. Davis and Co, James Lamb was a little bemused by this as the original partnership agreement made no provision for any new film, on the contrary the partnership was limited strictly to the production of *Boy and the Bridge*. McClory never made any bones about this fact; yes he had entered into partnership with Bryce for the sole purpose of making *Boy and the Bridge*. But of course it was Bryce's idea to plough on making further films, principally 007. Lamb called Bryce about what he'd found and was informed by his client that the Bond film was not a part of the original partnership agreement and that he was presently drawing up a new arrangement covering Bond, and that it should therefore not be made a part of Xanadu.

Bryce patently knew that the Bond film was mentioned on Xanadu's accounts and that Rosser-James regarded the Bond project as part of the partnership assets. So in order to give Rosser-James some basis to exclude the Bond film, Bryce decided to write a letter to the accountant stating the intentions of himself and McClory with respect to Bond. The letter indicated that the film was outside of the operations of the partnership agreement covering Xanadu. Reasonable enough if that was what the two partners had agreed, except McClory claimed he knew nothing of Bryce's intentions and was at no time party to the writing of what he regarded to be a "misleading letter."

Bryce also telephoned Rosser-James telling him that his relationship with McClory was confined only to *Boy and the Bridge* and that the film rights to James Bond were his alone, acquired personally from Fleming. As for his continued association with McClory, Bryce explained to Rosser-James that he'd only been engaged as his agent for the purposes of producing the 007 script and budget. McClory was to reject each and every one of these statements and later wrote to Bryce seething at his position in Xanadu being relegated to that of an agent. "I must say Ivar, I was surprised to hear you refer to my role in the enterprise as your agent. You must know, Ivar that apart from our being partners, I was, and always have been, the producer on this project."

But Rosser-James was taken in and duly amended the accounts, in his own words "to conform with the arrangements about which Mr Bryce told me on the telephone." The accounts now went under the heading: "Ivar Bryce trading as Xanadu Productions – James Bond Production." According to McClory, Bryce never discussed these changes with him therefore his action in instructing Rosser-James to change the accounts to show an incorrect relationship was done on his own initiative and without consultation or McClory's agreement, and in the full knowledge that the Bond film was a partnership project. "I believe that this telephone conversation was intended deliberately to mislead the firm's accountants in order to create a situation whereby Bryce would be left the sole proprietor of the valuable right to make the first James Bond film," wrote McClory. "And so that he and Mr Fleming would be free and able to go ahead free from any contractual liability to myself."

Meanwhile, McClory had sent Whittingham's script to Michael Todd and aroused the interest of the son of legendary Hollywood figure, Samuel Goldwyn. His involvement sent alarm bells ringing in Bryce's camp. "Goldwyn seems to have got into the act," Laurence Evans wrote to MCA New York. Fleming himself wrote to them confirming that "Goldwyn has indeed got into the picture but I am going to close my ears and eyes to the whole situation until advised otherwise. It takes up too much time and energy."

To help McClory in his bid to find backers, Whittingham's agents, Christopher Mann, had produced a relatively favourable report on the screenplay calling it "very good" with a "rattling good plot. It has the intellectual appeal of a good thriller. Personally I found the last third, which is simple action, rather a bore to read, but presumably it will screen well and is what the customers want and, in relation to Bond, what they expect."

McClory also continued to pursue a cast and crew. In April, he was planning to fly to Paris to see Brigitte Bardot. Did McClory see her as the perfect Domino? Bardot was approached again to play Bond's leading lady in George Lazenby's debut *On Her Majesty's Secret Service*. She turned it down in favour of a starring role in *Shalako* opposite – Sean Connery. Looking for the perfect cinematographer McClory was offered, ironically by MCA, Jack Hildyard, who'd suddenly become free after *Cleopatra* had shut down at Pinewood due to poor weather conditions, later to relocate to Rome. Also available was Freddie Young, soon to become one of Britain's greatest cameramen, shooting *Lawrence of Arabia* and *Doctor Zhivago* for David Lean. He would also lens *You Only Live Twice*.

A potential director was Alexander MacKendrick of *The Ladykillers* and *Whisky Galore* fame, who'd just been fired by Carl Foreman from *The Guns of Navarone*. "Whereabouts at present unknown," reported Leigh Aman. "Personally I do not think him at all suitable." Aman was still championing one of his early choices, Guy Hamilton. McClory also met with John Huston, but the Hollywood veteran was already committed to other projects. The Irishman was certainly setting his hopes high as he also tried to interest Sir Carol Reed and David Lean in directing the Bond picture. "Failing either Carol Reed or David Lean being available," McClory wrote on 13 April to Douglas Netter, who worked for the Sam Goldwyn organisation, "I think I shall have to look towards your native shores for a director as I do not consider any other director in this country suitable for this subject. And if possible the first approach should be made towards Alfred Hitchcock."

At this time, Douglas Netter was one of McClory's most valued contacts. Through him he hoped to interest Goldwyn in taking on the Bond picture. At the time Goldwyn had a production deal with Columbia where executive Mike Frankovich was also keen on the Bond movie, but at the right price and certainly not McClory's pie in the sky figure of $3m. A suggested $750,000 sounded more reasonable but McClory strongly believed that it was practically impossible to make *Thunderball* in the Bahamas for such a figure.

From late February onwards, Whittingham had been tightening, altering and improving his script into its final form. Reading his previous draft, the writer was convinced that two major changes needed making. First, he was sure that McClory's argument that a bona fide NATO pilot could never be a security risk and open to blackmail was well founded. "I agree with your suggestion that the real NATO observer should be impersonated and supplanted by a plastic surgery transformed impostor," he wrote. Second, Whittingham was now sure that his heroine, Gaby, would never be able to set off an atom bomb. "And that if she is allowed to do so in the story, it will lower its credence value to a point of hilarity. It should be a mad scientist with a mission to save humanity from itself, who does the trick."

By mid-May the shooting script was complete and McClory sent it off to Frankovich at Columbia with the hope "that everyone will work towards our being able to do this picture together." Though cleaner and more efficient, Whittingham's finished screenplay is not that noticeably different from the previous draft. One of the biggest changes happens early on and that's the use of a double to impersonate Petachi. We learn of the Mafia's planned deception when Martelli is welcomed aboard Largo's yacht. "Tell us about Antonio. How is he?" Largo asks. "A completely changed man," Martelli answers, showing his boss before and after photographs. "It's almost unbelievable what plastic surgery can do these days." Largo says. The operation itself took eight months and the surgeon has been liquidated as a precaution. So too is Martelli, as before, becoming shark bait.

Having a plastic double was extremely effective and McClory thought it added a new and intriguing aspect to the story. The makers of the 1965 film certainly thought so, whereas Fleming in his novel went back to Petachi as a NATO pilot open to blackmail.

In the next scene, we see Antonio in a NATO officer uniform getting out of a taxi in London. Entering a swanky apartment block, he finds flat 24 and rings the bell. "The man who is standing

Chapter 17: SIX MONTHS TO SAVE BOND

there, staring at him, might be his identical twin," writes Whittingham. "This is the true Petachi. We catch the look of complete astonishment on Petachi's face; then Antonio pushes forward into the apartment and the door slams shut. Camera holds on the closed door. We hear the sounds of a struggle and then a dull thud." From the murdered body Antonio retrieves personal belongings and his pass. He is now Petachi.

Whittingham also introduced a nice little scene of commuters on a packed train discussing the bomber's disappearance, which is all over the newspapers. "What are the Air Ministry doing about it? That's what I want to know." We then cut to the Air Ministry and their desperate search for the missing aircraft. A message arrives, the body of Petachi has been found dead in his flat just off the Strand. "But I saw him on to the plane," says the Air Commandant. Cue a baffled silence.

In this script Whittingham also heightens the significance of the scientist hired by Largo to detonate the bomb. Called Galante, he is a religious maniac and his motives and personality is defined in this interchange between Largo and henchman Janni. "He's an atomic scientist who wants to save the world. A second Jesus Christ," says Largo. "Save the world from what?" asks Janni. "From self-destruction." "How?" "By exploding an atom bomb," says Largo. They both laugh, believing Galante to be deranged, but obviously useful to their plans. "No, he really thinks it," continues Largo. "As a warning to mankind. The most Christian act since the crucifixion. So we told him that maybe we could provide him with the opportunity."

It's an interesting character change, and a topical one. The late 1950s saw the birth of the anti-nuclear movement (CND had just been formed) and the very real fear that the proliferation of atomic weapons had put the world on the brink of atomic disaster. It leads to one unnerving scene where Galante describes what the world would be like after an all-out nuclear attack: "The death of the world would not, in all areas, be sudden. In most areas it would be less merciful, long and drawn out, by starvation, poison, degeneration of the organs and tissues and disease."

Whittingham also makes Gaby less money grabbing here. When she confronts Largo about his bomb plan she refuses to be bribed by his promise of a share in the loot. Later she enters Galante's cabin and tries to persuade the scientist to destroy the bomb. Cleverly pandering to his religious madness Gaby says that he can still make his point about the dangers of nuclear proliferation because the resulting explosion will create global news. Instead of playing God, his role would be more like Jesus Christ, in that he would be performing the ultimate sacrifice.

After the underwater battle, Largo again makes his escape by plane, bribing Galante to come with him. As Bond and Gaby watch the plane disappear into the horizon there's a sudden flash and huge explosion. So Gaby's trick worked; Galante pressed the button. Actually by having Galante and not Gaby blow themselves up lessens the impact of the ending. Though at least, it does leave Bond with the girl as the credits roll. One wonders why Whittingham changed his mind. Maybe it was a joint decision that having Bond's leading lady kill herself was just too downbeat an ending.

Armed with the finished shooting script, and having been given the opportunity by Bryce of finding finance for the film elsewhere, McClory began to earnestly pursue potential backers. He'd been told that however attractive a film project may be no one would touch it if there was any hint of possible trouble about its copyright. In order to deal with the copyright aspect of the Bond property it was crucial McClory obtain the agreement under which Fleming had given the rights to make the first James Bond film to Bryce, on behalf of Xanadu. "I would be very grateful if you could express this to me as soon as possible," McClory wrote Bryce on 13 April. He received no reply although the importance of the letter must have been abundantly clear to Bryce.

By 10 June a reply was still not forthcoming and so McClory wrote to remind Bryce to urgently send the agreement to him. "This is very necessary in order that they (potential backers etc) can be sure that no copyrights are infringed in any way." Again hearing nothing, McClory went to see Bryce at his Essex home on 17 June. There he told him face to face that he would be unable to comply with the March arrangement, wherein he was allotted six months to find finance, unless he could have a copy of the agreement between Bryce/Xanadu and Fleming. McClory told Bryce that neither he nor his agents were able to enter into negotiations with companies over *Thunderball* without it. Bryce told McClory that his agreement with Fleming was in New York and he would try to arrange to get a copy sent over. McClory felt that even at this late stage it was clear that tactics were being adopted to prevent him making use of the time he'd been given to arrange the necessary financing.

Despite repeated demands to see Fleming's 8 July 1959 letter, in which he gave Xanadu the right to make the first James Bond film, McClory did not view it until after he began court proceedings when it was obliged by law that all relevant documents be disclosed. Reading the letter, McClory claimed someone had tampered with it. The word "the first" had been crossed off and the word "a" placed above it, thus giving the impression that it was the right to make a James Bond film and not "the first" James Bond film. There's a big difference. On all occasions, according to McClory, Bryce, in obvious reference to this document, told him that, "We have the right to make the *first* James Bond film." In a telephone call to McClory on 8 July Bryce was still making reassurances that this was the case.

So who had doctored the letter? McClory never found out, but believed the alteration must have been made sometime after April 1960, since correspondence between MCA lawyers around that time still referred to the document as giving the right to make "the first" James Bond film.

On 20 June McClory sent Fleming Whittingham's final script, but he didn't seem to be in any great rush to read it. This was to be the last correspondence between the two men. Occupying Fleming's mind now was his *Thunderball* novel, the typescript of which he was about to send off to his publishers, Jonathan Cape. As usual he also sent the whole thing over to William Plomer to seek his advice. Plomer wrote enthusiastically back on 9 August, "I have enjoyed it immensely and think it a fine addition to the Bond canon. If less in fantasy, it is stronger in alarmingly realistic up-to-dateness. The highest spots are perhaps the diet clinic and the underwater battle." When McClory eventually saw this correspondence he noted Plomer's words, "stronger in alarmingly realistic up-to-dateness." This, McClory argued was "due to the efforts of myself and Whittingham to set the character James Bond against a story which was seemingly realistic as opposed to the apparent fantasy of most of Fleming's works."

Plomer's positive reaction came as a great sense of relief to Fleming, as he wrote in his reply dated 16 August: "Your approval was all the more stunning this year as I really had got thoroughly fed up with *Thunderball* and was quite certain you would tell me to re-write the whole thing. Obviously your critical faculty is on the decline!"

Jonathan Cape, too, were well satisfied with Fleming's latest literary efforts: "I am inclined to believe that the rather more realistic approach and absence of excruciating incidents is an advantage. The underwater scenes, the little bit of gambling, the sidelights on catering economics are all excellently done and exactly what is expected of you," wrote Michael Howard, one of the company's directors. "Really you have done it again quite superbly and you need have no qualms at all. Congratulations!"

Again McClory, upon discovery of this letter, seized upon Howard's comments that, like Plomer, he'd found favour with Fleming's more realistic approach to the story. Also the absence of what the publisher described as "excruciating incidents." That, McClory took to mean passages in previous books such as the beating of Bond's testicles in *Casino Royale* with a carpet beater, "Which I abhor," wrote McClory. "It is these acts of sadism which both Whittingham and I attempted to and did in fact keep out of the script of *Thunderball* and we too were entirely responsible for the more realistic approach. Both of these advantages therefore to the novel are entirely due to the action of Whittingham and myself when preparing and writing the film script."

So pleased was Howard that he announced his intentions to at least double Fleming's sales with *Thunderball*. "This means a really mammoth operation, and there's honestly not a moment to lose." Howard wanted the manuscript at the printers before the end of September if they were to meet their publication date of March 1961. That gave Fleming just a few weeks to finish revising his typescript.

On 22 August Fleming replied to Howard, "A thousand thanks for your cheering letter and I will now get down to the corrections I hadn't already made. The final draft should be with you this week."

Fleming had also heard that his American publisher, Viking, was pleased with the book. "So at least some of my fears were unjustified, and naturally I am pleased with your plans to give it a real shove this time." Fleming also raised another point with Howard: "I think readers, and certainly reviewers, must be getting rather fed up with our paeans of reviewing praise on the back of the jacket. Can you think of any new way to say what a splendid chap I am without all these quotations? Anyway the reviews of *For Your Eyes Only* weren't all that hot."

(FROM FLEMING)

16th August 1960.

     A thousand thanks for your communications, white and green.

     Your approval was all the more stunning this year as I really had got thoroughly fed up with 'Thunderball' and was quite certain you would tell me to re-write the whole thing. Obviously your critical faculty is on the decline!

     I gratefully note all your cuts and digs and accept them all with the exception of 'mimosaic', a word which I saw somewhere and have taken to my heart. Do please let me leave this in if only to make my readers read at least one of my words twice over.

William Plomer Esq.,
Rossida,
Stonefields,
Rustington,
Sussex.

Fleming responds to William Plomer's encouraging letter about his novel, *Thunderball*.

CHAPTER 18
CASINO ROYALE SPOILS THE PARTY

In the first week of July, McClory read a newspaper article that made his heart stop beating. Fleming's first James Bond novel, *Casino Royale*, was to be made into a feature film by 20th Century Fox under the direction of Gregory Ratoff and with Peter Finch as 007. This was of course contrary to Bryce's statement to McClory that they had the right to make the *first* Bond movie. He then received a phone call from Douglas Netter in New York, who had been negotiating with Samuel Goldwyn Jr. and Mike Frankovich in regard to *Thunderball*. It was bad news; McClory would be unable to set up the film until after *Casino Royale* had been made. Even then the future of *Thunderball* was dependent on that film's box office performance. Netter also told McClory that he had been disturbed by reports circulating in the film trade around New York that the Irishman would not have the rights to *Thunderball* after October.

Had the supposedly secret March deal between McClory and Bryce that gave the Irishman six months to raise finance been deliberately revealed with the intention of dissuading any of the major studios to enter into negotiations with him? McClory also subsequently learnt that Fleming's agents, MCA, were at the same time openly discussing with film companies the setting up of Bond movies. This completely undermined the possibility of McClory placing or convincing potentially interested parties that he alone had the sole rights to make the first Bond film.

Angry and mystified over Ratoff's plans for a *Casino Royale* movie, McClory called Bryce on 8 July for clarification and reassurance that they definitely had first shot at James Bond. "We have," Bryce replied. "But I don't know the effect of this activity on *Casino Royale*, because Ratoff did buy the rights of *Casino Royale* immediately it was written, and he bought *Moonraker* but Ian bought it back for $5,000. Ian was under the impression *Casino Royale* wouldn't be made and wasn't worth buying back. But we have the rights to do the first one, Ian has said that twice over." McClory told Bryce that negotiations over *Thunderball* were going pretty well in New York but had stalled because of the *Casino Royale* announcement. "You think it's serious?" asked Bryce. "Yes. It will be absolutely impossible to put *Thunderball* together until after." Bryce admitted that Fleming had feared that might be the case when he read about Ratoff's plans in the papers. "But we have the agreement to make the first James Bond picture." Bryce again stated. "We definitely have that. But Ratoff has the rights to *Casino Royale*. So he has a nuisance value."

McClory felt it was more than a nuisance value and seriously crippled his chances of launching *Thunderball*. Also if Ratoff had the rights to make *Casino Royale*, surely this meant McClory and Bryce did not in fact have the right to make a Bond film before anyone else. "Couldn't we still be first?" asked Bryce. "The people in New York don't want to proceed until they see what happens about *Casino Royale*," said McClory. "I don't know quite what I can do," said Bryce. "It was quite a surprise and shock to everyone. I suppose Ratoff heard our plans and decided to go ahead. Ian understood they wouldn't do it because it is set, as you know, around a casino and not suitable for filming." An interesting note, that Fleming himself believed *Casino Royale* would make a poor Bond film.

McClory again raised the issue of Bryce's reluctance to hand over his agreement with Fleming, and the importance of seeing it. "The agreement is quite clear," Bryce reassured. "Perhaps you can have a word with Ian," asked McClory. "I have. But Ian said how quickly is Kevin going to do this." McClory then repeated the plea he'd made to Bryce in Nassau that six months was too short a period to try to set up a picture and that the only reason he'd agreed to it was the assurance that he had the sole and exclusive rights to Bond. Bryce's reply to this was that he'd always believed that was the case.

McClory now feared the worst; that despite Bryce's constant reassurances Xanadu did not in fact have first lien on the character James Bond. He now regretted the March deal, which he had only done on the understanding that Bryce had complete ownership of Bond. After filming *Boy and the Bridge*, when Xanadu had decided to make a Bond film, McClory claimed that he pointed out to Bryce that it would take months before a script was completed and they should require protection against Fleming selling novels already written to another film company. A rival Bond film, even worse a poorly executed Bond film, would render their project worthless. It was then that Bryce first reassured McClory that he had acquired the right for them to make the very first Bond film. "I did not consider at that time, in view of my relationship with both Bryce and Fleming, that it was necessary for me to see the agreement," wrote McClory. "I accepted my partner's word, which at that date I had never had any reason to doubt and which now appears to have been a serious error on my part." It was now patently obvious to McClory that he would not be able to enter into any negotiations with a studio or raise finance for *Thunderball* until this matter of copyright had been cleared up.

Bryce and his New York accountants, Arthur Anderson and Co, had been waiting in vain for the tax returns to arrive ever since Ernest Cuneo's stern letter to McClory asking him to sort out the necessary tax returns for Xanadu, as he was obliged to do under the original partnership agreement. By early September the certified financial statements were still not forthcoming. Such information was necessary in order to complete both the required tax returns of Xanadu Productions and also the personal tax return of Bryce for the calendar year 1959. The United States Internal Revenue Service had been unusually co-operative in granting several extensions of time for the filing of the returns but had now finally lost patience.

When Bryce's accountants tried reaching McClory they were told that he was on holiday abroad for an indefinite period and a forwarding address was not known. In desperation they wrote to Rosser-James at B. Davis and Co, Xanadu's accountants, asking that every effort be made to contact McClory "so that the certified statements can be completed and forwarded to us as soon as possible." Eventually, McClory was tracked down to John Huston's manor house in County Galway and a stern letter sent off to him: "Mr McClory has proved a rather elusive person in connection with the queries," Rosser-James admitted to Arthur Anderson & Co. "And I can only hope that your letter has done the trick." It didn't.

Bryce obviously thought McClory was being elusive too. In a letter dated 13 September to Fleming he claimed to "have heard nothing from Kevin for months." Bryce was seething over the tax situation. "He hasn't signed the *Boy and the Bridge* accounts (under American law accounts had to be signed by

Chapter 18: CASINO ROYALE SPOILS THE PARTY

the 'General Partner', McClory's title with Xanadu) or authorised the London accountants to certify them, thus making enormous tax losses to Jo (Mrs Bryce) and me here." McClory's complaints that Bryce had hindered him in his negotiations over raising finance for *Thunderball* were ridiculed too. "How he could claim that I have prevented him from performing his part of the agreement is beyond me. I have done and given him everything he has asked for two and a half years."

Significantly Bryce's letter contained a warning to Fleming. In recent weeks, Bryce had been discussing developments with Ernest Cuneo. One of the sharpest legal brains in America, Cuneo could only foresee a judicial minefield for Fleming were he to publish *Thunderball* as his own work; all three parties knowing full well that it was mostly devised by Whittingham and McClory. "Ernie thinks that Kevin may claim authorship of *Thunderball*, when you publish it!" wrote Bryce. "In any case, according to all existing documents, all rights in the script revert to me (us) in October unless he has secured the financing, as I understand it." The reference in the letter to the script reverting to "me (us)" seemed to McClory further evidence of a secret partnership existing between Bryce and Fleming.

Having not heard from McClory "for months," just a day after writing to Fleming, Bryce received a letter from the Irishman that made his blood boil. "I am really disturbed about the situation with Ian Fleming," McClory began, before going on to say that the first thing potential backers asked him when he brought up the subject of the Bond project was what the restrictions were on Fleming hiring out the James Bond character to competing films, and exactly what rights Xanadu had acquired from the author. Much of McClory's angst stemmed from Fox's proposed film of *Casino Royale*. "Everyone is very much concerned about Fleming being able to permit the making of other James Bond pictures which can be shown before or whilst *Thunderball* is in distribution."

McClory had heard that Bryce had instructed his solicitor, Laurence Harbottle, to establish a proper agreement with Fleming that would clarify what rights Xanadu had in the Bond character. "It is essential to the interests of both of us that you should get Fleming tied down so that we know exactly where we are. I therefore beg of you to instruct Harbottle to proceed to finalise the agreement with Fleming as soon as possible and let me have a copy." Only armed with this, did McClory see a way for him to go forward in his reassurances with film companies.

Bryce did not to reply to McClory, instead he wrote immediately to Fleming: "I don't know what Kevin is talking about or what he means, but it is obvious that he is going to try and be difficult, come October." This of course saw the termination of the six-month time limit.

Hearing nothing and only having the March deal with under a month to go, McClory wrote again to Bryce on 26 September concerning the proposed Fleming agreement and his hope that it had been settled. "Because as I stated in my previous letter I cannot do anything with the property until we know how we stand." Again McClory received no reply, later deducing from this silence that "neither Bryce nor Fleming wished me to be able to abide by the terms of the March deal. In fact every obstacle to my complying with this had been put in my path, and I do not now believe Bryce signed the memorandum in good faith."

That memorandum expired on 30 October. McClory's time was up. He had not been successful in setting up the film with any studio. He had lost, but he had no intention of admitting defeat. On 18 November Bryce's solicitor, Laurence Harbottle, in a letter to McClory's own solicitor Edwin Davis, drew attention to the fact that the six-month period had ended and therefore he should assign his rights in the Bond property to Bryce. As agreed in the memorandum McClory was to receive some appropriate compensation. "Mr Bryce would not wish to be unreasonable about this," wrote Harbottle. "But I should be glad if you would let me know what contribution to the enterprise Mr McClory thinks he has made. It seems clear to me that all the finance which has been provided has been found by Mr Bryce." This incensed the Irishman. Hadn't he been engaged in producing, writing and setting up the pre-production stages of the movie, of which Bryce was certainly aware? "In my opinion this letter from Harbottle tries completely to minimise my contribution to this project," McClory said at the trial.

Harbottle also stated that it was Bryce's view that Xanadu Productions ought never to have been concerned with *Thunderball*, indeed that the Bond project had only been brought into the orbit of Xanadu by McClory. "It is not accepted that James Bond is any responsibility of Xanadu except insofar as he has made it so." This was completely at odds with the facts as the Bond project was brought into Xanadu as a result of discussions and an oral agreement between Bryce and McClory. "I feel that Bryce had deliberately misled his solicitor, as Bryce was certainly aware that from the very beginning this was a partnership venture," wrote McClory.

McClory had no intention of assigning his rights in the Bond property over to Bryce, oblivious to the legal dispute that was bound to follow. "I think we should meet to decide your future course of action." His solicitor wrote him after learning his decision: "Harbottle's letter clearly shows that Bryce is not with you, but against you." After all the reason for McClory's failure to comply with the directive of the March agreement, he reasoned, was largely due to the unwillingness of Bryce to allow him access to a copy of his agreement with Fleming. But Harbottle wasn't buying that. "I am not at all convinced that formal documents between Fleming and Bryce are the answer." He wrote to McClory's solicitor, Edwin Davis. Nor did he believe that McClory ever gained the interest of any studio in the setting up of *Thunderball*. "And if there had been real interest I personally doubt whether the lack of documents actually in McClory's hands would have been relevant."

This opinion ran counter to McClory's experience and counter to the view of legal experts involved in the matter, among them Philip McNair, legal adviser to MCA, Fleming's own agent, who in a letter dated 27 April 1960, said, "There must be documents of title between Fleming and Bryce and Bryce and McClory to satisfy whoever is to put up the finance for the film." Bryce knew the significance of such a document, being informed by Robert Fenn of MCA that McClory would be unable to set up the film without it. Fleming also knew of the letter's importance and that McClory required it, and yet never once suggested Bryce should let his partner have it to enable the film to go forward.

And far from having gained no interest in the film from studios, McClory made it known that interest had been shown by Romulus Films, who had produced much of John Huston's recent output, British Lion and Columbia Pictures. McClory had been sent a cable from Douglas Netter assessing the prospect of a distribution deal for *Thunderball* with Columbia as, "very good indeed." But discussions with these companies eventually became impossible because the agreement between Fleming and Bryce was withheld from him. As Netter's court statement read, "The script was very good and because of that I ranked the prospects as excellent. Finance and distribution, however, were dependent on technical clearance of the copyright position. In the end the difficulties over title to the project prevented a satisfactory outcome."

Apart from not getting the agreement, what detracted further from McClory's chances of arranging finance was the fact that while he was dealing with British Lion and Columbia Fleming was, unknown to him, in negotiation with MCA, a competitive organisation. This, McClory felt, was calculated to, and did undermine his chances of setting up *Thunderball*. He wrote, "Although on the surface Fleming sought to give me the impression he was working with me, behind my back he was clearly working against me." On 19 October Douglas Netter informed McClory of continuing rumours. "That the James Bond stories are being offered to others here in the United States."

The stink of injunctions and lawsuits now filled the air and Fleming could smell it and was getting worried. He wrote to Robert Fenn of MCA setting out what he believed the situation to be, that McClory looked likely to base his claim on the *Thunderball* novel on the ownership by Xanadu of Whittingham's script. Fleming argued that his book was "different in many details from Whittingham's final script." Also that it could be shown that Ernest Cuneo's original story line, as set down in his memo, was the property of Bryce. "Who gave it to me to produce the first treatment which was paid for by Bryce and not by Xanadu. It was only by the engagement of Whittingham by McClory acting for Xanadu that the script, but not the story line, became

Chapter 18: CASINO ROYALE SPOILS THE PARTY

Xanadu's property." This, though, was in direct contradiction to a letter Fleming wrote to agent Alaric Jacob in October 1959 when he said his treatment "has been bought by Kevin McClory's backers, Xanadu Productions."

Fleming admitted in his letter to Fenn that during the evolution of the *Thunderball* story there had been "an interchange of ideas," some of which he had included in his novel. "But I don't think this in any way interferes with my basic copyright in the story of which the script is only an off-shoot." This theory, said Fleming, was supported by Whittingham's first draft continuity treatment, which acknowledged on the title page: "Story by Ian Fleming." A credit McClory was later to dismiss as having only been there to exploit and trade on Fleming's name as a novelist and Bond's creator.

McClory, of course, claimed that far more ideas emanating from Whittingham and himself found their way into Fleming's book than the author was letting on. And he disagreed that Fleming had a basic copyright in the story, when in fact the story was a development of Whittingham and McClory's joint work in evolving and writing the script. And the copyright in the script belonged to Xanadu, as Fleming readily admitted. And it was from this that his novel was written, claimed McClory.

At the time of Fleming's letter to Fenn (29 November) it was clear that he knew the copyright position on his novel was far from clear and envisaged being faced with an injunction, as Cuneo had warned. "I hope you will be able to clear this copyright problem without more ado as otherwise we shall be faced with injunctions by McClory which will be a great nuisance value vis-à-vis not only the *Thunderball* film, but particularly the *Thunderball* which is due to be published in March."

Around this time, news reached McClory that Patrick Broome, an employee of Bryce and the man who had taken the script off his hands at Nassau airport, was spreading dirty rumours about him. He'd been talking to mutual acquaintances about Bryce not being able to settle his tax situation because of McClory's refusal to sign the company accounts. In his anger McClory wrote Bryce on 8 December: "I must ask you Ivar, as Pat is very much a member of your household, to ask him not to discuss my business with anybody. This is not the first time that stories have come back to me which he has spread and which obviously have no foundation. If this continues, and I feel that this is in any way malicious, I will obviously have to take steps to protect myself against it." Again McClory pleaded his innocence over the tax situation, that at no time had he deliberately withheld the accounting. Such "unfair and unjust" stories, he said, "could seriously affect my career and my work."

McClory then raised another thorny issue with Bryce: the letters he'd written requesting the agreement with Fleming - "none of which you have even had the courtesy to reply to. Even though you must have known that the request made in these letters had a direct bearing on my future and my career." McClory took the dimmest view of this and the rumours Broome had been spreading. Such events, he confessed to Bryce, surprised him "in view of our partnership, and generally the spirit that a partnership means." With regard to James Bond, McClory had more bitter words to say: "I can only say Ivar, that your own conscience and Ian's conscience can tell you how damaging your behaviour over this could have been to me professionally."

The point remained though that despite repeated reminders McClory still hadn't signed Xanadu's accounts, and perhaps Bryce had resorted to such lengths as rumour mongering to embarrass the Irishman into action by calling public attention to it. Whatever the case, it worked. On 9 December McClory walked into the London offices of Xanadu and was immediately handed the accounts in the hall by a clerk who recognised him. Knowing the accounts to be urgently needed, and in a hurry himself, McClory only briefly looked at the figures before signing. It was, though, all too brief a look because he failed to notice, nor had he been forewarned, that the accounts had been altered at the request of Bryce. "Of course had I noticed that Bryce was incorrectly shown as the sole proprietor of a business of which we were and had been at all times joint proprietors I should have most strongly objected," wrote McClory. Indeed, when the alteration was drawn to his attention some months later, McClory was so incensed that he stormed into the office of company accountant Rosser-James to demand an explanation. "I was particularly incensed," he wrote later, "by what I considered to be a deliberate deception and an abortive attempt to exclude me as a partner in the James Bond venture." McClory used the word "abortive" because the doctored accounts did not completely conceal the truth.

On 19 December, and unknown to McClory, Fleming signed a contract with Jonathan Cape for the publication of the *Thunderball* novel. Fleming warranted to the publishers that the book was an original work and was in no way whatever a violation of any existing copyright. It seemed inconceivable that an author of Fleming's experience would have given this warranty in face of what he knew about the copyright situation, and the fears he had already expressed about the possibility of an injunction. Nevertheless, this is what he did. It was also equally inconceivable in the circumstances that he did not inform his publishers of the situation. During the trial the publishers swore in an affidavit that they had no knowledge of any of the matters relating to the question of copyright. They in fact knew very well.

CHAPTER 19
PUBLISH AND BE DAMNED

On 21 December McClory received a remarkable offer. Ian Fleming was prepared to sanction an "under the table" deal and pay £2,000 in cash for the Irishman's rights concerning the book *Thunderball*. Fleming later denied ever having made such an offer, whether under, over, or round the table. Bryce also emphatically denied the story. But McClory recalled being, "a little nauseated" by the suggestion.

The incident occurred at Moyn's Park, Bryce's UK residence, where McClory had been invited to discuss the ongoing situation. Shown into the drawing room, he was greeted warmly by Bryce who remained "ultra charming" all evening, according to McClory. As for the Irishman, he was happy to play the role of genial guest, "although inwardly I was a little wary."

A second offer was then made. Would McClory sign a document assigning his rights in the film script over to Bryce for the nominal consideration of one pound, with the reassurance that he would receive a percentage of the profits? It was a bit of a cheek, McClory thought, making all these offers when Bryce had deliberately withheld the agreement with Fleming that stopped him setting up the film. Bryce denied that accusation, giving his reason for not replying to McClory's requests as not wanting to get involved. And in any case, his solicitor Laurence Harbottle had had a copy of the agreement the whole time and all McClory had to do was get in touch with him and ask for it. McClory said he had done this, but with no success.

McClory came to the meeting armed with another accusation. An article had appeared in the London Evening Standard newspaper in September reporting his decision not to make the Bond film because he had refused to take the inferior position of associate producer. "Only three people were aware of this information," McClory pointed out, "Yourself, Fleming and myself." When questioned about who had given him the story the journalist only said that it was someone closely related to the facts. McClory told Bryce that he considered this to be a plant and merely another obstacle put in his path and planned talking to his lawyer about it. "It's not necessary to discuss this between lawyers, but between ourselves just like we have everything else in a nice friendly fashion," said Bryce, who had become quite agitated. "Look," said McClory. "The reason why we're in such a mess is because we have discussed everything in such a friendly fashion and not in a business-like manner."

Bryce was anxious to resolve matters as peaceably as possible and offered a payment in return for the copyright McClory held in regard to *Thunderball*. All he had to do was let Bryce know what percentage of the value in the project he considered his contribution was worth. Leaving for New York just after Christmas, McClory wrote Bryce telling him that it was impossible to assess this until he saw an advance copy of Fleming's novel to see how many of his and Whittingham's ideas had been used. And he still needed to see that letter of agreement from Fleming. McClory received no reply. Instead his solicitor received a letter from Harbottle formally demanding McClory's rights in the Bond screenplay. "Our client is anxious that there should be no delay in resolving the position," said Harbottle. "We have instructions therefore to take further steps in the matter if the assignment is not completed by the 20th January 1961." Bryce's patience obviously had come to an end. With no desire to wait for McClory's answer (whenever that might have been), he had now put the whole matter in the hands of the law to get the rights into his possession.

Also mentioned was the $15,000 loan Bryce had given McClory early in 1959. "I have instructions to proceed to recover this sum as well as the rights," said Harbottle. Next he pressed upon Edwin Davis, McClory's solicitor, to prevail upon his client to make "some sensible suggestion" which could then be considered as Bryce was still not "closed to the possibility of making a payment. I hope that your client will see that he can only gain by putting an end to the confusion in this matter."

With the copyright situation still unresolved between McClory and Bryce, MCA's Robert Fenn wrote to the director and chairman of Jonathan Cape, George Wren Howard, on 30 December. He began his letter with a whopping understatement: "A slight difficulty has arisen over the copyright position on *Thunderball*." Fenn went on to explain McClory's connection with the Bond story and that he was now legally bound to reassign the rights to Bryce/Fleming. "But he has not in fact done so yet," Fenn emphasised. "The full legal position is rather complicated, but there is no doubt that McClory is bound to hand back the rights. The only doubt is would we be able to get his signature to a document."

Howard was rather bemused by Fenn's letter and didn't pretend to understand what had or what was presently going on, and though grateful for being informed, believed it to be no business of his to try and sort out. "I hope that McClory, whoever he may be, does not in fact any longer own any rights," Howard wrote to Peter Janson-Smith, who acted for Fleming in all matters concerning book publications, on 3 January 1961. "But I am afraid that he may still have some nuisance value." This letter clearly demonstrates that Jonathan Cape and Wren Howard did know of the possibility of difficulty over copyright prior to the *Thunderball* trial. This was contrary to their later sworn affidavits. In other words, one of Britain's biggest and most respected publishers of the time lied under oath.

With Jonathan Cape's plans for publishing *Thunderball* so far advanced, Howard saw it as nothing short of, "disastrous if anything occurred to oblige us to postpone publication." In fact the decision to halt publication rested on the shoulders of only one man, Fleming himself. And he quickly made it plain that he had no intention of stopping *Thunderball* from hitting bookshelves. In the view of Philip McNair, of MCA's legal department, it was a case now, with the threat of possible injunctions hanging over their heads, "of taking a calculated risk as to which way McClory can or will jump."

The fact that Fleming sanctioned the publication of his novel *Thunderball*, well knowing there might be a claim for infringement of copyright and that an injunction might be sought was either an act of gross stupidity or plain arrogance. In the words of McClory's lawyer: "From this might be inferred a motive sufficiently wrong to constitute malice."

Back from the States in mid January, McClory was surprised that Bryce had not sent him an advance copy of *Thunderball*, nor the Fleming agreement, both of which he needed if he were to reach any decision in regard to the Bond property. But why on earth should he now sign the Assignment? And why did Bryce think the Irishman would even contemplate doing so. It was his

Chapter 19: PUBLISH AND BE DAMNED

> XANADU PRODUCTIONS
>
> 59 Sloane Street,
> London, S.W.1.
>
> 15th March, 1961.
>
> Messrs. Jonathan Cape Ltd.,
> 30 Bedford Square,
> W.C.1.
>
> Dear Sirs,
>
> I have just received a copy of "THUNDERBALL", authorship of which is claimed by Ian Fleming. In my opinion it infringes the copyright of scripts which are the property of myself and Mr. Ivar Bryce carrying on business as Xanadu Productions, and infringes copyrights which are invested in me personally, and also copyrights to which I claim authorship.
>
> If publication is proceeded with I shall have no hesitation in applying to the Courts for an Injunction.
>
> Yours faithfully,
>
> KEVIN McCLORY

McClory's letter to Fleming's publisher, Jonathan Cape, claiming that the *Thunderball* novel infringes his copyright.

Court document detailing McClory and Whittingham's bid to prevent publication of the *Thunderball* novel in 1961.

> 1961 M.No.989
>
> IN THE HIGH COURT OF JUSTICE
> CHANCERY DIVISION
> GROUP B
>
> BETWEEN:
>
> KEVIN O'DONOVAN McCLORY and
> JACK WHITTINGHAM   Plaintiffs
>
> - and -
>
> IAN FLEMING, JONATHAN CAPE
> LIMITED   and
> JOHN F   C   BRYCE   Defendants
>
> TAKE NOTICE that this Honourable Court will be moved before the Honourable Mr. Justice Wilberforce on Friday the 24th day of March, 1961, at the sitting of the Court or so soon thereafter as Counsel can be heard by Counsel on behalf of the above-named Plaintiffs for an order until judgment in this action or until further order to restrain the Defendants Fleming and Jonathan Cape Limited and each of the by themselves and their respective agents and servants or otherwise from reproducing, publishing, selling, offering for sale or distributing any copies of a novel entitled "Thunderball" and from authorizing any of the acts aforesaid without the consent of the Plaintiffs or of either of them and to restrain the Defendants Fleming and Jonathan Cape Limited and each of them by themselves and their respective servants and agents from representing to the public that the novel entitled "Thunderball" is the sole or exclusive work of the Defendant Ian Fleming or for such further or other order as to the Court may seem proper.
>
> DATED this 21st day of March, 1961.
>
> Yours, etc.
>
> To: the Defendants, Ian Fleming   GORDON, DADDS & CO.
> and Jonathan Cape Limited.   Of 80 Brook Street,
>   London, W.1.
>   Solicitors for the
>   Plaintiffs.

belief that Bryce had not lived up to the memorandum both men signed in March and had deliberately withheld, though he knew it to be essential, the one document which could have enabled McClory to negotiate with potential backers, "and had allowed himself to be persuaded by Fleming to conspire against our partnership." McClory also had no intention of signing away the results of all the work and effort he had put into the project for just one pound! And the promise of a percentage deal? "A promise from a man whose word I could no longer accept and whose integrity, I am bound to say with regret, I now doubted."

At last, on 2 March Harbottle sent Edwin Davis an advance copy of *Thunderball*. It was forwarded, in Harbottle's words, "without prejudice," and with the hope that both parties could come to some arrangement. Harbottle had already expressed his views to Davis that legal proceedings, "would be a great mistake and ought to be avoided if possible."

For some reason, it took another eight days before McClory was informed that the book was in his solicitor's possession. Immediately he made his way to the office and collected the copy on 10 March. He wasn't best pleased by what he read. Fleming, in his view, had blatantly used a substantial part of the film scripts without acknowledging either Whittingham or himself. "Both Kevin and my father were shocked and horrified," says Sylvan Mason, "because they'd been going around saying they were writing the James Bond film and everybody was getting more and more excited about it."

On 15 March, McClory banged out a no nonsense letter to Jonathan Cape: "I have just received a copy of *Thunderball* authorship of which is claimed by Ian Fleming. In my opinion it infringes the copyright of scripts which are the property of myself and Mr. Ivar Bryce carrying on business as Xanadu Productions, and infringes copyrights which are invested in me personally, and also copyrights to which I claim authorship. If publication is proceeded with I shall have no hesitation in applying to the courts for an injunction."

Hearing no satisfactory reply by 21 March, McClory decided to sue. Ian Fleming, one of the most successful novelists of the 20th century, who had been accused of everything from snobbery to sadism, now stood accused of plagiarism.

The hearing took place on 24 March in London's High Court with Mr Justice Wilberforce presiding. Counsel for McClory was Mr Skone-James, who explained to the court that James Bond was "A Sherlock Holmes type, except that he is not a detective. He is a secret agent. He has a large following of readers of this type of work." Continuing his outline of the book's plot Skone-James said, "Then there is a girl..." Judge Wilberforce interrupted, amid laughter, "Ah, I was waiting for that."

Basically McClory was out to stop Jonathan Cape from publishing *Thunderball*, set for 27 March, and representing it as the sole work of Fleming. In his sworn affidavit McClory stated that he was first told by Bryce in December 1960 that Fleming was bringing out a novel using some parts of the scripts. McClory had also claimed that Fleming mentioned this fact to him as early as March 1960. McClory was suspiciously fuzzy on when exactly he first knew of Fleming's intentions in respect of his *Thunderball* novel. "Bryce indicated to me that Fleming would in his novel acknowledge the use of the script and of the assistance rendered therein by myself and Whittingham, and would also pay me a suitable royalty. I understood at this time that only a small part of the script was being used in the novel."

Not only had Fleming failed to make any acknowledgement, but he'd also used a great deal more of the film script than McClory had been given to understand. "There is, of course, a great deal of material in the novel that is not in any of the scripts," McClory's affidavit admitted. "On the other hand, I am satisfied that the plot and a very large number of the details and incidents of the book are derived from one or other of the scripts, of which I and Whittingham claim to be joint authors. And very little, if any, of the novel appears to be derived from Fleming's original script."

McClory's affidavit concluded: "I still have a firm conviction that a successful film could be made from the film script. I claim that I still have rights in such a proposed film."

Chapter 19: PUBLISH AND BE DAMNED

Joining McClory in the court action was Jack Whittingham. "Dad just went along with it really," says Sylvan. "Kevin was the main motivator. But my father did feel outraged at what had happened. And he was very fond of Kevin, who at this stage had not let him down. So Dad went into it as a co-plaintiff. He felt very strongly about it." Whittingham had nothing much to win by suing, having assigned all copyright in his scripts to McClory and been paid, but he had plenty to lose. He feared that because it was widely known in the film community that he'd written the *Thunderball* script, if the book was published minus any acknowledgement of his work people might deduce that it was left out deliberately because it was in some way of poor quality. Such an inference would reflect badly upon his reliability and integrity as a screenwriter.

Incredulously, Jonathan Cape's George Wren Howard stated that prior to receipt of McClory's affidavit neither his company, nor indeed Bryce, had any knowledge of the affair. This was a blatant lie, as Howard was in direct communication with MCA about McClory's copyright claims. Howard said he'd still not received any copies of the various scripts and accordingly had not had any opportunity of comparing Fleming's novel with them. But he vigorously defended the integrity of *Thunderball*. "My company does not admit that any use has been made by Fleming of any material or work of Whittingham or McClory and does not admit that the Fleming novel owes any of its plot or incident to any skill or experience of McClory."

Howard further claimed that when he received McClory's letter of 15 March, this was the first communication his company had received from the Irishman, or anyone, of any claim by him in respect of the *Thunderball* novel. This was another lie, as Robert Fenn's earlier letter to him testifies. Yet by then all arrangements for its publication had long been completed; over £2,000 spent on advance advertising, 130 review copies posted and 32,000 copies shipped to booksellers home and abroad. "In the circumstances," Howard stated, "my company took no action to stop publication of the book on receipt of McClory's letter, especially as that letter gave no details of the scripts or copyrights alleged to be infringed or of the copyrights in which he claimed authorship."

Howard concluded that Cape would suffer great damage if the court were now to stop publication. Such a delay, he argued, would destroy their chances of any subsequent successful publication as interest would be dissipated and all value and effect of costly advertising lost. Moreover, to stop publication would involve sending some 1,467 telegrams and cables around the world. Howard was looking at Jonathan Cape suffering a very heavy financial loss if McClory got his way.

Sun-tanned after recently returning from Jamaica, and wearing an immaculate blue flannel suit, blue shirt and blue and white polka-dot bow tie, Fleming sat at the back of the court room listening as he was accused of plagiarism. He must have winced when Skone-James reminded the judge of the law of the land, that if there were a work of joint authorship no one author could licence exploitation of the work without the consent of the others. "Alternatively," James continued, "we say that the film screenplay in the latter stages of the development of the production was in fact wholly written by Jack Whittingham." Indeed Skone-James went on to point out that the only real contribution of Fleming to the plot was the character of James Bond himself – "A useful adjunct, I agree."

After just 90 minutes, Judge Wilberforce decided that since the accused had not had sufficient time to mount a defence and that publication of *Thunderball* was already so well advanced it couldn't be stopped, McClory and Whittingham's application was refused. "Quite ghastly," Fleming said to waiting reporters as he strolled away from the court. "I'm sure Bond never had to go through anything like this."

The battle had been lost, but McClory fully intended to win the war and pursue matters further by bringing another action against Fleming and Bryce claiming damages for breach of copyright. "I would hope to convince you," Skone-James told the judge, "without very much difficulty, that this novel owes a great deal to the film script." Judge Wilberforce replied, "I think, on the evidence before me, that that appears to be so." Fleming's counsel then protested that a lot of evidence had been read out which might be taken to reflect adversely on his client, who had not yet had an opportunity of putting his case and wished to make it clear that he did not accept all the relevant details. No doubt Fleming was perturbed by the press interest the hearing had garnered. "The whole truth remains to be investigated," said the judge.

And so a future trial was assured. But all parties would have to wait two years, for much was about to happen in the world of James Bond.

CHAPTER 20
ENTER BROCCOLI AND SALTZMAN

Helped no doubt by all the publicity surrounding the court case, the *Thunderball* novel was a huge success. "Published all over the civilised world," reported The Times, adding "and possibly the uncivilised world too." Despite the controversy surrounding it, purists cite *Thunderball* as one of Fleming's best novels. It has a grand scope absent from his other books. It's a big story with large characters expertly drawn. "The mixture – of good living, sex and violent action – is as before," said The Times, "but this is a highly polished performance, with an ingenious plot well documented and plenty of excitement." The only problem is the novel can't be attributed totally to Fleming. Some of the more observant critics spotted this, detecting differences from Bond's earlier literary installments. In particular there were fewer episodes of sadism. The reason for that, said McClory, was that the novel was based on the screenplay, which had to appeal to a general cinema audience, not Fleming's usual readership.

For some time friends and associates of Fleming had been concerned about his health and feared that the legal problems over his new book would only serve to exacerbate it. On 12 April, a little over two weeks after the failed book injunction, Fleming suffered a major heart attack. During the regular Tuesday morning conference at the Sunday Times, he suddenly keeled over and went so white that one of his colleagues was convinced he was dying. Fleming was rushed to the London Clinic, where he remained for a month. He was far from idle there. While recuperating he wrote his now classic children's story *Chitty Chitty Bang Bang*, which would later be made into a much-loved family film. Doctors saw the heart attack as a warning and told Fleming to moderate his smoking and drinking. But how could the creator of James Bond not live life to the fullest? Upon leaving hospital, Fleming chose to ignore professional advice, telling friends that he didn't intend to spend the rest of his days not being able to enjoy himself. He did in fact offer a compromise, cutting down from 60 cigarettes a day to a more modest 20.

As for his alcoholic intake, Fleming came up with a brilliant ruse. Ordered to give up drinking altogether Fleming talked his doctor into allowing him one drink only per day and that drink should be exactly one proper measure (a fluid ounce). Fleming went to great lengths to research which drink contained the most alcohol per ounce and discovered it to be Green Chartreuse. So he drank that.

Fleming spent that May in France recuperating with his wife. Whilst there, the big Bond movie breakthrough he'd always craved for happened. In London American-born producer Harry Saltzman was close to the end of a six-month option he had on all the Bond books, save *Casino Royale*. Writer Wolf Mankowitz introduced Saltzman to another London based American producer, Albert R. Broccoli, who was also interested in Bond, and together they created Eon Productions with the express intention of finally bringing 007 to the screen. But every studio in Hollywood turned them down. Luckily Broccoli had connections in United Artists and on 21 June 1961 he and Saltzman met studio executives to discuss the project. On that very same day a deal was struck, Broccoli and Saltzman were in business with a promised budget of a million dollars for their opening Bond movie.

With the *Thunderball* novel recently published and acclaimed as a big success, it followed that Broccoli and Saltzman chose this title to be the debut Bond screen adventure. Richard Maibaum, a colleague of Broccolis, was hired to write a new script based on the novel. So here was a screenplay, based on a novel that was itself based on another screenplay! It's obvious from this first draft (dated 18 August 1961) that the marriage of Maibaum with Fleming's source material was a match made in heaven. Clearly Maibaum loved the literary world of James Bond and his script is faithful to the novel, although he does improve somewhat upon the plotting. Bond is given a far more credible reason for heading to Nassau than the book, where M simply sends him to the Bahamas in the belief that this area is the most likely landing site for the plane. Maibaum's Bond sees Petacchi at Shrublands and later discovers that he was on the hijacked flight. After SPECTRE agent Count Lippe tries to kill Bond, and is himself assassinated for jeopardising Blofeld's overall plan, Bond realises sinister forces are at work. Learning that Petacchi's sister is in Nassau, Bond requests to go there for his assignment. This plot device, later modified for the film, helps enormously with the story's plausibility. It also makes Bond central to the early detective work on the case. Yet this angle was initially objected to by Maibaum's bosses as being "all too coincidental," and that Bond be sent to Nassau simply because he'd recently had a mission in Jamaica!

Maibaum makes other plot improvements, notably when Domino tells Bond that she first met Largo through her brother. Suddenly it's clear to Bond: Largo knew all along of the Domino/Petacchi relationship and still went ahead and killed him. The only random event in the script is Bond's chance encounter with Count Lippe at Shrublands, which sets the whole ball rolling.

There are weaknesses in the script, such as the slow pace of the first half. It isn't until page 58 that Bond leaves for Nassau – in other words almost an hour of screen time. Once in Nassau the action pretty much follows the novel, with a few exceptions that never made it into the finished film. For example, Bond and Felix Leiter visit Largo's home, Palmyra, under cover of night and steal into his boathouse. There they find treasure chests filled with Spanish doubloons, which both deduce to be Largo's ready-made treasure hunt alibi.

There are interesting hand-written notes all over Maibaum's script, presumably from Broccoli or Saltzman. "Do not like the ending at all," reads one. "What happened to all the sex associated with Bond?" reads another. Maibaum had included a tame love scene between Domino and Bond, similar to the novel, but didn't have them actually making love. This, of course, was rectified.

Whoever wrote these notes and suggestions obviously knew what they were talking about because many of them ended up in the later film. It's also clear that they must have read Whittingham's *Thunderball* script, not least because of the wholesale lifting of the idea to use a double to impersonate Petacchi. McClory believed that Broccoli and Saltzman had acted illegally in commissioning Maibaum to write a screenplay based on the *Thunderball* novel, since it was in litigation at the time and Fleming had no right to sell it. In any case, Maibaum's screenplay saw another significant advancement in the film life of the *Thunderball* material, successfully merging as it did some of the aspects of Whittingham's script

Chapter 20: ENTER BROCCOLI AND SALTZMAN

with Fleming's novel. It's also believed that this was the screenplay Sean Connery first read when he was offered the Bond role.

Maibaum had no sooner presented his screenplay, than United Artists' lawyers, who'd been researching *Thunderball*'s legal problems, warned Broccoli and Saltzman not to touch it. Still desperate to launch the 007 series with *Thunderball* the producers approached McClory in the hope of brokering some kind of deal. So at the end of August, McClory attended a two-hour meeting at the London offices of Eon Productions. Broccoli and Saltzman told him that United Artists had the right to make four films from four Fleming books and they were contemplating making *Dr. No*, but would prefer to go with *Thunderball*. However, in view of the pending trial they were not prepared to undertake that film unless a compromise was reached. McClory had begun explaining that Xanadu had the right to make the first James Bond film when Saltzman butted in, saying that this was not the case as years before the film rights to *Casino Royale* had been granted by Fleming and were still held by another company. McClory admitted this was so but had been led to understand that Fleming would buy those film rights back in view of his obligation to Xanadu.

Saltzman was having none of McClory's claims. He'd taken legal advice and the opinion of his attorneys in America was that as a result of the contract between United Artists and Fleming he and Broccoli were quite in order to proceed making Bond films. One fascinating feature of that contract, revealed during this meeting, was the existence of an indemnity clause that should damages be claimed against United Artists as a result of McClory's legal action, and such a claim be successful, then United Artists could recover those costs from Fleming and Bryce personally.

McClory explained in detail his own case and his conviction that it would succeed when it came to trial. He also informed the producers that a recent offer from Bryce of £10,000 to relinquish his rights in *Thunderball* was not a realistic figure. Broccoli offered to act as an intermediary between the two rival parties in the hope of breaking the impasse. He and Saltzman exited the room, leaving McClory alone with his solicitor to discuss the matter. When the producers returned, McClory informed them that he would settle only for a payment of £75,000 (a minimum of £800,000 in today's money). McClory was bluffing for secretly he was prepared to accept just £40,000. Both producers said that this was completely unrealistic and Broccoli refused to make an approach to the other side on the basis of such a figure. Broccoli also doubted whether Saltzman would do the same. Interestingly, Saltzman was non-committal in his reply. In that case, said McClory, the meeting was at an end.

Afterwards, McClory discussed with his solicitor the possibility that Broccoli and Saltzman would immediately inform the other side of the figure he had in mind for settlement and that it was more than likely that an approach from Bryce would materialise within days. It never did. And *Thunderball* was ditched in favour of *Dr. No*.

When approached to direct the inaugural Bond adventure, Terence Young agreed on the condition that he be allowed to film either *Thunderball*, *From Russia with Love* or *Dr. No*. By coincidence those were the three Bond films Young actually ended up making, but in the reverse order. "And as it turned out," he later said, "*Thunderball* was an immensely expensive picture and if we had started the series with *Thunderball* I think it would have been poorly made, it would have looked cheap, we never would have been able to make it properly. So I think the miracle was that we started with *Dr. No*, which was the most modest in production conception, and also the story lent itself best of all to setting the tone of what was going to be the whole series." Young was absolutely right.

Again Richard Maibaum was hired to write the screenplay for *Dr. No*, which turned out to be a smash hit when it opened in October 1962. But one wonders what McClory made of its success, feeling as he did that he owned the right to make the first Bond picture. His friend Jeremy Vaughan was actually present at the morning press show of *Dr. No* in London and recalls how perilously close it came to disaster. "Everybody in the cinema pissed themselves with laughter. And Terence Young was pulling his hair out because it wasn't meant to be a comedy. All of us slightly cynical lot thought it was hilarious. But little did anyone know that history was made."

Jack Whittingham and his wife Margot arrive at the High Court as the *Thunderball* trial begins.

CHAPTER 21
THE COURT CASE THAT KILLED IAN FLEMING

On 20 November 1963, a month after the British release of the second James Bond film *From Russia with Love*, the *Thunderball* trial began. Could McClory prove that his copyright in the *Thunderball* film scripts had been infringed by Fleming's novel? With box office tills ringing for Broccoli and Saltzman and the Fleming books selling better than ever, much was riding on the outcome.

Not long after his failed book injunction and to prepare for his court battle to come, McClory had employed the services of solicitors Gordon Dadds & Co, who upon looking at the case exclaimed, "You haven't got a hope in hell of winning this. We should try and settle." It was not what McClory wanted to hear and he went away to re-evaluate what to do next. Salvation came from a most unlikely source – Jack Whittingham's daughter Sylvan. After completing a secretarial course, Sylvan had come to London in search of work. Walking into the Strand offices of temp agency Alfred Marks, she was told a vacancy existed for an assistant secretary at the solicitors Oswald, Hickson, Collier and Co in nearby Surrey Street. "I spent my days typing out contracts and court notes and smoking cigarettes that cost 1/6 a packet. I was paid seven pounds a week. It was my first job. My boss, Mr Payne, one of the partners, had all sorts of interesting and high profile clients and I would go back home and tell Dad, guess who came in today. So Dad started to take an interest in Oswald, Hickson, Collier and Co and made a few enquires. The upshot of it all was that he and Kevin took the *Thunderball* case to them."

Specifically they took the case to one Peter Carter-Ruck, the firm's senior partner and one of the country's top libel lawyers with a fearsome reputation and an unrivalled client list that included Winston Churchill and Lord Rothermere. He looked at the case and saw that they had something. "It was very clear to me that Kevin had been exceedingly badly treated," Carter-Ruck later wrote. "Morally he had the strongest possible case; legally it was a matter of determining from all the documentation available that there had been a binding agreement on which we could sue."

The action would involve Carter-Ruck and his assistants in a prodigious amount of work and documentation over the course of almost two years, from the time he was hired in December 1961.

The brief to counsel occupied the equivalent of 400 pages of an average book. There were nearly 1,000 letters in the correspondence covering six years from 1957 to 1963, over 100 categories of documents and 18 witnesses. "Really, Peter was the perfect person for the job," claims Sylvan. "He was meticulous and a very, very clever man. He went through the *Thunderball* novel with a fine tooth-comb with Kevin and Dad. He also had all the script drafts and he prepared a huge document, which detailed every single bit that had been lifted from the screenplay. There were over 200 pages in which something had been taken from the screenplay and put in the book."

With the trial looming and growing in size and complexity all the time, anxiety began to overtake Jack Whittingham and he became severely worried about what the consequences would be if they lost. "He saw that it wasn't going to be open and shut," says Sylvan. "Fleming and Co were fighting back hard and he could see the costs mounting up. Daddy knew the law, he'd studied to be a lawyer, and was talking to Peter Carter-Ruck a lot and knew there was no guarantee that they would win. It was a 50/50 gamble. Do you keep what you've got and be grateful for it, or do you risk losing it all. He had two children at boarding school, a nice house in Surrey and a good career. He didn't want to jeopardise that. He started to get very nervous."

Whittingham knew that if he lost he would be financially wiped out. And as he no longer had any rights in the screenplay, having assigned them to McClory, but was still liable to half of the court costs should they be defeated, Jack had everything to lose while McClory had everything to gain. McClory also had the advantage of a new and very rich wife in Bobo Sigrist, whose considerable family fortune was largely responsible for him bringing the case and being able to follow it through. Bobo's mother, Beatrice, was an immensely rich widow whose husband had founded the Hawker Aircraft firm. McClory first met Bobo in Nassau and was almost twice her age. Aged 17, Bobo had eloped with her first husband, interior decorator Greg Huarez. The marriage was not consummated and lasted only a few days. On the morning after the wedding, Bobo awoke to find Greg Huarez wearing a hairnet! Even at 17, Bobo was a target for fortune hunters (even gay ones). McClory also benefited from contributions from his South African millionaire friend Johnny Schlesinger. Poor Jack Whittingham had no such capital to draw on. "In the end, I don't know who advised Dad or if he came to the conclusion himself, but he pulled out as co-plaintiff and decided to support Kevin as a principal witness," says Sylvan. "He was advised by Peter Carter-Ruck that he would have a good case of his own at the end should McClory win. That was the safer option for him."

Carter-Ruck himself knew it was a difficult and immense case but one that he and his team felt they should win, both legally and morally. The hope was, though, to achieve a satisfactory out of court settlement and thus save the need to go to trial. In late July, a dialogue opened up between the two sets of lawyers and McClory was offered numerous incentives to drop the case. These included: a screen credit for his script contribution, £10,000 damages, a profit share in *Thunderball* and to be engaged as associate producer. McClory made it clear that he was not prepared to contemplate any settlement that did not install him as the film's full producer. He knew that "associate producer" was merely a token job title with barely any influence. Plus in order to properly evaluate what was on the table, some information was required. This included profit and royalty statements for both the hardback and paperback editions of *Thunderball*, similar data in respect of the sale of serial, overseas and TV rights and how much Fleming received for selling the film rights in his books to Broccoli and Saltzman. All of these figures Fleming's solicitors were simply not willing to concede.

As for McClory's request to be producer, Broccoli and Saltzman had no intention of sharing the producing chores on *Thunderball* and so the offer of associate producer was the only one on the table. He had just six days to accept otherwise Broccoli and Saltzman, wrote Fleming's solicitor, "will not make a film of *Thunderball* now, which in practice would probably mean never." So, did Broccoli and Saltzman intend to follow *From Russia with Love* with *Thunderball* and were implying that McClory's only hope of ever seeing the film on screen was by accepting the lowly position of associate producer? If so, their

Chapter 21: THE COURT CASE THAT KILLED IAN FLEMING

Ian Fleming Is Sued Over 'Thunderball'

JUDGE HEARS OF HOW BOND 'ANNUALLY SAVES WORLD'

IAN FLEMING, author of the James Bond books, was a defendant to-day in a High Court action alleging infringement of copyright brought by a film producer.

The judge, Mr. Justice Ungoed-Thomas, was told that the action concerning the novel "Thunderball" would be an immense case.

Plaintiff was film producer and director Kevin O'Donovan McClory, of Chesham-street, Victoria.

Mr. Fleming, of Victoria-square, Victoria, and his co-defendants, Jonathan Cape, Ltd., of Bedford-square, and Mr. John F. C. Bryce, financier, of Lennox-gardens, denied infringement.

Mr. W. L. Mars-Jones, Q.C., for Mr McClory, reading a précis of the novel to the judge, described Bond as "An undercover agent in the British Secret Service—tough, hard-hitting, hard-drinking, hard-living and amoral, who at regular annual intervals saves the citizens of this country and the whole free-world from the most incredible disasters."

Mr. Justice Ungoed-Thomas: I have been saved myself.

CAPACITY
Surviving Torture

"Two of the reasons," continued Mr. Mars-Jones, "are: he has a licence to kill and an infinite capacity for surviving torture."

Mr. McClory had wide experience in the film industry.

"He was on the way to the top—being one of the youngest producer-directors—until he became enmeshed in the events with which this case is concerned," said counsel.

Jonathan Cape, Ltd., handled the James Bond books in the hard-backed editions. Two Bond films, "Dr. No" and "From Russia With Love," had been made with fantastic success and this had had a dramatic effect on the sales of the books, which were also sold in paperbacks.

Mr. Bryce, a man of considerable wealth, had homes in Nassau, Vermont, New York, London, and Steeple Bumpstead, Essex.

COMPLEXITY
Plea Failed

Closely associated with him was Mr. Ernest Cuneo, a member of the New York bar who figured prominently in the case.

Mr. McClory sought a multiplicity of relief: for breach of copyright, breach of confidence, conversion, breach of contract, false representation of authorship and slander of title.

The novel "Thunderball" was published by Jonathan Cape, Ltd., early in 1961, after Mr. McClory had tried to get a court order to stop publication. His application failed because of the complexity of the matter.

Mr. Mars Jones continued that it would be necessary for the judge to read the novel.

Outlining the plot he said it dealt with "Spectre," an organisation of the world's most daring and vicious criminals. They planned to steal a Nato bomber carrying two atomic bombs and hold up the governments of Britain and the U.S.A. for £100 million ransom. If the ransom were not paid they threatened to blow up a military establishment and then plant the other near a city.

Their plot was foiled by James Bond after a series of underwater skin-diving adventures set in the Bahamas.

CRITICS
Differences

Mr. Mars-Jones said the novel was serialised in the *Daily Express*, and later published in paper-back form all over the civilised world, and possibly the uncivilised world too.

It had a mixed reception from the critics, as most of the Bond novels did, but some of the more observant critics detected differences from the earlier novels. In particular, there were fewer excruciating episodes.

Mr. Mars-Jones continued: "The critics were right. This novel was different from Mr. Fleming's other novels. And the reason, according to Mr. McClory, is that it was based on a draft screen-play of 'Thunderball,' which then had the title 'James Bond of the Secret Service.'"

In the plot of that screenplay and earlier treatments Mr. Fleming certainly had a hand, but Mr. McClory and a screen writer named Jack Whittingham also had a substantial contribution.

"I hope to satisfy you that that work was of joint authorship, but that Mr. McClory and Mr. Whittingham made a far bigger contribution than Mr. Fleming," continued counsel.

There was no acknowledgement in the book to indicate that Mr. McClory or Mr. Whittingham had had any part in the conception or development of the plot.

Mr. Ernest Cuneo's contribution was acknowledged with the words, "to Ernest Cuneo, muse." Mr. Cuneo's contribution did not compare with that of Mr. McClory and Mr. Whittingham.

SCRIPT
Three People

If the intention of the inscription to Ernest Cuneo was to give the world the impression that the inspiration of the story came from him, that was contrary to the evidence which would be called for Mr. McClory.

Mr. Mars-Jones said he understood the defence contention to be that Mr. McClory contributed no copyright material to the film script.

Counsel maintained that when three people hammered out a film script, it did not matter whose hand held the pen. It was still a work of joint authorship.

Mr. Kevin McClory and his wife in London to-day.

Mr. Ian Fleming to-day.

The court case naturally made newspaper headlines.

ultimatum backfired. McClory would have none of it and a trial was now unavoidable. And *Goldfinger* replaced *Thunderball* as third in the 007 series.

The "spectre" of going to trial had been an intermittent worry at the back of Fleming's mind for the past two years. As the date approached he wrote to his friend William Plomer commenting wearily that he was winding himself up "like a toy soldier for this blasted case with McClory. I dare say that a diet of T.N.T pills and gin will see me through, but it's a bloody nuisance." The T.N.T pills to which Fleming referred were nitro-glycerine pills prescribed to prevent another heart attack.

Fleming and Bryce had assembled a formidable legal team, including John Whitford, a copyright expert. While Carter-Ruck had brought in William Mars-Jones QC and veteran of the 1961 book injunction Skone-James, who also happened to be the author of the leading textbook on copyright. McClory was taking no chances in assembling the best legal brains money could buy. And, of course, he had plenty of money.

The *Thunderball* trial took place at the Chancery Division of the High Court in London and became one of the media events of the year. Journalists lined up outside the courts every day as the leading players in this legal drama made their entrances and exits.

Fleming and Bryce would arrive each morning by taxi, accompanied by Ernest Cuneo who'd flown from the US to provide advice and moral support. After hours in a stuffy court room sat on hard wooden benches, hearing evidence most of which they disagreed with, Fleming and his team would retire to a nearby pub, The George, where they always had a table booked for lunch at one o'clock.

Counsel for McClory, Mr Mars-Jones, opened the case by describing the character of James Bond as "an undercover agent in the British Secret Service – tough, hard-hitting, hard drinking, hard-living and amoral, who at regular intervals saves the citizens of this country and the whole free world from the most incredible disasters." The judge then butted in: "I have been saved myself." Jones went on to praise McClory, calling him one of cinema's youngest producer/directors, "on the way to the top until he became enmeshed in the events with which this case is concerned."

McClory's strategy was to satisfy the judge that the *Thunderball* novel was totally derivative of scripts written by Jack Whittingham, ownership of which McClory claimed for himself. Fleming denied the allegation. In fact he went further, stating that it was McClory's idea to write the book in the first place. Fleming claimed that in November 1959 McClory telephoned him at the offices of the Sunday Times requesting that a novel be written based on the Whittingham screenplay in the belief that it would help the film's prospects, secure advance publicity and increase the chances of getting financial backing. Finding new plot ideas difficult to come by Fleming readily agreed and so turned his next Bond novel into *Thunderball*.

This new admission that Fleming wrote *Thunderball* at the request and with the full knowledge and consent of McClory, formed a major part of the author's defence. Fleming happily admitted McClory's important role in the development of the project and that numerous script conferences took place at which ideas came from everyone. Some he adopted in the book, some he didn't. "When I put Mr Fleming in the witness box," said Sir Andrew Clark, his QC, "I propose to ask him what incidents in his novel he took from suggestions by Mr McClory and Mr Whittingham, and then it would be open to my friends to cross-examine him on that. My whole case is that the novel was written to boost the screenplay, and it could not do that if it did not reproduce the incidents in the screenplay." Whether this made McClory a co-author was a matter of law, Clark added.

If then Fleming admitted that his novel did indeed reproduce a number of the incidents in the film scripts, the reason being because McClory wanted him to write the book in order to promote the film, why then did Fleming change certain characters and events or seek to disguise their origin? McClory argued that it was because Fleming knew full well that his book trespassed upon the screenplays and he was deliberately trying to hide the fact. To prove this McClory and Whittingham wrote a fascinating report, a checklist almost, of events that Fleming either changed or disguised. Most of the salient points are reproduced below:

1: Fleming changed most of the names of the characters in his book. "Leads to confusion and seems a deliberate attempt to camouflage his borrowings from our work," said the report. For example, Gaby became Domino, Mafia chief Bastico and Trapani turned into Blofeld, scientist Galante into Kotze, and others besides. "How can this possibly help to exploit the film?"

2: In the novel, Fleming had Bond trail Largo's yacht in a Polaris submarine, not a gunboat as in the script. This after it had been agreed in story conferences that from a production point of view a submarine was impossible, due to costs. This change, quoted the report "was damaging to the exploitation of the film. Did Fleming really imagine that he would be able to borrow a Polaris submarine for filming purposes? Is this exploitation of the film values!"

Moreover, from a cinematic point of view, the screenplay version of the climactic scene where Bond's men drop from a plane into the sea battle was "practicable and visual. Fleming's substitute by

Chapter 21: THE COURT CASE THAT KILLED IAN FLEMING

which Bond's men had to emerge from a submarine and locate the enemy was bad film and in fact makes nonsense." Underwater swimmers being unable to see the enemy from so far a distance and unable to catch them up either as Largo's men were using mechanical propulsion units. Again, if Fleming was writing the book in order to promote the script, why make such a bad change.

3: Fleming totally removed the entire opening sequence which had been agreed by all parties (the arrival of the Mafia informant and his subsequent killing) and which the author himself adopted in his own revised treatment. "He substituted it with a sequence in a health clinic, which had no bearing upon the rest of the story. We can only assume that this was another smoke screen laid down in an attempt to make his novel appear different from the screenplay. Or does Fleming call this exploitation, too!"

4: It was also agreed in conference that the villainous forces in the story should be the Mafia. In his novel Fleming reverted to SPECTRE. "This was another confusion – presumably used as another smoke screen." He also moved the HQ of the gang from Palermo to Paris. "Smoke screen," said the report.

5. The report further asked why Fleming renamed Largo's home from Xanadu to Palmyra. "We spent days carefully picking locations at and near Xanadu. By changing this location a great deal was lost from the screenplay. Was Fleming anxious that no mention of Xanadu should be made in his novel in case the evidence of our recce should be detected."

6. Fleming also substituted Largo's luxury yacht for a speedy hydrofoil. Why? asked the report. "Visually in a film this would reveal the secret compartment by the raising of the hull above the water so giving the game away. Another smoke screen?"

The report finished with a general comment: "It is quite obvious to us that Fleming would have found it impossible to produce his novel without trespassing upon many vital sections of our plot. In fact he hung his whole story on our plot. Having done so, wherever possible he changed the names of characters and locations, he altered the continuity, and inserted quite unnecessary irrelevancies such as the health clinic and quantities of other padding in an attempt to disguise the fact that he was pirating our work. If this is explained away by him as an attempt to exploit the film, our answer must be that he has done untold damage to the much better and more dramatic story as told by the screenplay."

Naturally Fleming didn't agree with the report's conclusions, but his argument that McClory asked him to write the novel made no sense anyway. If it was true, why was Fleming discussing with MCA the possibility of an injunction being sought against him. And wasn't it his own, as well as Bryce's defence, that McClory had no rights in *Thunderball*. So if he had no rights in the story how could McClory request Fleming to write a novel based on the script in the first place?

Despite the holes in this argument, Fleming claimed that the origins of the *Thunderball* story never came from McClory in any case, but from Ernest Cuneo. In a letter to MCA's Robert Fenn, dated 29 November 1960, Fleming said that when Bryce told Cuneo his intention of making a Bond film the American sat down "and scribbled off a suggested plot involving the Mafia and the theft of an atom bomb. His three pages have been broadly followed, first by me and, based on my suggested treatment, by Jack Whittingham." McClory pounced on this. The Cuneo memo never had the Mafia as its villains, nor the actual "theft" of an atom bomb (the bomb was provided by an unidentified foreign power). Plus it was McClory's suggestion to use underwater locations in the Bahamas and an atomic weapon for a Bond plot during meetings attended by Cuneo. Only then did Cuneo later write his memo to Bryce using those ingredients. McClory also thought it inaccurate to say that both Fleming and Whittingham had broadly followed Cuneo's memo. "There is absolutely no comparison between Cuneo's suggestions based on our thoughts and Fleming's novel or Whittingham's script."

In his letter to Fenn, Fleming also stated that he turned Cuneo's plot outline into his first draft treatment and it was decided to turn that into a script. After various conferences Fleming then produced his second treatment. It was this that Whittingham used as the basis for his screenplay. Again, McClory found holes in this story. It had not been agreed to script Fleming's first treatment. "Xanadu decided that Fleming's treatment was implausible and impracticable," wrote McClory. "And both Whittingham and I agreed to try to rectify this by changing the plot." The whole night club and

Bond's ludicrous infiltration as a burglar alarm repairman was excised, for example. Fleming agreed to these changes and his second treatment incorporated the new plot elements. Whittingham then produced the final screenplay. "Fleming played a very minor part in the writing of this script and in fact the few ideas that he produced in the main had to be removed from the screenplay," was McClory's recollection.

Fleming saw it as highly significant that when Cuneo heard his memo was to form the basis of the *Thunderball* novel, he sold it to Bryce for a nominal one-dollar fee. "I am pretty certain this was a sale from Cuneo to Bryce and not by Cuneo to Xanadu," Fleming wrote Fenn. Not surprisingly McClory took it to mean the exact opposite: that because Bryce was a partner in Xanadu at the point of sale Cuneo's memo became partnership property. So even if Fleming was claiming that the Cuneo memo formed the basis to his novel, that memo in fact evolved as a direct result of discussions between Bryce, Cuneo and McClory and now belonged to Xanadu anyway!

Ultimately though, it didn't really matter if Fleming based *Thunderball* on Cuneo's outline or ripped of wholesale Whittingham's script unless McClory could prove the validity of his partnership with Bryce. This was the whole crux of the case. Could McClory prove that the 6 May 1958 agreement to form Xanadu for the purpose of making *Boy and the Bridge* also applied to the projected Bond film and that therefore a new or continuing partnership existed?

McClory revealed that it was Bryce's idea for the company to pursue further film projects and during discussions said things like, "shall we do this" or "shall we do that." It was always *we* not *I*. "The whole trend of our relationship was that of a continuing partnership or a new partnership," McClory claimed. "And no other construction could be put upon the discussions which took place between us." Those discussions ultimately led to Bryce's idea that they make a picture based on his friend Ian Fleming's fictional hero James Bond. And McClory agreed.

Bryce, in his defence, rejected that argument completely. His partnership with McClory was expressly formed for no other purpose than for *Boy and the Bridge*. Yes, he admitted, a Bond film script was written and McClory was attached as producer, but this in no way created any binding or enforceable contractual relationship between them. McClory disagreed and the evidence overwhelmingly backed him up as the following examples clearly show:

1: The name Xanadu Productions was used by McClory with the full knowledge and approval of Bryce in connection with all arrangements made for the Bond film and many routine correspondences on behalf of the film were written on Xanadu headed notepaper.

2: Bank accounts were opened in the name "Xanadu Productions: James Bond Account," again with the approval of Bryce. Cheques, receipts and invoices were shown at the trial bearing out the existence of two separate accounts operated by Xanadu, one for *Boy and the Bridge* and one for Bond, both of which McClory had the power to draw monies. "There was no suggestion at any time," said Xanadu accountant William Rosser-James in his court statement, "that in operating this account McClory was other than a partner in exactly the same way as in the case of the *Boy and the Bridge* account."

3: Leigh Aman and others were with the knowledge of Bryce, engaged in various activities on behalf of Xanadu in connection with the Bond film.

4: Jack Whittingham was engaged on behalf of Xanadu and paid for his services through the Bond bank accounts, with the knowledge of Bryce.

5: Bryce wrote to the Colonial Secretary of Nassau in March 1959 stating that he and "my partner Kevin McClory" were interested in making pictures in the Bahamas, with particular reference to the Bond film. McClory said this showed Xanadu intended to continue making films.

6: For the proposed Xanadu Bahamas company, Bryce had installed McClory as company director and producer "in charge of all filmmaking activities."

7: Ernest Cuneo's memo and rough story line for a projected Bond film stated that it was to be a Xanadu production.

8: On a number of occasions in the presence of various witnesses (all of whom were prepared to

Chapter 21: THE COURT CASE THAT KILLED IAN FLEMING

appear at the trial) Bryce referred to McClory as his partner in connection with the Bond project. These witnesses included McClory's brother Desmond O'Donovan, Leigh Aman, Douglas Netter, Jack Whittingham and the actor Trevor Howard.

9: It was widely known in film circles that the Bond film was to be produced by McClory. Various press releases around the time of *Boy and the Bridge*, approved by Bryce, referred to himself and McClory as being partners and their intention to make ongoing features. Indeed the premiere brochure of *Boy and the Bridge* stated that their second film was now in preparation and was "based on an adventure of Ian Fleming's character James Bond."

Fleming also expressly denied that at any time did he believe that a partnership existed between McClory and Bryce in respect of the Bond film. Again the evidence proved Fleming just as much a liar as Bryce. Why then did Fleming write on the title page of his second treatment that the story was the "property of Xanadu?" Why in a letter to Bryce dated 2 July 1959 did he refer to the project as "Kevin's Bond film?" Why in his cable to Eric Ambler asking for Hitchcock's participation did Fleming say that the Bond film was to be made by Xanadu? Why in a letter to McClory on 15 June 1959 did Fleming express his wish that the Irishman should be the "sole mouthpiece on the project?" And hadn't Fleming himself, in his 2 July 1959 letter to Bryce, agreed to the proposition that Xanadu make a Bond film?

Fleming's dealings with MCA, his request that Bryce send him a copy of the original Xanadu partnership contract with McClory, as well as Xanadu's contract with Whittingham, also clearly showed that Fleming understood the Bond project to be a partnership proposition. Furthermore, McClory claimed that as early as June 1958, just a month after the Xanadu partnership was formed, Fleming contacted Bryce suggesting that his own company Glidrose Productions Limited (which owned the copyright to the Bond novels) should come into Xanadu as a junior partner.

In court, numerous other letters were read out; all pointing to the fact that McClory was heavily involved in the production of the proposed Bond movie as Bryce's partner. The letters also revealed that while Bryce maintained the appearance of a solid partnership, behind McClory's back he was in secret communication with Fleming and plotting to undermine the Irishman and finally oust him from the project. "There was a gradual lowering of Mr McClory's status," as lawyer Mars-Jones put it. The spotlight fell on one letter in particular from October 1959. In it, Fleming mentioned the possibility of Hitchcock buying the Bond film and giving Bryce and himself shares that would mean a certain fortune for them both. "They were discussing selling the whole thing, lock, stock and barrel to Hitchcock, while Mr McClory was being cut out of the whole deal," said Mars-Jones.

Whittingham also proved a vital witness in exposing Bryce's lies about his partnership with McClory. It was in November 1959 when Whittingham was first introduced to Bryce and recalled in his court statement that Bryce was then a keen collaborator in the Bond film. "At all times I could not have got other than the impression that Bryce and McClory were partners, co-directors or colleagues in a joint enterprise. I would certainly have described them as hand in glove."

Although he had backed out as a plaintiff in the case, Whittingham was true to his word and intended to loyally support McClory, despite considerable ill health. While in the Bahamas on a reconnaissance trip for the film Whittingham had suffered a coronary. Snorkelling one day, he'd come out of the sea with a pain down his left arm. Returning to London his doctor rushed him to hospital where he was ordered to lie still for three weeks and given so much morphine for the pain that his family feared he might become addicted. Fortunately he didn't. "But after the heart attack he suffered constant angina," remembers Sylvan. "I used to live in terror of him dropping dead. You'd be sitting at the table and he'd suddenly stoop over, the colour would drain from his face and he'd be fumbling for his tablets. These pills took about a minute to work and we would sit there, almost unable to breath, terrified, until he relaxed again. It used to frighten me a lot."

Despite living with the painful after effects of angina, which the court case only exacerbated, Whittingham was determined to travel to London from his Surrey home and attend every single day

Chapter 21: THE COURT CASE THAT KILLED IAN FLEMING

JAMES BOND IN A 'THUNDERBALL' CLASH

WHODUNNIT?

The James Bond plot thickens

A 'James Bond' case

IAN FLEMING IS SUED BY FILM MAN

Ian Fleming is sued over 'Thunderb...

James Bond — Ian

BOND'S CREATOR
Author Ian Fleming, pictured yesterday. He created the character of secret agent Bond in his books

AGENT 007 GOES TO COURT

Page from a scrapbook kept by Jack Whittingham over the course of the trial.

Chapter 21: THE COURT CASE THAT KILLED IAN FLEMING

of the trial. His evidence was to prove vital, notably in explaining to what extent McClory was involved in the script. "We worked in very close collaboration," ran Whittingham's statement. "I discussed scenes with him which I had written and proposed to write. There were also occasions when he outlined a series of incidents or scenes which he suggested and I wrote them into the script. In fact Mr McClory contributed a great deal to the script and Fleming very little and indeed he only attended script conferences on two occasions."

It was damning evidence, but at what price had it been given? "My bedroom was next to Dad's at home and I used to hear him crying out in pain at night," Sylvan recalls. "But he'd be back in court the next day. It was an enormous struggle for him, but he would not let Kevin down. He should never have been in court. It was against doctor's orders. But there were two things going on. There was the desire to stand up for Kevin, because he believed he was absolutely in the right. And there was his own reputation at stake, and ambition in that he hoped to go on with this project. Those were the two motivations, which I think are very human. It wasn't anything against Fleming because both men liked each other enormously."

Incredibly, despite the high stakes and enormous pressures surrounding the court case and his testimony against them, Fleming and Bryce remained affable towards Whittingham throughout its duration. Whittingham and Fleming, particularly, remained on good terms. Sylvan recalls never hearing her father say anything against him. And no evidence exists that Fleming ever said a negative word against Whittingham. Both men really were cut from the same cloth, sharing similar backgrounds and education. They also shared a love of women, drinking to excess and smoking, which largely contributed to the heart problem that both men were simultaneously suffering from. It was all very different with McClory. He was from a totally different world than Fleming and must have resented his privileged roots and Eton education, while Fleming no doubt looked down upon McClory's own humble origins. McClory would label Fleming "cynical" and "a snob." Not surprisingly both men had found it hard to work together and frequently clashed. One suspects that half of McClory's motive for his court battle was to put one over on the upper classes, as represented by Fleming and Bryce.

Another important element of the trail was the agreement in writing dated 17 March 1960 made between Bryce and McClory. This stated that should the Irishman be unable to arrange financing for the film in six months (by 30 October) he had to assign any rights he owned in the scripts back to Bryce, who would then be free to exploit them, as he wished. So when McClory's big gamble to attract a Hollywood backer in 007 failed, Bryce claimed that all rights in the *Thunderball* film scripts became vested in him. But despite repeated requests, McClory refused to hand them over. Why? It was simple, said McClory. Had he known what was now being revealed during the trial (Bryce and Fleming's plans and manoeuvres behind his back, their secret talks with MCA, the keeping of highly pertinent information from him, etc), he would never have signed the March document. "Indeed it is inconceivable that anybody in the industry in their right senses would have done so," he wrote.

Bryce's counterclaim against McClory focused largely on this point – that McClory had no longer any copyright interests in the scripts. Also by persisting in his claims he'd precluded Bryce from exploiting them, in particular at the time most propitious for the sale of the film rights namely upon the publication of the *Thunderball* novel. Thus Bryce himself was seeking damages for breach of contract, and the return of $15,000 he had lent McClory in early 1959, which had been payable at the end of that year and which had thus far not been forthcoming. Although the original terms of that loan provided for the repayment to come from McClory's profits of the Bond film.

Naturally, McClory contested Bryce on these points. Yes, he had signed the 17 March agreement, but it was decided that an appropriate payment was to be made to him if the Bond film was ever made outside of his involvement. The terms of such compensation were never agreed at the meeting but left to the men's respective lawyers to negotiate and arrange at a later date. This never happened. Thus, McClory contended, the March agreement was not legally binding and therefore any agreement constituted by it was void.

If, however, the March agreement was proved to be binding, McClory argued, then it was an implied term thereof that Bryce should use his best endeavours to assist him in obtaining the necessary financing by 30 October, or alternatively should not take any action to jeopardise such a task. Bryce, said McClory, had failed to comply with this condition. In particular, Bryce had failed to disclose the details of his agreement with Fleming, although frequently requested to do so. "It was obviously of critical importance to McClory to have the agreement asset," said the Irishman's lawyer in court, "which Bryce and his advisers had been so evasive and about which Bryce had been so deceitful." This was breach of contract, said McClory; ergo Bryce was not entitled to the rights.

At the trial, Bryce admitted that he did fail to disclose the Fleming agreement, but offered no explanation as to why. McClory had always known of its existence but at no time during his partnership with Bryce was he ever privy to its contents. He recalled how at the onset of their Bond adventure he'd pointed out to Bryce that if they were going to write a new Bond story specially for the screen, Xanadu had to make sure that none of Fleming's books were made into films either: In other words, that Fleming hadn't sold off rights in one or other of his novels to competing producers who might make a 007 movie before them, thus rendering their own production valueless. This is of course what happened with *Casino Royale*, which Fleming had either forgotten he'd sold to Gregory Ratoff or simply neglected to mention when giving Xanadu their rights. This was always McClory's fear. But Bryce informed his partner on more than one occasion that Fleming had indeed, by letter, given Xanadu the rights to make the FIRST Bond movie. "I did not ask to see the documentary proof of this," McClory wrote,. "as I trusted Bryce implicitly." Later McClory had great cause to question both his trust in Bryce and to demand to see a copy of Fleming's letter of 8 July, all to no avail.

It was only during the commencement of his legal proceedings against Fleming and Bryce, that McClory was shown the agreement. It made for illuminating reading. When Bryce informed McClory in December 1959 that he no longer wished to bankroll the Bond film after delivery of Whittingham's script he also stated that Fleming, in the 8 July agreement, had consented to the use of his character on two conditions; namely formation of a company and the actual making of the film. According to Bryce both conditions had failed and any production of the Whittingham script was now subject to the consent, approval and re-negotiation with Fleming. Without a completely new arrangement the screenplay would not be marketable. In case McClory was in the dark over his position, Ernest Cuneo re-enforced it with one of his customarily blunt letters, dated 28 January 1960: "It would be a criminal fraud to offer James Bond without Ian's consent. And a mere glance at the memo will indicate that nothing can be done without Ivar's ownership either. It is for them to decide what they wish to do, if anything, with their property."

The thing was, McClory had been given no opportunity to take a "mere glance" at the memo and therefore did not have an opportunity of judging whether or not Bryce's statements were correct. But upon reading the Fleming agreement at the trial McClory could plainly see that Bryce's statements, "were totally incorrect." McClory saw that the Fleming letter of 8 July contained neither of the alleged conditions. It did not prescribe as a condition the formation of a movie company; merely that in exchange for $50,000 worth of shares in Xanadu, Fleming would give the right to make the first Bond movie. It was, however, implied that such a company would be formed within a reasonable time period; Fleming took that to mean no more than one year. No such company was ever formed and accordingly, said Fleming, the agreement was void. However McClory's counsel pointed out that the agreement with Fleming was signed on 8 July 1959 and Bryce's letter of 18 December 1959 was only five months later, and so certainly within the reasonable period in which the company might have been incorporated.

There was also no condition implied or expressed in Fleming's 8 July letter that a film actually had to be made. And there was certainly no condition that production of the Whittingham script would be subject to any re-negotiations with Fleming. And as for Bryce's opinion that the Whittingham script was not marketable and couldn't be exhibited for possible financing without a completely new deal

Chapter 21: THE COURT CASE THAT KILLED IAN FLEMING

with Fleming, this was absurd, said McClory. Hadn't Bryce, all during this period, been exhibiting the script to MCA for just such a purpose? So Bryce had used the fact that McClory never saw the 8 July agreement to impose new restrictions and demands upon their partnership, knowing that minus the facts McClory could raise no objections.

Fleming had always argued that the 8 July agreement was personal to Bryce anyway and incapable of assignment. While Bryce claimed that because it was his money that paid for Whittingham's script, so the finished product was his property, McClory argued that the right to make the first James Bond movie was acquired from Fleming by Bryce, not personally, but on behalf of Xanadu Productions. Therefore it was an asset of the partnership. But could he prove it?

Besides Whittingham, others were prepared to back up McClory too, including Leigh Aman. Ironically at the time of the trial, Aman was production supervisor for Woodfall, a film company formed in 1956 by playwright John Osborne, director Tony Richardson and one Harry Saltzman. Aman's court statements were unequivocal in his belief that Bryce and McClory, "were partners carrying precisely equal authority." And it was his impression that both were to be partners in the Bond film "in exactly the same way as they were during the production of *Boy and the Bridge*." Douglas Netter, of Samuel Goldwyn Productions, said much the same thing: "It was clearly implied that the Bond project was to be another venture of their partnership, Xanadu."

Xanadu's accountant, William Rosser-James, also made a statement that he'd come away from conversations with Bryce and McClory holding the impression that "Xanadu was going to make more films and that the Bond film was to be made as a continuation of the original partnership."

Among several supporters on the sideline for Fleming and Bryce was Charles Wacker III. Ironically, Wacker was also on friendly terms with McClory and had come in from Chicago hoping, as a relatively neutral observer, to maybe act as a go-between and help the protagonists reach some last minute agreement. But there seemed little scope for compromise. Three days into the case McClory informed Wacker he was prepared to give Bryce one last chance to make a deal. This ultimatum was discussed and rejected by Fleming and Bryce.

All the more strange then, what was to happen on the trial's ninth day. McClory had just taken the stand and was giving evidence when, as Peter Carter-Ruck later recorded, "The hearing was unexpectedly and somewhat dramatically adjourned after Leading Counsel on both sides had seen the judge in his private rooms." It was Friday afternoon and the hearing was adjourned until the following Monday morning, 2 December. There followed a weekend of conferences with various lawyers and solicitors, leading to a meeting in the offices of Fleming's solicitors, Farrer & Co, on the Sunday afternoon. Fleming arrived accompanied by his wife Ann; Bryce was with Cuneo, and McClory with Bobo, his brother Desmond O'Donovan and Jack Whittingham. There were also sundry solicitors. Carter-Ruck quickly detected an atmosphere of, "muted hostility."

Everyone was shown into a large room with chairs set out in a circle but with no table in the centre. After the formalities, Carter-Ruck opened the proceedings by outlining briefly the terms upon which McClory was prepared to settle his action. This would involve the payment of his costs and the vesting in McClory of the film rights in *Thunderball*. The copyright in both the finished picture and the film scripts should be his as well, plus a sum by way of damages to recompense him for the mental anguish and physical inconvenience he had been caused. A figure was mentioned. "So great," Bryce later wrote "as to draw a gasp even from that sophisticated group." It was a figure of £50,000. In less than 10 minutes it was agreed in principle to come to terms.

Why after nearly three years of expensive legal wrangling did Fleming and Bryce so quickly throw in the towel after just nine days in court? And without either of them, or their witnesses, taking the stand? Technically both men decided to settle, but since Bryce was financing the action it was his opinion that counted most. There are several possible explanations. One was money. Peter Carter-Ruck himself pointed to the fact that after nearly two weeks in court the costs were mounting steeply. But Bryce was a very rich man; and anyway as soon as Broccoli and Saltzman heard of his intention to settle they offered to underwrite the costs of continuing the case for a further fortnight. Both producers had kept a very close eye on developments and were understandably loath to see someone else emerge with ownership of any Bond film rights.

The second factor was Fleming's health. Like Whittingham, Fleming was ill as the court proceedings dragged on, though he attended every day. Having already suffered one serious heart attack Bryce was worried that the stress of the trial would bring on another one. Only a handful of closest friends knew how really ill Fleming was and had been for these past two years. In early 1962, Ernest Cuneo had dinner with Fleming and reported to Bryce that their mutual friend, "looks well and seems to be his old energetic self, but his eyes reveal he has had an ordeal." Another friend, Blanche Blackwell, had come to realise that he was "fighting like a tiger to live, but everything was against it." Movingly Fleming himself had reached a similar conclusion, writing in his notebook, "Suddenly you reach the age when it crosses your mind to say no to pleasure."

After days of wrestling with his conscience Bryce finally decided to settle, rather than watch his friend endure the days to come. There is evidence that Fleming's health was in an even worse state than previously thought. In a family letter from 1967, Jack Whittingham wrote that Bryce had revealed to him, "that Fleming had two very bad heart attacks during the court case."

Another and much more controversial, and previously never revealed, reason for the quick settlement is the revelation that McClory may have had in his personal possession an incriminating letter against his opponents. Bryce's sudden decision to settle, so this theory goes, was to prevent the letter seeing daylight and causing public embarrassment both to Fleming and himself. Significantly, at the close of the trial, Bryce's QC handed a letter to the judge saying, "I think it would be unwise for me to comment publicly on this letter." After reading it the judge observed, "All I can say about this is that I am very surprised to see it." The contents and author of the letter were never made public.

As a side-note to this, Bryce when writing to Fleming would sometimes begin his letter with the endearment "Dear Boy." Even more strangely, in one letter to McClory, Bryce signed off with the words "love and kisses." Hardly the language one would use in a letter to another man.

But most probably the reason for the rushed settlement was the fact that McClory's case was incontrovertible. Carter-Ruck felt victory was in large measure due to William Mars-Jones' opening speech, which lasted a total of 28 hours and eight minutes, and placed all the evidence before the court. Concluding his brief, Mars-Jones felt it pertinent, in relation to the conduct of Fleming and Bryce towards McClory, to quote Macmillan, then Prime Minister, "What greater moral crime can there be than to deceive those naturally inclined to trust you, those who work with you, serve with you and are your colleagues?"

If Bryce and Fleming were hoping McClory would fall down in the witness box, they were sadly mistaken. With all of Fleming's connections – Eton, Sandhurst, naval intelligence, everyone figured McClory, an Irishman in an English court, didn't stand a chance. But he showed incredible command of the hundreds of letters in the case, which he'd committed to memory, and was indeed able to demonstrate that his partnership with Bryce in Xanadu had endured to include the Bond film. Fleming and Bryce had underestimated their foe. As Whittingham's son Jonathan later observed, "Fleming et al never believed that Kevin had either the nerve or the financial muscle to dare go the whole course. They were dead wrong." Now they were to pay the consequences.

McClory's victory and revenge over the men who had sidelined him was considerable. Fleming would keep ownership of the *Thunderball* novel, but his publishers were to add the message: "Based on a screen treatment by Kevin McClory, Jack Whittingham and the author" to the title page of all future editions. It's there still today. McClory, in return, was awarded the film and television rights to the book, as well as the copyright to all existing related scripts and treatments.

The wording of the Deed of Assignment, executed on 31 December 1963, is worthy of note and would prove highly significant in years to come. Fleming, Bryce and Jonathan Cape assigned to McClory "all the copyright in the film scripts and the exclusive right to re-produce any part of the novel in films

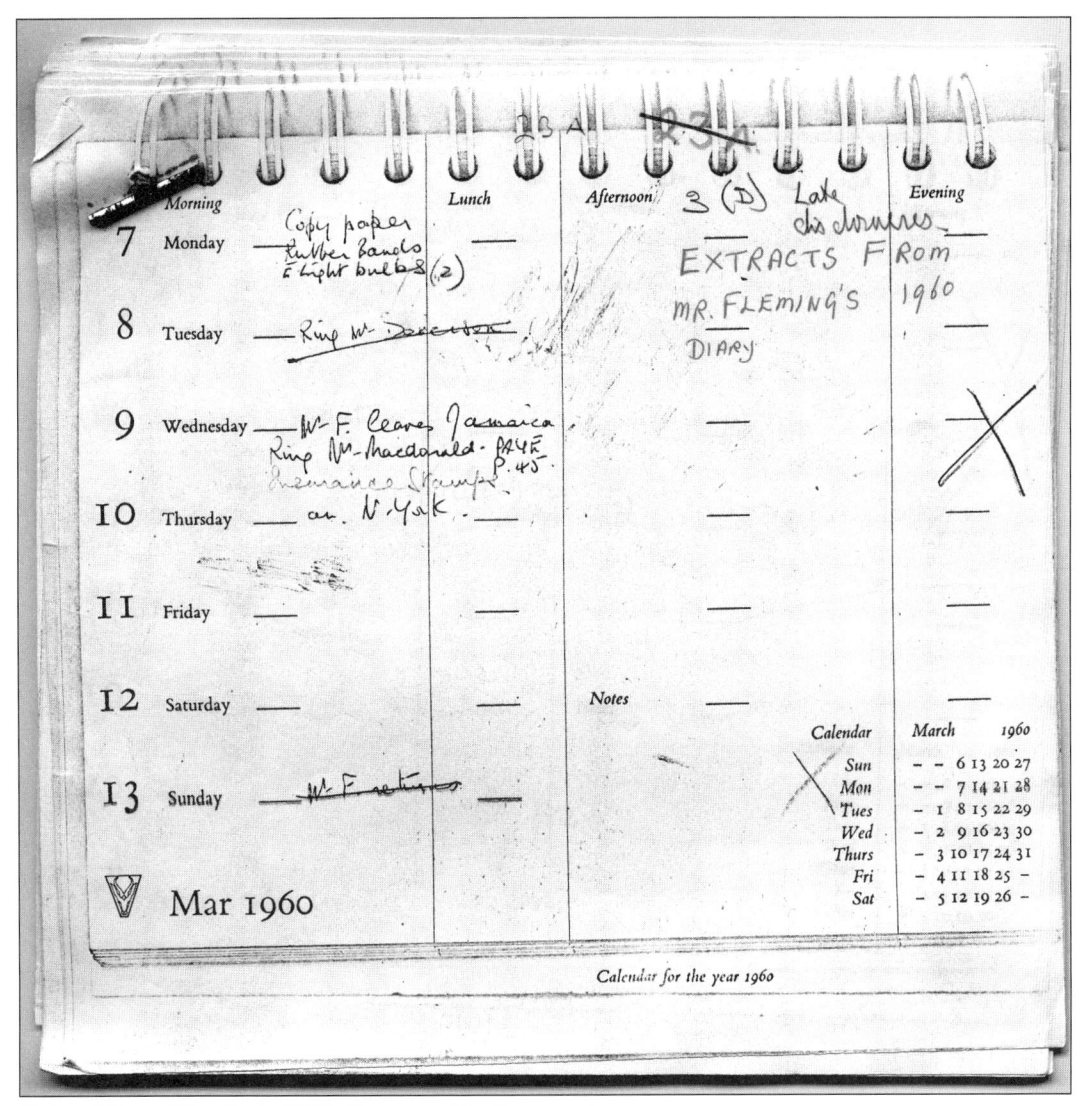

Chapter 21: THE COURT CASE THAT KILLED IAN FLEMING

Extract from Fleming's 1960 diary used in the court case.

and for the purpose of making such films to make scripts." Fleming also granted McClory "the exclusive right to use the character James Bond as a character in any such scripts or film of *Thunderball*."

In addition McClory got his own court costs paid (thought to be in the region of £17,500) and was awarded damages. In his book, *You Only Live Once: Memories of Ian Fleming*, Bryce explained how he forfeited a murderous slice of his personal assets to pay all the court costs.

After the trial, McClory celebrated his victory at a nearby pub with Bobo and friend and fellow Irishman Peter O'Toole. "Now I can look forward to making the best James Bond film ever produced," he told reporters. He also revealed the main reason why he brought the court action: "To wipe out the thought of anyone in the profession that I was trying to cash-in on the name of James Bond."

Incredibly, according to Sylvan, McClory was privately far from satisfied by the settlement and put all the blame on Peter Carter-Ruck, the man who organised it. "Kevin never forgave him for it actually. He thought he'd been sold out. Kevin always thought that Peter got in league with Broccoli and Saltzman. But Peter said he only met the Bond producers once at a cocktail party, so it was ridiculous.

But Kevin was a bit paranoid. He felt he should have had a better deal. I don't know how you get a better deal than that. I mean, he clearly won the case."

As for Fleming, after the trial he attempted to put a brave face on for the world, telling waiting reporters, "I am glad the whole expensive misunderstanding has now been disposed of. It's a pity it ever had to come to court." But inside he must have felt wounded and humiliated. To another reporter he tried to hide the fact with typical humour saying that he had found the case rather dull: "I feel Bond would have done something to liven it up. Like shooting the judge!"

And Bryce convinced himself that Fleming was happy with the case outcome. But a close friend who dined with Fleming the evening after the settlement later revealed that the writer bitterly denounced Bryce's perfidy. Ann was not happy too. She scrawled in her husband's personal copy of *Diamonds Are Forever*, which had a dedication to Bryce inside, the words: "Dedicated to Ivar Bryce. The man who betrayed Ian in the *Thunderball* case." In a letter to Evelyn Waugh, dated 6 December 1963, Ann expressed her feelings about the trial more succinctly: "Goodness I miss the Old Bailey, the case did Ian a power of good, no smoking in court and one hour for a simple lunch. It was sad for him having to settle. Our solicitors say we're all right, but one can never tell. So maybe we'll have to sell up."

Seeing that the whole ghastly business had lowered his spirits, friends of Fleming tried to cheer him up. John Betjeman wrote to commiserate but also to congratulate him on the movie version of *From Russia with Love*, which he'd just seen and loved, comparing Bond to a jet-setting Sherlock Holmes. "Write on, fight on," he championed.

As it turned out Bryce's concern over Fleming's health was later to be horribly justified. On 12 August 1964, just nine months after the *Thunderball* trial, Fleming suffered a massive heart attack and died. He was 56. Perhaps he never realised just how much of a strain the case had put on his already fragile health. A gentleman to the last, as the ambulance arrived to take him to hospital he said, "I am sorry to trouble you chaps."

Fleming died at the height of his earning powers, with his books selling around the world in undreamed of quantities. He also witnessed the popularity of the first two 007 movies. But he never lived to see his creation become a cinematic phenomenon and cultural icon thanks to the unprecedented success of, ironically enough, the story that had caused him much of those health problems in the first place – *Thunderball*.

CHAPTER 22
BOND GOES HEAD TO HEAD

After what had been amongst the most extraordinary media cases of the 20th century, McClory was left in the privileged position, one that any other independent movie producer would have sold his granny for, of having the means to make his own 007 film. The fact that Broccoli and Saltzman already had a well-established series underway that was proving highly popular seemed not to daunt or trouble him at all. To emphasise the point he dashed off to Saville Row, Bond's very own sartorial hunting ground, and had suits made with "007" marked on the inside breast pockets.

McClory wasted little time in setting his Bond film in motion. Flying into Dublin in December 1963 to spend Christmas with John Huston at his mansion in County Galway, the McClory's looked like any other holiday couple, with Kevin pushing a pram and Bobo holding two inconspicuous pieces of hand luggage. Except that one of them, a black box, contained McClory's total court winnings. Waiting reporters were told of his plans to set up his own production company called Branwell, named after his five-month-old son. It was backed by an American distribution organisation with a capital of £800,000. Not surprisingly *Thunderball* was to be its inaugural production. Bramwell was to be a real family business, with Bobo named Vice President and McClory's son as Company President. "He is now the youngest mogul in the film business," his father joked.

It wasn't long before stories began emerging in the press about who would play 007 in McClory's renegade Bond film, which was ready to go before cameras in March 1964, the same month as *Goldfinger*. Two names mentioned were the Australian actor Rod Taylor, recent star of Hitchcock's *The Birds*, and Laurence Harvey, who'd made his name in the kitchen sink drama *Room at the Top* before moving on to Hollywood and films like *The Alamo* and *The Manchurian Candidate*. Harvey seemed the favourite and on 7 January revealed that he had been asked and was considering the offer. "I think the script is marvellous and I would be delighted to portray Bond."

McClory was now in Rome choosing a suitable starlet to co-star with his new Bond. Just days after Honor Blackman had been chosen to play Pussy Galore in *Goldfinger*, McClory named Sylva Koscina, a 29 year old Yugoslav-born, Italian-bred actress, to star in *Thunderball* as Domino. He'd approached her

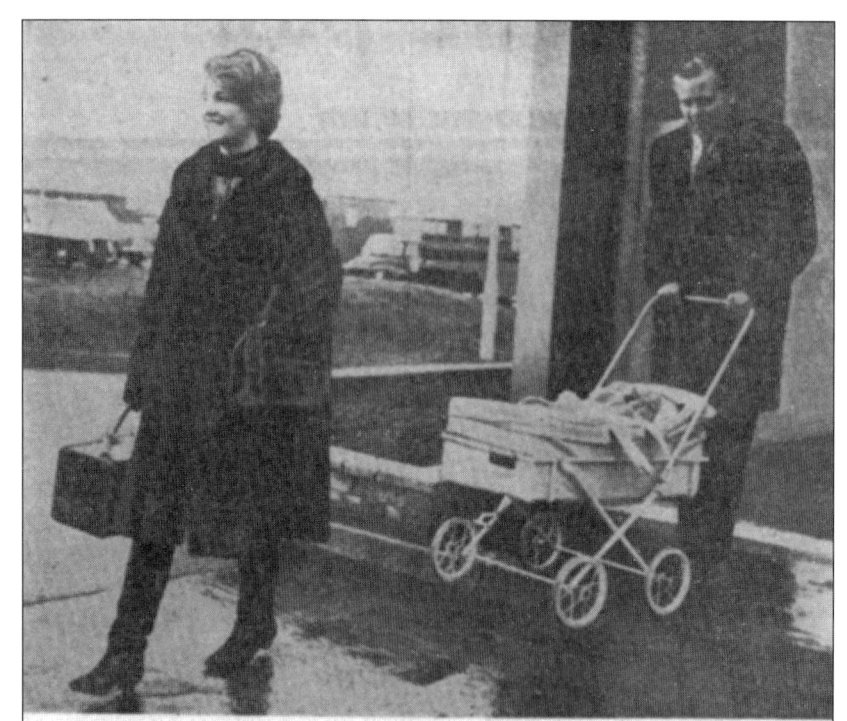

Press clipping of McClory and Bobo flying to Dublin with their court case winnings.

JAMES BOND CASH FLIES OUT. Kevin McClory, 39, the film producer, pushes the pram and his wife carries a black box as they leave London yesterday to fly to Dublin. In the box Mrs. McClory carried £52,500. This is understood to be the money her husband received as a result of his three-year legal fight involving copyright interests in the James Bond thriller "Thunderball" and his rights to make a film about it. Mr. Ian Fleming, creator of James Bond, was among the defendants of the action which ended with a settlement in the High Court last week.

on the set of her latest film saying, "You're the perfect Bond type, tough, as though you can carry a machine gun with ease, yet lusciously attractive." Sylva was understandably interested.

After years making Italian movies, notably Steve Reeves Hercules epics, Sylva had just made her English-speaking debut in the Bond spoof *Hot Enough for June*, opposite Dirk Bogarde. In the week of her public debut in Britain at the Royal Film Performance in London's West End, critic Barry Norman interviewed Sylva for his newspaper column, commenting on her engaging personality and English accent that "is not so much broken as shattered and eccentrically put together again." Ironically another guest that evening of 25 February was Honor Blackman. The Duke of Edinburgh was understandably confused at being presented with two competing Bond girls and asked Honor when she was flying off to the Bahamas. "No, that's the other James Bond film," she corrected him. "Mine is with Sean Connery."

The press, not surprisingly, had a field day with the prospect of competing 007 movies. "Stand by for the battle of the Bonds" was one headline. Film journalists had never before heard of two independent film companies prepared to film two different movies at the same time each featuring the same hero. It would happen again in 1983 and involve the same protagonists (McClory and Broccoli), the same character (Bond) and the same movie *Thunderball*.

But the big question everybody was asking was would the public accept another actor as Bond, now that Connery had so completely made the part his own. Harvey and Taylor were soon out of the running and McClory was hinting that whoever played Bond, "It will not be an American actor. But you can take it from me that my Bond will be a big 'animal type' actor." Influenced perhaps by Fleming's suggestion years before that Richard Burton would be his ideal Bond, McClory approached the hellraising Welsh superstar. He'd already told reporters that he wanted to cast his Bond from the very top acting drawer, likely candidates being Peter O'Toole and Burton – "Or alternatively to do an offbeat

Chapter 22: BOND GOES HEAD TO HEAD

Bond with Peter Sellers." This was a bizarre piece of casting, but it found resonance somewhere as three years later Sellers would indeed be cast in the Bond spoof *Casino Royale*.

Late in February, McClory flew to Toronto where Richard Burton had opened in a pre-Broadway run of Hamlet. Burton was reportedly "very amused" with the idea of him playing the super spy and more than curious about the £75,000 newspapers were suggesting was to be his pay packet. "Richard would be absolutely fantastic as James Bond," McClory told reporters. "He IS James Bond." McClory felt the Welshman was much closer to Fleming's original image of the English character, as opposed to the Scottish Connery.

A few days later on 21 February, McClory revealed that after four days of talks with Burton, "we are mutually agreed on all points." The start date of *Thunderball* had now shifted from March to June when Burton's schedule was free. "Everything appears right for him to step into the part," said McClory. "Only the contract has to be signed."

As Connery began work on his third stint as 007, his fears growing of becoming typecast, the notion of someone else tackling the role had become an appealing one. "Although I think they'd be crazy to do it," he said. "There was talk of Burton doing one, and I said he must be out of his mind. It would be like putting his head on a chopping block. Whatever he did he couldn't make the films more successful than they are. Even if David Lean made one, there's no guarantee it would do any better."

Connery was right. Despite the interest of Burton, the casting of Sylva Koscina and American backing, McClory must have felt that his 007 project was caught between a rock and a hard place. By the time he won the rights to *Thunderball*, he had lost the opportunity to put out a successful film first and independent of Broccoli and Saltzman. Three highly successful Bond pictures had already been made; a formula had been established in the public's mind. The opening gun barrel, the Bond theme music and, most importantly, Connery, would all be missing from McClory's production. The only real chance he had was to join ranks with the American producers he threatened to rival. "I needed somebody who was very strong for Bond if I was going to come up with someone else other than Sean," McClory said. "But deep down I knew I wanted Sean." McClory's agents Christopher Mann also gave Connery as the reason why their client had now decided not to make the Bond film on his own. "He wanted to make the best. And the best is with Sean Connery."

Broccoli and Saltzman too naturally felt that a rival Bond production at this early stage would harm their own series. And so it was almost by mutual consent that the two forces joined together. In September 1964 Broccoli flew to Dublin where he and McClory met at the airport and a deal was struck. It was certainly a good week for the Bond producers, the thorny question of McClory had been dealt with and *Goldfinger* had opened to capacity crowds. The clamour for the next 007 installment would soon reach fever pitch.

The White House
Oxshott
Surrey

6th May 1961

Dear Ian

I do hope that you are mending well, doing all you are told, and none of the forbidden things you would like to be doing! My main consolation was morphine, and I?m not too sure that I haven?t been hooked!

Following the suggestion in your letter, I have asked Freddie Holdaway, who is the legal adviser to my agents - Christopher Mann - to get in touch with your lawyers, and this has been done. But very understandingly, he was told that you are not to be in contact with the outside world for a while.

I am recovering slowly and impatiently and hope to be off on my travels for a new film at Whitsun.

Best wishes for a complete and speedy recovery.

Yours

Jack

As from the Clinic
4 Old Mitre Court
Fleet Street, EC4

10th May 1961

Dear Jack

I am horrified to hear that you have been on morphine and not only that, but that you are already contemplating your next stint at Whitsun. Is this really wise, or can you take the new thing on in a fairly leisurely fashion? It seems to me that you are getting back into your professional stride a bit quickly!

I am so glad that your legal adviser is now in touch with my solicitor. I don?t wish to sound ominous or to pre-judge anything, but I do think from what I hear from the legal cohorts on our side, that a graceful composure of such differences as you and I may have between each other might be wisdom.

However, as I say, this is all on the ?Old boy? wave and the main thing is that we should both be in good heart (!) again as soon as possible.

Again with warm thanks for your kindly letter

Yours

Ian

Correspondence between Jack Whittingham and Ian Fleming not long after the publication of *Thunderball*.

CHAPTER 23
THE FORGOTTEN MAN

Less than a week after McClory won his court battle with Fleming, Jack Whittingham put into action his own case against the author. Disappointment still remained that the Bond screenplay had been taken out of his hands, and if nothing else wanted to put the record straight about who was its originator. Whittingham had so far received nothing from the whole enterprise, except his original fee, but thanks to McClory's court victory now had a clear-cut case for personal damages and issued a writ against Fleming on 9 December 1963. It looked an open and shut case, all the papers and documents were exactly the same ones that had proved McClory's claim. Nothing could go wrong, could it?

In his claim Whittingham stated that he was solely responsible for the writing of the full screenplay to *Thunderball*. His involvement on it was widely known in the film making community. He recalled numerous film personalities popping into McClory's London home while they were undertaking story conferences, including the likes of Trevor Howard, Richard Harris and John Huston. His screenwriting colleagues also knew what he was currently engaged on, as did his old boss at Ealing, Sir Michael Balcon. "I can only say that in general everyone who knew me at that time and who I met was aware of the fact that I was writing this James Bond subject."

From his long experience of the film business, Whittingham had expected that there would be an acknowledgement in the event of a book being made from his film screenplay. And it still grieved him that despite being fully aware of his contribution, Fleming went ahead with his claim of being the sole author. He had also "deliberately and improperly" concealed from him the fact that he was writing a book based on the *Thunderball* screenplay, and worse, disputed Whittingham's two and a half-year involvement in the project right up until the commencement of McClory's court case. Because of this, Whittingham was gravely injured in his personal and professional reputation and now claimed damages for libel and for malicious falsehood.

It was Whittingham's sincere view that Fleming could not have written the novel *Thunderball* without tremendously leaning on the screenplay "which was in the main my work, with a considerable number of contributions by McClory and few, if any, by Fleming." To help his case Whittingham used documents drawn up by him and McClory at the original trial detailing some of the material both men conceived which ended up in the book.

1: In Fleming's first treatment, Domino was an English police agent working undercover in Largo's night club and later as a BOAC hostess. Whittingham changed Domino's name to Gaby, made her Italian and the mistress of Largo, thus giving her a much bigger role in the story. In his novel Fleming changed the name back to Domino but kept her Italian nationality, although had her sent to a girl's school in Cheltenham. "But he still left her as the character I had drawn," claimed Whittingham. "The girlfriend of the gangster who was used as a cat's-paw."

2: Fleming adopted the idea of an aircraft on a NATO training flight taken over by blackmailers. The hi-jacking idea was first suggested at a script conference attended by Whittingham, McClory and Fleming, who then put it into his second treatment and ultimately in his novel.

3: In Cuneo's original story line there was only one bomb. In Whittingham's scripts there are two. In Fleming's novel there are also two bombs.

4: In Fleming's original treatment he had the Mafia shown as men dressed up with rosettes and having a good time with the girls on a trade convention in the Bahamas. "I did not believe that this would be credible," wrote Whittingham. "As Mafia leaders would be spotted too easily." Instead Whittingham showed the Mafia bosses only at a meeting in Sicily. Fleming adopted this idea in his novel, changing the Mafia for SPECTRE and having SPECTRE's leaders shown only at their secret HQ.

5: The character of Petachi was raised in a story conference and Fleming immediately inserted him into his second draft. Petachi appears in the novel.

6: In Fleming's treatment, Bond was sent to the Bahamas on M's hunch that the trouble lay there. In Whittingham's screenplay Bond was but one of numerous agents assigned round the globe. In the novel this alteration was used.

7: The use of tarpaulin to cover the wreck of the bomber which otherwise would be easily seen in the clear Bahamian waters was also a product of a script conference and appears in the book. Fleming's only previous mention of a tarpaulin in his treatment was as a covering for the bomb – not the aircraft.

8: The idea of hiding a bomb in an underwater cave arose when McClory wrote to Fleming about his location recce in Nassau. Fleming adopted this idea in his book.

9: It was McClory's idea that underwater sleds should remove the bombs. Fleming's idea was to use webbing, but in his novel he used sleds.

10: The reconnaissance by aircraft, the discovery of the sunken plane and the taking of Petachi's identity disc arose as a result of a script conference with Whittingham, McClory and Fleming; as was the subsequent scene where Bond discloses to Domino that her brother was murdered by Largo and produces the identity disc as proof. Fleming adopted all of this in the novel.

11: The throwing of grenades at Bond while he is on an underwater scouting mission around Largo's yacht was lifted by Fleming from Whittingham's script and put in the novel.

In all, Whittingham and McClory claimed there to be 40 different incidents, descriptions and material taken from the various scripts and used in the Fleming novel. "Fleming was careful to use very little of my dialogue," said Whittingham. "The substance of the novel originated from my plot, but the detail and different dialogue was added by him. The plot of the novel is in most respects the same as the plot of the screenplay."

Then in August 1964, right in the middle of court proceedings, Fleming dropped dead from a massive heart attack. "I was with my father when he heard the news and he was convinced that he'd killed him," recalls Sylvan. "He was very shocked and suffered from terrible guilt as he felt he had contributed to Fleming's stress during the trial."

Fleming's sudden death also meant that Whittingham's case for damages was scrapped. You can't sue a dead man for plagiarism. Whittingham was left with nothing except a large bill for costs, which he had to dig into his own pocket to cover. The man for whom Jack Whittingham had battled through

Above: Whittingham and his wife Margot relaxing on their boat Domani in retirement in Malta. Right: Sean Connery gave what is perhaps his most assured and stylish performance as 007 in *Thunderball*.

Above: Jack Whittingham's personal ticket to the *Thunderball* premiere.

Top: The *Thunderball* women on location in Nassau: Martine Beswick, Claudine Auger and Luciana Paluzzi. Above Left: The stunning Luciana Paluzzi as Fiona. *(Photograph courtesy Luciana Paluzzi Solomon)*. Above Right: Publicity shot of Mollie Peters.

Stunning pre-production paintings highlighting scenes and sets from the proposed Bond film *Warhead*. Published here for the first time.

Pre-production painting highlighting a set from the proposed Bond film *Warhead*.

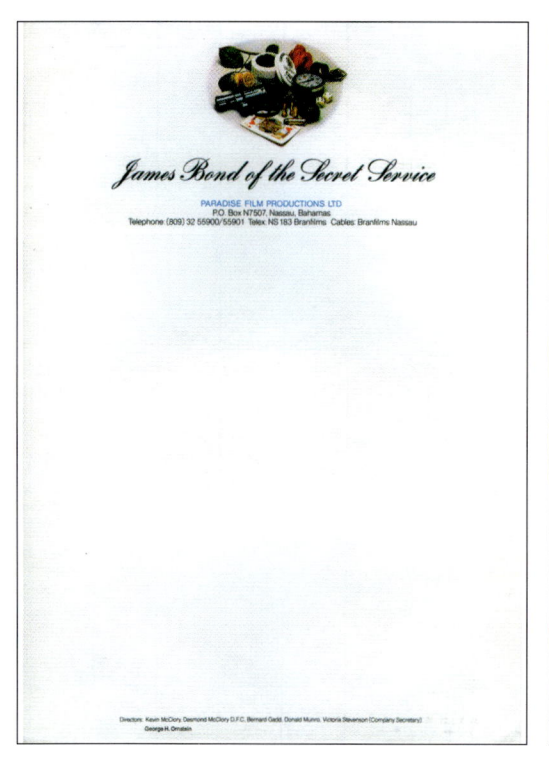

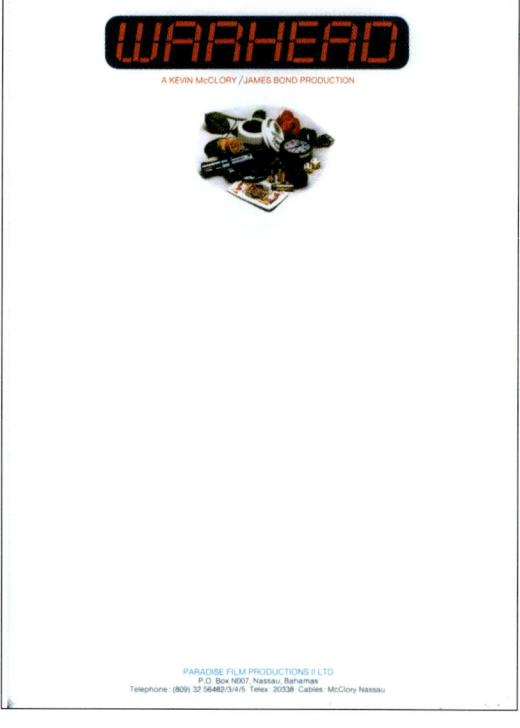

Left: Letterhead paper for 'James Bond of the Secret Service.' Right : McClory's own letterhead paper intended for *Warhead*.

Above: McClory's business card.

Top Left: On a location recce for *Warhead* Connery visits the Statue of Liberty, earmarked for one of the film's big action sequences.

Right: Connery ascending the stairs inside the Statue of Liberty.

Bottom: Connery takes a boat tour round Hudson Bay in New York, scene of another *Warhead* action sequence. Note the Twin Towers in the background.

Top Left and Right: The final scene of *Never Say Never Again* was shot at McClory's home in the Bahamas. In these shots Connery and Kim Basinger relax in-between set-ups.

Above: Here Rowan Atkinson waits for his entrance.

Left: Looking dapper, even in horrendous yellow shorts, McClory relaxes in Nassau.

Top Left: Connery and his wife Micheline on location. **Top Right:** Japanese film ticket.
Bottom: Connery relaxes at McClory's house, near the Jacuzzi.

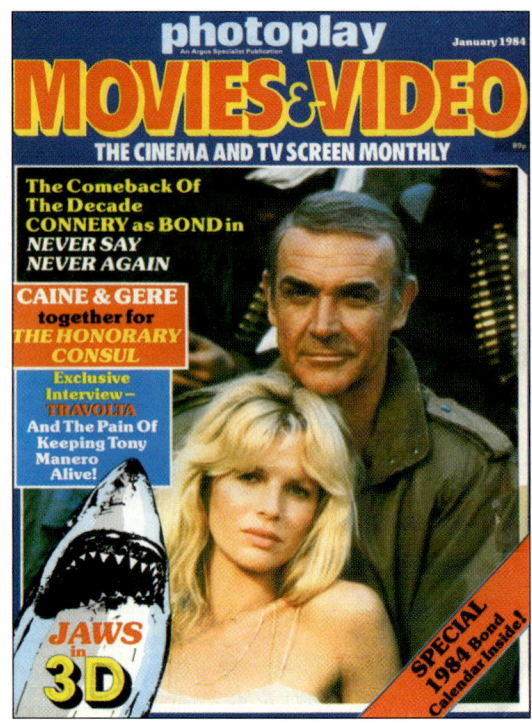

Above: Magazines around the world hailed the return of Connery as Bond.

Top Left: Kevin McClory's estate in the Bahamas stands empty and unkempt in the mid-80s.

Left: The 'Never Say Never Again' bar location at the Atlantic Hotel in Nassau circa mid-80s.

Bottom Left: The bomb-sled submarine from Thunderball found rotting in the garden of McClory's Bahamas house. The last known photograph of this iconic vehicle.

Below: The Vulcan bomber model from *Thunderball* used for the crash-landing sequence, found in the garage of McClory's Bahamas home. McClory's dog provides scale.

excessive pain levels to support during his trial was nowhere to be seen when he now needed his help and that bred deep resentment within the Whittingham family against Kevin McClory.

The result of McClory's deal with Broccoli and Saltzman also meant abandoning Whittingham completely. His son, Jonathan recalled in a letter that "At various times my mother expressed anger and resentment towards Kevin in that he had made at least verbal promises to Jack that if he helped Kevin as a witness (at the trial), then Jack would benefit from Kevin in the eventual production of *Thunderball*." In other words, Whittingham would be involved as screenwriter. It never happened. Richard Maibaum was hired instead. Did McClory fight for Jack's involvement in meetings with Broccoli and Saltzman or did he easily cave in to their demands that it had to be Maibaum. It isn't clear. Certainly Whittingham had no idea of this new arrangement because McClory hadn't bothered to tell him. "We hardly heard from McClory again after his case was won," says Sylvan. "I think Dad only met with him once more in his remaining lifetime. By then dad was busy on other films and thought, well I've done my work, been paid for it. He didn't really know what was going on. What he didn't realise was that Broccoli and Saltzman would insist on using Richard Maibaum to adapt the screenplay to the format which had by now evolved, which was sort of understandable."

Although a kick in the teeth for Whittingham's work to be re-imagined by another writer, by this stage Maibaum's winning formula of Bond screenplays was self-apparent. Terence Young had also introduced a tongue in cheek humour into the films that was largely absent from Whittingham's original screenplay, and indeed from Fleming's books. It was also a new decade, the swinging sixties, and styles and tastes had changed considerably from when Whittingham had written his screenplay back in the staid late 50s.

Perhaps what's harder to understand is why a second writer, John Hopkins, was hired to revise the Maibaum script. It wouldn't have been beyond Broccoli or Saltzman, or for McClory to insist that if another writer was needed, that it be Whittingham. "It would have been a very nice gesture," says Sylvan. "Or to give the screenplay credit to the three of them. But that was down to Kevin, he was just cow towing to Broccoli and Saltzman. He didn't consider Dad at all. And Dad didn't stand up for himself because he didn't know what was going on. Kevin could've easily told him what was happening, as a friend."

Broccoli and Saltzman did come up with an interesting way to credit the numerous contributors to *Thunderball*'s remarkable evolution to the screen. Sold as Ian Fleming's *Thunderball*, the screenplay was attributed to Maibaum and Hopkins, but with the added credits: 'Based on an original screenplay by Jack Whittingham. Original story by Kevin McClory, Jack Whittingham and Ian Fleming.' Ironically, Ernest Cuneo, who wrote the original story memo, was left out completely.

When *Thunderball* opened, Jack Whittingham attended an early screening with his son, Jonathan, who still remembers that occasion and the pride he felt that this was a crowning achievement for his father. But when the movie was over, everybody's feelings had dramatically changed. "You see Dad didn't have the sole screenwriting credit on it," says Sylvan. "He found out by going to that screening. It was very cruel. That's when he realised he'd been totally abandoned by Kevin."

Whittingham carried on writing screenplays, notably episodes of TV's *Danger Man* and the Disney film *The Prince and the Pauper*. But his career was never again to reach the celebratory heights it had achieved in the 1950s. "Jack was a nice guy," says Jeremy Vaughan. "And was well respected in the business and very competent as a screenwriter, but I don't think the whole *Thunderball* experience did him any good, either on a professional or personal level. I think he was very shook up by the whole thing."

Because of his failing health (he was still having trouble with his heart), Whittingham and his wife Margot had moved to Malta. 1960 was the year that Jack took up sailing. "Something he had always wanted to do," says Sylvan. "And he did this in his own inimitable way." Going to the London Boat Show Jack ordered a 30-foot sailing boat and bought six books on "How to Sail a Boat." He'd go out in terrible weather and get into dreadful pickles as he learnt to sail in some of the trickiest waters in the world – the English Channel – full of cross currents and rush hour traffic.

Personal letter from Walt Disney complimenting Whittingham on his work on the Disney production *Prince and the Pauper.*

> WALT DISNEY
>
> April 25, 1962.
>
> Dear Jack Whittingham -
>
> I am glad you approved the cutting we did on THE PRINCE AND THE PAUPER. It went off very well as a three-part television show in this country and the comments were very favorable -- especially from those who viewed it on color sets, but then the reactions were also good from the audience with black and white sets. All-in-all, it turned out very well.
>
> It was nice to hear from you again and we enjoyed working with you and I, too, hope we can meet up again one of these days.
>
> Sincerely,
>
> Walt Disney
>
> Mr. Jack Whittingham,
> The White House,
> Oxshott, Surrey,
> England -
>
> WD:DV

After several months of this Jack replaced his sailing boat for "Domani" – a 40-foot ketch and set off for Malta with Margot. The journey was beset by difficulties. Before they had even cleared Southampton the engine stalled and the fierce weather blew them back across the Bay of Biscay overnight and it had to be crossed again the next day. During the journey there were several severe storms. One of them sheared off the main mast.

"The journey took six weeks to complete," claims Sylvan. "My mother sat clutching her jewellry box the whole way expecting to drown at any minute." When they finally arrived in Malta no one was more surprised to see them than the coastal authorities as they were "missing presumed drowned." Because of Jack's fame as a screenwriter the Maltese papers made a front-page story over the incident.

Sylvan has other memories of her father's boat, principally his smuggling activities: "Whenever he arrived back from trips to France, the customs officer who came on board to inspect would find 'The Skipper' exhausted and asleep on the main galley berth. My mother would show them round. What

Chapter 23: THE FORGOTTEN MAN

they didn't realise was that under the seemingly sleeping body was a stash of duty free Gin and Gauloise Disque Bleu cigarettes. Both of which Jack consumed in large quantities."

It was on Malta that Jack began writing a screenplay based on the life of Ian Fleming. "He had Fleming as a Reuters correspondent travelling on this train across Russia," recalls Sylvan. "Fleming was sitting in a compartment and this alter ego, like a ghost, would come out of him and this whole adventure took place. That was how Dad played it - that Fleming had this other life, this alter-ego, that was Bond." Sadly the project never went ahead, partly because it would have needed the approval of Ann, Fleming's widow, and the studio would not take a risk of litigation whilst she was still alive.

In 1971, Whittingham underwent an operation for throat cancer, but continued to smoke in spite of doctor's advice. The subject of *Thunderball* was rarely ever mentioned, as Sylvan recalls. "He didn't talk about it much and the family chose not to look at it. It was a sad subject. He always liked Fleming and felt bad about what happened. He still felt he'd contributed to his death in some way. Although he never regretted the course of action he took. He was always affectionate towards Kevin too, just very hurt by him. He felt very let down by Kevin."

McClory was to see Jack Whittingham only once more in the writer's life and then only because he wanted something from him. "We all felt very badly that Dad was not included in the enormous success that *Thunderball* went on to enjoy," says Sylvan. "His health was weakened by the whole episode and his spirit saddened by having been left behind, abandoned. So the family has no good feelings about McClory at all. Maybe Kevin felt like that because he saw Dad as just a hired hand that had been paid to do a job and that was it. But Dad was much more than that. Remember they'd been friends and Dad had supported and stood by him. Kevin wouldn't have won the case without Dad, or Peter Carter-Ruck, or indirectly without me. It was lack of consideration. Legally Kevin could leave Dad behind, but what about morally? I've got letters from Kevin saying that morally Dad was owed a lot more than what he was paid. But he wanted the Ian Fleming camp to pay it."

Aged only 62 Jack Whittingham died of a heart attack on Malta in 1973, his contribution to the cinematic legacy of James Bond all but forgotten and unrecognised.

MALTA NEWS

3d. THURSDAY, OCTOBER 28, 1965 No. 370

GALES, FOG, HURRICANES
STORMY TRIP FOR 007 SCREEN WRITER

BY Ivor Tilney

THE MARINA, Wednesday

IF ever a yacht's crew were glad to berth in sunny Malta it must be Mr. Jack Whittingham, his wife Margot and 19-year-old son Jonathan. They arrived at the marina earlier this week from England after a fighting voyage of nearly five weeks aboard their 17-ton ketch Domani during which time they ran the gauntlet of three hurricanes and teething troubles which beset the £10,000 yacht on its maiden trip.

Mr. Whittingham is well known in the film world in Britain as a screen writer. He has the screen play credits for the latest James Bond film "Thunderball" which has its premiere in London in December and which Mr. Whittingham will be attending. He also wrote the script for "Mandy", "Divided Hearts", "The Hunted", "West of Zanzibar" and about 30 other films.

While Mr. Whittingham, his wife and son were sailing out to Malta, their 21-year-old daughter, Sylvan, was in the news in Britain.

Blonde Sylvan has just made her first record, a pop number called "We Don't Be-

long" which has been re'eased in the U.K. and is doing very well. Sylvan wrote the song herself. She was unable to accompany the family on their Mediterranean cruise, because she may be making more records.

Jack Whittingham said, "We had hardly left Dartmouth when we ran into fog in the Channel. We reached Brest in the teeth of a Force 8 gale in the Bay of Biscay. We were caught with the sails up in a huge Atlantic swell. The engine decided to pack up but we finally arrived off the Spanish coast with the mast almost in the water. A tremendous thunderstorm and gale raged and we were carried some good 50 miles out into the Atlantic."

Mr. Whittingham said they were about to enter Vigo when the yacht was struck by Hurricane Carol.

He said, "We doubled the watches and managed to tie up in Vigo. We sailed in calmer weather down the coast of Portugal to Gibraltar where we arrived on October 4." There Mr. Christopher Smith, a Bristol undergraduate, who had been helping to sail the yacht, left for England to resume his 'varsity studies.

The Whittinghams stayed in Gibraltar for a week awaiting repairs for the generator and damaged auto-pilot. When they sailed again the steering seized up.

Mr. Whittingham said, "I managed to repair this and we pressed on only to run into another violent Force 8 gale off Almeria for two nights.

"We made for Bizerta and left there in blinding rain. We ran into another fierce thunderstorm and Force 9 gale off Pantelleria. We were really relieved and happy to see the Maltese coast."

Mr. Jack Whittingham, Margot and Johnatan on the Domani at the Marina.

Jack Whittingham's near-fatal nautical adventure makes the front pages of this Malta newspaper.

CHAPTER 24
SLEEPING WITH THE ENEMY

So why did the Bond producers give in to McClory and make a deal? "We didn't want anyone else to make *Thunderball*," Broccoli said simply. "We had the feeling that if anyone else came in and made their own Bond film, it would have been bad for our series. After *Goldfinger* we naturally felt that we knew more about Bond than anyone else." He was proven more than right when in 1967 American producer Charles Feldman made *Casino Royale* (the only other Bond novel outside of Eon's ownership) and turned it into a spoof and assorted freak show. Broccoli could sense a not dissimilar thing happening with *Thunderball*. So they had no choice but to get into bed with McClory.

Because of his court victory, McClory would receive sole producer credit on the film, Broccoli and Saltzman would be executive producers, but in reality all three men would essentially act as producers. It was also reported that McClory would receive 20% of the film's profits. But most significant of all was the fact that even though the 1965 *Thunderball* film would remain copyrighted in the Eon fold, McClory would retain ownership of all the script materials. All he had to do was promise not to exercise his rights in them and make another Bond film for at least ten years. This he was only too happy to agree to, believing Bond would still be very much alive in a decade's time and he could one day make further 007 films. But just why did Broccoli and Saltzman agree to this? Did they have no choice; did they miss it in the small print or simply disregard its importance, perhaps thinking that in ten year's time Bond might be beyond its sell by date? If so, it was a decision that came back to haunt them.

McClory also agreed to the deal on the understanding that *Thunderball* was the next film on Eon's schedule, allowing him to cash in quick on the current Bond boom. The producers had hoped to follow *Goldfinger* with *On Her Majesty's Secret Service*, but were forced by McClory to forge straight on with *Thunderball*. In October the co-production deal to make *Thunderball* was publicly announced. McClory was understandably ebullient. Broccoli and Saltzman less so.

Maibaum's 1961 script for *Thunderball* was dusted off and by mid-January 1965 a shooting script was complete, featuring revisions by John Hopkins, whose career began on the seminal British television cop series *Z-Cars*. Hopkins would later write the screenplay for the harrowing Sean Connery police drama *The Offence* (1972).

Returning to *Thunderball* after a four-year gap and with three Bond scripts already to his credit, Maibaum had learnt what audiences wanted and to some extent tailored the new script to public taste and expectation. Comparing the filmed *Thunderball* script with the one he'd earlier written, Maibaum realised just how much he'd been influenced by audience reaction. "In re-writing it four years later, I had to remember the proven public delight in jokes, gadgetry and so forth," he said. "Now the two are completely different. Because now we know exactly what it is that the public love about Bond, and how they best like to see the stories treated in the cinema."

Maibaum was also keenly conscious of the fact that James Bond was no longer a mere character, but a phenomenon, a trademark, and elements of his script illustrate this. Describing the opening shot of the pre-credit funeral sequence he wrote: "Here stand two people looking down, apart from the crowd, yet interested. One of them is an elegant Frenchwoman in her late twenties, and beside her, that idol of the intelligentsia, that opiate of the oppressed and working classes, James Bond." Many sections of the script are infused with a self-reflective quality, a self-assured quality. When a character gets into a big car, the writer adds, "Presumably from Ford Motors." The firm had premiered their new Mustang in *Goldfinger*, so Maibaum just assumed the product tie-in would carry over into *Thunderball*. It did. Later he describes how Bond quickly gets out of his jet pack: "It should take him no longer to do this than a golfer with a collapsible trolley or a secret agent in Istanbul with a folding sniper's rifle."

Maibaum and Hopkins' script for *Thunderball* also went through a vast number of changes. In the pre-credit sequence, Bond doesn't drive his Aston Martin but a Ford Thunderbird. The Junkanoo festival is missing from an early draft, as is Fiona's death at the Kiss Kiss club. In a later script, the Junkanoo does appear and incredulously Bond is forced to wear a costume as Fiona and her thugs lead him out of the hotel. When a waiter passes them in the corridor wheeling a room service trolley Bond grabs a small spirit stove as a weapon before fleeing, only to be shot in the leg, as in the film. There's also no mention of Bond discovering the dead body of the pilot in bandages at Shrublands and then fighting off Count Lippe's henchman. Instead, while saying goodbye to Patricia on leaving the clinic, Bond sees the "mysterious" body brought out to an ambulance covered in a blanket, which falls away to reveal his face.

The Fiona/Largo skeet-shooting scene was originally longer with more dialogue about the wisdom of killing Bond. It also included the revelation that Largo "found" Fiona and made her into what she is within SPECTRE. The scene on love beach where Bond tells Domino of her brother's death was also intended to be much longer and in the original script contained more emotional punch than the version ultimately filmed. In the night assault on Largo's house Palmyra, Pinder joins Bond only to be killed in the ensuing gun battle. Bond was still to have made his exit via the shark pool, but his line was to have been, "Sorry, loves. You'll have to order something else. I'm off."

One great idea that was ultimately scrapped would have had actors famous for playing movie or TV secret agents appearing in cameo roles as the other 00 agents during the big conference scene where M briefs the entire 00 section. Following this scene Bond breaks into the dead pilot's flat and finds the beach photo with him and Domino, plus a stack of letters from Nassau. Thus Bond makes the connection between the pilot and his sister and asks M to send him to the Bahamas. In the film the beach photo is already in the file Bond is given. In the flat Fiona is watching from the shadows, prepared to stab 007 with her lipstick stiletto, but Bond leaves before she deems such drastic action necessary. Another interesting SPECTRE gadget that never made it into the movie was a pistol that used compressed air to fire hypodermic bullets, which could kill or stun.

By now, McClory had given up any faint hope he may still have harboured about directing *Thunderball*. Terence Young had helmed the opening Bonds *Dr. No* and *From Russia with Love*, very much helping define the cinematic 007. When first hired, Fleming approached Young at the press launch and said, "So they've decided on you to fuck up my work." Actually the two men did grow into enormous friends, both hailing from much the same kind of world, the world of private schools, privilege and cocktail parties. Though Young did once refer to Fleming as "a pompous son of a bitch. Immensely arrogant."

Beginning pre-production on *Goldfinger*, when Young was denied a slice of the profits he left disgruntled and was replaced by Guy Hamilton. And it was to Hamilton that the producers first turned to direct *Thunderball*. "I was spending a weekend in Las Vegas and Cubby and Kevin McClory came out to see me," the director recalls. "McClory was an old mate of mine because we'd worked on *The African Queen* together, and he pushed the script into my hands and I said, "Honestly fellas, I've run out of ideas because Bond takes a lot out of you and I have nothing fresh to add. So I'll have to pass." I think they were sorry about that, and I went on with my life and did various other things." Those other things included directing the second Harry Palmer movie *Funeral in Berlin* (1966) and the epic *Battle of Britain* (1969), both produced by Harry Saltzman, before returning to the Bond fold for *Diamonds are Forever*.

Hamilton remembers reading the *Thunderball* script and being impressed, but having one major reservation: "I thought the script was excellent apart from all the underwater stuff which I've always been a bit nervous about because I think everything that takes place underwater is very, very slow. That was my only criticism." With Hamilton not interested Terence Young reconciled his financial difficulties with Eon and reclaimed the director's chair. Backing him up was the creative team that had been responsible for the three previous Bonds, production designer Ken Adam, Cinematographer Ted Moore, editor Peter Hunt, Special effects man John Stears and composer John Barry.

At last *Thunderball* was ready to go before the cameras.

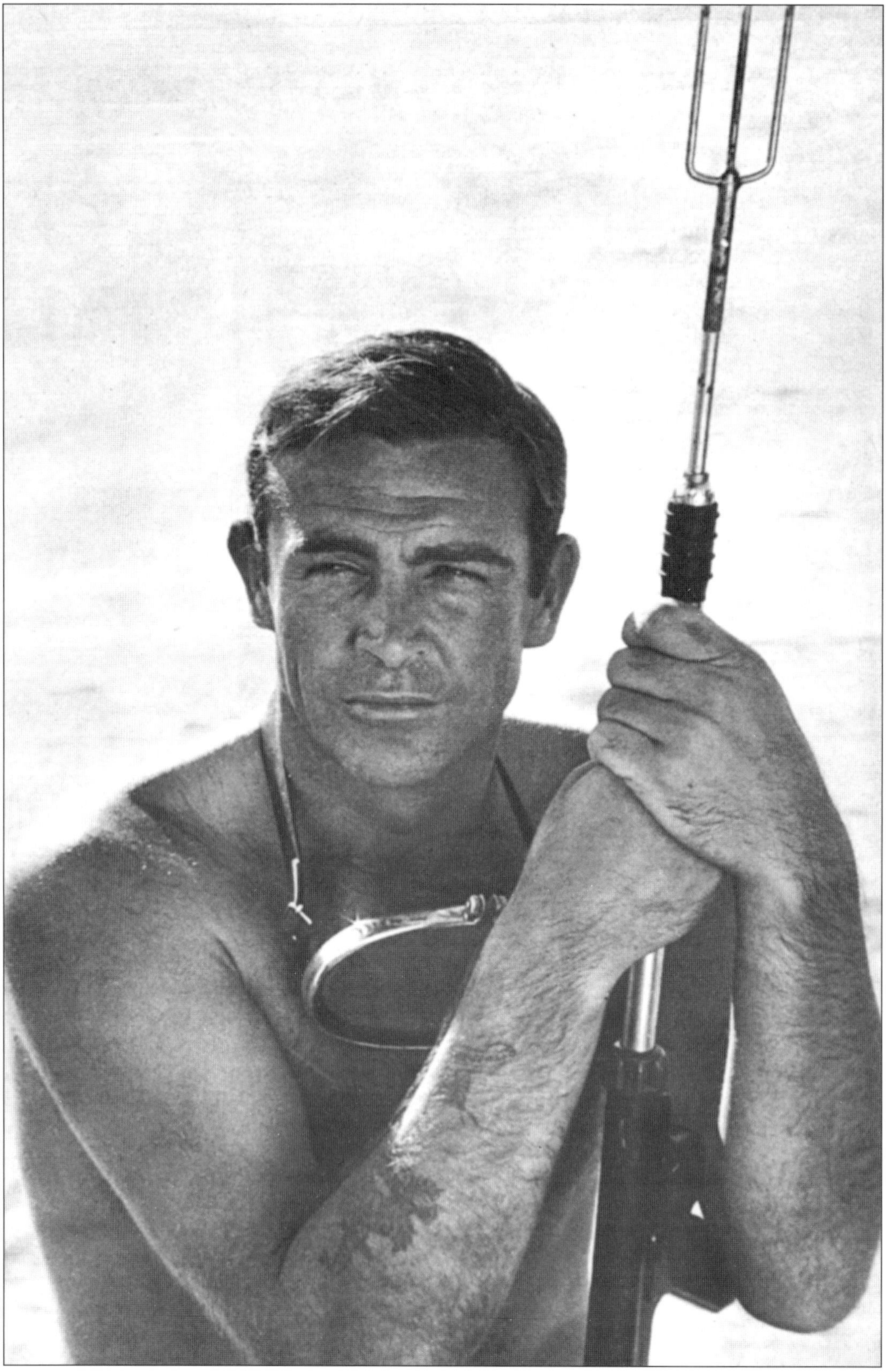

CHAPTER 25
18 WEEKS OF SWIMMING, SLUGGING AND NECKING

By 1965 Sean Connery was the most famous man on the planet. After playing James Bond in three successful movies, he graced more magazine covers than the Beatles and received 1500 fan letters a week. Thanks to *Goldfinger*'s triumphant box office performance Connery was named the number one box office attraction in America, an achievement for a British movie star that has not been matched before or since. But such fame had a price as life came to resemble a freak show for this most private of men. It became almost impossible for him to walk the streets or go to public places. At that year's Cannes Film Festival he left early after being unable to enjoy a simple meal in his hotel without being harassed by hordes of fans and reporters.

As the 007 franchise grew, the burden became almost intolerable and Connery began referring to the character as his personal Frankenstein monster. "If you were Sean's friend in those days," Michael Caine once recalled, "then you didn't mention the subject of Bond. Never." In the 60s, Ken Adam enjoyed a very good relationship with Connery and saw first hand how his identification with Bond was overtaking his life: "We were so close. Sean was one of my best friends and already on *Goldfinger* he was stopped in the street and people would say, 'Oh, Mr Bond.' And he hated that. Hated it! He'd say,. 'I'm not Mr Bond. I'm an actor called Sean Connery.' In a way it was silly because Bond made him and he's turned out to be a very, very good actor. But you know, everybody should be so lucky."

There were early warning signs. Arriving in New York for the opening of *From Russia with Love* with Terence Young, Connery was hustled through an airport side entrance by security guards due to the overwhelming crowds. One elderly lady broke ranks to ask for his autograph. "Sean, sign the bloody thing," urged Young. The woman took one look at the signature and ranted, "No! I wanted James Bond." Connery's face crumbled. "It was the first time this had ever happened to Sean," Young said. "It suddenly occurred to him that he was no longer a human being. He was a symbol."

It was with some reluctance then that Connery returned for his fourth outing as Bond. Especially having just worked with the acclaimed American director Sidney Lumet on *The Hill*, a gritty drama about the treatment of British prisoners in a WW2 military prison in North Africa, for which he'd given

```
                              - 1 -
     From: WESTON DRURY JNR.              2nd February 1965.

                         "T H U N D E R B A L L"

                              Cast List
```

CHARACTER	ARTIST	ADDRESS	AGENT
✓ JAMES BOND	SEAN CONNERY	Acacia House, Centre Avenue, Acton, W. 3 SHE: 9773	R. Hatton GRO: 3957
✓ MADAME BOITIER	ROSE ALBA	1 Mornington Place, London, N.W. 1 EUS: 6567	Joan Rees KEN: 9158
✓ "Q"	DESMOND LLEWELYN	Whitelands, Battle, Sussex. BATTLE: 2121	Bryan Drew GER: 4502
✓ MONEYPENNY	LOIS MAXWELL	27 Cadogan Court, Draycott Avenue, S. W. 3 KEN: 0010	Fraser & Dunlop REG: 7311
✓ "M"	BERNARD LEE	17 Oaklands Avenue, Isleworth, Middx. ISLEWORTH: 8675	GAC Redway HYD: 5581
✓ LIPPE	GUY DOLEMAN	10A Albert Hall Mansions, S. W. 7 KEN: 6064 (Messages KEN: 1925)	Al Parker GRO: 4232
ATTENDANT (at Shrublands)	TOM BOWMAN	35 Elmstead Gardens, Worcester Park, Surrey. DER: 7513	Pam Simons REG: 2308
✓ PATRICIA	MOLLY PETERS	26 Ladbroke Square, W. 11 PARK: 5861	Pat Larthe TEM: 2663
✓ PALAZZI	PAUL STASSINO	Flat 2, 29 Chartfield Avenue, S. W. 15 PUT: 3044	London Mgmt HYD: 2456 & HYD: 5041
RECEPTIONIST (At Shrublands)	JANETTE ROWSELL	76 Wendover Court, Chiltern Street, W. 1 WEL: 3437 (Messages PER: 9635)	Joseph & Wagg MAY: 1048/9

Thunderball cast list. Note the actor's home addresses.

Chapter 25: 18 WEEKS OF SWIMMING, SLUGGING AND NECKING

arguably the performance of his life. These were the kind of films Connery wanted to make, not Bond, so before a foot of film was exposed on *Thunderball* he was already counting the days left in "bondage" and looking forward to stretching his acting skills in other more challenging roles. "My only grumble about the Bond films is that they don't tax one as an actor," Connery complained as he geared up for the *Thunderball* shoot. "All one really needs is the constitution of a rugby player to get through 18 weeks of swimming, slugging and necking."

After the blockbuster success of *Goldfinger*, money was flooding into the coffers of Eon. It was reported in 1965 that the first three Bond films were earning £1,000 every hour, day and night. There were stories that Stanley Sopel, who worked uncredited on the 60s Bonds as associate producer, was forever flying to Switzerland with suitcases of money to put in banks. For *Thunderball*, United Artists gave Saltzman and Broccoli virtual carte blanche with the studio's finances, allocating them with the enormous budget of $5.5m, a million more than *Goldfinger* and seven times as much as *Dr. No*! The theory from the start of *Thunderball* was more of the same, only bigger. The success of 007 had spawned legions of imitators on TV and film and the producers knew they had to demonstrate that Bond movies had blockbuster qualities their rivals could never replicate. And so *Thunderball* became the first 007 "epic." Even by today's standards, especially when viewed on the cinema screen, the sheer size and scope of the film never fails to impress.

The now legendary pre-credit sequence was the first thing to go before the cameras on 16 February. Chateau D'Anet was the backdrop to the action, a sumptuous building 40 miles outside Paris. As originally scripted by Maibaum, the location was a strip joint in Hong Kong where a beautiful girl dressed from head to toe like a peacock sits in a golden cage above a large dance floor. Bond follows the dancer into a dressing room and starts putting on the charm before suddenly punching her full in the face. The peacock head falls off revealing a man beneath, the enemy agent Bond is after. Maibaum subsequently shifted the action to the funeral of one colonel Jacques Boitier and has Bond watching proceedings from a safe distance, with a glamourous assistant. "Is there anything else our French station can do for monsieur Bond," she not so innocently asks. "Later, perhaps," says he.

Tracking the deceased's widow back to her chateau, Bond offers his sincere condolences, only then to stun the audience by walloping the poor woman full in the kisser. It turns out, however, to be a SPECTRE agent masquerading as the widow at his own funeral. The ensuing fight, with Bond stuntman extraordinaire Bob Simmons in drag, has to be one of the most frenzied in the whole series with both men practically demolishing the room, and closing with Bond breaking Boitier's neck with a poker. Bond was to have strangled Boitier with the elastic from the bra he's wearing as part of his disguise, which has come off in the tussle. Wisely this was altered.

Pausing only to throw some flowers over the corpse, Bond races to the roof, dons a jet pack and flies off in true Superman style to land safely beside his trusty Aston Martin, brought back for an encore after its success in *Goldfinger*. Impressive today, this stunt must have looked like something out of *Star Wars* for audiences 40 years ago. And not surprisingly the jet pack has become one of Bond's most famous gadgets, even making an amusing re-appearance in 2002's *Die Another Day*.

The Bell Textron jet pack actually worked, and was a US army prototype developed for battlefield use, and the sole model of its kind in the world. The only two pilots qualified to fly it were brought to France especially for the sequence and wouldn't let the equipment out of their sight for a second. One of them, Bill Suitor, doubled for Connery during the short flight and was asked to fly without a helmet as it was felt Bond would look more debonair without headgear. Only too aware of the risks the pilot refused.

But there were other risks that the pilot faced. "The jet pack was a very dangerous prop," recalls Ken Adam. "Because you had no timing device on it, you had to go by your own stop watch. And you had only a limited amount of fuel. So if you ran out of fuel you'd had it, you didn't have a parachute or anything like that."

For Connery's close ups, a replica jet pack was built by Bert Luxford, one of Pinewood's resident engineers who'd assisted with technical and mechanical problems on earlier Bonds. Attached to a rig,

Connery and the pack could be raised or lowered on cue with concealed CO_2 canisters simulating the rocket thrusters. After landing, Bond bundles the machine into the Aston's boot and fends off pursuing baddies by shooting jets of water out of the exhaust pipes. A great gag, but totally illogical. As John Brosnan wittily pointed out in his seminal book *James Bond in the Cinema*: "To be capable of squirting out that much water at such high pressure, Bond's car would need to contain a storage tank of vast proportions. When we remember all the other infernal devices that it's supposed to contain – machine guns, ejector seat etc – it's surprising that there is still room for the engine."

The effect was startlingly simple to achieve. A fire engine sat out of camera range feeding two hoses through to the rear of the car where each was bolted to the chassis. At the required moment the hoses were activated and – whoosh – out came the water. The three actors playing the pursuing agents didn't really need to act as the sheer force of the water knocked them off their feet like pins in a bowling alley. The whole thing was achieved in two takes.

CHAPTER 26
BEAUTIES AND THE BEAST

Whilst in Paris, the producers took the opportunity of unveiling to the press local girl Claudine Auger as the new Bond girl. A former Miss France, a title she won aged just 16, much to the consternation of her parents, Claudine was also a Miss World runner up. "I don't know who was the most excited when I finally heard I had won the Bond role," she told reporters. "My husband, my parents, my sister or myself. My sister screamed with joy, for Sean Connery is her favourite star. His pictures are all over her bedroom."

The role of Domino had been hotly contested with 600 girls considered and 150 auditioning, including French Hammer heroine Yvonne Monlaur, former Miss Italy Maria Grazia Buccella and Gloria Paul, who made do with a role in Morecambe and Wise's Bond spoof *The Intelligence Men* instead. But the usually shrewd Saltzman and Broccoli were guilty of letting much bigger fish slip through their fingers. One early candidate for Domino was Julie Christie, then relatively unknown. Cubby and his wife first spotted the actress on television late in 1964 and thought she was not only beautiful but also highly talented and invited her to meet Saltzman and Young. "She was very nervous," Cubby later recalled. "She came in wearing a pair of jeans and she was terribly dishevelled and didn't look at all like she did on television. In fact I couldn't believe it was the same girl." Young felt sorry for Christie. Eon's stuffy London office was evidently not the right environment for such a shy young woman to meet movie power brokers. "There were a lot of people hanging around the office in those days mentally undressing every girl who walked in, and I immediately thought this chick wasn't destined for such an atmosphere. She had class and was more than a pretty face."

In the end, the deciding factor against casting Julie Christie, in a role where she would spend most of her time in a bikini, was the smallness of her bust. Broccoli and Saltzman had a winning formula, which was that Bond girls had to have big tits. Simple as that. In the end it was a lucky accident for Julie because had she made *Thunderball* she might have lost out on the role that made her the most famous British actress of the 60s, Anya in *Doctor Zhivago*.

Broccoli also vigorously pursued Raquel Welch to play Domino after seeing her on the cover of Life magazine. Rumour has it that Welch did indeed sign for the Bond film but 20th Century Fox supremo Richard Zanuck persuaded Broccoli to release the actress for his sci-fi epic *Fantastic Voyage*. Faye Dunaway too almost signed on to play Domino but had a late change of heart, deciding to make her feature debut in *The Happening* instead. Apparently Eon furnished the future Oscar-winning actress with plane tickets to London. But she never showed.

Claudine Auger decided on an acting career while attending college in Paris. She made her film debut in *Le Testament d'Orphee* in 1959, just one month after being elected Miss France. Claudine's *Thunderball* screen test took place on a hastily erected beach set on a sound stage at Pinewood. For a woman who proudly admitted walking naked around her Paris home, Claudine no doubt won over the producers by showing off her best assets in a very revealing bikini of her own design. "Somehow I always felt I would become Domino," she later claimed. "I had read the book about seven times and knew her inside out." Still that didn't stop her from being petrified on her first couple of days filming.

Fleming described Domino as: "Independent, a girl of authority and character. She might sleep with men, obviously did, but it would be on her terms and not on theirs." Well cast, the stunningly beautiful Claudine admirably portrays the rich bitch qualities of Domino and also the inner sadness of a pampered but unloved woman caught up in a dark world. But the film Domino is a much less multi faceted creation than Fleming's literary one; an altogether less fierce and more benign girl, mainly due to the requirements of a stereotypical Bond girl and Claudine's limited screen experience at the time. Bond naturally wastes little time in seducing Domino, first encountering her underwater when he retrieves her stuck foot from a piece of coral. A vast improvement over the book's dull first meeting in Nassau high street. On dry land, they have lunch together and there's a classic bit of repartee when Bond notices her name on an ankle bracelet. "What sharp little eyes you've got," teases Domino. "Wait till you get to my teeth," replies Bond.

After *Thunderball*, Claudine married an English businessman and worked sporadically in film and television, finding at first that she was being offered just inferior duplicates of Bond babe characters. "Once you are a Bond girl you are a Bond girl for life," she once lamented. Although Claudine rarely talks about her Bond experience, politely refusing this author an interview, she remains proud of *Thunderball* and of having been one of the more independent of Bond's conquests. "I believe we showed that the Bond women are the women of the nuclear age. They are free and they make love when they want to without worrying about it afterwards." Bond women of the 60s didn't need to burn their bras to show how independent they were from men; they just shot them in the back with harpoon guns or put black widow spiders in their beds.

Pictures from the period show Claudine happily larking about with Connery on the set, a few even show her happy in the company of the other actresses in the film. But the reality was very different, according to Luciana Paluzzi, who played bad girl Fiona in *Thunderball*: "She was always on her high horse. I don't know what was the matter with her. She was not friendly, always a little distant. And it wasn't just with me. She was just like that all the time. Like she was the queen. I don't know if she realised that during the making of *Thunderball*, I never mentioned her name. Years later, when Vanity Fair magazine did a big pictorial on the Bond girls, shot by Annie Leibovitz, we all met in the studio in New York. It was so much fun. The only one who arrived and said that she wasn't feeling well, and never showed up, made people wait for hours, was Claudine."

After casting beauty, the producers needed their beast. Fleming described Largo as a pirate/adventurer, a modern-day smuggler and womaniser. But behind his playboy image lurks a psychopath. In one chilling sequence from the book, understandably cut for the film, he shoots one of his men three times in the face for saying something out of line. The literary image of Largo immediately brings to mind someone like Anthony Quinn, who'd have been marvellous in the role. The eventual choice, Italian actor Adolfo Celi, certainly made for a visually striking villain with his snow-white hair and black eye patch, following in the tradition of physically grotesque Bond super baddies: Dr. No's metal hands, Goldfinger's obesity, Scaramanga's three nipples, Stromberg's webbed-fingers etc.

Chapter 26: BEAUTIES AND THE BEAST

Born in 1922, Celi was a prolific actor in European cinema and was travelling back from Hollywood after making the Frank Sinatra war picture, *Von Ryan's Express* when he happened to buy *Thunderball* in the airport lounge to read on the flight home. Thinking how great it would be to play Largo, Celi was later staying in Paris when his agent told him to go see a producer at the George V hotel. It was Saltzman. "We talked about Bond," Celi reminisced later. "And they offered me a role in the new Bond film. 'Which book?' I asked. When they told me I laughed. 'Oh *Thunderball*. I know everything about that.' Life is so very funny. So strange. Destiny is so complicated."

Celi and Connery kept in touch after *Thunderball*, meeting for example in 1981 when both were working in London; Connery on *Outland* and Celi playing the Pope in the controversial BBC drama series *The Borgias*. "Sean is remembered as Bond," Celi said. "Because he imposed a new kind of virility, a new style of courting women and a new style of action." Celi also appeared briefly in Connery's 1976 thriller *The Next Man*. He died in 1986.

Once the pre-credit sequence was wrapped, the Bond crew took up residence for the next month at Pinewood working on one of the film's most important sequences – Shrublands. After his exertions in France, Bond relaxes at a private heath farm where he uncovers SPECTRE's diabolical scheme for world domination. Shrublands was based on Fleming's own experiences in the spring of 1956 when he was a recuperating patient at Enton Hall, a large Victorian mansion in the heart of the Surrey stockbroker belt. Ken Adam and production manager David Middlemas visited Enton Hall and found it to be old, run down and highly uncinematic. Looking for something more streamlined and modern they came across the head office of the British Aluminium Company in Chalfont Park, Buckinghamshire. They'd found their Shrublands.

At the health farm, Bond achieves the first of his three "conquests" in the film, with physical therapist Patricia Fearing, who isn't averse to a bit of mink glove massaging. On Young's advice Mollie Peters was cast. Since spying her as an extra in a crowd scene on his film *The Amorous Adventures of Moll Flanders* (1965), Young had championed the career of the former pin up and nude photo model. "Molly has that rarest of all screen qualities – instant sex!" he once raved. "Just like Rita Hayworth – but so very few other stars."

Molly was understandably nervous when she arrived at Pinewood for her screen test, as she'd never in fact stepped onto a sound stage before. "And standing in the corner of the studio was Sean Connery. And I remember Terence saying, 'Now, of course, darling you know Sean.' I didn't know Sean. I was in awe of Sean. I pretended I did, but I didn't. And that was my first meeting with Sean Connery."

Molly remembers that numerous other girls tested for the role, most notably Suzanna Leigh, who in the following year co-starred with Elvis in *Paradise, Hawaiian Style* and made the Bond spoof *Deadlier than the Male*. Molly's own test couldn't have gone any better. "Afterwards I got a round of applause from the crew all over the set. And when I came off, this man came and sat next to me and said, would I be prepared to be blonde for this film, because I was a natural brunette. And I said, I'd be green or pink, or whatever. And that man was Kevin McClory."

All of Molly's scenes in *Thunderball* were played opposite Connery and she built up a good relationship with him. "He was always straight, always direct and didn't suffer fools gladly. He was also very protective. I remember that I'd had some personal problem and we were just about to do one of the bed scenes when I started crying. Sean thought that someone had upset me on the film set and came over and put his arm round me and said, 'Who upset you? Tell me who did it?' I said. 'No one.' He said. 'Well somebody must have. Tell me who did it?' And I said, 'No, it's a personal thing.' So he was very protective of me and I thought that was great. To me he was like a big brother."

Feeling nervous throughout most of her time on the film, not helped by the constant script changes going on, Molly's nerves were put to the most severe test when Bond leads her into a sauna room, disrobes her, then pushes her bare buttocks onto the glass. It's one of the most suggestive scenes ever in a Bond film and up to that time the series' first flash of real nudity. Molly remembers it vividly: "I was given two pieces of strategically placed sticky tape for my top half, and sticky tape for my bottom half. And I thought this was more obscene if anything to have your boobs covered with bits of sticky tape, so I took that off. Terence Young cleared the set, only essential people stayed, and we shot it a number of times. And Sean was sort of fooling about. At one point he had a bowler hat on and was doing Groucho Marx walks. I think it might have been his way of relaxing me, trying to make me laugh. Although I had done glamour posing before in front of cameras, to be acting in front of a world famous male was a little bit intimidating."

It remains a wonderful scene, beautifully played, though it did cause confusion later on when Molly's young son caught the film on television. "He used to ask was Sean Connery his dad because Sean Connery kissed me. 'No!' His father used to say." It's also an incredibly chauvinistic moment. Bond has just faced near-death in an out of control traction machine and threatens to tell Patricia's employers, with the result she'd be sacked, unless his carnal desires are satisfied. In essence, sexual blackmail, though you'd hardly call it rape, Molly argues. "Bond says he's going to tell and my character is saying, oh you wouldn't. And then obviously knowing what he's all about seemed to go in the sauna room quite readily, I thought. But as a character Bond, or at least he used to be, was pretty sadistic, gratifying himself. Women were mostly objects."

Molly turns Patricia into a warmly remembered character, displaying a winning combination of naivete and burning sexuality. There's a great in-joke in her last scene as she wistfully sees Bond drive away from Shrublands asking when they might see each other again. "Another time, another place,." he replies – a reference to a pre-Bond Connery picture that co-starred Lana Turner, who wouldn't have made a bad Bond girl herself.

CHAPTER 27
BOND HITS THE BAHAMAS

On 22 March, *Thunderball* moved big time to the Bahamas, 102 actors and crew. But according to actor Earl Cameron, who played Pinder, Bond's Bahamian ally, there was a problem when the customs in Nassau impounded all of the movie equipment. "But Cubby Broccoli said, 'Look, make up your mind because if you don't want us to make the film here we'll go somewhere else to make it.' So he just frightened them and they let it go, of course."

In Nassau, Kevin McClory came into his own as producer. Living as he did on the island, he'd many contacts among the community's richest movers and shakers and was able to smooth the way for the production and provide access to many desirable locations. Extensive use, for instance, was made of Paradise Island, then a massive property and leisure development owned by the millionaire Huntingdon Hartford. It was a stretch of the island that so enchanted Sean Connery, that he now resides there. But on the whole McClory's producing marriage with Broccoli and Saltzman didn't work. There was a feeling that he was merely being tolerated for the duration of this one film. "Kevin didn't fit in well with the Bond team," admits Ken Adam. "He had occasionally some good ideas, but he must have felt too that he wasn't one of the boys. Nobody unfortunately took him very seriously. He was in a strange way a friend of mine because I knew him as a boom swinger at Shepperton Studios and then again on *Around the World in 80 Days*, when I got him the job with Mike Todd. There was something always which I felt sorry for with Kevin because he had a stammer, and when somebody has a physical problem like that, you feel more sympathy for that person."

Connery's arrival in Nassau was under a black cloud of personal turmoil. Just weeks before he and his wife, actress Diane Cilento, in the glare of publicity, had announced a trial separation. They'd been married just three years. After a few nights at the Hilton hotel, Connery returned to the family home, only to then jet off again to the Bahamas. Feeling miserable in London while her husband frolicked in the sun, Diane, along with their young son Jason, flew to join him. This sudden appearance on location, some guessed, was to keep a watchful eye on Claudine Auger, after the inevitable rumours that she and Connery were having an affair. As one columnist put it, "All the girls in Nassau kept begging Sean to play golf – or anything with them. But since Diane arrived, the girls have gone back into the bushes. Nothing like a wife to snap everybody to."

Despite residing in a rented bungalow on the appropriately named Love Beach, the couple engaged in some blistering rows, with Diane more than capable of holding her own. When Michael Caine visited the couple, he and Connery went out while Diane prepared lunch. Turning up two hours late Connery popped his head round the door announcing, "darling, we're home," only to see the meal Diane had cooked flying through the air towards him. Both he and Caine stood in the kitchen covered in gravy and green beans.

It was also on *Thunderball* where the pressure of Bondmania started to take its toll on Connery and the frustration with his alter ego reached breaking point. "I find that fame tends to turn one from an actor and a human being into a piece of merchandise, a public institution," he grumbled at the time. "Well, I don't intend to undergo that metamorphosis." It surprised no one when Connery announced after *Thunderball* that his next Bond would indeed be his last. "I felt an enormous sympathy for Sean," Desmond Llewelyn later recalled. "He really did live under a microscope. Both fans and press pursued him relentlessly." In the Bahamas fans, mostly American students on holiday, followed the crew around everywhere, even when they put out to sea. Resting in a boat between takes, Connery suddenly became aware that it had been encircled by over 200 fans treading water. "Speak to us," one of them shouted. "You're our leader and we're your people. Speak." Connery told them to fuck off.

Connery's on/off relationship with the producers had also more or less broken down, particularly with Saltzman. "Even on *Goldfinger*, as far as I can remember, Sean was very bitter against them," recalls Richard Jenkins, who worked as an assistant director on the early Bonds, "because they'd got him on a three or a four film contract and they absolutely refused to negotiate. Even though he had been tremendously popular and they were making huge amounts of money they wouldn't share it. I think Terence told me that. And on *Thunderball* it was really Terence and Sean against Harry and Cubby, with Kevin McClory as the good guy as far as Sean and Terence were concerned."

The two producers had grown increasingly less fond of each other too now that Bond was a money making behemoth. As Connery cynically noted, "They are not exactly enamoured of each other, probably because they're both sitting on fifty million dollars and looking across the desk at each other thinking 'That bugger's got half of what should be all mine.'" He even joked that both men would have played Bond themselves if they could have in order to save money. During filming one rarely saw them together on the set. Only in the rarefied air of Eon's office in London's posh Mayfair were the two seen together, facing each other across a huge desk with their own phones because they didn't want one to be agreeing something that the other wasn't privy to. It was another reason why both formed the Swiss-based company Danjaq, so that neither of them could withdraw any large amounts of money before getting approval from the other person.

Luciana Paluzzi remembers that office only too well after a memorable trip there after winning the role of bad girl Fiona. "My agent had negotiated my fee and I said to her, but it's so little. They said, that's all we could get. So the first time I went to London I remember walking into Harry and Cubby's office to ask for better pay, to tell them that my agent was an idiot, that he didn't know what he was talking about. Their secretary saw me and said. 'They're both on the phone but go in, they'll be off in a minute.' So I'm sitting in this chair and the two of them are talking business, but Harry was screaming at the top of his voice. 'And you tell your client that if he doesn't want to do this role there are a hundred people outside my door lining up to do it.' And he slammed the phone down. Then he turned to me, Cubby by this time had finished, and they both said. 'Come over Luciana, what can we do for you?' And I thought I was going to die because the timing of my request was so bad. I had to muster all my courage to ask for a rise, and I thought they were going to explode and that I was going to be on the receiving end of another screaming session. And Cubby said to me. 'You're not happy, what do you want?' So I

Chapter 27: BOND HITS THE BAHAMAS

asked for double. And they looked at me and then they looked at each other and said, 'Ok.' And I couldn't believe it."

Broccoli and Saltzman complemented each other perfectly. Michael Caine (whom Saltzman cast as Harry Palmer) saw their partnership as being that of good cop, bad cop. "Cubby gives you the cigarette and Harry knocks it out of your mouth." Broccoli was the more laid-back of the two, while Saltzman was temperamental and mercurial. "The received wisdom was always that Cubby was the nice one and looked after everybody, and Harry was the blunt one," says Richard Jenkins. "And it's true that Saltzman had quite a temper. I recall one incident. In those days parking at Pinewood wasn't an exact science with cars parked everywhere and one morning Harry couldn't find a place and he stormed onto the studio stages shouting and screaming. Cubby was the one that would spend more time on the set, chatting with people, telling stories to the prop guys. But behind your back, I'm not at all sure whether he did feel much for the crew. *Thunderball* was the one that we all eventually got a bonus on, nine months after it came out. There was a huge furore because United Artists' staff got a bonus because *Thunderball* did such good business, and I think the technician's union shamed Harry and Cubby into giving us, the crew, a bonus."

Looking back at that period there are conflicting views about these two highly individual men who were chalk and cheese in personality but together were cinema's greatest producing team. "Cubby was friendly, cuddly. I liked him," remembers Mollie Peters. "Sort of dad-like, as far as I was concerned. Harry, I didn't really ever get to know." Actor Earl Cameron saw it this way: "On the film there would be an attitude of, if they said Cubby's coming tomorrow, oh great. If they said, Harry's coming tomorrow, oh shit. That was the attitude of the crew. They didn't like him at all. He wasn't a nice man. Cubby was well loved. He was a really nice man. A charming man. I liked working with Cubby." Ken Adam too, although he was enormously fond of both men, speaks in more glowing terms of Broccoli. "Though he was enormously volatile, Harry was a showman, brought up in showbusiness. He came up maybe with ten bad ideas, but then one idea was brilliant. Whereas Cubby was more one of the boys, always. I remember once I wanted to look at a really dangerous location in the jungles of Guatemala in a tiny plane and I said, 'Cubby, I'm going by myself.' He said, 'No I'm coming with you.' He would never let me go by myself."

To be fair to Saltzman, Richard Jenkins does recall one illuminating occasion on *Goldfinger*, filming the pre-credit sequence on the backlot at Pinewood. Only recently married, Jenkins' young wife was afraid of being left alone at home all night so had come along to watch. When filming broke for dinner the production manager refused her any food, as she was not allied to the production. An angry Jenkins complained to the producers, and it was Saltzman who insisted she sit at the main table with all the other wives. "Family was important to Harry. He was a great family man."

Veteran Bond stunt man George Leech also sticks up for Saltzman, although he never got to know him especially well, as opposed to Broccoli who he always could have a chat with. "I remember something Bob Simmons told me. He said, 'Harry is the nicer of the two. He gives the impression that he's the tough sod, but he's nicer than Cubby.' So he always gave the impression of being a hard, wheeler-dealer did Harry. But I never personally got to know him. He was just someone you saw on the set occasionally."

One of Connery's major gripes with Broccoli and Saltzman was that as 007 got bigger it became increasingly difficult to plan other projects because the films were taking longer and longer to make. Huge chunks were being taken out of his life that he felt could be better spent playing more artistically rewarding parts. And the schedule on *Thunderball* was punishing. At one time he worked 15 consecutive nights shooting from 6.30pm until six in the morning. "And then I'd go back and try to have some free time to sleep, but the hotel was full of journalists and photographers. I'd get messages, telephone calls. And I was left to handle everything myself."

The Bahamas was literally flooded with media representatives fighting to get a glimpse of Connery in action. "The Bond series was such a huge success all over the world by the time of *Thunderball*," remembers Luciana Paluzzi. "I remember when we were in Nassau, they had two huge planes that came in with photographers and journalists from Europe. First came one plane and they were there for a week, and then later on another plane brought the second batch in, and we had 60 photographers and journalists on the set doing interviews between takes. It was really wild."

Connery though refused all interviews bar one, his now infamous Playboy interview where he argued over the merits of hitting women, a quote that's been resurrected ad nauseum, each time igniting fresh controversy. On set, Connery was never less than the ultimate professional but once work was over he didn't want his free time taken up with endless interviews and posing for photographs. One day was indicative of his attitude. After the final "cut" was called, Connery, oblivious to the crowds roped off watching on the beach, removed his toupee and threw it at the hairdresser like a Frisbee. "That's it, I'm off."

There was another reason why Connery refused to play ball with the media. He still hadn't forgotten how they treated him back in 1962 when he won the role, asking snide and stupid questions like, "How did your training driving a milk truck prepare you for this picture?" On *Thunderball* a press delegation complained to Terence Young about Connery's attitude: "Now that he's important he won't do any interviews," they whined. "Why is he being so unpleasant?" They got this response: "He's not unpleasant, you were. You started it, after all. Sean's never changed, he's been like this all the time, and you're the people that provoked him. You tried to make a monkey out of him and now he doesn't need you."

With Connery ignoring the press, they were quick to seize on another story – Bond girls. Along with Claudine and Molly, another two stunning actresses had been cast and luckily for the media's clicking cameras they seemed to spend most of their time in bikinis.

The character of Fiona Volpe did not feature in either Whittingham's script or Fleming's novel. Maibaum said he created the role because in his opinion, Largo was not the grandest of Fleming's baddies, never reaching the villainous heights of a Goldfinger or a Dr. No, so felt the forces of evil directed against Bond needed enlarging. Thus the Bond series' first *femme fatale* was born. Subsequent variations on the same character have appeared periodically in Bond films, notably May Day in *A View to a Kill* and Onatopp in *GoldenEye*, but Fiona is by far the most successful. The role of Fiona, SPECTRE's black widow assassin, was way ahead of its time, very much a free spirit and more than able to hold her own in a man's world. Her first meeting with Bond is memorable. She picks him up in her blue Ford Mustang sports car on the road back to Nassau, but Bond can't resist the temptation to indulge in a little word-play, or perhaps foreplay, as he asks, "How far do you go?"

As Fiona, Italian actress Luciana Paluzzi gives a commanding performance of a woman of brazen sexuality cloaked in evil. The sexual frisson in her scenes with Connery is quite electric, best of all when he discovers her in his bath! Asking for something to put on Bond offers her a pair of slippers. It's the best sight gag in the entire Bond canon. Inevitably it leads to them having sex, but the mood doesn't last long as Fiona soon has him at gunpoint. Bond, realising he hasn't won her over to the cause of good as he'd previously managed with Pussy Galore, spitefully announces that what he did was for king and country. "You don't think it gave me any pleasure, do you?" He gets a slap in the face for that one.

Brought in by Terence Young, who'd directed the actress before in *No Time to Die* in 1958, Luciana originally tested for Domino. "And that was scary," she recalls, "because there must have been 100 girls testing for all the roles. It was like a mad house at Pinewood." Luciana did her test and went back to Rome and didn't hear a word for months. "Finally one day I got a call from Cubby and he said. 'Luciana, I have bad news and I have good news.' I always like to hear the bad news first, so Cubby said, 'You will not be able to play the role of Domino.' And I said, 'Why?' Because I thought I did a very good test. And he said, 'Because the policy now of the Bond series is to launch a new girl who isn't very well known to the public in each movie and you've already made a lot of movies, and so it's not a launching of somebody new. So don't feel offended because that's the only reason why we've decided not to give you that role.' My heart sank. I was so upset. Then I said, 'OK, what's the good news?' He said, 'Well, because you did such a terrific test we want you to play Fiona.' And I said, 'That's fantastic, I like that role better." I thought that the villainess was much more fun to play. The ingenue, those kind of roles come and go and sometimes they don't leave any impression, but the role of the villainess for me was the best role, so I was very excited."

Making her screen debut in *Three Coins in the Fountain* (1954), Luciana went on to briefly become a Rank contract player, starring most prominently opposite Stanley Baker in *Sea Fury* (1958). Later film appearances included the 1966 Man from UNCLE caper *To Trap a Spy*, where she attempted to kill Napoleon Solo, and *The Klansman* (1974) with Richard Burton, again directed by Terence Young. Luciana retired from movies in 1980; her scintillating performance as Fiona had sadly not lead to a successful film career. "We knew *Thunderball* was going to be a success, but you never know what happens to you after. It was an incredible experience and it propelled me all over the covers of magazines and all of that, which was fantastic. Then I found some snobbish directors like Visconti or Fellini, this kind of art director, wouldn't have anything to do with me because I was in a Bond picture. I'm not complaining, but this is what happened. I wasn't considered for pictures of a certain stature because nobody wanted to have a Bond girl in their movie."

Luciana did, however, remain in touch with Connery, seeing him as recently as Christmas 2005 at their old *Thunderball* stomping ground of the Bahamas. She also became friendly with Roger Moore, once having both James Bonds over as dinner guests at her Beverly Hills home.

From *femme fatale*, we move to that other mainstay of the Bond series, the "sacrificial lamb." Usually a woman, this is a character on Bond's side that is bumped off by the bad guys enforcing the audience's desire to see him triumph: the Masterson sisters in *Goldfinger*, Aki in *You Only Live Twice*, Plenty O'Toole in *Diamonds Are Forever*, Paris Carver in *Tomorrow Never Dies* etc. In *Thunderball*, the sacrificial lamb is Paula Caplan, Bond's Bahamian contact, who when captured takes cyanide rather than face torture or let the side down.

Like Fiona, Paula Caplan was created for the film, one thinks merely to beef up the babe quota, and was played by Kingston born Martine Beswick. After winning Miss Jamaica in 1961 Martine used the prize money to come to London to be a fashion model. Terence Young spotted her while casting for *Dr. No*, but advised she needed drama lessons before he could use her. True to his word, a year later he cast Martine in her first film role as one of the fighting gypsy girls in *From Russia with Love*. With her casting in *Thunderball*, Martine joined a select group of actors who have appeared in Bond films as different characters. But the role of Paula is horribly underwritten, leaving her with hardly anything to do save look great in a bikini, which one has to say she does rather well. One nice little scene involving Paula was sadly cut from the script. At her first meeting with Bond in a beach front bar she traces "007" in the sand with her foot as recognition.

Funnily, Martine had been so long in England that her skin had grown pale and upon arriving in Nassau she was ordered to lie in the sun for the first two weeks in order to get an even suntan. "What a job," she later recalled.

In subsequent years Martine carved a name for herself as a Hammer scream queen with roles in *One Million Years BC* (1966), *Slave Girls* (1967) and most notably *Dr Jekyll and Sister Hyde* (1971).

Everyone recalls the shooting of *Thunderball* with great fondness, especially the stylishness of the production, the first class hotels and the chauffeured cars. That was Young's influence. "Usually on a film set at lunch or dinner time they have a caravan or a canteen where the actors are served, it's nothing special, it's very easy going," says Luciana. "But with Terence, when we worked on the beach he would have white tents put out at night with tables with flowers and candlelight. This was like all fantasies come true making *Thunderball*. Champagne was flowing all the time. At night if we were working we could have champagne whenever we wanted. And that was very much Terence, I just can't see Woody Allen doing that." Terence Young was a throwback to a more glamourous age of filmmaking and he reflected that style in his Bond pictures. "Terence had wonderful elegance and refinement, that was his personality," as Mollie Peters observed. "And he took it over into the films as far as I could see. And Sean, I could see picked it all up and used it. They were always seemingly together Terence and Sean."

Assistant director Richard Jenkins also saw the close bond that existed between director and star: "Terence had a very good relationship with Sean and really Harry and Cubby were so lucky that he directed the first Bond film. I liked Terence very much. He was a very sophisticated man and had great style. He always wore a suit, owned two Bentleys and had a lovely villa in the South of France. And he was very kind to me and actually became godfather to my first son."

Young became even closer to Luciana Paluzzi. "Terence was like my father because my father died many, many years ago. When I got married for the second time he flew to New York from Rome where he was making a film just to give me away. We had an incredible relationship. He was like family to me. I just loved and adored the man."

Terence was a born bon vivant who mixed in high circles with the ease and grace of a lord of the realm. One afternoon he was in the camera boat with Connery and Claudine Auger when a huge yacht came alongside. Young made out the figure of a man on deck in a white suit wearing the Cordon of the Legion d'Honneur, a massive award in France which DeGaulle and only a few others had. "So this guy has to be a pretty big fish," Young announced. The man shouted across at them that he'd heard they were filming and wanted to meet Young, as they had some mutual friends. "I've brought you a present," he said stepping aboard and producing a big magnum of Dom Perignon. He got some glasses out of a fridge, filled them with ice, and when he started pouring the champagne over them Young screamed, "No, no, no. No champagne and ice!" The man said, "My friend, I shall never teach you to direct pictures, you should never teach me to drink wine. I am the Count de Vogue and I own Moet et Chandon. We make Dom Perignon." One suspects this sort of thing happened to Young all the time. It's a nice Bondian tip, too. If ever your champagne gets warm, put ice in it for 30 seconds; then remove it. Hey presto, it's chilled again.

Young also shared with Connery a schoolboy sense of humour and a liking for practical jokes, as Luciana remembers. "In the scene with myself and Sean in the car where I pick him up on the Nassau road and drive very fast, we shot it two or three times. And when we went to see the dailies, Terence had substituted the back projection film of a winding road for the sea, we were floating in the middle of the ocean. It was so funny. Then another time, there is a scene where Sean is making a drink all dressed up behind a bar that's like a table, you can see through it. Then we go to the dailies and he'd asked the cameraman to pan down and he was in his underwear and socks. And Terence used to play these funny jokes on the set all the time and that's why everybody loved him because he had a great sense of humour."

CHAPTER 28
THE MACHINES TAKE OVER

Although he'd reconciled the money wrangles with Broccoli and Saltzman that had precluded him from directing *Goldfinger*, *Thunderball* was actually a film Young didn't much care to make. "We started to repeat ourselves. We started picking the best moments from the previous films and saying, 'Let's do something like that.' We were getting old hat and quite mechanical." Young saw that the writing was on the wall, that the urbane style he'd created for Bond was becoming swamped by technology. *Thunderball* has been singled out as the moment when the makers lost touch with Fleming's literary hero and the special world of the novels, when Bond as a character became a push-button superman. Credibility also started to go out of the window as the situations Bond found himself in became increasingly far fetched. This is a little unfair as really the die had already been cast in *Goldfinger*; after the trick Aston Martin there was no turning back. But even Maibaum admitted that with *Thunderball* the series "really did become larger than life. It became enormous, more fantastical, almost comic strip. And once we'd done that there was just no way of bringing them down."

Connery has often made the same complaint. "As the films got bigger and more expensive they became more involved with hardware than people." Already thoroughly pissed off with Bond taking over his private life, now even the simple pleasure of playing the part was losing interest for him with the character dwarfed by gadgets galore. And *Thunderball* is simply awash with machines, super vehicles and gizmos. A large proportion of the budget was spent on realising them for the screen and they still look impressive even by today's standards.

Undoubtedly the star of the show was Largo's private yacht the Disco Volante (Italian for 'flying saucer'). The script merely called for a super fast yacht and when the producers couldn't find one impressive enough Ken Adam decided to make his own. "By chance when I was in New York with Harry Saltzman he found an ad that there was a hydrofoil for sale in Puerto Rico. So we went to Puerto Rico and bought this thing for $10,000. It was in dry dock and looked pretty rough, but they're built out of aluminium so I knew nothing could go wrong."

Called The Flying Fish, it had once ferried passengers between Venezuela and Mexico. Now the craft sailed to a Miami shipyard where it underwent a complete overhaul and refurbishment. "My idea was that this had to be a big yacht," says Adam. "I've always been interested in boats, along with sports cars and aeroplanes, so I came up with this idea of doubling the length of the hydrofoil, and at the same time redesigning it, by having a catamaran body attached around it." And so a huge cocoon, some 50ft long, was created and fitted out with a yellow smokestack, lifeboats and a functional sun deck. The whole thing was powered by a 1,320 HP Mercedes Benz diesel engine. "The naval expert had serious doubts," remembers Adam. "He said you can't have it solidly attached because in the first bit of bad sea it will break. And somebody came up with the idea of putting two one-inch diameter slip bolts on either side. That was the only thing that held those two halves together. And you can't tell in the film. As I've always found, eventually, the most difficult things that we were all shit scared over work better because you take more care."

But the real coup de grace is that at the drop of a switch the hydrofoil is capable of escape by jettisoning its rear body, which then stays behind to fight a rearguard action to foil pursuers. It's a virtual floating arsenal equipped with the type of armaments you'd find on a destroyer, including an anti-aircraft cannon, heavy machine guns and armour plating. People thought the shedding of the cocoon just wouldn't work and for a while they were right as during rehearsals the damn thing refused to budge. "For about five days in a row it wouldn't come apart," Young recalled, "even with men with axes and hammers hitting the goddamn thing." Fearful of huge problems ahead, Young put aside several days to film this important sequence. On the first morning, with a helicopter following, speedboats attacking and three cameras mounted on an enormous barge, Young yelled action. "And the Disco Volante came by and clean as a whistle, the front came off, the back remained, and that was it! We had nothing else to do, so Sean and I went off and played golf! We didn't have anything else to shoot."

Of course this is a Bond film so the whole thing gets blown up at the end; hitting some rocks Bond and Domino jump out just in time. Instead of using a model it was decided to obliterate the real thing, but that was going to take a helluva lot of explosives. The man who came to the rescue was Eon's unofficial military liaison General Charles Russhon. The retired US air force officer (some say also ex-CIA) had previously been instrumental in securing permission from the US army for the *Goldfinger* crew to film around Fort Knox (with a little extra string pulling from Robert Kennedy). As a "thank you" the crew mounted a sign on one of Fort Knox's admin blocks proclaiming: "Welcome General Russhon." An in-joke that's actually visible in the film. Russhon was a real character and endeared himself to many who worked under the Eon banner.

Russhon told effects maestro John Stears that he could get hold of some experimental rocket fuel to blast apart the Disco Volante, but it could only be delivered the night before filming, which meant no time for tests. It was suck it and see. Stears later explained what happened: "I hit the TX and I just couldn't believe it, the thing just disappeared in front of our eyes. I didn't know where the boat had gone. I thought we'd vaporised it. I looked up and there was a little black pinpoint in the sky. I said, 'I don't want to worry you guys but the boat is coming down on top of us.' By this time it was perfectly round, all bits and pieces, a very nasty mess coming down." Stears and his crew managed to survive but when they got back to Nassau all the windows were out in the main high street. That was 30 miles away! It was only the fact that Stears' crew was right on top of the explosion, laying down, that the blast went right over them. "It must have been the biggest explosion ever in a movie," Stears said. "Ever."

In addition to almost wiping out the effects team, Russhon helped secure the "skyhook" rescue gadgetry that scoops up Bond and Domino at the close of the film and contacted the US coast guard to participate in the final sea assault on the escaping Disco Volante. He also persuaded the US Navy aqua-paratroopers to jump free of charge for a simply stunning sequence where they bale out of planes over Miami into the ocean to do battle with Largo's frogmen. Normally the team is engaged in the recovery of Apollo astronauts after splashdown. As a thank you from the producers Russhon was awarded a cameo in *Thunderball*. He's the military official with Miss Moneypenny during the London briefing scenes.

Chapter 28: THE MACHINES TAKE OVER

Other pieces of hardware included Bond's underwater camera. Common today, small underwater cameras were unheard of in 1965, but it so happened that Nikon were working on ides for just such a device and the producers asked if they could use their prototype. Nikon jumped at the chance of being in a Bond movie and sent them a camera which was so well used during filming that Desmond Llewelyn, who owned it afterwards as a souvenir, had to keep it together using sticky tape.

Another gizmo was a pocket-sized re-breather containing several minutes of air, used memorably in Largo's shark pool and the underwater battle. Peter Lamont, then a senior draughtsman who graduated to production designer on later Bond films and won an Oscar for *Titanic*, recalls receiving a phone call one afternoon at his Pinewood office from a commander in the British Navy who'd just seen *Thunderball*. "We're very interested in the miniaturised breathing apparatus," this voice said. "Can you tell me how long the air lasted?" Lamont went, "Yes I can tell you exactly. As long as you can hold your breath." Lamont could visualise this poor man going white on the other end of the line. "What do you mean? Bond was underwater for three or four minutes." Lamont said, "Yes, but if you look at it carefully that's the skill of the editor. It didn't work. Believe me." "Thank you very much," said the officer and put the phone down.

The re-breather makes a nostalgic return in *On Her Majesty's Secret Service* when Bond offers his resignation and goes into his office to clear out his desk. Opening a suitcase he takes out Honey's knife from *Dr. No*, Red Grant's watch-garrote as seen in *From Russia with Love* and finally the re-breather. It's a great scene.

Unlike the re-breather most of the underwater gadgets and vehicles in the film actually did work and were the brainchild of Ken Adam. Because of the use of mostly outdoor locations there's little evidence in *Thunderball* of Adam's trademark gargantuan sets, a la the reactor room in *Dr. No* or the classic volcano interior from *You Only Live Twice*. But he still faced huge challenges. "*Thunderball* was a different type of Bond picture. Pinewood was shoved into the background and we had the majority of complicated building in the Bahamas. That's why I brought out my construction team of Ronnie Udell, Peter Murton and Peter Lamont and we created almost a studio out there. It was a completely different experience, a real one-off. I'd never done anything like it before or since. It was really the underwater dimension that was completely new for all of us. And very exciting."

Just as exciting was dreaming up suitably Bondian nautical craft, although Adam didn't believe anybody would be able to realise his fantastical designs. Then the production happened upon Jordan Klein in Miami who said, "Sure, we can build that." Those words gave Adam the confidence to really go to town on the underwater vehicles and on future Bonds too, knowing that whatever he designed someone, somewhere in the world could make it practical and bring it to life.

Jordan Klein was an award winning underwater filmmaker, inventor and engineer. Initially contacted by General Russhon about the possibility of building the underwater A-bomb carrier, Klein was eager to be involved, impressed by the ambitious nature of the project and the involvement of Ivan Tors, a production company specialising in underwater films and adventure TV shows like *Flipper* and *Sea Hunt*. "The only trouble was the Bond people were very difficult to get money out of," Klein recalls. "Russhon said, 'How do you want to get paid, half now and half before the bomb carrier gets shipped out of the US.' I said, 'That's reasonable.' Meanwhile no money came, and it was about three weeks into the work when Russhon finally showed up with a cheque for half. And we only had a month to make it. My assistant and I lived in my workshop building the damn thing day and night. We finished it and Russhon says, 'Can you ship it over.' And I said, 'Where's the money. I busted my arse here, all somebody had to do was take a piece of paper and sign their signature. This isn't working out too well.'"

The bomb carrier was eventually shipped out to the Bahamas but Klein, still owed half his money, decided to follow in his own plane and told the crew not to load it on the camera barge until his order. Production supervisor David Middlemas met Klein when he landed asking. "Where is it?" Klein replied, "It's sitting on the dock." "But the barge is leaving tomorrow," Middlemas pointed out. "Where's the money?" Klein said. "You know we're good for it," Middlemas responded. "Not at the rate you've been going," went Klein. Middlemas escorted Klein to where they were filming. It was the beach scene where Bond kills a baddie with his speargun and says, "I guess he got the point." There he was introduced to Saltzman who turned round and started yelling at Klein. "Where's the stuff? What's going on? I'm paying Ivan Tors all this money." Klein had to cut in and explain that he wasn't Ivan Tors but a separate contractor. "It got ridiculous," he says. "It got to be a scream out. And David told Saltzman, 'He won't let the thing go on the barge until he gets his money.' And then Saltzman starts yelling again, so I go to David, 'Listen, we're not getting anywhere. He's getting upset. I'm getting upset. Just tell me what's the problem. Don't you guys have the money?' 'Of course we have the money.' They said. 'So what's the trouble?' I asked. 'Well our trouble shooter General Russhon...' I said. 'You mean troublemaker. That guy has created problems for me from day one, not showing up when he's supposed to, missing meetings. The one lousy thing he had to do was give me a piece of paper with a name on it.' Finally Saltzman calms down and drives me to the office and gives me a cheque. Then I called the dock, who said. 'You phoned just in time because we're running out of space on the barge.' So that's how the bomb carrier eventually got there."

With the carrier now up and running Klein found himself stuck with the film because nobody could operate the damn thing properly. "They kept smashing it up and I was spending my nights instead of sleeping, patching it all up again for shooting in the morning. Finally they said, 'Who the hell can run this thing?' And I said, 'Well I can run it. I ran it when I tested it in Miami.' And the next thing I know I was driving the bomb carrier for the entire show." Klein is visible in the cockpit. He's the one wearing the gold Rolex.

Klein was also responsible for building the one-man sea-tows, which came armed with two front-mounted spear guns. "I figured these things needed a lot of power so I bought two and a half horse power DC landing gear motors from B29's. The first time I put the sea-tow in the water to test it I squeezed the trigger and it just took off, pulled my trunks down around my ankles and my face mask down around my neck. So I thought that's too much power. I altered it and in the end they worked fine. I still own one of them today."

CHAPTER 29
SPEARGUNS AND SHARKS

Not just involved with the props, Klein's expertise was exploited on the underwater unit, mainly as second cameraman working alongside the great Lamar Boren, the world's premiere underwater cameraman. On *Thunderball* Boren put to good use techniques he'd learnt on dozens of underwater jobs. To adjust the level of his camera he used his lungs almost like an elevator. To rise up he took deep breaths, to drop down he simply exhaled. By controlling his breathing in such a way he achieved a perfect balance, a factor that contributed to the steadiness of his camera and the clarity and effectiveness of *Thunderball*'s many underwater sequences. "Lamar was like a whale himself," Ken Adam recalls. "He was an enormous man. By this time he'd already spent 5,000 hours under the sea, mainly at the Great Barrier Reef in Australia. There was nothing he didn't know about sharks. And he kept saying to me, 'Ken, you know a shark is like any other wild animal, nine out of ten times it will do nothing to you. But there will be one who will.'"

Such talk didn't make Adam feel any easier about diving down under the ocean. On his first recce to the Bahamas he recalled seeing from a helicopter sharks swimming around. "And Kevin McClory said, 'There are no sharks in the Bahamas, Ken.' Then I found out that the year before they'd found a tiger shark dead with somebody inside in an RAF uniform. So I said, 'Don't give me that bullshit. The place is full of sharks!'"

Actually, Adam got quite used to the sharks; it was the barracudas he never acclimatised to. "They're unpleasant. And I'll never forget Cubby making fun of me. I used to swim every morning and one day Dick Maibaum joined me. And on that morning there was a barracuda lying dead still on the seabed. And I said, 'I'm not going in.' And Dick said, 'Are you scared of that little fish?' I said, 'Yes, I'm scared of that little fish.' Because the moment you tried to get in the water his jaws opened. And Cubby was standing on his hotel balcony watching and said, 'My God, what a bunch of heroes.'"

Despite the sharks and barracudas, shooting in the Bahamas remains one of the fondest memories of Adam's career. "We had a lot of fun on that picture because Terence was the sort of director who was full of fun and very sociable. Cubby was very sociable too and knew all the wealthy Americans in

Nassau. So the atmosphere was wonderful. I must say in terms of ambience the Bahamas was one of the most pleasant experiences for all of us."

The man responsible for choreographing and directing the underwater action was Ricou Browning, who once played the gill man in the 1954 cult classic *The Creature from the Black Lagoon*. No film in the history of the cinema had ever attempted the large-scale underwater sequences to be featured in *Thunderball*. Even by today's standards, they're hard to beat. But Browning wasn't at all daunted by the task. "I felt very confident about doing the sequences, as long as I could get the support required. And fortunately I got the support. Just before shooting started in the Bahamas I said to Terence Young, 'Do you want to go over the shots?' And he said, 'No Ricou, I know your background. I'm not going to tell you what to do or how to do it. Just do it. If I see the dailies and I don't like it, I'll let you know.' And I never heard from him. So we got along famously. And McClory was the same. I worked with him great. He was very co-operative in the sense that whatever needs I required, he helped me fight for them. You could tell that he was far more interested in the underwater scenes than any other portion of the film."

Browning was also instrumental in pointing the Bond team in the direction of Klein and Boren. All three had worked over the years for Ivan Tors, which had given them unique knowledge of the waters around the Bahamas. Browning also brought along his own special crew with whom he'd developed an intricate series of hand signals for directing divers underwater. "In those days we didn't have underwater communication systems so we used hand signals. I'd give a signal as to whether we were gonna shoot long shot, close up etc. Then I look at all the actors in front of the camera and make a circle, like an OK circle. If they're ready to shoot they give me an OK sign back. Then I tap the cameraman on the shoulder to give him a roll sign. And for a cut, I touch the cameraman and then go into the scene and just grab the divers to stop them from fighting or whatever they're doing."

The underwater team filmed mostly in shallow water between 15-20 feet and because of the lack of underwater communications, rehearsal and planning was essential. This was carried out on a large barge moored off the coast. "All the divers would dry land walk all of the scenes that we were going to do underwater," explains Browning. "And if everything went smoothly we'd stay under and just keep shooting, but if we had a serious problem we would just wrap it up, come on board the ship, discuss it again and go back down. And it seemed to work well that way. But because of the sheer number of divers that we needed some were brought over from Florida and although all of them were accomplished divers they knew very little about film work. So it took a lot of patience and trial and error to accomplish what we needed done."

Despite the plethora of underwater scenes, Connery rarely got his feet wet. "I think Sean's probably as professional as they get," says Klein. "But he's not particularly fond of the water, even less fond of animals beneath the surface of the water. We didn't actually use Sean for any of the swimming stuff. We doubled him with a guy named Frank Cousins who had almost an identical physique. All we did was use Sean for establishing shots, like looking left and right, swimming towards the camera, stuff like that, a lot of which was done in the pool. But Sean's smart. What does he need to do that stuff for that just slows down the production if they've got him off playing around underwater. So it was probably fortunate that he didn't want to be a diver."

The most dramatic underwater sequence, and the film's highlight, is the epic battle between Bond's orange-suited aqua paras and Largo's black suited SPECTRE frogmen. On the big screen especially it's truly eye-popping and ranks alongside the volcano assault in *You Only Live Twice* as the finest climax ever to grace a Bond film. Some 60 divers were employed in total, including one guy who turned out to be a Miami motorcycle cop on holiday. The battle itself was choreographed beforehand in a car park, much to the puzzlement of passing locals, and then filmed over the course of six days off Clifton Pier around an old wrecked US Navy landing craft.

Asked to help with the hiring of divers, Klein was also handed a camera and flittered around the mass of sprawling bodies picking up exciting shots wherever he could. "There was one scene that was

Chapter 29: SPEARGUNS AND SHARKS

the damnedest thing you ever saw. I was shooting tight on these two guys fighting and I saw a shark in the background and he's swimming toward us. I kept shooting and as the shark swam closer the two guys quit fighting and watched this thing. And then when the shark had passed by they commenced fighting again. You couldn't have set that up for a hundred grand."

However breathtaking this final battle undeniably is, Terence Young was never convinced by it. In later years he stated his dissatisfaction with the film's overall emphasis on underwater action calling it, "anti James Bond," because it slowed the pace of the movie down as people can't move more than four mph underwater. During editing Peter Hunt tried speeding up some of the underwater shots but they just looked ridiculous. "I thought that the first underwater scenes were delightful, especially the opening sequence where the frogmen recover the hijacked atomic bombs," Young later said. "But in the final fight we kept repeating ourselves. There was nothing you could do except fire a spear at somebody, pull his mask off, or cut his lifeline. So when you've done that stuff 45 times the audience is naturally going to clamour for something new."

To be fair, Klein and Browning picked their brains to come up with gag after gag to make the final battle a real spectacle, and succeeded gloriously. "We used everybody's ideas on how to shoot, kill and fight somebody," recalls Browning. "Everybody contributed. And we got great coverage on it and were able to create a pretty good fight. I recall that in the script there wasn't a lot of detail on the underwater battle, we pretty much had to create it ourselves. And I think the more the producers saw the dailies the more they encouraged me to get more action."

There are spear hits galore and some imaginative demises. And some shocking moments too, such as a frogman's facemask smashed open by the butt of a spear gun. The underwater pyrotechnics were courtesy of Klein. The most effective is a SPECTRE frogman hit with an explosive-charged spear. Unfortunately for diver Courtney Brown (who used to double Lloyd Bridges on *Sea Hunt*), the stunning effect proved all too realistic, as Klein recalls: "The idea was to place a piece of lead on the outside of his wet suit, spray it black so it matched up, and when the spear was fired, on a wire, it would strike the lead and create an explosive flash. But the riggers put the lead underneath his wet suit, instead of outside, so when it hit and exploded the water turned to steam between the suit and his body and the piece of lead. This guy went ballistic, naturally. He went nuts trying to rip the suit off to get away from the scolding water. And he's still got the scars."

There were other accidents too, according to Klein. "Ricou Browning got a spear shot through his calf. We took him to the doctor who looked at it, felt around the wound, looked again and then took the spear and shoved it all the way through, because it didn't go totally into the calf. And that makes my stomach feel funny just thinking about it. And then he unscrewed the head and pulled the spear out. Yeah that was fun."

The real star of the sequence is Bond's special underwater jet pack that shoots him around underwater like an aquatic superman. Again the prop was courtesy of Klein. "After the bomb carrier incident David Middlemas and I became fast friends. He was the only breath of sanity over there. They were getting ready to shoot Q's scenes and I said to him, 'What's Bond got for the underwater finale like the briefcase in *From Russia with Love* and the Aston Martin in *Goldfinger*? What's his special piece of stuff.' David says, 'Well, nothing. Why?' I said, 'I've got an idea to have a back pack that propels him though the water, lays a smokescreen, has a headlight and two explosive spears that he can fire.' David goes, 'Wow, that's great. But there's only one problem – it's Friday and we shoot Q's headquarters on Monday. What do you want to do?' I said, 'Give me $38,000. I'll build it and have it here Monday.' He said, 'That's impossible.' I said, 'Tell you what I'll do. If I don't show up with it at nine o'clock when you're going to shoot at Q's place, you don't have to pay me anything.' He said, 'That's a deal I can't refuse.' So I leaped on my plane and went home. Again I worked round the clock with my guy and we built the thing and I got it over there actually five minutes past nine."

Aesthetically the thing looked gorgeous, but underwater it was a bit of a flop according to Ricou Browning: "The backpack didn't work very well. The motor inside wasn't powerful enough to do the job. We could get no speed out of the equipment." To achieve the desired effect Connery's stunt double Frank Cousins was pulled along by a piano wire attached to a high speed motorboat. If Cousins had turned his face at any moment the force would have torn the mask from his face.

The climactic underwater battle notwithstanding, the biggest set piece filmed out in the Bahamas involved the hijacked bomber. A full-size mock up of a Vulcan, made of fibreglass and featuring a real cockpit taken from a scrapped plane, was sunk in 60 feet of water. For the sequence where it crashed into the sea a model was used and suspended on wires from two large specially built towers. Supervised by John Stears, who deservedly won an Oscar for *Thunderball*, he'd left his crew to start preparatory work only to return a week later to find none of the towers had been built. "What's the problem?" He asked. "We can't work out there John, the place is full of sharks." The rigger replied, "Give me a break." Said Stears, "There's only about six feet of water out there." Armed with a shark gun, just in case, Stears went out and sat on the tower to watch over his crew as they worked. Suddenly his assistant tapped him on the shoulder and said, "I didn't realise there were rocks around here." Stears reassured him that the area was all sand. "Well, there's a big rock down there." He said. "That isn't a rock, that's a lemon shark," yelled Stears. A 14-foot monster was swimming round the tower. "Oh, Guys," said Stears, as calmly as possible. "I think we'd better work at low tide when it's only two feet deep." Stears later found out that the coastline he'd chosen was notorious for where the sharks have their young, and it was the breeding season. Later, while shooting the model plane hitting the water from a camera barge, Stears and his crew suddenly became aware they had company. The sea around them was full not just of sharks, but whole shoals of barracuda!

The Vulcan plane and the atomic weapon used in *Thunderball* were unusually authentic. Because of Ken Adam's RAF history (after fleeing the Nazis in 1934 he became the only German to fly with the RAF as a fighter pilot during the war), the designer was invited to a Vulcan base in England. There he was accorded carte blanche to look at the bomber at close quarters and observe them in flight. Adam's assistant Peter Lamont was also invited to bomber command and shown round the most highly secretive areas by a squadron leader. "All the questions that you have asked me, if you look, all the answers are here," he said. Lamont also surreptitiously photographed some bombs using a secret camera. At the time the public really didn't know what nuclear weapons looked like, so Jordan Klein was able to construct his A-bombs based on the real thing.

Once the Vulcan descends underwater, Largo swims to the submerged cockpit and murders the pilot by cutting his air hose. To achieve this shot, diver Courtney Brown, having recovered from being scalded when the explosive spear hit effect failed, came in to double the actor, only to almost lose his life. Brown's air hose was to be cut for real and he was relying on a "bale out" bottle of air under his seat. On cue, Brown was supposed to struggle and thrash around until finally feigning death, then wait a few seconds and grab the tank and breathe. "Well he did it all perfectly," recalls Klein, who was shooting the scene from behind the cockpit seats. "I saw him doing all the struggling and I thought, man he's going crazy. Then he stopped and didn't move for a bit. I dropped the camera and looked and realised that the bale out bottle had fallen down past his reach and he was actually drowning. We put a mouthpiece in his mouth but he wasn't breathing, he was full of water. He was blue when we got him to the surface. We rushed him to hospital and they pumped him out and eventually got him breathing. And that was poor Courtney Brown again. So he left *Thunderball* with a scar and almost died."

After filming was completed on the Vulcan the producers ordered it to be destroyed, fearful of other filmmakers photographing it. So the entire bomber was wrapped in explosives and blown apart. When the crew dived down to take a look, all that remained was its framework, which over the years has since become a reef.

Above water the Bond crew utilised numerous Bahamian location sites. The tropical island really was the place to be in 1965, as only weeks before Connery and co arrived, the Beatles had been based in Nassau filming *Help!* Thanks to Ted Moore's sumptuous photography, *Thunderball* ranks amongst the

Chapter 29: SPEARGUNS AND SHARKS

most colourful and glorious looking Bond movies of all. "I think Ted Moore's one of the most underrated cinematographers," says Richard Jenkins. "However, he was frequently very bad tempered. But my older self now realises that was just stress and tension. But he did seem to have quite a liking for alcohol. One had to treat him almost like a star actor, try and work on his better self, to make sure everything was in place for him."

Downtown Nassau was the scene of the classic Junkanoo sequence. Held every year, the Junkanoo is Nassau's version of New Orleans' Mardi Gras, complete with elaborate floats, marching bands and a party in the street atmosphere. The producers felt this would make for a lively backdrop to the scene where Fiona and her thugs chase Bond. The only problem was that the Junkanoo normally took place on Boxing Day, and this was mid April. It was decided to specially re-stage the event, with an offer of £1,000 prize money for the best costume. Almost 600 locals turned up and the procession ended up extending for two miles along Bay Street, Nassau's main thoroughfare.

Even here in this sweaty, overcrowded location, Young endeavoured to bring a little luxury as Luciana recalls. "Usually when you're shooting in the street they say, ok here in this restaurant there is a room that they're giving us where you can change. No, we had a huge yacht that was anchored just beyond the street where we were able to change. This was like all fantasies come true making *Thunderball*."

Young's plan for the Junkanoo was for his camera crew to weave in and out of the crowds and the parade, but on no account to stop it. The results are some very candid moments, including several revellers holding placards with 007 plastered over them. Most famous of all is the shot of a dog pissing in the middle of the street. For years this was considered a blooper, left in by mistake, but according to editor Peter Hunt, the producers loved it. Hunt himself thought it to be in poor taste and left it on the cutting room floor. Running the sequence for Broccoli and Saltzman a few weeks later, both yelled, "Where's the dog Pete?" Hunt said, "You don't want that shot of the dog?" "Yes we do." So Hunt put it back in.

For two nights the Junkanoo eased up Bay Street to the constant rhythm of whistles and booms. A lot of extras only wore paper costumes and when they came lose because of sweat they'd simply strip off and heat them over flames to make them stiff again. Several times the cameras picked up crowds of people coming round a corner stark naked. On the second night the whistles and crashing drums had been going on for six hours and Young simply couldn't stand it any longer. "I've got a headache. You've got to stop the Junkanoo," he said, breaking his own rule. The crew stood there transfixed. Something like 45,000 spectators were watching by this time and everyone was afraid that all momentum might be lost. But Young was adamant he needed a break. Later that same evening Young was seen sipping champagne from a Styrofoam cup complaining, "God this is a rough location, my champagne is warm."

Moving onto Paradise Island locations included the world famous Cafe Martinique, an exclusive five star restaurant and nightclub that still stands today. In the film we see Nassau's social elite arriving in motor launches to enjoy a grand night out. These weren't any old extras, but the real thing. A pledge of £5,000 to the Bahamian Red Cross and the proceeds of a special gala screening of the film resulted in 200 of the town's richest residents turning out. Eon also threw in a bucket of the finest caviar and several cases of Dom Perignon champagne. One of the group included Henry Ford II, grandson of the world famous auto manufacturer and a friend of Young. Kevin McClory also makes a cameo appearance as the seated moustachioed gentleman smoking as Connery waltzes, as only he can, through the lobby into the casino.

The following baccarat game between Bond and Largo is one of the best-played scenes in the film; a verbal fencing duel between two powerful and dangerous men. After winning with ease, Largo's line "you seem to be unbeatable Mr Bond" is parried by a casual shrug from Connery. Bond style doesn't get much better than this. Probably only Steve McQueen could've matched the same kind of cinematic cool that Connery exudes here. Bond next invites Domino to dine and then dance with him and it is here where her shield comes down and she openly submits to his advances in one of the most romantic scenes in the series.

For another night club scene, where Bond ends up after escaping Fiona at the Junkanoo, the makers were looking for something a bit less refined than the Cafe Martinique, but couldn't find anything suitable on the island. In the end they decided to build their own open air club from bamboo, and Terence Young christened it The Kiss Kiss Club after Bond's Italian nick name of Mr Kiss Kiss Bang Bang. It was built with such skill that one member of the crew told local reporters, "Best damned night club on the island. They should have left it there."

The Kiss Kiss Club is where Fiona meets her death and it's a highlight of the film. As befits an adversary every bit as memorable as Red Grant or Oddjob, her demise was dramatically charged. Trapped on the dance floor, Bond knows that Fiona's henchmen have him surrounded and that behind a curtain near the band a gun is aimed at his heart. In a brilliantly edited sequence the two foes dance and swap witty barbs while the music reaches a tremendous crescendo. In the nick of time Bond swerves Fiona round just as the gun is fired so it's she who gets the bullet. Sitting her limp body next to a young couple Bond asks, "You don't mind if my friend sits this one out. She's just dead."

Palmyra, Largo's exotic mansion, lay further up the coast and was in reality the summer home of Nicholas Sullivan, a millionaire from Philadelphia. The estate was spotted from the air by Ken Adam during an early location recce. "The villa had two pools, one sea water and one fresh water. And I thought, this could be interesting for the shark sequence."

The Sullivans happily rented the property to the film crew but chose not to move out, much to everyone's surprise. They even invited guests to come over and watch the Bond team at work. It was truly bizarre, heavy cables lay everywhere, booms and lights, stunt men practising judo falls on each other, Connery hanging about between set-ups and at the edge of it all Mr and Mrs Sullivan and guests sitting in evening dress sipping cocktails. "I was worried," says Adam. "Because Mrs Sullivan was an alcoholic and I thought at night time she might fall into the pool holding the sharks. So I asked Cubby to station some guards there in case." Thankfully she never did fall in.

While Bond is investigating Palmyra at night he's disturbed by a guard and in a hectic fight both fall into the swimming pool. Largo presses a lever and a metal roof closes the two men in, while another lever opens a hatchway to an adjoining pool containing sharks. "Let them in," Largo smiles. For realism Connery needed to be seen swimming with the sharks but was understandably concerned and demanded protection. So Ken Adam built a corridor of Plexiglass to partition the pool and keep the sharks isolated. Still Connery wasn't satisfied. "Look," said Young. "The only way the sharks can get you is if they can jump in the air like dolphins." To which Connery replied, "How the fuck do you know they don't?" "You have my word for it," said Young. "Not good enough," went Connery. Nor was he much reassured by McClory, who'd personally experienced sharks in the ocean. "They aren't really dangerous," he said, "as long as you stay away from their business end."

After much persuading Connery finally agreed and got in the pool. Now probably wasn't the best time to tell him that there was a problem with the underwater corridor. "Unfortunately I could not get enough 8x4 sheets of Plexiglass," says Adam. "I couldn't get it in the Bahamas, I couldn't get it in Miami; it was impossible. So I had a four-foot gap. I didn't tell Sean this. So I stationed one of Ivan Tors divers down there. And of course the first thing the shark did was go straight through the gap. I don't know what happened to the guard. We all started screaming. And Sean never got out so quickly. I mean, he was walking on water."

But the scene had to be completed. In it Bond escapes the pool by heading down the tunnel only to be suddenly confronted by one of the sharks. Behind the camera was Klein. "So Sean's behind the Plexiglass and the shark's on the other side. We were only in about four feet of water. When the shark darted through I stood up and said, 'Sean, don't press your fingers against the Plexiglass because I can see your fingers are flat. It ain't gonna work.' So he says, 'I just want to be sure that it's there.' We resume the scene and he does it again. 'Sean, it doesn't look good.' He says, 'They're not going to be looking at my fingers anyhow' I said, 'You're probably right, but let's do one more.' And he did it again. So if you watch the film you're gonna see his fingers against the Plexiglass. But it's almost impossible to tell. If I hadn't told you that, you wouldn't notice them. So Sean was right, we didn't have to shoot it three times. But the ironic thing was, after the third take Sean stood up and asked how it was when something bumped into the back of him. He looked and it was a shark and he went nuts. 'That's it, the last take,' he said. 'I'm out of here.'"

In the end it was probably Young who came out of the experience worst. "My wife refused to go to bed with me for two weeks afterwards. She said, 'You stink of shark and rotten fish. Go and sleep somewhere else!'"

The sharks were obtained by the Miami seaquarium boat, an 80 foot long collection vessel that had a holding tank in the stern. They'd go out fishing every night and each shark brought back alive the producers paid $500. One of them was a huge tiger shark, over 14 feet long, probably a world record size. Klein used it for some of the scenes around the sunken bomber but had to re-shoot when the beast absconded and none of the remaining sharks matched it for size. The majority of the sharks were captured just off Love Beach, where Connery, Luciana and Ken Adam were all staying. "And we'd been swimming very happily there," says the designer. "After that we took more care."

Far from being dangerous, Klein approached the sharks as if he were herding cattle. Once caught sharks quickly become lethargic because in order to breathe they must have water passing through their gills. So Klein tied them up at night in the holding tank where they threshed about and quickly knackered themselves out. In the morning, they'd be moved gently through the ocean water to get a bit of energy back before being caught, tied to a rock and allowed to go nuts for a while until they slowed down again. "Then what you do is take the rope off their tail, put a guy on each dorsal fin and when the cameraman's ready you let the shark go and as soon as he clears the shot you all dive down and grab him again," says Klein. "You can do that maybe two or three times before the shark is back up to speed and has to be tied to the bottom again. Believe me you don't want to grab them when they're energised because they've got so much strength they'll tear you off. Once you do this with a specific shark you'll know exactly what he's going to do when you turn him loose. Some sharks will go down and away. Some swim up. Others will hook to the left or hook to the right. You can play the game. If we need one to go to the left we get Herman and not Charlie. But then some of them will just turn back and try and grab you. They're all different characters."

Besides the holding tank on the boat some sharks were held at the Sullivans' house in their sea water pool. "I've got a picture of Ivan Tors and myself standing in that pool with sharks swimming around," says Klein. "Ivan was a strange guy, he believed that if you treated animals right they'll treat you right and it didn't matter to him whether it was an elephant, a tiger or a shark. And I kept saying, 'Ivan, they don't know your name. From the knees down you look like anybody else.'"

British stuntman Bill Cummings felt much the same way about sharks. As the ill-fated Quist, a Largo henchman, he's thrown into the pool for failing a mission and lands on top of one of the monsters. "They're not really man eaters," the producers reassured him. "Well, they might give you a nasty suck," Cummings replied. After a hurried conference Cummings was offered £250 danger money and the stunt went ahead. Fortunately only one take was required. Another time, John Stears was in the pool attending to a special effect with what he thought was a dead shark when it suddenly leapt into life and started attacking the others. The next thing he knew he was being pushed about by seething sharks and the water was turning blood red. And all Terence Young was saying was, "Turn the cameras. This is fantastic." Stears screamed, "Get me out of here!"

None of the tiger sharks were drugged, nor were their jaws wired, they were the real thing. But on the whole the sharks were reluctant participants as the pool was so small they became listless and a few died. Special wranglers worked hard to keep them active, prodding them with long polls. McClory used to delight in getting into the pool himself until one shark got so tired of his presence that it turned and bit his poll, snapping it in two. After that McClory wasn't so keen about getting back into the shark pool. But the memory of the shark's captivity still rankles with Richard Jenkins. "I just remember the cruelty of us watching those sharks dying. We could see sort of tissue coming out of their mouths and them looking unwell. And there's this shot of Bond going through the tunnel and coming out with a bit of glass in-between them, so it wasn't really a very brave thing to do, especially with those dozy sharks. I just felt really bad about that."

CHAPTER 30
Q AND CO

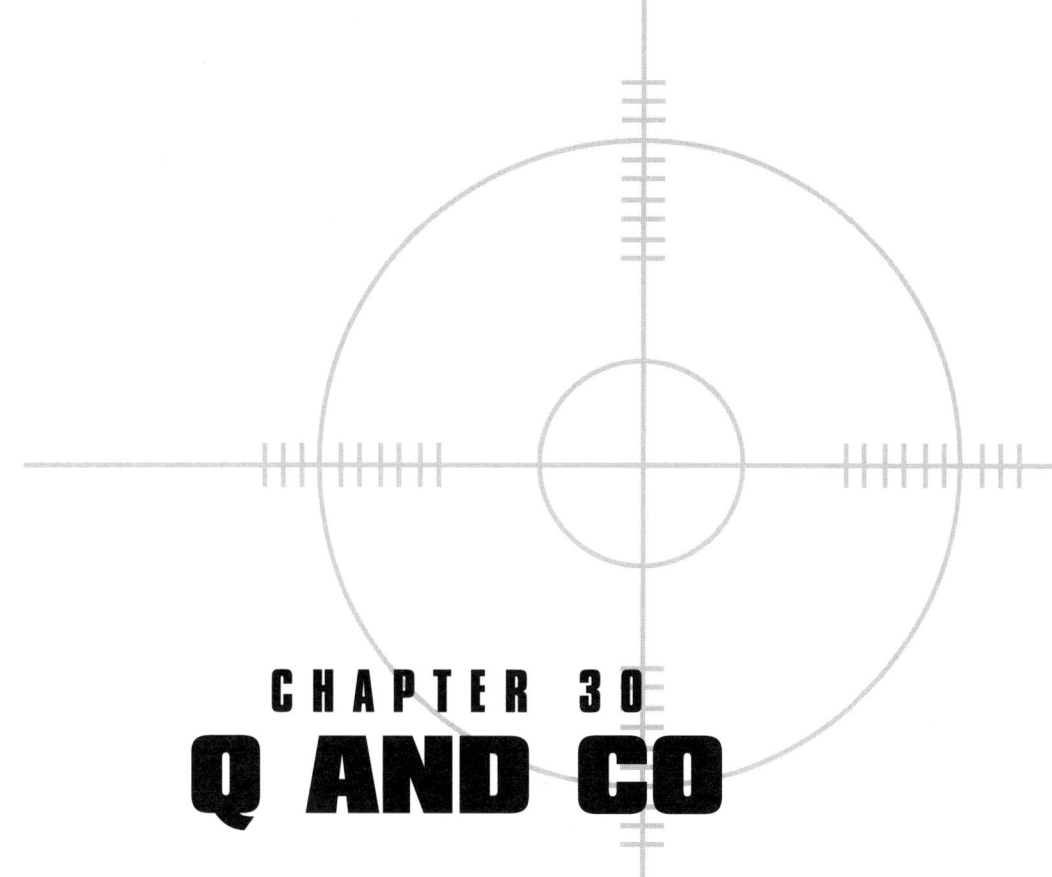

A fascinated observer during much of the shark filming was actor Desmond Llewelyn. He later recalled that it was the only time he ever saw Sean Connery "visibly scared." Llewelyn spent a lot of time in the Bahamas watching the filming and not acting at all. It was a glorified holiday really with Llewelyn in Nassau purely as rain cover. If the weather suddenly changed for the worst his scenes as Q would replace normal filming. But they never did.

Prior to everyone going out to the Bahamas, Llewelyn had dutifully turned up at Pinewood to do his brief scenes. He hung around all day while Young directed something else which was over-running. Late in the afternoon he was told to go home. "When am I going to be needed?" he asked. Nobody knew since the crew was heading next for Nassau. So Llewelyn just assumed his scenes would be done when they all came back. A week later the phone rang at home. "Get your bags packed, you're flying out to the Bahamas tomorrow. Q's scene is needed for wet weather cover and we're building a special duplicate set." When Llewelyn arrived and stepped out onto a melting runway and experienced the piercing heat he thought, "The prospect of rain looks about as likely as British Rail being on time." The production manager collared him. "Whatever you do, stay out of the sun, Desmond. We can't have you getting a tan. And don't leave the hotel without telling us first." Q couldn't have a suntan as in the story he's just arrived from London.

Waiting in the shade for rain was a boring existence and he grew understandably restless. Then the production office rang. "It's obvious the weather ain't gonna change, so we've booked you a flight back home." Not sure whether to be happy or sad Llewelyn started packing, but just then the sky darkened and spots of rain started to fall. The phone rang. "Thank God you haven't gone. Cubby's going mad. You're needed on location. It's raining." In the event, by the time he got there the sun was out again and he wasn't needed, but it made the producers nervous enough to ensure Llewelyn a paid-up stay in the Bahamas for the entire duration of the location shoot.

In the end, Llewelyn's one scene as Q was filmed back at Pinewood in May and it ranks amongst his best in the series firmly establishing the now traditional Q and 007 repartee. Though one witty line was erased, when Bond asks: "What have you got for me? An Aston Martin with water wings?" 12 years later, of course, Bond did get an underwater car. The scene also earned Llewelyn his first real bit of publicity. Merely one of the subsidiary characters prior to *Thunderball*, it was The Daily Mail that ran a photograph of Llewelyn surrounded by all the underwater paraphernalia. "Bond's Gadget Man" ran the headline. It was the first time the press had latched onto the character of Q and from then on he was to become, after Bond of course, the series' most popular and enduring figure.

Another character making a welcome reappearance in *Thunderball* was Felix Leiter, played by Rik Van Nutter. Out of all the actors to play Bond's CIA buddy (eight in total), the unfortunately named Nutter is by far the best. He was the correct age, physical type and had the youthful good looks that Fleming described. Unfortunately the script reduces him to the role of mere side-kick and there isn't the depth of friendship which exists in the novels. But it still remains the most believable Bond/Leiter relationship on screen.

Nutter was married at the time to Hollywood actress Anita Ekberg, whose own Bond claim to fame was having starred in *Call Me Bwana* produced by Broccoli and Saltzman. Famously her face appeared on the billboard poster in *From Russia with Love* where Kronsteen makes his escape from a trap door in her mouth. It was through the couple's friendship with Albert and Dana Broccoli that Nutter was cast. It was also envisioned that he continue playing the character, but when the writers couldn't find ways to put Leiter into the story line of the next two Bond films the idea was dropped.

As for the rest of the supporting cast, Bernard Lee is again wonderful as M and, of course, Lois Maxwell is as irreplaceable as ever as Miss Moneypenny. Bond's first encounter with SPECTRE villainy is Count Lippe, who tries to kill Bond at Shrublands by sabotaging a motorised traction table. Bond has his revenge by locking him in a sauna machine. Originally, Maibaum had Bond impersonating one of the cockney staff to fool Lippe and as he exits, with Lippe's cries fading into the distance, he was to have sung, "We're having a heat wave, a tropical heat wave." Guy Doleman, an actor who was much better at pompous authority figures, such as Harry Palmer's boss, rather vacuously played the role of Lippe.

Making only his second appearance in a Bond film is Blofeld. As in *From Russia with Love* his face is obscured and the character remains a mysterious figure. Audiences would have to wait until the next Bond adventure for him to be finally unveiled. Here he's played by actor Anthony Dawson (Professor Dent in *Dr. No*), while the menacing voice belongs to Eric Pohlmann.

In the small but integral role of Pinder, a Nassau-based agent helping Bond, was Earl Cameron, a Bahamian born actor who'd come to England in 1939 and fought prejudice to become the first black man to win a leading role in a British feature film (*Pool of London* in 1950). Cameron knew Broccoli, having worked with him on three previous pictures and had been the producer's first choice to play Quarrel in *Dr. No*. But at a meeting in Eon's office, Broccoli was overruled by Saltzman who wanted John Kitzmiller instead. "When I left the office that day," Cameron recalls, "I met Sean Connery outside. I knew Sean quite well because I'd worked with his wife Diane Cilento and he said, 'Are you going to be in the film?' 'It doesn't look like it, this guy Saltzman is very tricky,' I said. 'Yeah, tell me about it,' he said. 'How about yourself?' I asked Sean. 'I'm not sure.' So even Sean hadn't been signed yet. He was still waiting. This was early days."

On *Thunderball*, Broccoli saw to it that he finally did cast Cameron in a Bond and the actor was only too happy to fly out to the Bahamas and enjoyed the filming immensely. "There was a wonderful atmosphere, lots of parties. I was staying at the Nassau Beach Hotel and I remember one day I was on the beach and the second assistant came and said, 'Earl, I'm sorry, we're going to need you.' I said. 'Oh shit. Come on, man.' I was joking, but that's the way it was, it was a very glamourous production. But to tell you the truth I never took the part of Pinder seriously, because at the time I was getting some very good roles, and this was a very small part. But the idea of going to the Bahamas was a big temptation. I was seven weeks in Nassau. And I spent the best part of the time on the beach!"

Happy to be part of a Bond movie, Cameron hadn't realised just how huge they were until he finished his role and went to work on an American TV series also shooting at Pinewood. "And the guys playing the lead roles, who were very well known actors, they were all wide-eyed. They said, 'Come on, tell us what was Connery like.' They wanted to know everything about him, almost what kind of toothpaste he used. The Bonds were huge in the States."

Occupying another small role as one of Largo's henchmen, was veteran Bond stunt man George Leech. When Bob Simmons contacted him to work on *Thunderball* Leech was working on a film in Ireland. "I was choreographing a fight that took place in this freezing cold barn that had about three feet of water in it. Bob phoned me up and said, would you like to join us in the Bahamas. And I said, yes! So from freezing Ireland in a dirty old barn I was off to luxury on the sandy beaches of Nassau."

Leech is one of the unsung heroes of the early Bond movies and one of the few surviving links to the very first 007 epic *Dr. No*, in which he doubled Connery in the climactic fight in the reactor pool. Since then he's probably met his demise more times in Bond movies than any other stunt man. "In *Thunderball* I was cast as a radio operator on the Disco Volante and was killed by Connery. I was shot from the balcony of Fort Knox in *Goldfinger*. I was killed with a star dagger thrown by Connery in the volcano for *You Only Live Twice*. I was twice killed by Lazenby in *On Her Majesty's Secret Service*, once as a lab technician and then strangled as a skier. With Jaws I was dropped through the roof of a house in a car in *The Spy Who Loved Me*. And doubling Mr. Kidd in *Diamonds Are Forever* I was set on fire by Connery."

Those are the dirty and dangerous jobs that stunt men day in, day out are asked to perform. But the stunt business has its glamourous side too. One day on *Thunderball*, Bob Simmons had to double Connery being airlifted to safety. He was stuck in a dank and smelly cave, dressed in scuba gear with sweat pouring out of him under the tropical sun as the cameras took hours to set up. On stand-by in case of emergency was Leech and another stunt man. "And we were standing by on a luxury yacht sitting in the sunshine drinking gin and tonic and saying, 'Oh that poor sod. Look at Bobby.' And Bob was the top stunt man at the time, but he was sitting in amongst all that shit while we were living it up like two millionaires. So that's the good side of the business."

And then the crew upped and left paradise, leaving lasting memories upon those that had been there those few months. "Because I think Harry and Cubby knew *Thunderball* was going to be a success, there was no tension on the set, ever," Recalls Luciana. "You know sometimes when you work on a movie and the producers get upset because there is waste of time because something doesn't go right. We were in the Bahamas and huge clouds would sometimes obscure the sun and it didn't match the shot before so we had to sit and wait. Usually the producers are jumping up and down and looking at their watch. Nothing like that with Harry and Cubby. Truly it was the easiest and the most fun movie I've ever made."

McClory's very own Bond-like gadget, a water-borne car

CHAPTER 31
BACK TO PINEWOOD

The crew returned to Pinewood in May to finish the remaining interiors, including the frenzied climactic fist-fight aboard the Disco Volante, a partial replica of which had been built in the studio. An early Maibaum script called for Bond to gain access to the escaping hydrofoil from a pursuing hovercraft and then for scientist Kutze, once Bond and Domino have escaped, to destroy the ship by detonating the fuel tanks. The film was also to have ended with a neat gag as the credits rolled. The ransom is dropped by plane and the package sinks to the seabed where it is intercepted by a two-man SPECTRE sub. As the mechanical arm extends to grab the package – boom.

Also built at Pinewood were the two sets featured in the film that allowed Ken Adam to truly express himself, although not to degree he'd done on say *Goldfinger*. The first, SPECTRE's menacing headquarters, has become something of an iconic set. Adam explains the thinking behind it. "That came about because by this time I was getting fed up with board rooms. I'd done so many I thought what could I do? So I wanted to come up with something else. I decided I was going to do away with the boardroom table and each chair would have its own console. And I don't know whether it was myself or Terence who came up with the idea that the villain is electrocuted and disappears in the floor and the chair comes up empty. I think it probably was me because I have a quirky sense of humour in a way and I thought it would be funny. And it appealed to the American sense of humour enormously."

Another big set was the 00 briefing room. Here Adam took a straightforward, ornate room and went into Bond overdrive using absurdly large tapestries that slid upwards to reveal gargantuan wall maps. Today such an effect would be accomplished within hours by computer; then it was done for real. "There I decided, my God, think big. And I was very fortunate that I knew this great scenic artist called Ferdinand Bellan, who was brought over by the Kordas in pre-war days. He was a brilliant Hungarian scenic painter. I can't remember the exact dimensions, but probably those tapestries were about 50 or 60 feet by 40 feet. They were enormous. I found a little mediaeval tapestry and Ferdi copied and painted it. So when you have people like that, who are geniuses in their own way, you can try those things."

Back from the Bahamas the congenial atmosphere of filming in the tropics was certainly transplanted to London. After all, this was the swinging sixties and there were showbiz parties aplenty for the cast to enjoy. "Somebody had a flat near the Dorchester hotel and there used to be a number of supper parties," Mollie Peters recalls. "And I'd go along and Sean would be there, Michael Caine would be there, Claudine, Martine, Luciana, Harry, Cubby and Terence, of course. That was great. And I must be the only girl that didn't go out with Michael Caine in the 60s. He actually did ask me. He rang up and said, 'Put on something uncomfortable and come out with me.' And I said no."

Mollie didn't see Connery again after her scenes wrapped until Terence Young's memorial service in London some 30 years later. "But I didn't push through the crowd of guests to go and see him. I didn't think it was appropriate. Then I wrote to him telling him I didn't have any mementoes of us from *Thunderball* and he sent me two signed photographs back. Sean is a man I have great respect for."

Unlike Richard Jenkins, who worked with Connery on three Bonds and on other occasions, "we got on OK, but I never particularly liked him. In truth, I've never really liked actors at all. They're exceedingly self-centred; from how do they look, to how they're feeling. And Sean was not a generous man at all. I bought him drinks; he never bought me a drink because he's an actor so he doesn't want to spoil the line of his trousers by having money. But as an actor in that part, he was absolutely terrific, absolutely right for it."

Just before cameras stopped rolling on *Thunderball,* one of the film's most complex stunts was filmed – Bond's close encounter with Fiona's rocket-firing motorbike. Leaving Shrublands, Bond is followed by a revenge-seeking Count Lippe. But it's Lippe who becomes the hunted; as punishment for a botched assassination attempt on Bond, his own car is blown apart. Maibaum originally intended Fiona's bike not to fire rockets but to have a flame-thrower mounted on it. "A long jet-like burst of flame licks out from motorcycle and hits Lippe's car near gas tank... immediate explosion."

Due to the obvious danger inherent in the sequence it was impossible to shoot on a public highway so Silverstone was used, its famous racetrack "dressed" to appear as a motorway. But look carefully, in widescreen prints you can just make out a public grandstand in the distance. The motorbike used was a 120mph BSA Lightning, the most powerful model in the BSA range. Although not performing any stunts, Luciana Paluzzi was still taught how to ride the bike and revving up the engine during one test run lost control and smashed into a wall. Fortunately because of her skintight leather outfit she didn't suffer any serious injury.

It was left to Bert Luxford to modify the bike to Bond standards, while John Stears designed and installed the pyrotechnics, four Icarus rockets adapted to explode on impact, and very real! Two contained napalm, the other two ordinary black powder.

George Leech drove the Aston, while Bob Simmons took charge of Lippe's car, a Ford Skyliner. It nearly resulted in Simmon's death. The bike was to come up behind the Ford and blast it off the road. Although the rockets were real they could not be guaranteed to create a big enough explosion, so Simmons filled the boot of the car with five-gallon drums of gasoline wrapped in cordite which he could detonate at the right moment. Apart from protective clothing the only thing that separated Simmons from the resulting fireball was a sheet of Plexiglass. The driver's door was removed in case a quick exit was necessary.

With the fire brigade and an ambulance standing by, Terence Young called action. Leech took the Aston up to 30mph, with Simmons following behind. When the bike passed a predetermined point on the track the stunt rider triggered the missiles and Simmons set off the petrol in the boot demolishing the back of the car. The timing was perfect. But because of poor light the whole thing had to be filmed again the next day. Luckily, Stears had rigged a spare Ford. This time not everything went to plan. The rockets hit the Ford and the explosives went off, but Simmons suddenly became aware of thick black smoke and flame filling the car. The glass shield had failed. With his clothing already on fire Simmons rolled clear of the car, unseen by the rest of the crew. The car came to a rest with Lippe's dummy in the driving seat. The crew, including Young, thought the dummy was Simmons, still trapped inside and

Chapter 31: BACK TO PINEWOOD

being burnt alive. Realising what was happening Simmons softly crept up behind Young. "How was that Terence, alright?" Young spun around, a look of complete amazement on his face. "You bastard," he said, with feeling. "I thought you were dead."

Simmons himself later testified that the car stunt from *Thunderball* was one of the most dangerous he ever tackled. Yet he carried it off with a mixture of total professionalism and style that so characterised the man. "Bob was an extrovert and he loved his wine, women and song," says George Leech. "He spent all his money on booze and women. At the time he was the top stunt man, but he always had to fill himself up with whisky. That went on for years and finally it told on him. The drink finally crippled him. He just couldn't think clearly any more. It was so sad."

HARRY SALTZMAN AND ALBERT R. BROCCOLI PRESENT

SEAN CONNERY AS JAMES BOND 007 IN IAN FLEMING'S

THUNDERBALL

PRODUCED BY KEVIN McCLORY
DIRECTED BY TERENCE YOUNG

PANAVISION ® A UNITED ARTISTS RELEASE TECHNICOLOR ®

PUBLICITY OFFICES   27 HILL STREET LONDON W 1 ENGLAND   HYDE PARK 9011

CHAPTER 32
LAST MINUTE TINKERING

With *Thunderball* now in post-production, composer John Barry was brought back to hopefully emulate his blockbuster soundtrack for *Goldfinger*, which in America even knocked The Beatles off the No.1 slot on the album charts. With the film set for a December opening, record retailers demanded the LP be in stores prior to the Christmas season, resulting in an incredibly tight recording schedule. Amazingly Barry was still in the studio working when the soundtrack album was released, with the effect that it featured virtually no music from the second half of the movie. Barry and Bond fans had to wait over three decades for the complete soundtrack to finally become available.

There were problems with the theme song, too. Shirley Bassey's rendition of *Goldfinger* had established the formula of opening each Bond with a classic song belted out by a famous singer. Just how was Barry going to top a huge international hit? Believing in the maxim, "if it ain't broke, don't fix it," Shirley Bassey was once again hired. But Barry hated the title, *Thunderball*; what the hell did it mean? Flying from London to LA he read in some magazine that the Italian's nickname for Bond was Mr. Kiss Kiss Bang Bang. What a great title! Teaming up with lyricist Leslie Bricusse a dynamic song was created, two versions of which were recorded, one by Bassey and another by soul diva Dionne Warwick. Then just weeks before *Thunderball* was due to open, United Artists got nervous about a theme tune that didn't mention the film's title. A last minute replacement was sought. With Bricusse now tied-up writing for *Dr. Doolittle*, Barry got in Don Black as lyricist and a brand new song was forged. Tom Jones, who'd only recently burst onto the pop scene with his hit "It's Not Unusual" was asked to record the song. Famously, the strain of hitting and holding the final note almost caused the welsh superstar to pass out in the studio. The song made it to No.25 on the US billboard charts, a disappointment after *Goldfinger*'s No.8 position. More disappointingly, the song only reached No 35 in the UK. But the song remains a staple part of any Tom Jones concert.

Complementing Tom Jones' vocal on *Thunderball* is a dazzling title sequence from Maurice Binder, who after creating the legendary gun barrel opening shot and *Dr. No*'s hypnotic credits had been missing from the next two Bonds. Inspired by the film's underwater theme and remembering a woman he saw swimming in a tank above a bar in a Soho night club, Binder set about filming the raciest titles yet seen on cinema screens. Too provocative for the Spanish censors, as it happened, who excised most of the titillating bits. Shot in a studio tank at Pinewood, Binder persuaded three girls who'd previously swum in night-club tanks to strip naked and be photographed in black and white on a clear background. A deep blue colour was later added as an optical effect and the result is stunning. Binder's use of silhouette nudes and wild colours was a pattern that remained virtually unchanged for the remainder of the Bond titles he worked on till his death.

Binder's famous gun barrel sequence was also filmed again because of *Thunderball* being the first Bond film made in the Panavision widescreen process. The original walk, turn and fire at the camera for *Dr. No* was actually performed by Bob Simmons, not Connery. It was then reused on the subsequent two Bonds. So it's on *Thunderball* where Connery for the first time performs the famous gun barrel walk.

Other more substantial tinkering was needed when it became apparent that both Adolfo Celi and Claudine Auger's entire vocal performance would have to be dubbed. Robert Rietty (who later appeared as the Italian minister in *Never Say Never Again*) was hired to re-voice Celi, while actress Nikki van der Zyl came in to do Claudine. Nikki already had an association with the Bond films, having dubbed Ursula Andress in *Dr. No*. Amazingly the producers had considered Ursulas's voice not sexy enough! "She's a sexy looking woman," says Nikki. "But her voice actually didn't match the face, it's strange to say. It wasn't a sexual voice." Then, having narrowly lost out on the role of Tatiana to Daniela Bianchi in *From Russia with Love*, Nikki was next employed on *Goldfinger* as Gert Frobe's vocal coach. On the set Nikki got to know Connery well. "Sean's a very down to earth, very straight person. I remember from conversations I had with him that he didn't like all the paraphernalia of being James Bond and the fact that he had to wear a toupee. 'Why do I have to wear a piece,' he'd complain. This was Sean and that's why he endeared himself to me. Terence Young, I always found very aloof. I asked him for a small part in *Dr. No* and he said something not too friendly about my looks and Sean was there and looked at me and said, 'Well Nikki darling, I'd stop the traffic for you any day of the week.' Which was so sweet. He was such a lovable fellow. I was very fond of Sean."

Testament to Nikki's creative gift is that you'd never guess it wasn't Ursula speaking in *Dr. No* or Claudine in *Thunderball*. "But I made no money on those films," Nikki criticises. "They paid £50 a session and I usually managed to get it done in two sessions and that was it. I think I did Claudine's voice in a day. And I was paid pretty much the same amount on *Thunderball* as I was on *Dr. No*. I think that was unfair because by the time of *Thunderball* they knew they had a massive success on their hands. What they should have done was to offer people like myself a fair price for the job we were doing, which was half the performance of the artist. Certainly I think we helped to make the films the success they were."

Nikki became the queen of dubbing in the 60s, re-voicing Raquel Welch's grunts in *One Million Years BC*, Mie Hama in *You Only Live Twice* and Ursula Andress in both *Casino Royale* and *She*. But the fact that their voices had been dubbed was usually kept from the stars and performers like Nikki were sworn to secrecy. As a result Nikki has received little acclaim for her admittedly small, but significant, contribution to the Bond legend. "It's not just that you're not credited, but you're not paid anything either and that's unfair. Of course Broccoli and Saltzman were businessmen, they were in it for the money, but even businessmen should have ethics. If it was me I couldn't sleep at night knowing I'd made a whole lot of money on the back of somebody who was poor."

As *Thunderball* entered the final stages of post-production, Terence Young, who'd grown disenchanted with the film during the final weeks of shooting, left never to return to work for Broccoli or Saltzman again. *Thunderball* was his swansong as a Bond director. More than most Young had originated the style of the series and played a significant role in moulding Connery into the character of Bond. Many saw him as a Bond-like figure himself. "Terence had all the class and the mystery and the charm of James Bond," Says Luciana. "He probably would have made a great James Bond himself. Although physically he was maybe not as handsome as Sean was, but he had all the finesse and the humour of Bond. And he was bigger than life."

Chapter 32: LAST MINUTE TINKERING

For years, Young noted with pride that he not only directed the first Bond film (*Dr. No*), but also the best (*From Russia with Love*) and the most successful (*Thunderball*). When asked if he would ever consider returning, Young's answer was always the same, only if it was to direct the last ever Bond picture. But 007 outlived him. Young died in 1994.

With Young gone, the task of editing the mammoth film into a workable length was left in the more than capable hands of Peter Hunt. "There you are dear boy. Get on with it," Young had told him. Hunt had contributed greatly to the visual style and pacing of the early Bond films and later graduated to director with 1969s *On Her Majesty's Secret Service*. Although it doesn't have the lean narrative of *Goldfinger* or the taught suspense of *From Russia with Love* due to its sprawling *mise en scene*, Hunt did a spectacular job of keeping *Thunderball* moving along at a walloping pace. Inevitably some scenes ended up on the cutting room floor; Largo giving 007 a guided tour round the Disco Volante and the moment when Bond and Domino meet underwater and disappear behind a large rock for a spot of necking. A mass of bubbles is seen which was to have been followed by Domino's bikini top floating to the surface, but it was deemed too suggestive and cut.

Thunderball hits Oxford Street – one of the underwater props goes on display in a leading department store.

CHAPTER 33
THUNDERBALL UNLEASHED

Thunderball wasn't just a movie; it was an event - one of the most heavily promoted and anticipated films of the decade. With Bond now the pop culture icon of the age it wasn't surprising that in the months leading up to release he graced the covers of the world's biggest magazines - Life, Saturday Evening Post, Esquire and Playboy. While on US television, an hour-long special was devoted to him. Entitled *The Incredible World of James Bond*, it aired on NBC on 26 November and was the highest rated programme of the week. Connery declined a lucrative offer to host the show. Hollywood legend Joan Crawford, who was a board member at Pepsi, the show's sponsor, personally pleaded with him to change his mind, but to no avail.

Bond merchandise too was flooding the market, reaching a peak by Christmas that would never be equalled. It was estimated that the Licensing Corporation of America put out $250m worth of merchandising for *Thunderball*. The public's appetite for all things Bond was now insatiable. Far from being a licence to kill, 007 was more a licence to print money and global manufacturers fell over themselves to tie their products in with the Bond image. But Connery wasn't too enamoured of seeing his face flogging everything from bubble gum to dressing gowns. "The whole thing has become a Frankenstein's monster," he ranted. "The merchandising, the promotion, the pirating – they're thoroughly distasteful. It's a lot of rubbish!" Sour grapes perhaps, as he didn't receive a penny out of any of it.

Honouring an earlier pledge by Broccoli and Saltzman, *Thunderball* was shown publicly for the first time in Nassau. Ricou Browning remembers going to see it on McClory's invitation. It was the first time he'd seen the completed movie. "I was thrilled. I thought it was so well done and marvellously put together. I thought, this is going to be a hit. I was very proud to be a part of it." Days later the world premiere took place in New York on 21 December. From late November onwards Manhattan's Paramount Theatre had erected a special booth that showed the trailer for fans who gathered outside. For the premiere itself, the jet pack was launched from the Paramount's marquee on Broadway to the street below, whereupon the pilot and United Artist's publicists were met by police offers and arrested for staging the stunt without a licence.

Demand for the British opening on 29 December was so massive that it was decided to hold two premieres simultaneously, one at the London Pavilion in Piccadilly and the other at the Rialto just 100 yards away. Guests at the Pavilion included Claudine Auger, Luciana Paluzzi and Adolfo Celi, along with *Goldfinger* duo Honor Blackman and Tania Mallet. "The amount of people that were gathered outside the cinema was astounding," Luciana remembers. "The whole of Piccadilly Circus was closed to traffic. I've never seen so many people in my life. It was really sensational."

Meanwhile crowds at the Rialto saw Martine Beswick, Guy Doleman and Mollie Peters, who was overwhelmed when she first saw the picture. "I couldn't really take it all in, that that was me up there on the screen. As time has gone by, and seeing it many times since, I realise that *Thunderball*, apart from perhaps being a little bit long with some of the underwater stuff, was a very good film. It's put together well; it's not too gimmicky. There are characters that actually are characters and not just cut out cardboard. And it's very witty."

Adding to the glamour of the evening was the fact that many of the celebrities were chauffeur driven to the premiere from the "007 bar" at the Hilton Hotel in a fleet of, what else? Aston Martins! And the whole event finished with a plush supper dance at the Royal Garden Hotel in Kensington, which Mollie also remembers vividly. "There was a young singer there, Tom Jones, and he didn't really know anyone because he wasn't quite part of the film scene. And he spent most of the evening with my then husband, and myself I guess, because the guy was lonely. I'll always remember that. Later, of course, he became a world star."

But anyone expecting Sean Connery to turn up was gravely disappointed. He stayed at home, fed up with the Bond ballyhoo, and still having not forgotten what happened to him the previous year at the Paris premiere of *Goldfinger*. Driving an Aston Martin down the Champ's Elysee to the cinema as a publicity stunt a frenzied female fan jumped through the window and landed in his lap! Fans at the *Thunderball* premiere instead had to make do with life-size photos of the star, which were torn down from hoardings outside the London Pavilion. Strangely Harry Saltzman was also absent from the evening's festivities, as was Broccoli, understandably so as he was grieving the recent loss of his mother.

There was also a big premiere in Dublin, again attended by Mollie Peters. "And of course Kevin McClory was on his home ground there, and it was interesting to see people clamouring to *him*." It was very much a homecoming for the Irishman, the prodigal son returning a success, and with the world at his feet, seemingly. McClory's friend Jeremy Vaughan was invited too and remembers the occasion with humour. "Kevin gave me a small suite at the Gresham Hotel. And it was crazy. He told me I was going in car number two. I did what I was told and came down and got in this motorcade and we had to drive all the way up and down O'Connell Street to the cinema. But the cinema was next door to the bloody hotel! If you fell down outside the hotel you had your head in the cinema foyer. But no, we had to have this bloody motorcade. That's Kevin."

With the premieres over and done with, the critics pounced. Although it was only the fourth 007 epic, some were predicting the series had had its day. "There is a limit to the exploitation of any character or formula, and the Bond thrillers have just about reached that limit," warned the Financial Times critic, who nevertheless remained convinced the movie would make a fortune. "But the seeds of decay are already apparent in it. That *Thunderball* does in fact remain entertaining for a good deal of its length is due to some bright dialogue, crisp direction and to the ingenuity of the machinery. All the same there is no denying that there are glimpses of a Bond growing middle-aged and boring."

The Guardian expressed a similar view. "It is difficult to say for sure who killed James Bond, but one thing does seem clear – he is certainly dead." The blame for his demise rested on the plethora of gadgets and action set pieces. "The writers seem to have sat down, thought up a bundle of gimmicks – shark-filled swimming pools, electrified chairs etc – and then built the script around them." The New Statesman agreed. "The finest moments of *Thunderball* belong to the technicians rather than actors or writers." The Observer likened the new Bond to "a prodigious toyshop-cum-travel agency. The film is

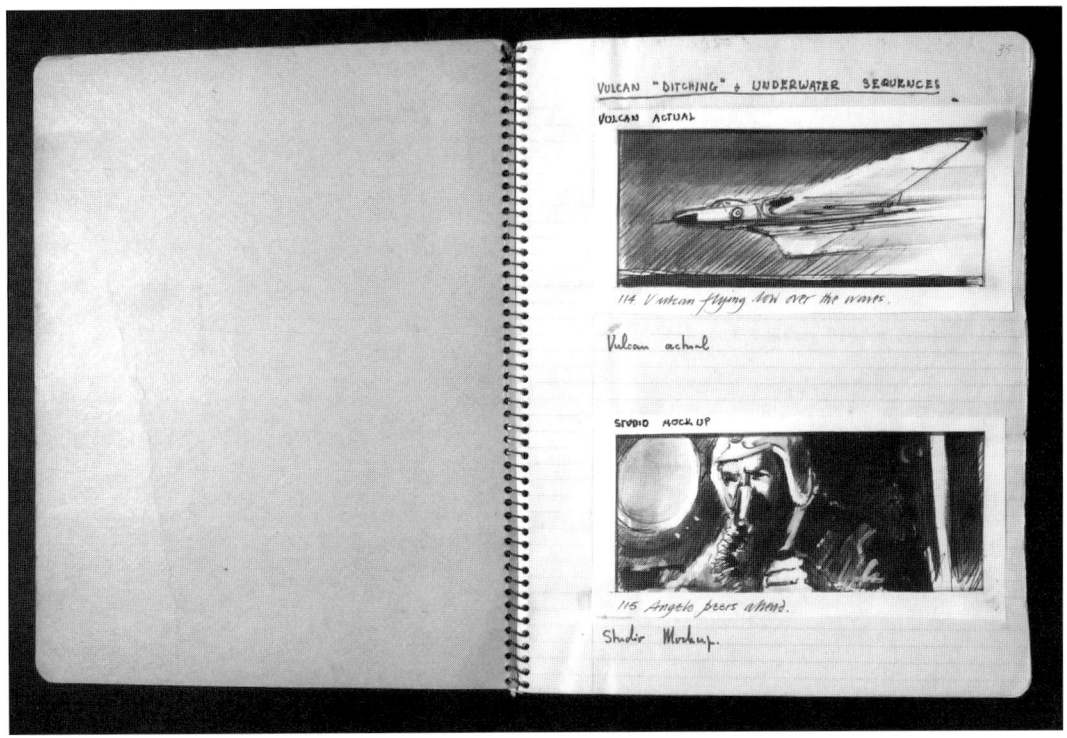

The storyboards for the Vulcan 'ditching' and other underwater sequences were pasted into this book and used by the filmmakers.

Left: McClory in the submerged Vulcan cockpit.

Above: Actress Anita Ekberg, wife of Rik Van Nutter (Felix Lieter) has a quiet meal with Connery on location.

140. A two man sub. accompanied by 4 swimmers

140. Swimming away - In B.G. 2 man sub arrives.

143b) Two men slide back hood and secure 1st bomb

The retrieval of the bombs from the ditched Vulcan by **SPECTRE** frogmen and the killing of Angelo by Largo are told in these original storyboards.

143c) Largo and men lower 2nd bomb.

139. As he appears above he offers Angelo a hand in a congratulatory gesture, and with the other draws a knife from his belt.

139a) and cuts Angelo's intake tube, watching him drown.

Above: Broccoli, Luciana Paluzzi and McClory enjoy an after-hours drink.

Below: Young and McClory work together in the water tank at Pinewood studios.

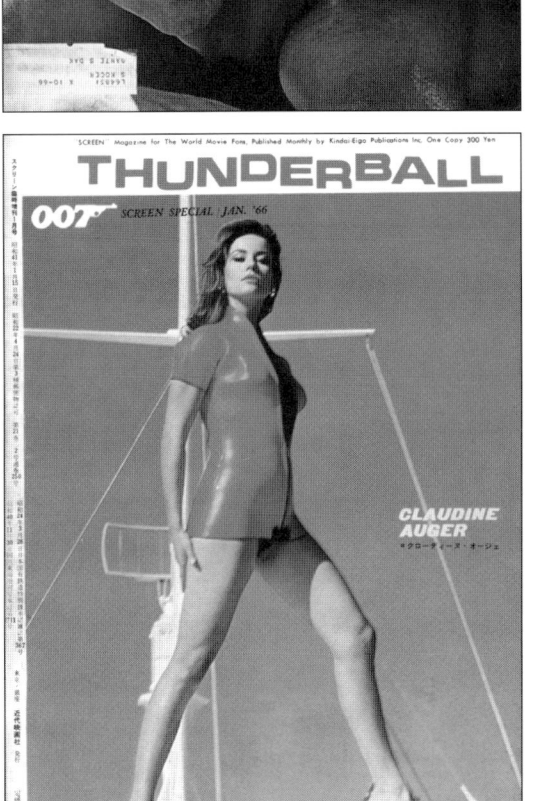

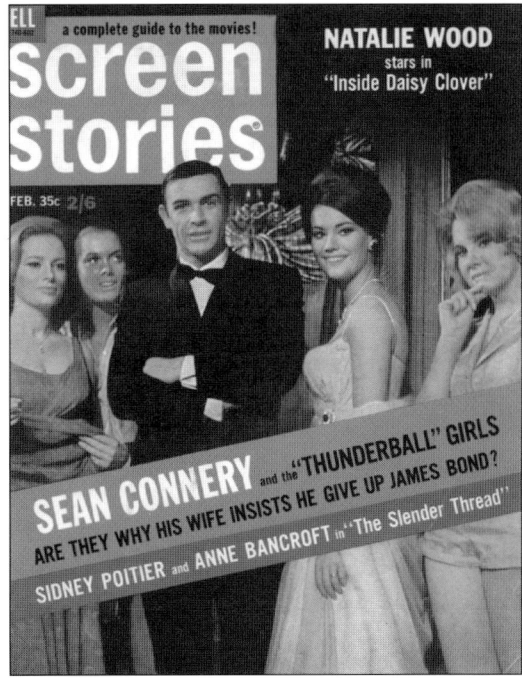

Thunderball makes the front pages of magazines around the world.

Above: Broccoli and other United Artists bigwigs attend a special advance showing of *Thunderball* in Tokyo.

Below: McClory and Broccoli are handsomely greeted when they arrive in Tokyo for a publicity tour for *Thunderball*.

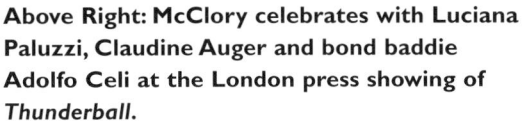

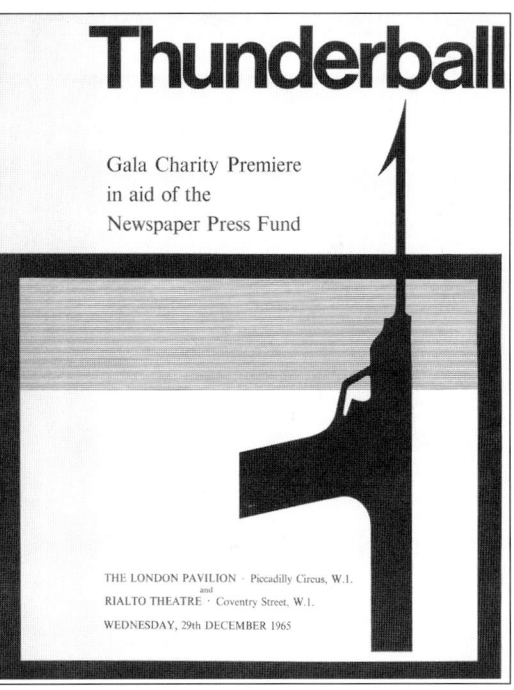

Above Right: McClory celebrates with Luciana Paluzzi, Claudine Auger and bond baddie Adolfo Celi at the London press showing of *Thunderball*.

Above Left: McClory and Broccoli at the Thunderball premiere. One gets the feeling that the two men really don't want to be in the same photograph.

Right: Whittingham's personal copy of the *Thunderball* premiere brochure.

Thunderball enjoyed a double premiere in London, showing at the London Pavilion and the nearby Rialto in Piccadilly Circus.

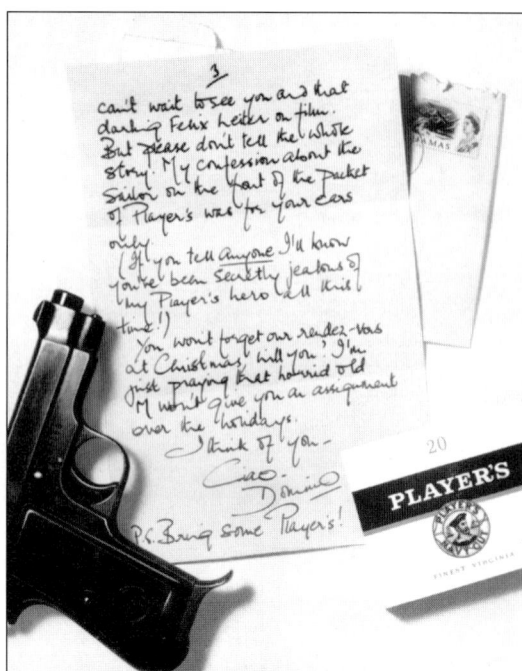

Two 007-related advertisements from the premiere brochure.

Thunderball

SUPPER DANCE

ROYAL GARDEN HOTEL
Kensington W 8

following the
gala premiere at the London Pavilion,
on the night of

Wednesday 29 December 1965

TABLE PLAN

Left: The post-premiere supper dance table plan.

Above: Claudine Auger and Young celebrate at the post *Thunderball* premiere party.

Above Left: Bobo, McClory and Luciana Paluzzi smile for the cameras after the triumphant opening night of *Thunderball*.

Above Right: The grand opening of *Thunderball* in Dublin.

Left: A proud McClory at the Dublin premiere poses for cameras.

"THUNDERBALL"
IS THE BIGGEST BOND OF ALL ✱
SHOWCASE THEATRES 1st SEVEN DAYS £96,303 †
(11 THEATRES)

THEATRES	GOLDFINGER	THUNDERBALL	THEATRES	GOLDFINGER	THUNDERBALL
BROMLEY ODEON	£5245	£6,606	NEW VICTORIA	£9004	£10,659
FINSBURY PARK ASTORIA	£6304 (6 DAYS ONLY)	£9,862	PURLEY ASTORIA	£4117	£5,526
HAMMERSMITH ODEON	£10127	£13,510	STREATHAM ODEON	£7165	£9,146
ILFORD ODEON	£6470	£8,575	WATFORD ODEON	£4704	£6,302
KINGSTON GRANADA	£5850	£8,009	† Includes **LONDON PAVILION** (1186 seats) **£11,986** & **RIALTO** (570 seats) **£6,122**		

✱ EVERYWHERE—'THUNDERBALL' IS ON ITS WAY TO BECOMING THE BIGGEST GROSSING ENTERTAINMENT IN FILM HISTORY!

ALL HOUSE RECORDS BROKEN IN EVERY SITUATION!

UNITED ARTISTS

THE NEXT JAMES BOND - 'YOU ONLY LIVE TWICE'

Trade paper announcement of *Thunderball*'s record breaking first week in London cinemas.

Connery, Len Deighton and McClory at the Irishman's home during their collaboration on the ill-fated Bond script 'James Bond of the Secret Service' later re-titled *Warhead*.

Above: Connery and *Never Say Never Again* producer Jack Schwartzman. The two men had a frosty relationship.

Right: Royal charity premiere brochure.

ROYAL CHARITY PREMIERE
in the presence of
HIS ROYAL HIGHNESS PRINCE ANDREW

To Aid
The Variety Club of Great Britain,
London Federation of Boys' Clubs
and
Bowles Outdoor Pursuits Centre

NEVER SAY NEVER AGAIN

at the Warner Theatre
Leicester Square,
Wednesday, December 14th
1983

Above: Sheet music for Sylvan's debut single.

Below: Publicity image for Sylvan's break into the pop world.

Top: Jack Whittingham congratulates his daughter on the start of her singing career.

Bottom: Sylvan and Englebert Humperdinck at a 60s pop function.

Above: In the recording studio with Morecombe and Wise.

Above Right: Sylvan at Kinfauns, the house she bought from George Harrison in 1969.

Centre Right: Peter Carter-Ruck at work at Sylvan's house one month before his death in November 2003.

Below: During her Wimbledon days as an official photographer, Sylvan poses with Bond might have been Cary Grant.

Above Left: Sylvan today. **Above Right:** Shortly before his death Peter Carter-Ruck enjoys a day apple picking in 2003 with Sylvan, her daughter Aimi and granddaughter Mia. *(Photo Massimo Nicastro)*

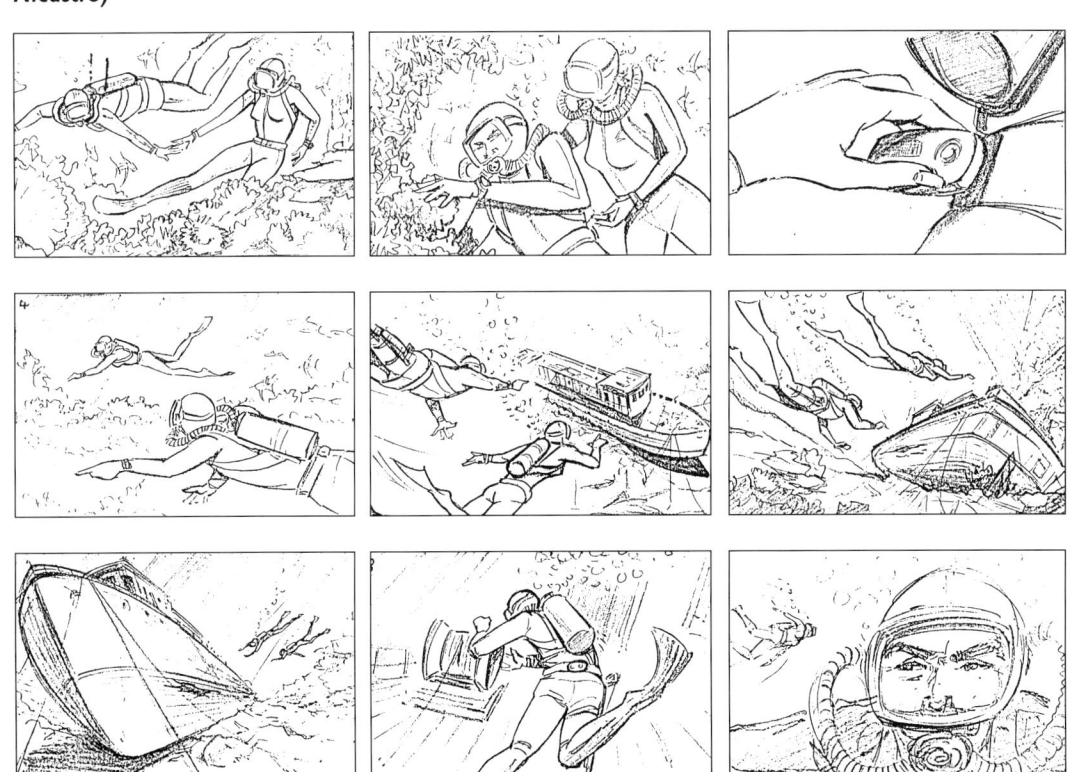

Storyboards for *Never Say Never Again* **showing the shipwreck shark attack on Bond.**

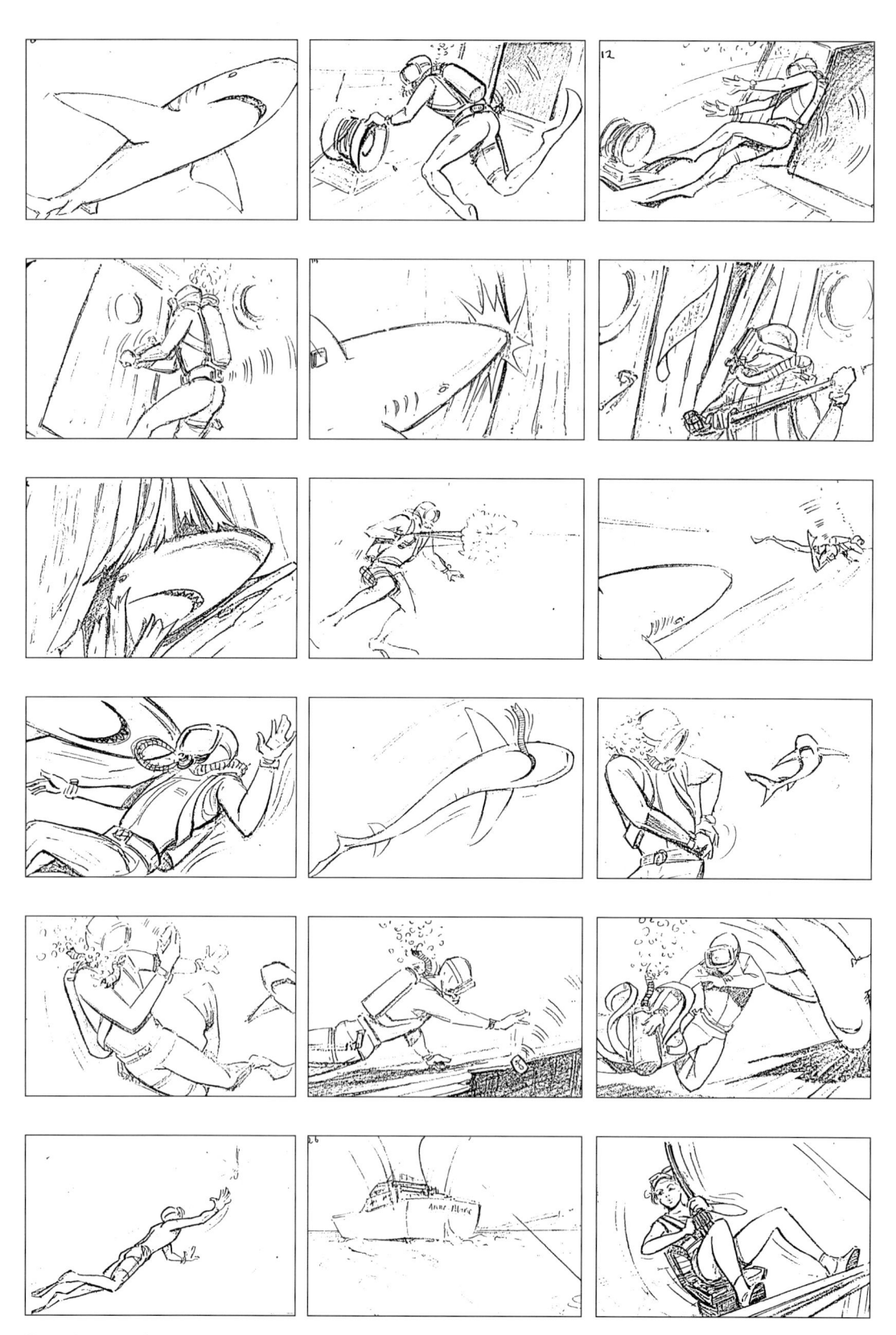

Storyboards for *Never Say Never Again* showing the shipwreck shark attack on Bond.

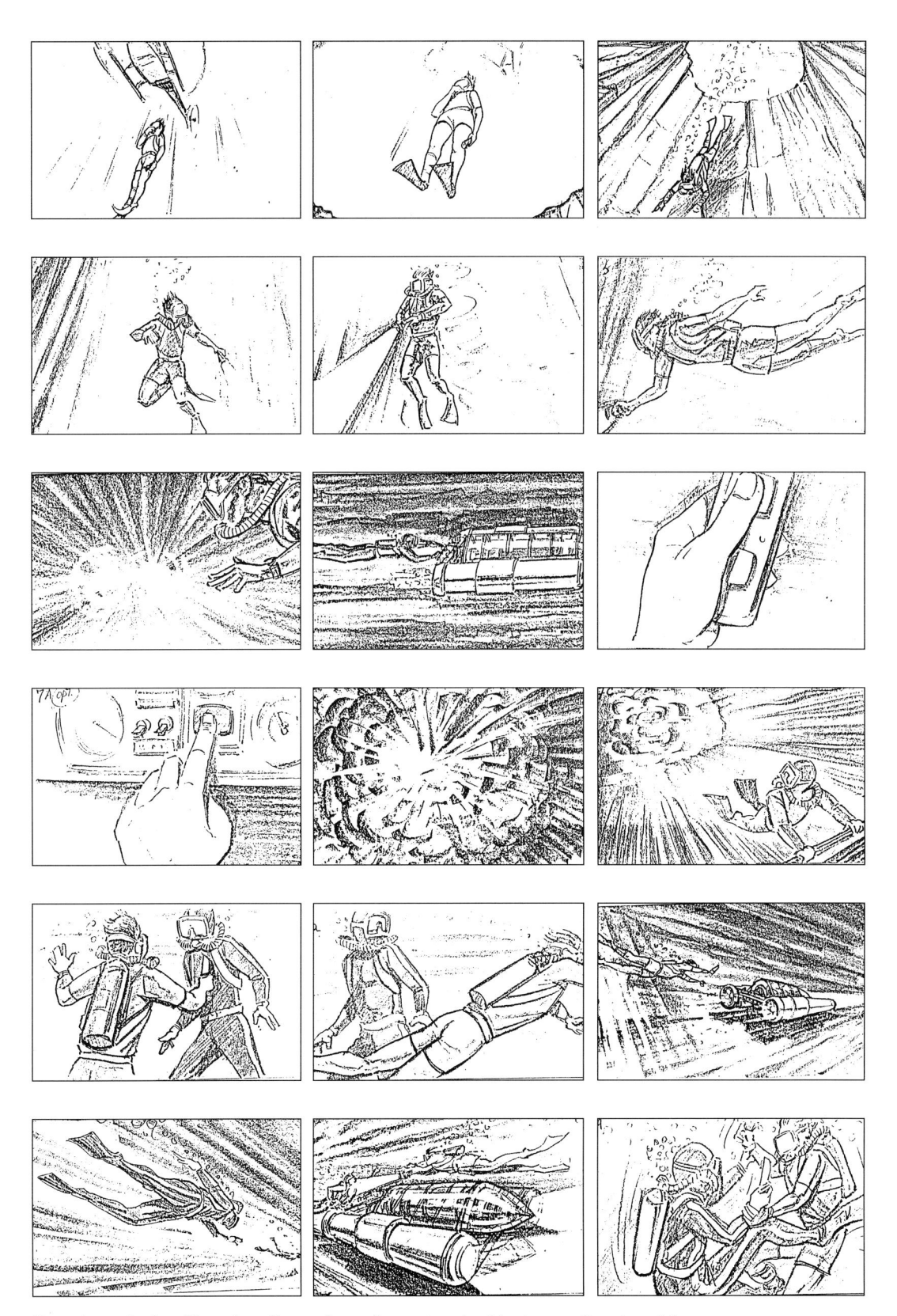

Storyboards detailing the climactic underwater duel between Bond and Largo.

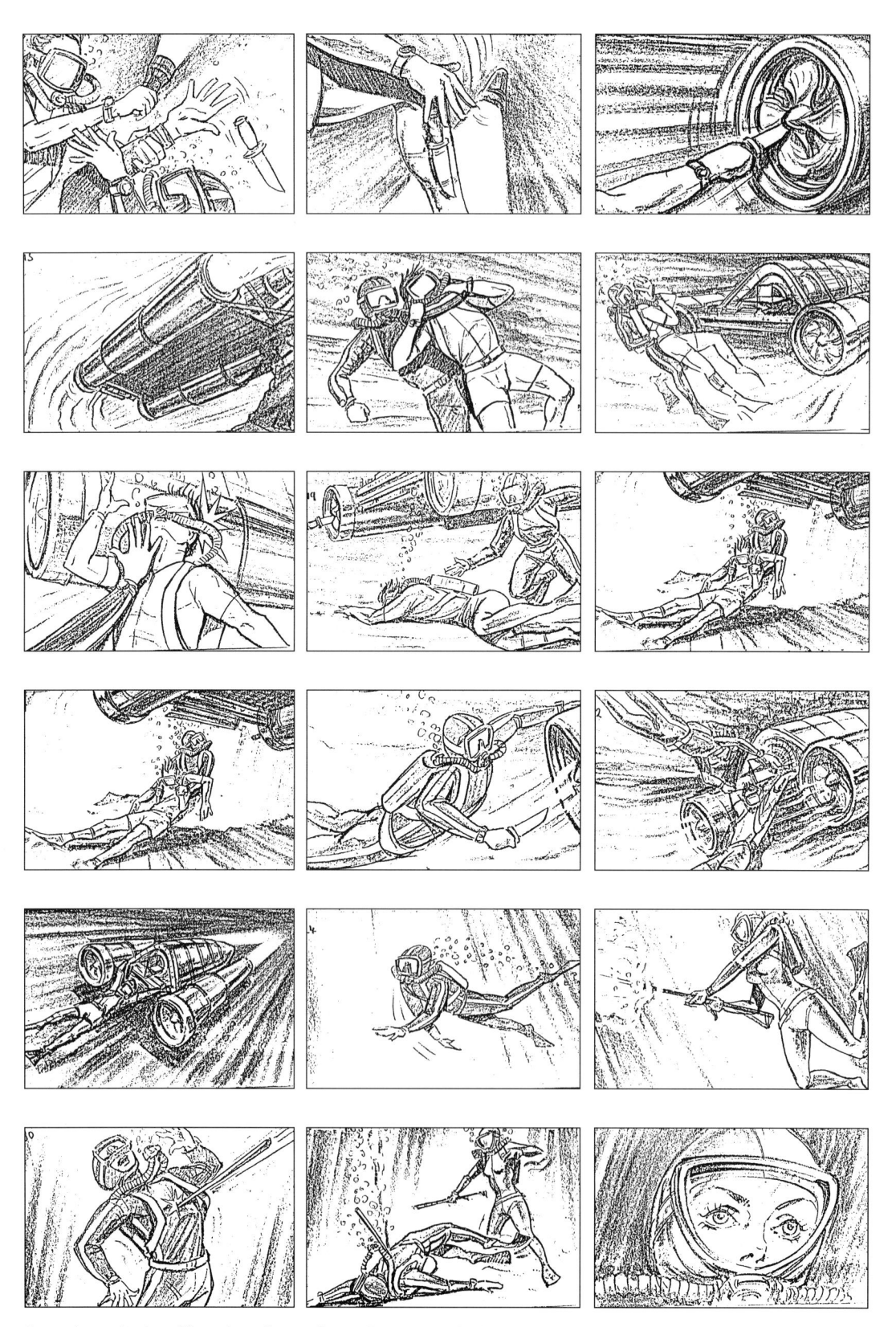

Storyboards detailing the climactic underwater duel between Bond and Largo.

Chapter 33: THUNDERBALL UNLEASHED

always jolly to watch but the toys have clearly taken over. Terence Young is the director who presides over the dissolution of his empire."

Others weren't impressed either. "Compared with *Goldfinger*, when the timing was perfect, *Thunderball*, though plushy and elaborate as ever, is slowish, stodgy stuff," was The Spectator's assessment, while The Times offered. "*Thunderball* does show alarming signs that the series is going to seed. Unless things pick up somewhat it will take more than a one-man jet pack to extract Bond with equal popular success from his next assignment." Films and Filming were to find fault in the overly long underwater scenes "which gives the impression of being a Robin Hood adventure in slow motion. Acknowledgement for these goes to Ivan Tors' studio, a pity Flipper wasn't included." As for the critic of the Sunday Telegraph, he found no story in *Thunderball*: "just a string of novelties briskly directed by Terence Young." Hardest of all was the critic from the Daily Sketch who found it, "faintly nauseating. It's a film full of arrogant wish-fulfilment – but without an atom of real satisfaction. Surely this must be the limit to merriment from mayhem."

But best of all was this roasting from guest critic David Sylvester in Harper's and Queen: "One of the attractive things about the Fleming books is that, however preposterous the story may be, it's told with a straight face. The books appeal to the fifteen year old in us; this film might be ideal for an audience of nine year old psychopaths."

But there were exceptions to the general negative press. "Laughter and thrills have never been so brilliantly combined," raved the Sunday Express. "Far and away the best bit of Bondery yet." In the deadpan presence of Connery, the News of the World felt Bond had "become the cinema's greatest folklore hero with the key to a bumper fun-book of escapism."

Significantly two of the leading film critics of the day were also impressed. Dilys Powell, writing in The Sunday Times complained that the film was largely over the top but, "In over two hours *Thunderball* includes not a minute's boredom. The cinema was a duller place before 007." And there was fulsome praise from The Evening Standard's Alexander Walker who called the film "The unbelievable ultimate in spectacle." Though his review did include words of caution: "Broccoli and Saltzman have given 007's adventures the extravagance and velocity of a comic strip and the only alarm may be whether they have overdone it."

As for Connery, he won some of his best notices ever for Bond. This from The Daily Mirror: "Connery is better than ever – a maturer, more self-assured hero who wears the role like a glove. A mink one." While no fan of the film itself, The Times had to admit that Connery, "as usual, presides with unshakeable confidence over the whole proceedings."

Critically, *Thunderball* fared better in the States. The New York Times raved, "The best of the lot. Connery is at his peak of coolness and nonchalance." The paper even named *Thunderball* among the ten best films of the year, along with more "revered" works like *The Pawnbroker* and *Kwaidan*. As for Time magazine, it could have been summing up the entire Bond canon when it said "*Thunderball* spreads a treasury of wish-fulfilling fantasy over a nickel's worth of plot."

When *Thunderball* opened around the UK at the beginning of January it played to capacity houses everywhere, breaking records with comparative ease. In some cinemas, tickets were even issued to customers willing to stand for sold out performances. In all over 15 million people went to see it upon first release, making *Thunderball* the 18th most successful film ever shown in the UK, according to the British Film Institute.

Richard Jenkins recalls seeing the film in Notting Hill with his wife and some friends: "I was standing in the queue and I said to them, 'Do you know that Sean Connery never wears underpants?' And the whole queue went quiet. But it was true; he never wore underpants for the films. It was in order not to spoil the line of his trousers. And I think that away from films he didn't wear them either. I guess like a Scotsman not wearing anything under his kilt."

Today it's difficult to comprehend the impact *Thunderball* had on world audiences. But Adolfo Celi, speaking to American 007 fanzine Bondage, summed it up impressively: "When I have been shooting films in the most god forsaken places of Africa or Asia, where nothing arrived from the western world, not even the word 'Jesus' or 'Mohammed.' But James Bond was regularly present. It was present everywhere. I've been welcomed with feasts in forlorn villages of Africa, where they had never seen or read anything, but where they had seen *Thunderball*."

Really *Thunderball* was the *Star Wars*, *Jurassic Park* and *Lord of the Rings* of its day. Records were smashed in every nation, where it played under some quite bizarre titles. *Calm Down, Mr Bond* in Holland; *Fireball* in Germany; *Operation Thunder* in France and Italy; *Agent 007 into the Fire* in Denmark; and in Japan – *Thunderball Fighting*.

As for its popularity in the USA, no Bond has equalled it since. The Paramount in New York became one of many cinemas to show the film 24 hours a day, seven days a week to cope with the crowds. One theatre manager was even threatened with divorce because he couldn't leave his cinema for days on end. In America alone, an incredible 58 million people saw *Thunderball*, giving it a domestic gross of $63.6m. A respectable figure even today, back in 1965 that was a phenomenal sum and enough to ensure its entrance to the all-time box office top ten list along with the likes of *Gone with the Wind* and *The Sound of Music*. Even more impressive is when *Thunderball*'s 1965 American gross is inflation adjusted to 2006 dollars, then it's in the region of $459m, a figure only a handful of films have ever attained.

As *Thunderball* opened around the world, several of the cast enjoyed glamourous publicity junkets. What stays vividly in Mollie Peters' mind was a trip she made with Martine Beswick to a film festival in Brazil. "Myself and Martine became friends there and we've been friends ever since. We had a great deal of fun together in Brazil. But the thing that really hit me was coming out of the cinema - people surged forward to touch me. And I found that very difficult because I thought, why? Was it because I was blonde and attractive and represented something that they haven't got? I just couldn't understand it. I felt awful about it, in fact, because I'd seen orphan children sleeping rough on the beaches. I didn't flinch away, but I just inwardly felt this is wrong."

Unfortunately due to a wrangle with her modelling agency, Mollie wasn't able to exploit her Bond girl status to pursue an acting career and eventually retired from the business. Originally, Terence Young wanted to sign her to his own company, but soon after *Thunderball* he went to live in Europe to escape the tax man. Then the William Morris agency voiced an interest but Mollie's agent refused to let her go. Sadly once she'd finally battled to free herself all impetus was lost. But Mollie still has great memories. "Looking back now it's as though it was never me, it was another woman. But it was a fantastic thing to have done, to have experienced. Just to be caught up in such a phenomenon as Bond. That's my own bit of immortality. And the amazing thing is that even now, 40 years after, I'm still getting letters and requests for autographs. I just think that's amazing. After all this time you've only got to mention you were in a Bond film, or someone mentions that you were, because I don't talk about it very much at all, you get. 'What! You kissed Sean Connery?'"

For Earl Cameron, it's much the same. Despite the smallness of his role the actor is amazed that four decades on he still receives fan mail. "Three years ago I got a letter from a guy in Holland who was coming to London and wanted to meet me and have an autograph and a picture taken. I thought, why not, I'm an easy sort of guy. So we made the arrangements and I went to his hotel and during coffee he introduced me to this guy from America. And it seemed to me that he'd told the guy from America that I was going to be at this hotel at a certain time and he'd flown from Washington just to get my autograph! That's the way I saw it. It seems ridiculous. But it meant so much to both of them."

For Luciana Paluzzi, *Thunderball* meant much more than just a successful film, she met her second husband Michael Solomon because of it; a marriage still going strong. "Michael wanted so much to meet me because he saw the scene in *Thunderball* where I shoot the rockets from the motorbike and you don't know if it's a man or a woman and then I get off the bike and pull the helmet off. Michael said, 'oh my God, this is the woman for me.'"

It's a testament to the skill of everybody involved in *Thunderball* that 40 years on, the film still works and is the least dated of the 60s Bond movies. It's particularly impressive on the big screen. Like

Chapter 33: THUNDERBALL UNLEASHED

Lawrence of Arabia, *Thunderball* was made for 70mm and can only be truly appreciated in a cinema; much of its epic sweep is dissipated on television. But not everyone looks back on it with artistic fondness. "If *Thunderball*'s on the telly I turn it off," says Richard Jenkins. "Looking at it now I'd think it was crap, I'm sure. The stories were ludicrous, but there was a certain chutzpah that made those early Bond films work."

What also makes the film a treat for Bond fans is that Connery is operating at the peak of his powers, turning in his best ever performance as 007. "By the time we did *Thunderball*, Sean *was* James Bond as no one else will ever be," Young later remarked. We also have the wittiest script ever written for a 007 movie and brilliant direction from Young, whose taste for brutal action, Hitchcockian atmosphere and glorious panache and style is displayed as never before. *Thunderball* struck the perfect balance between outlandish action and gadgets, humour, sex and the storytelling of Ian Fleming.

After the film's release, Connery remarked, "We have to be careful where we go next because I think with *Thunderball* we've reached the limit as far as size and gimmicks are concerned. What is needed now is a change of course, more attention to character and better dialogue." Oops, Connery certainly didn't get any character introspection with *You Only Live Twice*; just more of the same, only bigger. Young has admitted being partly at fault for heightening the importance of gadgets with *Thunderball*. "Sure, I contributed to the gadgetry that came in later. Why not admit it? I added to the decadence." His excuse was that he was powerless to stop it. It was a case of, if the producers want to flood the screen with underwater stuff, let's do it properly. "And they did," said Young. "They piled in as much as they could, but that's why I said after *Thunderball*. 'I think you don't want a director anymore, you want an MIT graduate to handle all the machines.'" If truth be told, it was really the public who came to demand more hi-tech hardware and gadgets with each successive Bond mission. "And I believe in giving the public what they want," said Young. "In a Bond film you aren't involved in *cinema verite* or *avant-garde*. One is involved in colossal fun."

And that's exactly what *Thunderball* was and few people reaped the benefits more than Kevin McClory. The personal fortune he made from the film is still unknown, but it was a phenomenal sum. "It's anybody's guess," says Jeremy Vaughan. "I think his cheques didn't bounce for quite a long time."

Then suddenly McClory disappeared from the public and showbiz radar, not emerging for another ten years. The story of Thunderball was really only just beginning.

WARHEAD

A KEVIN McCLORY PRODUCTION

CHAPTER 34
WARHEAD – THE BOND FILM THAT NEVER WAS

In the years following the release of *Thunderball* the world didn't hear very much of Kevin McClory. In truth, he was simply biding his time, waiting to strike. He returned to live in Ireland for a time and raised a family, did some farming, and bought a huge estate in County Kildare, Straffen House. The property was sold in 1988 for the highest price paid for an estate in Ireland. It became the K Club, the internationally renowned golf club where the 2006 Ryder Cup took place. The venue has since tripled in size since McClory's day.

Sadly, during this period his marriage to Bobo came to an end. "They had been married for quite some time," says Jeremy Vaughan. "I think she was besotted by Kevin because it took her a while to see through it all before she left him."

McClory ended up marrying the daughter of Vincent O'Brien, the racehorse trainer. "And that was a disaster," testifies Vaughan. "The girl was in tears most of the time she was involved with Kevin. I think he had the ability to be quite cruel. The O'Brien girl wasn't as strong a personality as Bobo was."

Vaughan was among many of McClory's old friends who lost contact with him during these "lost" years and never again resumed any sort of relationship afterwards. "The whole time that he spent in Ireland is shrouded in mystery," says Vaughan. "I have no information at all, but there were a lot of people in Ireland who were very suspicious of his activities and what he was doing with his money to fund things going on in the North. Kevin always played his Irish card from the minute I first knew him. He thought that sort of added to his armoury."

McClory had, though, remained in touch with Connery. The actor often visited McClory in Ireland and in September 1975 took part in a charity show the producer staged in aid of the Central Remedial Clinic in Dublin and the Variety Club of Ireland. McClory roped in other famous friends and hired a circus big top and put on what must have been quite an eclectic show for his paying audience. John Huston acted as ring master introducing various acts and special guests like Shirley MacLaine, Judy Geeson, Eric Clapton and Burgess Meredith. Connery, at one point in the show even dressed as Quasimodo, complete with hump and horror mask.

McClory re-emerged publicly in 1975, ironically in another court case and against old foe Ivar Bryce. In his biography of Fleming, *You Only Live Once*, Bryce alleged that the settlement of the 1963 *Thunderball* case was dictated solely by the state of health of Fleming at the time of the court hearing and that the claim by McClory lacked real substance. It was also alleged that McClory had paid Jack Whittingham to give evidence on his behalf at the trial. When McClory read the book it was with astonishment and distress. Bryce's statements were totally libellous and untrue. McClory didn't hesitate to sue on behalf of himself and Whittingham's distressed widow.

McClory's counsel at the trial was Mr Leon Brittan QC, later a prominent figure in Margaret Thatcher's Conservative government. His argument was simple: "There is not one word of truth of these disgraceful allegations which are totally devoid of any foundation whatsoever." It was also stated that it was "a matter of sadness to Mr McClory that the late Jack Whittingham is not here to defend himself against this wanton libel."

Bryce hurriedly agreed in court that he had withdrawn the allegations without reservation, acknowledged they were utterly without foundation, agreed to pay substantial damages to McClory and expressed sincere regret to the widow of the late Jack Whittingham that they were ever published. He hoped such an apology "would remove the unwarranted blemish upon the late Jack Whittingham's name."

All seemingly was resolved, except that Jack Whittingham's widow, whose distress McClory had made much of during the trial, knew nothing about the court case taken on her behalf, nor even of Bryce's book. "The family didn't find out about it for another 15 years when I got access to the court papers," says Sylvan. "Kevin hadn't had the courtesy to let us know about it." Nor did McClory feel any duty to pass on some of the money he'd been awarded for the slur, not only upon his name, but Whittinghams.

In January 1976 the ten year time restriction imposed on McClory by the Bond producers had elapsed and he was free to make further films based on the *Thunderball* film material. The Deeds of Assignment given him at the end of the 1963 court case were enough, in McClory's opinion, to allow him to proceed. After all hadn't he been granted, in the court's own words, "Exclusive right to use James Bond as a character in any such scripts or film of *Thunderball*." And, "The exclusive right to reproduce any part of the novel in films and for the purpose of making such films to make scripts."

Jettisoning once again Whittingham's original screenplay after all nearly 20 years had passed, McClory wanted something fresher to reflect the cinema of the late 70s, and yet had that cold war, spy tradition element to it. His inspired choice of scriptwriter was Len Deighton, the thriller novelist and creator of Harry Palmer, the famous anti-James Bond spy of the 60s brought to the screen by Harry Saltzman and immortalised by Michael Caine. Suitably taken with McClory's proposal Deighton agreed to come on board.

"I suggested calling the script 'Hammerhead' because I dreamed up the idea of mechanical sharks equipped with radar and various IT gimmicks that could be fitted into the hammer head shape. I went to New York, Tokyo and to Okinawa with Kevin, and in Florida met men who designed and built miniature subs. At first they had done it for fun, but later they were bought up by oil companies with underwater rigs that wanted a cheap way of inspecting the underwater apparatus. They became very rich and were great fun to be with.

"Kevin was something of an eccentric. I was arrested as I got off the plane but it turned out that the cop who arrested me was a NYPD detective who was a close friend of Kevin. To compensate for the joke, he had me made an honourary member of the NYPD.

"One evening, Kevin and I strolled down through Greenwich Village (where I once lived) and he spotted a fortune teller sign. He insisted that we had our fortunes told and seemed quite genuinely pleased to be told that everything was going to be great for him.

"In Tokyo, Kevin had not packed his bags in time enough to catch the plane. So he just told the hotel to keep his room for 10 days. The bill for that was astounding but Kevin didn't turn a hair even when the hotel manager was trying to talk him out of such extravagance.

"I wrote the script in my home in Ireland after all this world-wide research and - considering how much underwater material Kevin insisted upon having included – it wasn't too bad. When my script was in draft form, Sean and Kevin came up to our rural retreat, and it certainly looked as if it was all ready to roll.

"You have to take into account that Kevin was obsessed with scuba diving and underwater ideas. We had lunch with Jacques Cousteau (if I remember rightly) and Kevin wanted him to advise me on the script. Fortunately he didn't want to."

The natural born gambler in McClory now came to the fore. Despite quitting Bond after *You Only Live Twice*, and then tempted back in 1971 before quitting yet again, McClory wondered if the impossible could be achieved – Connery returning a second time as 007. Since his final Bond, *Diamonds are Forever*, Connery had been in the doldrums with films like *Zardoz* and *Ransom* proving box office poison. But after the career reviving role of Raisuli in *The Wind and the Lion*, followed by the classic *The Man Who Would be King*, things were looking good. So who needed Bond, certainly Connery didn't and the answer was a resounding no.

Undeterred McClory played his ace. Knowing that Connery hankered to one day direct and write movies McClory asked whether he might consider collaborating on the script. Connery thought about it and was intrigued enough to agree, not least because of the involvement of Deighton, whom he greatly respected. McClory claimed that it was Connery's special brand of humour that he wanted to instill into his Bond script, conscious of the fact that many of the throwaway lines in the early 007 films were the actor's own invention, and that he'd contributed to the scripts in other ways too. But surely the real motive was getting Connery's name attached to his Bond project any which way he could. And it worked. The entertainment world sat up and took notice. McClory must have also secretly hoped that as Connery worked on the script he'd start to care again about the character he'd previously labelled his own Frankenstein monster.

For the next few months the three men worked both in Ireland and at Connery's home in Marbella. "It was really a tremendous experience working with Sean as a writer," McClory later recalled. "Because he did not contribute just throwaway lines, he also got involved in the construction of the plot. And he's a very good storyteller. Therefore he's a good story writer, and he writes visually. He made enormous contributions and we all got along very well."

The fruit of their endeavours was the script "James Bond of the Secret Service." Almost immediately Eon objected to the title due to it sounding similar in nature to *On Her Majesty's Secret Service*. In the event McClory always preferred one word titles and came up instead with "Warhead." Seen as one of the great-unfilmed scripts in cinema history, described in Hollywood circles as *Star Wars* underwater, "Warhead" featured SPECTRE's most outlandish plan yet for world domination. The film opens with SPECTRE, by use of a jamming device, bringing down the plane carrying the Secretary General of the United Nations into the Bermuda Triangle. We watch as the aircraft sinks down to the seabed and joins a graveyard of other planes and ships.

Operating from a vast undersea base, Arkos, Largo sends a diver in a deep-sea suit, to retrieve nuclear warheads from a recently sunk Russian ship. But an American recovery vessel arrives ahead of schedule and Largo leaves him behind, despite his desperate pleading. The vast pressures at that depth cause the man's body to be slowly squeezed up into his helmet. Early in the film there was also to be a neat variation of the *Thunderball* SPECTRE meeting. Blofeld presides over progress reports from several agents and learns one of them is guilty of embezzlement. Instead of his chair being electrocuted, a glass tube surrounds the unfortunate man and exits him out into the sea.

The action switches to Shrublands, not a health farm but some kind of aquatic training facility based in the Bahamas. We meet various characters here, Bond, Felix Leiter, plus Fatima Blush, a beautiful oriental and fellow agent and her squeeze, Hellinger, a top CIA underwater expert with a distinctive scar running down the side of his face. At Shrublands, Bond and Leiter attend a meeting about the Secretary General's lost plane and the fact that the White House received word from

Chapter 34: WARHEAD – THE BOND FILM THAT NEVER WAS

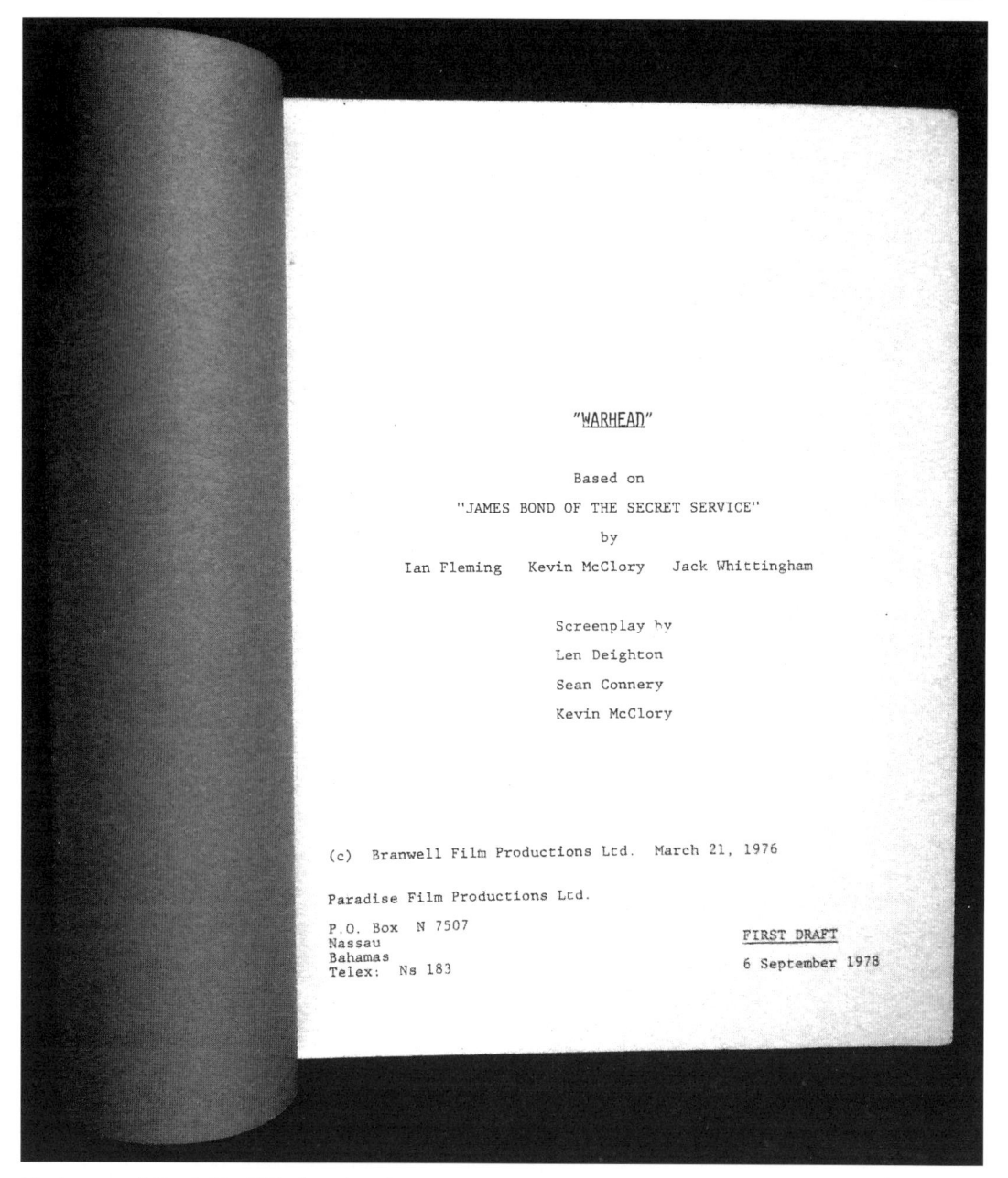

```
                        "WARHEAD"

                        Based on
              "JAMES BOND OF THE SECRET SERVICE"
                           by
         Ian Fleming   Kevin McClory   Jack Whittingham


                     Screenplay by
                     Len Deighton
                     Sean Connery
                     Kevin McClory




(c)  Branwell Film Productions Ltd.   March 21, 1976

Paradise Film Productions Ltd.

P.O. Box  N 7507
Nassau                                   FIRST DRAFT
Bahamas
Telex:  Ns 183                        6 September 1978
```

First page of the fabled Warhead script.

Blofeld threatening such an event minutes before it happened. Leiter also informs Bond that the Russians have just lost another submarine off the Azores and there's a chance of getting hold of some top secret decoding equipment that was on board. Hellinger is being flown out to the recovery vehicle within 24 hours.

That night, Fatima and Bomba, Largo's black muscle-bound henchman who, according to the script, "makes Muhammad Ali look like a fag," sneak fellow spy Petachi into Shrublands. Petachi has undergone plastic surgery in order to look like Hellinger. Bond, predictably in bed with Shrubland's masseuse, one

Chapter 34: WARHEAD - THE BOND FILM THAT NEVER WAS

Justine Lovesit, is disturbed by noises. Looking out of the window he observes Bomba standing outside Fatima's room. He investigates and Fatima "persuades" Bond to join her in a whirlpool. Hellinger overhears them together but is himself disturbed by Petachi and is more than surprised to see his double. Before he can cry out, Bomba steps out from the shadows and snaps his neck. Petachi, now assuming the persona of Hellinger, interrupts Bond and Fatima and reprimands the agent for fooling around with his girl.

Next day, Petachi takes Bond out hang-gliding but deliberately slows the speedboat down as they approach the shark pens so that Bond's feet skim the water. Just managing to avoid being eaten, Bond lands on a pier and jumps into the boat, overpowering Petachi. Later Petachi manages to escape and rendezvous with Fatima. He informs her that he wants more money for his SPECTRE mission. When Largo is informed he replies, "I'll see he gets it."

The American recovery vessel, with Petachi aboard, arrives in the Azores. Operating from inside an old dredger, Largo uses a jamming device to immobilise the American ship, while SPECTRE divers enter the Russian submarine and remove its nuclear warheads. Turning to Maslov, the obligatory scientist, Largo asks if the jamming device Petachi carried aboard the American ship has a self-destruct button. It does. "How is it activated?" Largo asks. "By pressing this button. Like this," says Largo as he pushes the button destroying the US recovery vessel, along with Petachi.

At MI6 headquarters, M and Q inform Bond of the missing warheads and suspicion points to SPECTRE. Bond returns home but an enemy agent, posing as a cleaning lady called Effie (the real name of Connery's mother!), has placed an explosive device inside his Aston Martin and then sneaks upstairs to place a bomb under his bed. Just then Fatima calls and Bond carries her upstairs and throws her onto the bed, flattening Effie. Bond and Fatima indulge in some seriously athletic sex, much to the discomfort of Effie. Afterwards Bond confronts Fatima about his suspicions that she may be a SPECTRE agent. Before she can answer a man suddenly drops in through the skylight. A fight ensues during which Fatima attempts to escape in Bond's Aston Martin. Effie runs into the garage but is too late to stop Fatima from turning on the ignition. BOOM!

Bond and Q fly out to Shrublands. M is waiting for them. The American president has received a message from SPECTRE claiming responsibility for the Bermuda Triangle and that it has the Russian warheads. If their ransom demands are not met a major city will be atomised and the remaining warheads will be exploded beneath the Antarctic ice cap to flood the world.

Bond and Leiter use jet packs to fly over to Shark Island, a laboratory owned by Largo, which uses sharks for cancer research. Sneaking into Largo's house, Bond sees who he thinks is Fatima, but it can't be - she's dead. The woman turns out to be Fatima's twin sister, Domino. She hates Largo and agrees to help Bond. While nosing around Maslov's laboratory Bond and Leiter discover mechanical sharks, but are captured and placed inside a decompression chamber. Not having heard from Bond for 24 hours M sends troops to Shark Island and rescues his agents. Luckily Domino tied her scarf around the controls to prevent the chamber from decompressing any further.

Back on Arkos, Largo and Maslov discuss the operation. A mechanical hammerhead shark will carry the warhead, while heat-seeking tiger sharks will act as escorts. Largo then discovers a homing device given to Domino by Bond and intends using her as bait for his pet sharks. Maslov intervenes and saves her. Back on Shrublands, the homer worked long enough to point to New York as being Largo's target. A mass evacuation of the city begins. All the buildings have been searched except the sewers. Bond asks for a team of aqua-marines to inspect them.

SPECTRE has commandeered the Statue of Liberty. Maslov arms the warhead on the hammerhead shark and lowers it into the water. Together with its tiger shark escort, it makes its way into the sewer system, its progress illuminated on a large map watched by Largo. Amid the news on TV of riots and looting there are reports of shark sightings in New York harbour. Bond realises the troops are inside the sewers and orders them to get out. But it's too late. They watch horrified as mutilated limbs float out amid toilet paper and sewage.

Bond hears that the sharks were seen coming from the direction of Ellis Island. He also recalls Blofeld's words in his threatening message: "liberty is our symbol." They must be in the Statue of Liberty. But first they've got to stop the sharks. With every manhole in Manhattan sealed by SPECTRE and robot sharks on guard at the sewer outlets, Bond and his team of men have to drill through a subway wall to get into the sewer system. Before going inside Bond is offered a gun by New York's chief of police. "A screwdriver is all I need." He then disappears into the blackness. Three policemen follow; the last one is Bomba.

One of the mechanical tiger sharks senses the presence of Bond and starts hunting him down. Bomba, who has quickly dispatched the two policemen, is also hot on his trail. Seconds before it strikes, Bond sees the flash of a fin and moves out of the way just as a huge set of jaws pounce. He seizes the metal rungs of a wall ladder and leaps up as the shark attacks again. But Bomba is waiting for him and kicks Bond back down into the maelstrom of the water and the threshing shark. Bond grabs its fin and is dragged down the narrow sewer at high speed, bashing against the side. With the screwdriver Bond opens its control panel and rips out wires and transistors. The shark's eyes flicker and go dark.

Bond climbs out onto a walkway. Using a Geiger counter he tracks down the hammerhead shark, only just discernible as it slowly cruises along. From out of the shadows Bomba strikes. A terrific and vicious fight ensues resulting in Bomba falling into the water to be ripped to pieces by tiger sharks. Bond then falls on the hammerhead and with his trusty screwdriver renders it and the bomb harmless.

Largo watches as the light on the map disappears and orders Maslov to activate the bomb's time mechanism. Bond is alarmed to see the words BOMB ACTIVATED appear on the shark's control panel. Panic-stricken he tries to defuse the warhead. Just when it looks like he's fighting a losing battle a hand reaches from behind him and switches it off. Bond is more than relieved to see it's Q.

A squadron of army helicopters attack the Statue of Liberty. With Leiter at the helm of a speed boat Bond water skis past the sharks in the harbour and thanks to a balloon device, raises into the air and lands on the Statue of Liberty. There he confronts Largo. From out of the sea the Arkos rises. Largo slides down a rope to land on its upper deck. Bond follows but the rope is cut and he falls into the water. Grabbing a foothold, Bond submerges with the Arkos and swims up through its inner pool. Again he confronts Largo and a misplaced gunshot shatters a glass tube and the sea starts spilling in.

Now out of control, the Arkos speeds perilously close to mountainous underwater hills along the Hudson Canyons. It hits a cliff-face and Domino is thrown backwards onto a control panel. A glass tube rises swiftly around Largo and jettisons him out into the swollen ocean. We see him descending into the darkness, madly clawing at the glass.

The Arkos continues its descent, while inside the water level is rising. Bond and Domino just make it to one of Largo's mini subs and escape as the Arkos is destroyed. Safe on the surface Bond and Domino cuddle up close. "Oh James," she sighs. Bond looks up at their reflection in the ceiling mirror and winks. We see the submarine float towards the horizon along with the strains of Rule Britannia.

Ecstatic over the industry reaction to the script (mega agent Irving "swifty" Lazar proclaimed it to be one of the most exciting scripts he'd ever read) McClory announced the film would begin shooting in February 1977 in the Bahamas with $22m in backing from Paramount studios. Rumours circulated that Orson Welles would play Blofeld, with Trevor Howard in the role of M. Richard Attenborough was favourite to direct.

But who was going to play Bond? That was the question an inquisitive world was asking, hoping against hope that the answer might be Connery. Having snared him first as one of the writers, McClory next tempted Connery by offering him the director's chair. But that wasn't enough for Paramount, they'd millions at stake and would settle for nothing less but Connery back as Bond. Amazingly, after much introspection, the actor agreed. "Why not?" said Micheline Connery, when her husband broached the subject to her. "What would you risk. After all these years it might be interesting." Coming from his wife Connery took it much more seriously than if anybody else had suggested it, and the more he thought about it the more he felt she was right. "There was also a certain amount of curiosity in me

Chapter 34: WARHEAD – THE BOND FILM THAT NEVER WAS

about the role," he later claimed. "Having been away from it so long." Connery probably surprised himself about how much he missed the old boy.

Connery's decision to return as Bond made headlines around the world. McClory equated his comeback to "Muhammad Ali, when he's at his most fit, when someone else is champion of the world, throwing his hat in to the ring."

The only people who didn't want Connery back were Eon and United Artists. And who could blame them as they were having problems of their own with the official 007 franchise. Connery's replacement Roger Moore had yet to fully settle into the role and his first two Bond efforts, *Live and Let Die*, but particularly *The Man with the Golden Gun*, hadn't exactly set the box office on fire. Worse, Harry Saltzman, owing to personal financial problems, had been forced to sell up his shares and interest in Bond, leaving Broccoli as sole producer of the series. Saltzman virtually disappeared from cinema soon after, working on just a few small-scale films. Once counted amongst the most powerful film producers in the world, by the time of his death in 1994 Saltzman had removed himself so far from Hollywood that his passing went barely noticed.

Deep in pre-production on *The Spy Who Loved Me*, Broccoli was incensed when news reached him of McClory's project. And his blood pressure didn't get any better when McClory suddenly filed an injunction to hold up filming on *Spy*. The Irishman claimed that its scenario was too similar to the Deighton/Connery script, featuring as it did an ocean-obsessed megalomaniac and a SPECTRE plot to destroy the world with the use of hijacked nuclear weapons. Broccoli meanwhile argued that McClory had no right to make a movie based on the original *Thunderball* scripts, as Fleming personally never gave him permission to do so.

McClory then played his trump card. According to his favourable decision in the 1963 court case, McClory claimed to own the film rights to SPECTRE, as it had been created solely for the intended *Thunderball* film. Only later was it incorporated into Fleming's novel. When Broccoli and Saltzman came to begin their Bond movie series they wisely decided to avoid the cliché use of Russians as baddies, finding a ready made criminal alternative in SPECTRE, who became the perfect umbrella organisation for the fantastical schemes pulled off by Fleming's gallery of rogues. Thus SPECTRE turned up in all of Connery's Bond pictures, with the exception of *Goldfinger*, even though they never featured in those original books. Broccoli, therefore, never had any right to use SPECTRE, claimed McClory, and had already illegally done so.

Thus far, SPECTRE had been mysteriously absent from Roger Moore 007 outings. But for *The Spy Who Loved Me*, Broccoli intended to pull out all the stops, including the villainous organisation's dramatic return. Updated to include members of the Bader-Meinhof gang, Japan's Red Army, Black September and other more modern terrorist organisations, this modern SPECTRE has no interest in blackmail and extortion, just mass destruction. The opening of *Spy* would have seen this new radical splinter group bursting into SPECTRE HQ and assassinating the old guard. But fearing the possibility of a long legal battle which would only hold up production Broccoli told his screenwriter Christopher Wood to remove all traces of SPECTRE from his script, replacing it with a pseudo Blofeld baddie in Stromberg and his SPECTRE-like private army. Interestingly, neither SPECTRE nor Blofeld have appeared since in any Eon Bond film. That's if one doesn't count the bald-headed, cat stroking psycho at the beginning of *For Your Eyes Only*, who is so obviously Blofeld, but never referred to as such. One wonders if by killing off this Blofeld, Broccoli was saying, we can do without SPECTRE.

McClory may have won this particular battle, but Broccoli fully intended to continue the campaign. He wasn't about to let a rival filmmaker spoil his well-earned monopoly on 007 and aided by United Artists and the Fleming Trust instigated legal proceedings to obstruct the progress of "Warhead" at every turn, essentially to keep the production in perpetual limbo. McClory made public his view that Broccoli and Eon knew full well that he had the right to make additional 007 films from the original *Thunderball* scripts, but were using the law as a delaying tactic. "They cannot stop this picture from being made, and they know it," he said. "Let them live with their consciences, if they have them."

McClory reminded people again of the agreement he entered into with Eon back in 1965, an understanding that ten years after *Thunderball*'s release, all the copyright in the original script materials would revert back to him. "Automatically and irrevocably," McClory told the press, "That is in this contract. This is signed by Saltzman and by Broccoli, so they're well aware of the situation." McClory also revealed that the contract contained a clause that any film or series of films he made that used substantial material from *Thunderball*, Eon and United Artists would receive 20% of the profits.

Despite accompanying McClory on a scouting mission to New York looking at potential location sites, including a visit to the Statue of Liberty itself, the legally cautious Connery was having second thoughts about the minefield McClory was forced to traverse. "I am now awaiting the outcome of the legal problems," the actor said in December 1978. "Before I put my nose into anything I want to know it is legally bona fide." Paramount too were getting nervous and the fierce legal obstacles posed by the combined big guns of Eon and United Artists ultimately led to the studio withdrawing their backing. But McClory persevered, proving to be a constant thorn in Eon's side; an irritating scratch just out of reach. In an interview, Broccoli referred to McClory as a, "former friend," momentarily forgetting perhaps that he was godfather to one of McClory's children. Things were getting personal, but the stakes were high.

Over the next few years, McClory made sporadic announcements that the Connery Bond film was imminent. He'd even begun fantasising about launching a completely separate series of Bond films, one of which he wanted to direct himself. "As long as we don't release the films at the same time, I don't think they would hurt each other," McClory said in 1979. "Our series will certainly be different than theirs and I think the market is big enough to support two James Bond series." But such talk just proved to be so much bluster and each rumour was met with jaded scepticism by 007 fans. By 1980, Connery too had had enough and bowed out, blaming the legal obstacles and the involvement of what seemed like an army of lawyers. It now looked like the impossible; Connery back as Bond, wasn't going to happen after all.

CHAPTER 35
CONNERY RETURNS

In the summer of 1981, the breakthrough finally came for McClory when his plight came to the attention of Jack Schwartzman, the former executive vice-president of Lorimar Pictures. New York born Schwartzman's background lay in tax and entertainment law and since leaving Lorimar he had set up his own production company, Taliafilm, named after his actress wife Talia Shire, sister of Francis Ford Coppola and famous as Mrs Balboa in the Rocky films. Schwartzman was contacted by an old friend, New York investment banker Philip Mengel, who happened to be McClory's financial adviser, and wondered if Schwartzman was interested in meeting his client. He was. Despite the legal problems, Connery back as Bond was too good a proposition for Schwartzman to pass up.

Schwartzman duly met with McClory and convinced himself that the Irishman did indeed have the rights to do what he'd been claiming for years; he just needed to present his case properly with some solid financial clout behind him to face off Broccoli's legal battalions. Shrewdly, Schwartzman decided to distance himself from the "Warhead" script, a subject of litigation now for five years. "I didn't want to be tarred with the same brush." Nor when he read it, did the script appeal to him. His plan was to go back to Fleming's original book, but update it to include 1980s technology, cruise missiles, computers etc. He knew that in order to thwart the tremendous legal obstacles in the way, any film made from McClory's rights would have to be a direct interpretation of the source materials. Eventually he persuaded McClory to allow him to option the rights to the project and proceed with an entirely new screenplay. The Deighton/Connery "Warhead" script was scrapped; it probably would have been too expensive to realise anyway. McClory too was left pretty much out in the cold, agreeing to give up creative control in return for a mere screen credit. So the Bond project fell under the auspices of Taliafilm. Schwartzman, and not McClory was now in charge.

Only a tenacious man like Schwartzman, with his experience as a Hollywood lawyer, could have successfully accomplished the seemingly insurmountable feat of turning McClory's oft-postponed and legally mired *Thunderball* remake into a workable project. He even had the gall to offer the film as a co-production with Eon. Broccoli understandably declined.

Attention turned next to Connery. Wary of getting his fingers burnt a second time, Connery approached this new development with caution, laying down a number of stipulations. First and most important, he was to be indemnified against any of the lawsuits that were still flying around. He also wanted script, director and cast approval. In other words, total creative control. Schwartzman agreed to everything and offered a fee of $3m, plus a percentage of the profits. It was too good to refuse.

Once announced that Connery was to return as Bond, and it actually looked likely to happen this time, the media went into a frenzy. It was as if the Beatles were about to reform. Certainly it was cinema's most unlikely comeback. After all this was a man who'd left the Bond role no less than on two separate occasions, each time vowing never to return; which made the proposed title of the film all the more ironic. It was actually Micheline who coined the now famous title *Never Say Never Again*. Connery liked it immediately. "It was romantic and pre-empted all the bullshit I knew would be written about my coming back to Bond."

But having fought so hard to escape the Bond image why, cynics were asking, was Connery so willing to return to it. "I don't think any role changes a man quite so much as Bond," he once said. "It's a cross, a privilege, a joke, a challenge. And as bloody intrusive as a nightmare." The fan intrusion in the Bahamas on *Thunderball* was superseded on location in Japan for *You Only Live Twice* when photo journalists followed Connery into the toilet. That was it, he wanted shot of the whole Bond circus. Since those days, when industry insiders quipped that on the subject of Bond, "Sean's considered the best three-second interview in the business," his attitude had mellowed considerably, having proved himself an accomplished actor outside the world of 007. So why come back? Was it purely the colossal pay cheque, or sweet revenge against old boss Broccoli who he still held a grudge against, feeling that his cut of the Bond profits were paltry compared to what the producers raked in. Maybe it was just a bid to boost a career that had once again suffered a succession of recent high profile flops like *Cuba*, *Outland* and *Five Days One Summer*.

With Connery installed once again as Bond and Roger Moore preparing to play the super spy for the sixth time in *Octopussy*, the most over-used media headline of the year was: "Battle of the Bonds." The two stars had been friends for years and would often be put in the awkward position of having to defend their film without insulting the other as the press tried to stoke up a bitter rivalry between them. "Whatever you read about the aggro between us in the newspapers from here on in," Connery reassured Moore, "don't believe it." In the end both met up in London in order to quash the speculation by posing together and issuing a joint statement. But the whole "who is the better Bond" debate raged on in magazines and newspapers around the world right up until the release of both films. At the meeting, the two Bonds discussed their respective movies, with Moore asking Connery. "So where are you going on location?" Connery, clearly looking forward to it, gloated, "South of France, the Bahamas. How about you?" Moore's face fell. "India." He said, resignedly.

Schwartzman had wrangled a healthy $34m budget from Warner Brothers on the strength of Connery's name alone and so the search was on for a director. According to Terence Young, Connery personally approached him with the job, but McClory had his doubts considering the film's close proximity to *Thunderball*. They wanted a fresh vision. Connery's next choice was *Superman* and future *Lethal Weapon* director Richard Donner. But he passed.

Connery turned instead to Irvin Kershner, the veteran director with whom he'd already worked, on 1966's *A Fine Madness*, an uneven comedy that was shot directly after *Thunderball*. Kershner was far from being a hardboiled, action film director but was highly respected in Hollywood and had just helmed the *Star Wars* sequel, *The Empire Strikes Back*. Still, he was surprised to get the call. "I really wasn't the type of director who did big films; it was very unusual for me. I really was very independent, doing mostly small films and suddenly here I was with this giant Bond film. I didn't say yes immediately. I had great reservations. Am I the right person to do it? Shouldn't they get an action director and try to do an all-action film? They asked me how I wanted to do the film and I said, I want to use Sean as the person he is, at the age he is. He shouldn't be a duplicate of what he was 13 years before. He'd

Chapter 35: CONNERY RETURNS

gotten older. I didn't want him hanging by one finger from a helicopter while it's moving along at 200 mph. And it took weeks before finally they said ok and I said ok."

All the time Connery had been phoning Kershner urging him to make the commitment. "Why don't you do it?" he'd plead. "This is gonna be my last Bond. The last one! We'll have some fun; we'll go to Paris and the Bahamas. What the hell!" In the end, it was Connery that tipped the balance for Kershner. "The only thing that made me do it was Sean Connery. I had tremendous respect for him. I think of him as a truly great film actor. If it had been another actor playing Bond I wouldn't have done it because I was never interested in Bond. In fact, up to that point I'd only seen two Bond films, *Dr. No* and *From Russia with Love*, which I liked."

Kershner's approach to the film was simple: yes there'd been many Bond films before, but as far as he was concerned *Never Say Never Again* might as well be the first. He wasn't out to copy anything. "I did not want to look at the Bond films. I didn't want to know what the formula was. I felt that we were making something different. Just from having seen a couple of Bond films I knew what the so-called formula was; licence to kill, plenty of women, action, that's about it. There's nothing else to them. I didn't think Fleming was a great writer at all. In fact, I thought he was a mediocre writer. I guess our film did follow naturally a sort of formulaic pattern, but I didn't try for it. I also wanted to make a contemporary film even though it was a James Bond film, which is kind of a throwback really to the 60s. So I made the character of Bond sort of a 60s character, but the film and the antagonist and the background is all today. It was a difficult fusion to make."

Kershner was further hampered by the fact that due to legal reasons he couldn't use many of the elements that had been created for the official Eon Bond series; elements which audiences were so familiar with. These included the famous opening gun barrel, the distinctive James Bond theme and Maurice Binder's visually erotic titles. If they had, Broccoli and his army of lawyers would have pounced.

Out to create something new for the world of Bond, Kershner found himself thwarted at nearly every turn. "We had a great deal of problems getting a script. One of the reasons was that we had to do the book, not impinge on the film that was done. And yet that film, *Thunderball*, was not very much like the book, they took tremendous freedoms. And of course to make a film we would have to take freedoms, and every time we tried to take freedoms Eon and United Artists would somehow get wind of it and start to sue us that we weren't using the book. We were kind of trapped in the middle, and there was no easy way out. It was an attorney's game going on and I just wanted to get a script and let them do the fighting in the courts."

The first of what turned out to be several writers to work on the film was an associate of Schwartzman's from his Lorimar days, Julian Plowden. Hired to deliver a script carefully tailored around the remake rights available, Plowden failed to make much headway so he himself recommended Lorenzo Semple Jr, a veteran screenwriter with several impressive credits to his name such as *Papillon*, *Flash Gordon* and a stint working on the camp 60s *Batman* TV series. Semple's script would make an amusing virtue of Bond/Connery's advanced years. It begins with Bond almost in semi-retirement and brought back to front line service after years as a teacher. There were also going to be scenes with Bond doing press ups in the bathroom before getting into bed with some young nymph. Included perhaps to pre-empt press reports that Connery, at 52, was too old for Bond, this approach was ultimately rejected. "I have not necessarily tried to play him as an older man and nor do I feel that one should attach any major importance to the age factor." Actually, for 52, Connery was supremely fit, having spent months working out in preparation for the film, and looked in overall better shape than he did in *Diamonds are Forever* 12 years previously.

Few people in the world knew more about playing Bond than Connery, so it was wise to let the man himself decide how best he should be portrayed. Charged with so much creative freedom, Connery was able for the first time to mould an entire Bond film to suit his own vision of the character and his world. From the outset he wanted to downplay the technology and gadgets and emphasise the human elements. His favourite film in the series had always been *From Russia with*

Love, which he thought had the best chemistry of espionage, action and characterisation. Right from the start, Connery insisted on quality. "I said that if we ever felt we were going to have to sacrifice that quality for expediency, I would rather not make the film." One of the areas where he felt they could get real class was in the calibre of the actors. For all its flaws, and there are many, *Never Say* triumphs in the acting department and a lot of the credit for that must go to Connery as no one was cast without his say so.

For the villain Largo (here called Maximillian, not Emilio), Kershner didn't want your everyday bad guy, "with a patch over the eye and a leer." He felt that the antagonist in a Bond film was almost as important as Bond himself and he laboured to get Largo right more than any other character in the film. "I wanted the antagonist to be contemporary, and a contemporary antagonist to me was a greedy businessman. The corporations have gotten away with murder and they're changing our world. In fact we should change the name of the United States to the Corporate Republic of North America because they're really running the government. It's money that gets people elected. So I decided the villain should be a businessman. He should also be a believable, powerful antagonist who could be said to be insane, but is not. If he's insane then he can make no choices. I wanted someone who could make choices, and his choice was power. With these big businessmen it's no longer money that motivates them, because they have all the money in the world, it's the power that they want. And that's how the character of Largo evolved."

After his stunning performance in the German film *Mephisto*, Klaus Maria Brandauer was being hailed as one of the best actors in Europe, "If not the world" argued Connery. Brandauer had yet to make an English language film but Connery felt the Austrian actor would prove stunning as Largo. He didn't disappoint and went on to win deserved plaudits. 'It's the kind of performance that should be shown in acting classes – understated, tense and full of intelligence,' said People magazine. 'He becomes one of the screen's most convincing psychotics.' In one scene, Domino asks Largo what would happen if she ever left him. He laughs and playacts, then suddenly his smiling face freezes into hypnotic stillness. "Then I cut your throat." And you know he means it. "Brandauer is a great actor," says Kershner. "I loved what he was doing with the character. He was on the verge of being a madman, but he wasn't. And that's what I wanted. But I had problems directing him because he was always testing the director. He's a very bright man. And he was constantly putting me through the hoop, and I'd have to jump, I had no choice. During the day I could kill him, and then as soon as I said cut, he'd come over and say, let's have dinner, come on let's talk about Shakespeare. So as soon as the shooting was over he was charming and the most interesting man you could want to be with."

To play Domino, Micheline Connery suggested Kim Basinger after bumping into her at a London hotel. Just embarking upon a film career after years as a top model, Basinger does reasonably well in what is a cardboard role, radiating a degree of vulnerability which is highly effective. Not according to one American critic though, who sneered. "Basinger is a singular embarrassment, not exhibiting the slightest wisp of acting talent." Bond's first encounter with Domino, when he sneaks into a health spa and pretends to be her masseur, is a highlight of the film and carries real sexual sparks. Spending most of her time half-naked in a bikini, skimpy leotard or sparse negligee, Basinger's role as Domino was the perfect springboard for the actress to become one of the sex bombs of 80s and early 90s cinema.

While Domino personifies innocence, Fatima Blush is pure evil. The character is no different really to Fiona from *Thunderball*, a femme fatale, but in the hands of Barbara Carrera she becomes an almost operatic villain who makes love to her victims before killing them. Barbara Carrera was a stunning Nicaraguan-born model and Playboy cover girl beginning to turn heads in Hollywood. Connery was later to favourably compare the actress with his number one Bond girl Ursula Andress in terms of, "sheer sexual impact." Ironically Barbara had just been offered the lead role in *Octopussy* when she attended a film festival in Manila and bumped into Irvin Kershner. "I asked what he was doing and he said, "Scouting locations for this new Bond film. Sean Connery's coming back." I said, "Whoa, that should be interesting." Then he said, "I'd like you to play Fatima." And the way he told me about her I was

Chapter 35: CONNERY RETURNS

```
                    EXAMPLE


                              LETTER OF HEALTH


                        FILM TITLE. NEVER SAY NEVER AGAIN


    TO WHOM IT MAY CONCERN


    I , KLAUS MARIA BRANDAUER born on 22 6 44
    declare myself to be in good physical condition and capable of
    performing my role in the above mentioned film production.



              Signed  [signature] *
              Dated   20 6 83

    * The actions in —
    → The shots UNDERWATER HAS TO BE
      AGREED BY MYSELF
```

Klaus Maria Brandauer's personal medical release form.

fascinated not only with the character, but I also thought, gosh, I'd prefer to do this Bond because of Sean Connery. People are going to be much more curious to see that."

Barbara accepted the part on the strength of Kershner's pitch alone and without even reading the screenplay. Flying to London to start pre-production she noticed someone on her flight was reading the script. "I was most curious so I went over. He turned out to be someone in the special effects team and let me read it afterwards. But when I read this character I was supposed to play, I was mortified because it was not at all like anything that Kershner had told me. Semple had written Fatima as a bald-headed dyke dressed in men's clothing! She was just horrible. Semple must have thought if a woman is going to be bad she has to be a dyke and really ugly. When I got off the plane instead of going to my hotel I had my driver take me directly to the studio and when I got there I was in tears. I said, 'Kersh, I've read the script and I will not play that character no matter how much you pay me, she's just horrible, horrible.' He said, 'Oh no, you weren't meant to see that script, we're not going to be using that character. Don't you worry about it; we're bringing in six more writers.'"

Despite the new influx of writers, the character of Fatima Blush did not progress well and so Barbara was left pretty much to her own devices. At first she had problems relating to what kind of a person an assassin is, what goes on inside their head. She knew Fatima enjoyed her line of work, but how do you feel good about going out and killing someone? "I worked on the character for about a month and then finally one day it came to me, the idea of Kali, the Hindu goddess. People think of Kali as very bad, she comes and she destroys things. But what Kali actually does is she destroys negativity. Wherever there is negativity she comes in as a storm, or fire, or pestilence. And then another thought came to me - black widow spiders. A black widow spider will always make love to its prey before it kills it. So I thought, Kali, black widow spider, what a good combination for this character, because Fatima makes love to her prey and then annihilates them, she takes them to the height of ecstasy and takes away their bad life and gives them a new life, a rebirth. So that was what was going through my head, and it gave me a tremendous energy, the type of energy that I needed for this character to feel good about going out and doing her job, of getting rid of people."

Although barred from using regular motifs like the gun barrel and Bond theme, the makers of *Never Say Never Again* were allowed to use the familiar Bond series office staff of M, Miss Moneypenny and Q, as these characters appeared in the *Thunderball* scripts. Yet they faced the unenviable dilemma of casting brand new faces in roles that the public had grown accustomed to over 20 years. How do you replace Bernard Lee, Lois Maxwell and Desmond Llewelyn. Answer? With some difficulty.

The new M is an insufferable technocrat that relies more on computers than the instincts of agents like Bond. It was Connery's idea to cast Edward Fox, a self-confessed Fleming fan, who plays the character as a bit of a fussy old maid. But it's an amusing performance.

In the person of Pamela Salem, Miss Moneypenny is even more infatuated with Bond than she is in the official series. Pamela had played a small part in Connery's excellent *The First Great Train Robbery* (1978) and he personally recommended her, "which was lovely of him. For me I really enjoyed the experience of working on something that is so much a part of British folklore and movie history. I had such a good time. But I was sorry I didn't get to one of the exotic locations. Miss Moneypenny stayed firmly in the office in London."

Perhaps the best piece of casting in the lower ranks is that of respected theatre actor Alec McCowen as a very different Q, who spends his days complaining about how his gadget workshop became run down after the 00 section was dispersed. Now Bond is back, he says, in one of the film's best lines, "I hope we'll have some gratuitous sex and violence." To which our James replies, "I certainly hope so too." When he saw the film Desmond Llewelyn commented, "I was most complimented and very flattered that Alec played Q in a totally different way. It was a very funny performance."

Making a welcome return after a 10-year gap from his last appearance in *Live and Let Die* was Felix Leiter, Bond's CIA buddy. There was much less of an identification problem with this character, having always been played by different actors, but therein lay the trouble, thought Connery. Did anyone really remember who played Felix in *Goldfinger*? No. The character had hardly ever created much of an impression. To change all that Connery suggested casting black actor Bernie Casey. Making Felix Leiter black would certainly get him noticed, and therefore be more memorable, but they forgot to do anything else with the character and Casey, a former American football player, struggles in an underwritten role. He and Connery, however, do spark off each other quite nicely.

Also making a long overdue re-appearance in a Bond film was super villain Blofeld, the first time in fact since *Diamonds are Forever* over ten years before. Played down the years by such accomplished actors as Donald Pleasance, Telly Savalas and Charles Gray, *Never Say* pulled out all the stops by hiring esteemed European star Max von Sydow. Still most famous for his role as the Priest in *The Exorcist,*

Chapter 35: CONNERY RETURNS

Sydow appears in only a few scenes and makes little impression, but does hint at a modicum of velveteen evil.

Once again, Blofeld is out for world domination, hijacking cruise missiles this time round. The hijacking is also handled differently to the 1965 film. Domino's brother Jack Petachi has been turned into a heroin addict by SPECTRE and undergone surgery on his right eye in order for it to be the exact replica of the US president. This allows Petachi to override a security system protecting the device which arms atomic bombs on an English NATO base. The two missiles subsequently veer off course, hit the ocean and are picked up by Largo's men. Kershner particularly revelled in the atomic hijacking theme of *Never Say*. "I wanted to put in a contemporary theme which bothered me at the time, and that was that the American military said, our atom bombs, our nukes are perfectly safe; they're protected, nobody can get to them. Well this is bullshit, and the terrorists are going to prove it one of these days. That's why I liked the fact that the nukes are stolen. So for me the picture did have a message, of sorts. I was having a go at the military."

Kim Basinger relaxing off set.

CHAPTER 36
LAST TANGO IN NICE

With the cast in place and everything seemingly ready to go, there were still major problems with the script. One day in the canteen at Elstree Studios, Kershner bumped into comedy writers Dick Clement and Ian La Frenais, famous for their classic BBC sitcoms *The Likely Lads* and *Porridge*. La Frenais knew the director vaguely and asked what he was up to. "I'm doing this Bond film. It needs a re-write. Are you free?" "Could be," came the reply. But then nothing happened. "And we were rather disappointed," recalls Clement. "Because we had worked on one Bond film before, doing a tiny rewrite on *Moonraker*. We had to go to Paris, that was the best part, and we got some nice dinners and stayed in a fabulous hotel. But I can't remember what the hell we wrote. I know there was in that film the most lethal stage instruction in the history of screenwriting, which was: NB, in a bracket, from this point everybody is weightless. It was one of those simple one-line things that can add millions to a budget at the stroke of a pen. Truthfully we weren't involved much on *Moonraker*, you're never involved much at the end of a Bond film because basically that's when all the track-suited extras come in and start keeling over in dozens, and there's not a lot of dialogue apart from ... two minutes and counting."

Months went by and still nothing was heard. "And I just happened to say to my agent one day," says Clement, "'why don't you call and see who got that job, they really needed a rewrite on that Bond film?'. And he called back and said, 'They still need a rewrite and no one's been assigned. Are you interested?' And Ian and I said, God yes. This has happened to us a few times and it's very exciting when you're suddenly called in on a situation where you know the script's in trouble. It's a bit like being a plumber when somebody's basement's flooded; people are very pleased to see you because maybe you can pump it out and you didn't cause it in the first place. You're in a win-win situation to a great extent."

By the time the writers touched down at Nice airport, the film had been shooting for three weeks, since 27 September 1982. It was an historic day, when Connery stepped onto a film set as James Bond for the first time in 11 years. He even received an instantaneous round of applause from the crew. "I sat there and thought, even with all the travail, it's been worth it," said Schwartzman. "And when I finally saw him on film, I knew it had been justified."

Upon their arrival in France, Clement and La Frenais heard there had been at least ten rewrites of the Semple screenplay. Schwartzman even received help from his brother in law, Francis Ford Coppola, who took a look at the material and actually produced a full script. "I heard that Coppola had written it as a favour," says Clement, "just so that they had one in their hip pocket. I think he did it before us. But obviously you can't switch scripts in mid-stream; not when you've got a massive movie with three units shooting sharks and different things all over the place, you've got to stick to the game plan. The truth is it's very hard to re-write movies while they're being shot, it's never a good sign."

The writers were further hampered by the extraordinary circumstances in which the film was being made, not least the spectre of litigation that hung over the production like acid rain. "People were saying, this film will never be released," says Clement. "They were absolutely categorically saying, it will never be released because we'll make damn sure it isn't. That's what we were hearing." Kershner puts it even more succinctly. "It was iffy all the way because we were being sued by Broccoli's company every day."

An American insurance company had been hired to approve every script rewrite because the makers were running scared of being sued. In other words, any rewrite by Clement and La Frenais had to please not only the director, but also the producer, the star, the insurance company and ultimately the studio. The scope for any creativity to blossom in such a situation was almost zero.

Before starting work on the script, Clement and La Frenais first sat in on dailies. Most of what they saw involved Klaus Maria Brandauer and Kim Basinger, notably the scene with the jade sculpture that Largo smashes. "And they were very, very long scenes and I kept muttering to Ian in the dark, that'll never be in the movie, because it was just so long and turgid. They were really ponderous scenes. It was as if the actors didn't trust the script at that point, with some reason."

But it wasn't just the script that had Clement worried. "Ian and myself quickly discovered that this was a very strange film indeed. There were so many factions involved. We also discovered that Jack Schwartzman was terrified of Sean and tended to leave the room when he came into it. And there was no love lost from the other direction either. Sean had no time for Jack. So there were these factions going on, and in the middle of it there was Kershner who was trying to make a movie."

The largely British crew were shooting all along the sun drenched Cote d'Azur, taking in such sites as the casino at Monte Carlo and various villas of the rich and famous. The action highlight of the film is a pulse-racing chase through the streets of Nice with Bond on a supped-up motorbike chasing an escaping Fatima in a nifty red Renault. Accustomed to automatic rather than stick shift, Barbara Carrera had her most difficult moments of the whole shoot driving that car. "I wrecked about eight gear boxes and created such havoc. They had me shoot this thing before I shot anything else and I wasn't ready. At one point I couldn't get it into gear and I ran into a vegetable cart and all this poor man's vegetables were all over the street. It was horrible."

In one stunning shot, Bond's bike literally jumps over a car in front of it. But Kershner had even grander plans for the machine. "When it reached a certain speed I wanted wings on the two sides of it to unfold and because it has a rocket engine it can actually fly over buildings. It can't keep flying, but it can do these long hops, way up in the air and over two streets and down. This was an image that I had from the beginning and it was drawn on my storyboards. So I asked for it and they said they were going to build it. And the day before shooting they finally said they had it, so the truck came by and they wheeled it out for me. And I said, 'Ok, show me the wings.' They said, 'There are no wings.' I said, 'Why not?' They said, 'The producer said it was too expensive.' And so without telling me they just eliminated it. And there was nothing I could do with it. So I had Bond do a little jump over a canal instead, but it was nothing."

For the whole shoot, Kershner contests that he was always having to compromise over how much of his own personal vision he could impose on the movie. He and Schwartzman had divergent views about what the film should be and although Kershner tried to maintain what he could of his vision, he could only do so much especially since the studio sided with the producer, whether he was right or wrong. "I had to compromise every day. Every day there was frustration for me. And of course nobody

Chapter 36: LAST TANGO IN NICE

realises that you're compromising. Why, because you can't lose the respect of the crew and the actors. They have to feel that you know what you're doing and you're getting what you want, otherwise they get very insecure. So I suffered alone, with my assistant director David Tomblin at my side. He was the only one who knew. He said, 'What are you going to do about this?' I said, 'What the hell can I do, we've got to shoot.' He said, 'We'll make it work.' And that was it. He was the only one I could talk to."

It was a situation that obviously affected the quality of the finished product. Amazingly Kershner calculates that *Never Say Never Again* could have been at least 60% a better movie. "All I see when I see the film now is the compromises, things that I couldn't get. It's like if you're a wardrobe person, you look at a film and all you see is that the star's shoelace is loose and they're going to trip at any moment. That's all they're watching. Well, I can see my compromises all through the film and it was a big disappointment to me."

In Nice, Barbara Carrera rented a luxurious 13-room villa to help her get in the right mood to play the exotic Fatima. "It looked right out of Bond and I thought, this is perfect for Fatima." Barbara had now totally immersed herself in the role, making it known to the crew that once she was in make up and on the set they had to treat her like the character. "Don't ever call me Barbara, I said, just call me Fatima. And they were wonderful with this; they kept it going for the whole shoot."

Barbara even went to the lengths of designing her own wardrobe. Not surprising since her background was fashion, having started out as a model aged 15. "I had definite ideas about this character. I wanted her to be just outrageous. I didn't want her to look like normal people. I went to Yves St. Laurent and all the designers but didn't see anything that was outrageous enough for Fatima. So I ended up just telling the costume designer what I wanted and he created these wonderful outfits." For Barbara the clothes Fatima wore were really an extension of her personality and crucial to the overall performance. "Every part of her outfit was a weapon. I don't think audiences ever realised this, but I knew it and so it helped me. For instance she wore a black pill box hat at the casino. If one looks closely at that hat it's covered with lots of little jewels. Well, they're all sharp little weapons, little daggers, things that could be used as weapons. Also her fingernails were like daggers. And her stiletto heels were a weapon. Those stilettos made me as tall as Sean, so I was looking eye to eye with him. The only problem I had was with Klaus Maria Brandauer. When he first saw me in my outfit and stilettos he freaked out because I was towering over him."

Barbara's dedication endeared her to the whole crew and soon Fatima was everyone's favourite character on the movie. "They all liked Fatima very much and got involved with her. One day we decided she should have a pet, so everyone thought, what kind of a pet? David Tomblin said she should have a cobra. So the next day they brought out this glass box with all these cobras in it. They looked so evil. And up until then I couldn't even look at a picture of a snake, let alone touch one. I told them, I like your idea for a snake, but a cobra? It looks so deadly. Let's use a different kind of snake. So we ended up with a baby boa constrictor. It was eight feet long, but it was still a baby, so I felt comfortable. And by the time we filmed the scenes I was already in Fatima's skin so I was able to do the things I did with that snake, like kissing it and putting it around my shoulders."

A willing ally in the creation of Fatima was Kershner. His help and guidance is something the actress has never forgotten. "To me he's the greatest because he was the first director who allowed me to pull out all the stops. He allowed me to take control of this character. When I came to him with ideas he did not reject them, in fact he listened and then he enhanced them. I've never had that relationship with a director again. As an actor one yearns for this kind of work where one can be very creative and have the support of those around you to help you to be creative. And I had that on this film. It was the first and the last."

Besides Connery, one of the few members of the production crew with previous Bond experience was action co-ordinator Vic Armstrong, who as a stunt man worked on *You Only Live Twice*, skimming down on a rope as a ninja in the famous climactic shoot-out in Blofeld's volcano base. Later he doubled George Lazenby in *On Her Majesty's Secret Service* and Roger Moore in *Live and Let Die*. Armstrong

"NEVER SAY NEVER AGAIN"

REEL 3

Bond's speech in Shrublands Corridor should be (off stage).

SHRUBLANDS CORRIDOR - MORNING

Doctor suggests that a herbal sedative will put Bond right. Bond replies:

       BOND

"I can hardly wait."

REEL 5

      SMALL FAWCETT (calling out)

"Mr. Bond.....Mr. Bond."

       BOND

"Well tell me.....(What's the score with Largo?)

       BOND

"Doesn't this boat belong to Mr. Largo?"

   (As he turns placemat at Bar)

REEL 7

       NICOLE

"3-2-5 Nicole - assigned to MI-6."

       BOND

"Call me James."

       NICOLE

"I found a villa for us in Ville Franche. The yacht is anchored in the bay below. This package came for you from Algernon. (?)

       BOND

"Thank you."

       NICOLE

"He said to remind you - that the pen is mightier than the sword.

Script revisions by Clement and La Frenais.

was as amazed as anyone about Connery's return to Bondage and was thrilled to be involved, despite it leading to serious personal injury. "In the South of France I quickly got into the action doubling Sean, with my wife Wendy doubling Kim Basinger, in a scene where Bond rescues Domino on horseback and they're both chased around a castle by Arab baddies. At one point I burst through a group of riders, but my stirrup caught a horse on the shoulder and it turned my foot completely, dislocating my ankle.

The pain was atrocious. As I rode back, my face ashen white, nearly vomiting in agony because my foot had come out of its socket, I saw a bunch of medics rushing over. But it wasn't for me; one of the other riders had landed on a wall and broken his back so that obviously took priority. By the end of the day my bloody ankle had blown up like a balloon and I couldn't work so the boys took me to hospital. 'Do what you like,' I said. 'But don't put a plaster-cast on because I'm working tomorrow.' The doctor shook his head. 'No, you can't work.' I said, 'Of course I can, I'm only sitting on a horse for the next few weeks, galloping around the South of France, I'll be fine.' So they reluctantly just put a bandage on, even though by now my leg had gone black from the knee to the sole of my feet. I arrived on the set the next day on crutches and every time I got on the horse the doctor had to pump me full of painkillers."

After glimpsing Connery only briefly on *You Only Live Twice* way back in 1966, *Never Say* was the first time Vic Armstrong had really worked with the superstar, though they'd go on to make several pictures together like *Indiana Jones and the Last Crusade* and *Entrapment*. "Connery is great. If you're a stunt man he's a fabulous guy to double for because he doesn't want to do much at all; quite rightly so, he does the acting, you do the stunting, the complete opposite of people like Harrison and Tom Cruise. Sean would much rather go and play golf. He was great to work for, very professional; he wanted to know how everything was going to work in the action and fight scenes. Famously he doesn't suffer fools, if you're wasting his time, which is precious to him, the same as anybody, he gets very antsy, but as long as you're professional and he knows you're doing a good job he's fine. He was good fun to work with."

As the crew wrapped in France and were preparing to leave for the next location, the Bahamas, Clement and La Frenais were heading back to London. "I'm standing next to Kershner at the airport," Clement recalls. "And by now I'd read the whole script and we'd done a few little rewrites to do with the French bit, but we could see that there was a lot of other stuff that really needed help. And I said, 'Do you like your opening sequence?' And Kershner stroked his beard and said, 'Not especially, why, you got a better one?'"

The opening sequence, as written by Semple, took place at a spectacular medieval jousting tournament. When one of the contestants is viciously murdered a fellow knight gives chase to the assassin. Both men, on horseback, vault over a fence and into a modern-day parking lot. Jumping car after car the knight finally catches the killer and eliminates him. He then removes his helmet and guess what? It's James Bond. This could have been one of the most unusual openings to a 007 movie ever. But Clement didn't think so. "I remember saying to Kershner, 'Your film's main trump card is that you've got the real James Bond, and you've got a tin can on his head for the first five minutes. It seems to me that it would be stupid not to take advantage of the fact that you've got the real guy.' Kershner said, 'Then why don't you write a new opening?' And we said, ok."

Back in London the writers started thinking up ideas for a brand new teaser when Clement got an urgent midnight call. "We need you in the Bahamas tomorrow." Boarding an 8am British Airways flight to Nassau the next morning the lucky pair found themselves sharing first class with Kim Basinger. "This stuff doesn't happen very often in screenwriting," Clement testifies. "And I'll never forget this flight. There was a very camp steward and he said, 'I'll bring you some better wine when we take off because I know who you are.' So he was looking after us. And then he said, 'Let's hope we get in the air.' I said, 'What do you mean?' He said, 'No I shouldn't have said anything.' I said, 'Come on you've got to tell us now.' He said, 'It's just that this pilot has never flown the Atlantic before. He's been on Mediterranean routes.' We said, 'All right, at least we know.' So the plane takes off and the steward's standing there and he went, 'Oh didn't he do well.' And this is all true. I couldn't make this up. And then a little bit later the announcement comes on. 'This is Captain Matthews. We've reached our altitude of 37,000 feet and we're continuing our course across the Mediterranean… I mean the Atlantic.' Well, when he said that our steward nearly lost it completely."

Clement and La Frenais' new opening had Bond on a training mission to rescue a kidnap victim held by guerrillas in a jungle hideout. The whole sequence was played against the background of a stopwatch going tick, tick, tick. "In the worst post production decision in movie history, in my humble opinion, they put a song over this," rages Clement. "It was a sad, pale imitation of, 'oh it's a Bond film so we've got to have a song.' Trust me, when it had a ticking stopwatch over it that sequence had tension. You put a song over it, nobody's tense. It was a terrible decision. It was really dumb. We saw that sequence and it got the film off to a great start. There was Sean looking great, like a man of action. Wham, bang, thank you man. And it worked. A lot better than knights with tin cans on their heads. That really upset us when we saw the movie because we said, this was really exciting and now it isn't. It totally threw the tension away."

The new sequence also addressed the age factor, which Semple had drawn too heavily upon in early script drafts. "You see Bond looking absolutely fantastic," says Clement. "And then having his boss say, 'Only 26 seconds, you're slipping Mr Bond.' So it was dealing, in a way, with that whole question of age. And we did talk about how to deal with the age factor and decided in the end to send him to a health farm to straighten himself out."

Besides pitching the new opening, something else about the script had caught Clement's eye in Nice. "I said to Kershner, 'Is there any particular reason why Bond goes to the Bahamas because it's very unclear in the script why he goes there?' And Kershner said, 'Well we'd better find one because there's three units shooting there as we speak.' They had an underwater unit, a second unit and obviously the first unit was about to go out there. So I think maybe that, and the opening sequence were two reasons why they thought that maybe they did need us."

CHAPTER 37
BAHAMIAN BALLS-UP

Arriving in Nassau, Clement sensed with interest that the uneasy atmosphere in France had carried over into the Bahamas. "There were these terrible rows in the evening. At the end of each day there was a huge debate about what was going wrong. And we'd sit in on these meetings until they started to get ugly and then we would get up and say we'll just go and make the dinner reservations. So we would go and get a bottle of red wine, start drinking it and wait to see who turned up. And it tended to be Sean. He'd come in and say, 'bloody Mickey Mouse outfit,' and grumble at us. He found it very unprofessional."

Spirits were low among the crew as well, so it was decided to put an assembly together of some 30 minutes of cut footage. The motorbike chase had been filmed and the action looked good, and it did give everyone a boost when they saw it. But this solution was akin to putting an Elastoplast on a bullet. The production had now degenerated into a diabolical fiasco. Schwartzman had never produced a film before. His only other credit prior to *Never Say Never Again* was as executive producer on Peter Sellers' penultimate picture *Being There*, so starting one's solo producing career with an action blockbuster was sheer madness, as well as professional suicide. "He was way out of his depth," says Clement. "And I felt sorry for him. When a film is unhappy the unhappiness waves over everybody. When you've got a power vacuum there's people rushing in to fill it. And Sean knew Schwartzman was out of his depth and was pissed off."

To counterbalance Schwartzman's lack of experience, the behind the scenes talent on *Never Say Never Again* couldn't have been any better. There was top cameraman Douglas Slocombe, assistant director David Tomblin, whom Steven Spielberg would later call the finest in the world, and veteran second unit director Michael Moore, fresh from *Raiders of the Lost Ark*. But Schwartzman still lost his way and the film was irrevocably damaged as a result. "It was not a well organised film at all, in fact it was kind of dis-organised," admits Kershner, who'd just made *The Empire Strikes Back* so must have been used to the rigors and demands of a mammoth movie. "But *Empire* was organised. Even though the unexpected is constantly happening on a big picture, especially when you have 64 sets to build,

```
MOVEMENT ORDER FOR ARRIVAL OF CREW TO NASSAU


THURSDAY, 9th June, 1983

Les Dilley                          Art Director

SUNDAY, 12th June, 1983

Peter Grant                         Property Master

TUESDAY, 14th June, 1983    UP 247 at 17:00 Hours

Harold Schneider            Completion Bond Representative
Ilona Herman                Makeup
Sue Love                    Hairdresser

WEDNESDAY, 15th June, 1983

Sean Connery

Ocean Films Crew    EA 47 at 17:40 Hours

Al Giddings
Rosemary Chastney
Terry Thompson
Walt Clayton
Rich Mula
Chuck Nicklin
Henk van Beever
Dan McSweeney

THURSDAY, 16th June, 1983   EA 47 (Eastern) at 17:40 Hours

Kim Basinger + 1
Ron Snyder

Peter Swann                 Assistant Director
Jim Swann
Philip Pickford             Wardrobe Master
Doug Green                  SPFX Man
John Newman

FRIDAY, 17th June, 1983

Klaus Brandauer
```

Movement order for the crew's arrival on Nassau.

it was huge – *Empire*, but it was organised, which means that I could do my work. With *Never Say*, it was disorganised."

Outside forces too conspired to scupper the film; everything from weather problems to car crashes that didn't work. As the production fell heavily behind schedule rumours flew around that this Bond was in deep trouble. "I think people should judge the film, not the process," was Schwartzman's defence. The producer also blamed Kershner's indecisiveness for causing further delays and confusion, and soon the budget had mushroomed to $36m. "But I saw a tremendous wastage of money; it made me sick," says Kershner. "Because if you're not organised on a big picture the money just flows out. It's like turning on a faucet, and you wonder how the hell to turn it off. Of course the director takes a lot of crap because of it. But I can't do all the organising for a film like this, I have to have the people around me that I can count on, so I can do my work. The only person I could count on during the whole picture, in terms of organisation, was my assistant, Dave Tomblin. He was fabulous. Without him I could never have finished the picture. Indeed the picture wouldn't have been finished."

Kershner gives a good example of the sort of incompetence that he was facing sometimes on a daily basis. He sent a second unit crew out to the Bahamas to shoot underwater scenes using a double for Bond, just swimming shots that could be inserted later into the main action. "They spent quite a bit of money and took about a month shooting it. Beforehand I'd asked them to get all the pictures they could of Sean to see exactly what he looked like and to shoot his body double. I came to the Bahamas from France and wanted to see everything they shot. At my hotel they started running the rushes and I almost died. 'What's that?' They said, 'That's Bond swimming.' I said, 'That's not Bond swimming, that's a young man, doesn't look like Bond at all.' They said, 'Well we copied the pictures.' It transpired that the production outfit had sent them photos of Sean, but they were from *Thunderball*. His body was different, quite different. After all, he was almost 20 years older. I went crazy and said, 'We're throwing out every foot of this film. I don't want to save one frame, you can't save it; it's ridiculous.' And I stormed out. Walking down the hallway a man passed me carrying some scuba equipment and I went, 'Whoa, who are you?' He said, 'I hold the camera for the cameraman underwater.' And I said, 'Turn around.' He turned around. He was a perfect duplicate for Sean. So I brought him back into the room and said, 'Here, re-shoot every chance you get with this man.' And they shot him and of course it matches perfectly. And he'd been behind the camera the whole time."

Faults apart, Schwartzman did contribute creatively to the film. It was his idea for Largo to challenge Bond to a deadly video game duel; a sort of updated version of Fleming's classic casino showdowns. Bond purists may have balked, but it's actually one of the film's few genuinely tense moments. Schwartzman's business relationship with the brother of Arab billionaire Adnon Khashoggi also helped secure use of his yacht, the Nabila, for ten days of shooting. At almost 300 feet long, with a helicopter pad, swimming pool, cinema, discotheque, two saunas and 11 guest suites, the Nabila was a perfect stand in for Largo's ocean faring HQ, the Flying Saucer.

To be fair on Schwartzman, he did admit his shortcomings after the film's release: "I totally underestimated what I was getting into. There were substantial cost overruns, all of which came out of my own pocket. So, in effect, I paid the price of my own shortcomings." Had he the chance to do it all over again, Schwartzman admitted he'd make the same picture but spend the money more efficiently, plus develop better relationships with his team. I guess mostly with Connery. Producer and star took an instant dislike to each other, which lasted for the duration of filming. "They had a very, very poor relationship," admits Kershner. "It goes beyond what you can imagine." Barbara Carrera noticed this too. "Sean and the producer just didn't get along at all. They hated each other." It didn't help that Schwartzman often upped and left the production, with few knowing where he'd gone. "He'd leave all the time," confirms Clement. "He was scared of Connery. There was such tension around the set."

For Connery, the filming of *Never Say Never Again* wasn't the joy it should have been. Instead of basking in his return as Bond he felt the whole enterprise was jeopardised by a producer that was "totally incompetent, a real ass." One of the major gripes Connery had about his 60s Bonds was their lengthy schedules, but ironically here he was saddled with a limping production that seemed as long as the other six he'd made put together. "There was so much incompetence, ineptitude and dissension that the film could have disintegrated," he later blasted. "It was like working in a toilet. What I could have done was just let it bury itself. I could have walked away with an enormous amount of money and the film would never have been finished. But once I was in there, I ended up getting in the middle of every decision. The assistant director and myself really produced that picture."

The whole *Never Say* experience left Connery drained and disillusioned. After filming he took the longest sabbatical of his career, not making another picture for three years. As for Schwartzman he went on to produce only a handful of other movies before his untimely death from cancer in 1994.

Connery, at times, also found himself at odds with Kershner, even occasionally taking personal charge of scenes from the director. "I'd done six Bonds and this was his first," he excused. On creative matters they didn't always see eye to eye, but Kershner is a believer in the best actors challenging their director. It's up to the director to know the answers, and today Kershner has nothing but fond memories of their collaboration. "Sean is the greatest professional I've ever worked with. No matter what is going wrong, no matter what you're trying to do, he's there to help. The only thing that he demands is that if you tell him he gets off that day at 5.30, he wants to go at 5.30 because he's got a golf game going. I don't blame him for it because he's there on the set when you need him and he knows every line. He's quite wonderful."

Barbara Carrera too has nothing but the fondest memories of Connery. "It was great working with Sean. He was the Bond I'd grown up with as a child. And when I looked at him I just saw Bond, so that was great, I didn't need to act. Nor did I seek help from him, but early on in the shooting he gave me a little piece of advice. He said, God helps those who help themselves. And so I took that literally and took total control of my character."

Notwithstanding the incompetence and obscene waste of money that led Connery at one point to tell a reporter that he should have killed Schwartzman, what incensed the actor above everything else was that the script was never right. "You see, he'd been burned before over the Richard Lester film *Cuba*," says Clement. "On that he kept saying, the script isn't there, the script isn't there. And they went on the floor and it didn't work. And the truth is, if the script isn't really there before you go on the floor, you're in dead trouble. And Sean was pretty mad because he felt that he kept telling Schwartzman, you've got to get the script right, and they hadn't. So he was mad because they shouldn't have been in this position."

The poor quality of the script was even affecting the way the actors behaved, notably Brandauer, according to Clement. "Brandauer, who can be a very fine actor, was doing the sort of things that actors do when they don't trust the text; in other words, falling back on every trick that they've ever done. I thought he was dreadful in the film, particularly in the dailies. For somebody who can be a great actor, it was terrible. And poor Kim Basinger had very little to do, except look decorative. She really had a shitty part. The sensible thing really would have been to delay the shoot for three months and get the script right. But sensible things don't always happen in films, usually you have to go when the money's there. If a script isn't ready you're in trouble because there is a real limit to what you can fix on the floor. I think if you're trying to change more than 5% you're in trouble and we were changing at least 30%, and fairly radically."

It's difficult to underestimate Clement and La Frenais' contribution to *Never Say Never Again*. Their fingerprints are all over the opening 40 minutes, the entire health farm sequence (where they resurrected the old gag from *Porridge* about giving a urine sample in a beaker. "From here?"), through to the Bahamas section. They also invented a totally new character in Small-Fawcett, Bond's bumbling British contact in Nassau, played by Rowan Atkinson in his film debut. "That character came about because we thought the film needed some comic relief around there," says Clement. "And while we were writing him we thought, this is kind of Rowan Atkinson. Of course the Americans had never heard of him and Rowan had never been across the Atlantic before. I'm not sure the character completely works in the movie. But there are some nice bits."

Connery was particularly pleased with the British style comedy input from Clement and La Frenais, later using them for much the same purpose on his action hit *The Rock*. But despite working on *Never Say Never Again* for three months, a restriction imposed by the Writers Guild of America precluded their receiving a credit on the finished film. Lorenzo Semple Jr gets sole authorship. "Very often you don't have a beef when you don't get a credit on a movie because usually you know going in it's not gonna happen," says Clement. "But with this one we really felt we'd earned a credit. We fought for it and Sean backed us up, and we still lost. Which happens. But Sean made it known in interviews that we worked on the script which we were very grateful for."

Chapter 37: BAHAMIAN BALLS-UP

In the Bahamas, the film was further bogged down by intricate underwater sequences, although these were on a far less ambitious scale than *Thunderball*. Again the filmmakers turned to Ricou Browning to direct them, the most hazardous being Bond's close encounter with a school of sharks around a sunken fishing boat. "Actually the wreck of that ship was about two football fields away from where we sank the Vulcan bomber in *Thunderball*," Browning reveals. "And the framework of the aircraft was still sitting there. It had turned into a reef."

At first, according to Kershner, the idea was to use fake sharks, but he was told they would be too expensive to build. "So we simply sent out a boat every night and caught a tiger shark, which had to be at least 13 feet long. We kept it in a tank on the ship and then put a rope around it and lowered it down to our sunken ship where it was used for a few seconds at a time. And then the next day we got another one. So those were real sharks. And they look it."

No one had attempted to film sharks inside an underwater set before, but much of the impact of the sequence was lost when elements of the action ended up on the cutting room floor, such as when Bond dispatches the first shark with a spear gun. "I wasn't completely thrilled with the editing of the shark scene," Browning complains. "As a matter of fact it made me mad because I thought the footage they cut out was excellent. It followed exactly what I told them I would shoot; they understood that, but I think somebody decided they didn't want to see a shark get killed. And there were other things too that were edited not to my satisfaction. Maybe the picture was running long and they had to cut somewhere so they cut the underwater stuff. That's probably the reason."

While not the memorable experience *Thunderball* had been, *Never Say Never Again* did afford Browning the chance to hook up again with Connery. "He was very easy to work with. If Sean knows you know what you're doing he doesn't give you a hard time and co-operates 100%. I got along great with him. I think Sean was kind of the glue on that picture. He held it all together."

In the Bahamas, Vic Armstrong took time out from filming to indulge in a bit of scuba diving with the shark team and learnt the awful way they train sharks in films. "I found it very cruel. People talk about looking after the welfare of other animals in movies but because sharks are killers or fish they don't seem to have any pity for them. Once caught, a rope was put around their tails and they were tied to rocks so they couldn't swim anywhere. In order to breathe sharks must have water passing through their gills, without it they fill up with carbon monoxide and end up dying or getting very dopey. It's like leaving somebody in a car full of fumes and then pulling them out at the last minute when they're on the edge of dying. So the unit had these dopey sharks and two or three divers would just throw them like arrows through this sunken wreck; it was terrible and they killed a lot in the process."

Armstrong went diving one day with his wife Wendy (the daughter of veteran Bond stunt man George Leech), a great swimmer but nervous about the deadlier things that live in the sea. "Exploring this wreck I looked about and saw two divers carrying a 12-foot shark towards the set to do some rehearsals. I turned round to tell Wendy and she wasn't there, just a stream of bubbles, she was about thirty feet above me going like a rocket to the surface. I carried on and stroked this tiger shark. What a beautiful creature it was and quite an experience to meet a real man killer up close."

Besides coordinating the action, Armstrong doubled Connery in the opening jungle training exercise and in the controversial stunt when Bond leaps off a castle battlement on horseback and falls into the ocean. This was achieved by putting Armstrong, a stuntwoman doubling Domino, plus the horse on top of a 40 foot tower inside a box that could be tilted forward, just like the old shows on Coney Island where horses fell out of traps into water tanks.

The tower had walls built on the side and around the box so the horse couldn't see where he was and on the day of the stunt, Armstrong walked him up the tower into the box and hitched himself into the saddle. "On action, the box was designed to tilt forward, sliding the horse down and these doors at the front were to open to release us into space. But on action, everybody was so highly sprung, the guy operating the doors panicked and pressed the button too early. The horse had been quite calm until this moment, then suddenly saw where he was and went, 'whoa, no way,' and backed off completely. Now, of course, the box wouldn't tilt because all the weight of the horse was in the back. The crew reached over to try and chase him forward but all they did was beat me over the head. In the end everyone manually lifted the box up and as we slid out the horse's last reaction was to try and rear up in a bid to come out backwards, so I held his head as we went down absolutely vertically. Almost immediately the stuntwoman jumped clear while I rode him all the way down, stepping off as we smashed into the water. I deliberately stayed underwater as long as I could because I didn't want the horse trampling on my head, but when I broke the surface he'd already swum ashore."

The horse had been given weeks of endurance training in order to build up enough energy to swim clear, but during the stunt, as the crew walked the horse up the ramp, a bunch of holiday makers watching nearby started booing and hissing believing the film crew were being cruel to the animal. The RSPCA certainly agreed and when the film was shown in Britain they complained so vigorously that the sequence was cut out.

It would be almost 15 years before Vic Armstrong returned to Bondage, this time with the official series and in the capacity of second unit director on the last three Pierce Brosnan 007 movies. But due to the controversy surrounding *Never Say Never Again* having been made outside of the Broccoli family, he was never allowed to mention it. "Barbara Broccoli and Michael G. Wilson always frowned when I spoke about that film. 'Don't swear in front of us.' They'd say."

With work in the Bahamas completed, the crew flew to London's Elstree Studios to film interiors, including the impressive "Well of Allah" underwater cavern set that features prominently in the climax. The final reel of *Never Say Never Again* differs markedly from that of *Thunderball*. SPECTRE no longer plans to obliterate Miami, but somehow have managed to plant one of the stolen bombs under the White House. The other threatens the West's oil supplies in the Middle East, so the climax shifts to North Africa. There is no big underwater battle, just a few marines led by Felix Leiter that defeat SPECTRE in an underground temple. All pretty uninspired stuff. And the final showdown between Bond and Largo is a boring underwater duel.

There's also something very stodgy about the final third of *Never Say*, and one can't help feeling that killing off Fatima Blush too early was a mistake. Such is her impact on the film that it almost can't recover from her leaving it. "Fatima had this bombastic energy," says Barbara. "This energy that was unworldly; maybe it was Kali. And it was kind of missed. And I'm sorry about that. In a way I didn't think that would help me too much in my career because it made me a little bit afraid that certain big male stars would not want to work with me." One can't help feeling, with Hollywood being the insecure business it is, that this is exactly what happened because Barbara's career faded after *Never Say*, when surely it should have risen, notwithstanding her deserved Golden Globe nomination. "But I could not believe the reaction to Fatima from the public. I did not anticipate it. She's the kind of character I discovered over the years that everybody loves. Even though she's so bad, everybody loves her. Children loved her, nuns and priests loved her. I met this guru and she told me, I couldn't wait to see what bad things this character was going to do next. Even though she was so wicked, she was full of light. People found her very appealing. I don't know why to this day, but everybody liked her."

Despite her inability to capitalise on her Bond appearance, Barbara looks back fondly on the film today: "I had the time of my life, I loved every moment of it. I couldn't wait to wake up the next morning to go to work. It was a truly wonderful experience for me. And I think it's one of the better Bond films. I think it's very entertaining. They could have spent less time with all of the underwater stuff at the end, which kind of slowed it up a little bit, but all in all it was a very good film."

Also in England, location work took place in Luton, where a manor house stood in for Shrublands health farm. Here Bond makes the first of a frightening number of seductions. Actress Prunella Gee took on the role of masseuse Patricia, essayed by Mollie Peters in *Thunderball*, and confessed that playing a Bond girl was nowhere near as glamourous as it sounded. With almost everyone else going to the Bahamas and the South of France she was landed with ten days in freezing cold Luton.

Chapter 37: BAHAMIAN BALLS-UP

Oblivious to all the machinations that had gone on in France and the Bahamas, what Prunella saw was enough for her to label the production as "complete chaos. The schedules were all up the creek." She observed arguments and differences of opinion between Connery, Kershner and Schwartzman, though sensed that it was Connery who held the upper hand throughout. So far as she could gather Connery was also very much responsible for the humour in the film, going back to his hotel and working on the script at night, changing lines to get slightly more double-entendres into their scenes together.

Clement and La Frenais were around too for the English shooting, and after their stint in Nice and Nassau managed to cop yet another perk off the movie. "There was a whole debate about which wine Bond was to have," says Clement. "We researched this copiously and we specified Cheval Blanc 62, I think. And we said to the prop guy, 'By the way it's written in the small print that we get the wine when you've finished with it because I'm sure you won't open it.' And the prop guy came up to us and said, 'We couldn't get the 62, is the 63 alright?' It was very alright."

Looking back, Clement describes working on *Never Say Never Again* as. "a dream gig. And Connery was great. I remember saying to Sean once, 'In the script you have a bonk in the morning, then you've got this whole underwater sequence where you wrestle with sharks, and you come out and you have another bonk in the afternoon. That proves something.' 'Yeah,' he said. 'That proves it's a movie.'"

When the cameras stopped rolling finally on *Never Say* there was a collective sigh of relief. "Logistically the film was a nightmare," says Kershner. "Shooting in five countries was very, very difficult. I was flying around from place to place and setting things up and rushing over to another country and setting things up and rushing off somewhere else. It was kind of a nightmare."

Barbara Carrera – publicity pose at McClory's Bahamas' home.

CHAPTER 38
THE BITTEREST PILL

Originally, Schwartzman had hoped to bring *Never Say Never Again* out in direct competition with Eon's summer Bond *Octopussy*, but delays in filming meant a winter debut was now more likely. There were also problems in the editing stages and some interesting scenes were cut out. When Fatima plants the bomb under Bond's hotel room bed, she goes to reception to check that he'll return in time to be killed. "When is Mr Bond expected?" she asks the clerk. "Five," he replies. "Dead on five," Fatima responds. Then after Largo's death, Bond and Domino were to escape in a helicopter with SPECTRE's mini-TV communicator. Suddenly, Blofeld appears on the screen asking for Largo, his No. 1. "Sorry," Bond replies. "You've got the wrong number; it's 007." A startled Blofeld is then scratched by his cat, whose claws are dripping in poison. As Bond casts the monitor out of the window, we watch Blofeld's screaming face plummet toward the sea below.

Legal problems also threatened to scupper the film. The trustees of the Fleming estate, financially assisted by Eon and MGM, the studio who had recently purchased United Artists, brought an injunction against Schwartzman to stop the release of *Never Say*, much to Connery's chagrin. "Now that they've had their innings, as it were, with *Octopussy*, I can't imagine why they persist." But persist Broccoli did. Close to the American opening of *Never Say* Eon petitioned the High Court of London in a final 11th hour bid to stop its release. But their legal team failed. By waiting until the film was ready to go into cinemas they'd undercut any chance of stopping it. The judge simply asked, "Why did you wait until now?" The financial stakes were so high even the law wasn't prepared to put the brakes on it.

Never Say Never Again premièred in Los Angeles on 7 October 1983, with Connery in attendance. Then as now, October was a dead time to open a movie, but despite that self-inflicted handicap, the film set attendance records for the greatest Fall movie opening in US history with a weekend take of $10m. And when the reviews came out even Connery couldn't have wished for better. Undoubtedly they're some of the finest notices ever for a Bond film. "*Never Say Never Again* falls only a desperate hair short of being the best Bond movie in recorded history," said the San

Francisco Chronicle. The Chicago-Sun Times thought Connery back as Bond was "One of those small showbusiness miracles that never happen. There was never a Beatles reunion. But here by God, is Sean Connery as Sir James Bond."

For once, the London opening of a film on 14 December, was a more glamourous occasion than its Hollywood counterpart. Connery again attended, with McClory and Kershner. Special guests included ex-Bond girl Barbara Bach, with husband Ringo Starr, former Prime Minister Harold Wilson and Prince Andrew. Prior to its British release Connery had embarked upon the most gruelling publicity campaign of his entire career. He'd taken *Never Say* around the world and in the UK subjected himself to interview after interview on TV, radio and print culminating in a Q&A session before a live audience at the National Film Theatre, who'd been holding a season of his films.

The UK press reacted equally enthusiastically to the film. Starburst magazine was typical of the critic's views: "A definite hark back to the halcyon days of the Fleming series… superb entertainment." As for Roger Moore, his only printed comment on *Never Say* was typically self-mocking: "It's the first time I've ever been panned for a film I wasn't in." But in box office terms, Moore enjoyed the last laugh with *Octopussy*'s US gross of $67m outpacing *Never Say*'s $55m; although that was a figure that wouldn't be beaten by another Bond film until 1995's *GoldenEye*. World wide *Never Say* took over $100m, working particularly well in Europe and Japan.

Kershner was most surprised by the reaction in Russia. It was the time of Gorbachev and Glasnost, so they were beginning to loosen up, but it was still very much a Communist state. Few if any Western films had arrived in the country, but a new policy allowed for some to be shown in selected cinemas. "And they asked me to bring over *Never Say Never Again*. They showed it in the largest theatre in Moscow. Before the film started I got up on the stage and I looked at these grim faces. The first five rows were full of military officers. And I said, 'Look, this film must not be taken seriously, it is a comedy, in essence; it's supposed to have witticism; it's supposed to be funny; it's supposed to have tension, but don't think of it, as you do with Russian films, as being some metaphor that I'm hiding behind. What you see is what you get.' The film started and there was this woman translator sitting up in the balcony with our script reading everybody's lines, including Bond's! I thought, this is awful, awful. But they laughed at every single witty moment. It surprised me because when I showed the film in New York I had a few giggles. When I showed it in the Mid-West I didn't get one laugh, not one. They didn't get it. They didn't see the humour of it. Yet in Russia the critics afterwards talked about what a relief it was to see an American film that didn't take itself seriously. For example, the tango scene when Bond tells Domino that her brother is dead but to keep dancing, well in Russia they burst out laughing, they saw the humour of it. In America, nothing. In America, it has to be very obvious for them to get it. Back then American audiences were not accustomed to irony."

Never Say ranks up there with *Thunderball* as one of the wittiest Bond films. There are some great double entendres, ironic asides and just plain funny lines, which is just as well because in many other respects the picture just doesn't work. Watching it is always an anti-climactic experience because it's not the film it could and should have been. "In the final analysis, the film fails to achieve its true potential," wrote the British James Bond Fan Club. "And after 13 years and numerous false starts it is a bitter pill to swallow."

So what's wrong with it? Here goes: The direction is too often lethargic, the story is disjointed and the score by Michel Legrand (chosen over Schwartzman's preferred choice of James Horner) seems as if it's wandered in from a different movie completely. Indeed in the mid 90s there were rumours that Schwartzman hoped to release a laser disc version of *Never Say* that not only incorporated extensive footage cut from the film, but a brand new score. But most glaring of all, *Never Say* just doesn't have the feel and epic-scope of an Eon-Bond movie. "I don't think anybody would say it's one of the best Bond films," says Dick Clement. "Of course it did have Sean, and that helped it enormously." Connery certainly holds the picture together with a wonderfully debonair and laid back performance. He's the best thing about the film, which otherwise would have been a very undistinguished adventure

Chapter 38: THE BITTEREST PILL

yarn. As Bond historian Steven Jay Rubin sums up, "It's long. We've seen most of the action before in *Thunderball*. It has the worst musical score in the series, and the climax is boring, but *Never Say Never Again* is a Sean Connery Bond movie and when he's on screen the movie works. Fortunately he's on screen a lot."

That even a half way decent film emerged from such a calamitous production is in itself a minor miracle. "And it's a great tribute to Sean's star power," says Clement. "I remember watching Sean in the dailies where he's in the warehouse and Fatima Blush is about to blow him away, and in every take, even the space between the words, something was happening with Sean. You'd look at him and say, he's very good. You just could see a real movie actor doing his stuff."

and also should be financially compensated for the illegal use of their work.

As far as the Whittingham heirs are concerned, the legal issue from the opposition will be the same as last time, i.e Jack Whittingham was a writer 'for hire', and was paid.) I take a much more moral AND PRACTICAL VIEW OF THE THEFT OF INTELLECTUAL PROPERTY, ~~piece of the copying of others work~~ and the profiting by so doing. ~~And~~ I feel that Jacks heirs should benefit not just by credit but in a monetary way, As at this point I am exploring the various options open to me I do not know the route I shall take or the amount involved, but I am sure that there would be no difficulty in our sitting down and coming to an arrangement on this, as................... You called at this moment, I shall close now and look forward to hearing from you.

Warm wishes

Kevin McClory

OK to Send to Jonathan.

Part of McClory's 1989 letter to Sylvan.

Sylvan's brother, Jonathan, responds to McClory.

Box 135, Heriot Bay,
British Columbia,
Canada, V0P 1H0.

June 5th 1989.

Dear Kevin,
    The last time we met, I was a small boy. I remember sitting at our kitchen table building plastic models of bomber-planes and being interrogated by my father as to the crew requirements and other technical details which I very convincingly managed to make up on the spur of the moment and for which Jack appeared to be extremely grateful. I also remember being crammed into the back of what I think was a red Ford Mustang and being taken up to London to see, I think, Lawrence of Arabia. My one other relevant memory is of a basement flat, a beautiful woman and a plastic model of an underwater diver with a harpoon gun. I never quite forgave my father for not asking you to give me the model.(Of the underwater diver).
    I have recieved a copy of your letter to Suilven and I am prompted to respond. I have one comment to make and one question to ask.
    Having absolutely nothing to do with the film world, I must confess that it is of little relevance to me what the people in that particular industry choose to believe regarding the authorship of Thunderball. I know what I know. Please don't take this comment as a sign of callous disrespect for the memory of my dear father.It is merely a rational and practical view of my own world when placed in context with a world so far removed as to appear invisible. I won't deny that, given the opportunity, I will search the indexes of specific books for mention of Jack's name and be thrilled to find it . The comments that have been written have not always been so thrilling- Ivor Bryce's book made me quite angry.
    However, to be quite honest with you, the suggestion that the heirs to Jack's estate should be entitled to some financial compensation for as yet unspecified damages, is extremely thought-provoking.
    In your last paragraph you say:"I take a much more moral and practical view of the theft of intellectual property, and the profiting by so doing. I feel that Jack's heirs should benefit not just by credit but in a monetary way." The question burns in my brain. If that statement truly represents your feelings and beliefs, Kevin, then perhaps you will be kind enough to explain to Suilven and myself, why arrangements for either royalties or payments were not made prior to the production of the film " Never say never again" ? The credits were clearly forthcoming. The money was not.
    Aside from any arrangement that we three may agree to regarding the release of any papers for your scrutiny and possible use, I feel that in order to demonstrate your genuine credibility, you must first very clearly adress the question asked in this letter.
    I am sending this to Suilven for her approval to send this to you. I realise that it may appear somewhat blunt and to the point. I apologize for that, but I am , after all, the son of a Yorkshireman.

Jonathan.

CHAPTER 39
McCLORY BOUNCES BACK

Encouraged by the success of *Never Say Never Again,* McClory was keen to launch a series of 007 films based on the *Thunderball* scripts to rival the official movies. Eon and Broccoli's legal team had foreseen such an eventuality when their injunction to hold up the release of *Never Say* was rejected by a judge. They had appealed against the verdict to the Appellate court but after five days of argument, three Lord Justices upheld the original decision. The implications of such a ruling and the repercussions it might have were not lost on Eon's legal team. "By your Lordships' decision," barrister Mr John Mummery said. "The defendants (meaning McClory and Schwartzman) may well say in future that they are entitled to make other films of James Bond without restriction. If that is so, that could have serious effects on the financial interests of the plaintiffs (Eon) and the film companies with whom they have been associated for the last 20 years." He was right.

Going ahead with more Bond films was one thing, but McClory would have to do it without Sean Connery, who had already told reporters his intention of never again stepping into Bond's shoes. And this time it appeared he really meant it. In February 1984 McClory announced the first of his intended new Bond movies would go under the title of SPECTRE. It never materialised.

Hollywood didn't hear anything more from McClory until 1988 when he announced the production of "Warhead 8", which would see the reintroduction of Bond's arch foes SPECTRE and Blofeld. "Bond fans throughout the world will be delighted with the return of the original villains," McClory said, adding his claim that Eon and Broccoli never had any rights to use the SPECTRE organisation or its chief, Blofeld, in any of their Bond movies save *Thunderball*. "Broccoli duped film audiences for 27 years with cover-up of illegal use of SPECTRE in early Bond films," ran a McClory press release. The Irishman also started touting round Hollywood the notion of a series of James Bond versus SPECTRE animated adventures. It led to nothing, but not long afterwards *James Bond Jr* appeared - a 60+ episode cartoon series, sanctioned by Broccoli, that featured Bond's nephew. The cartoon was almost certainly meant as a counter point to McClory's project and helped to diminish the value of any future McClory animated projects.

Meanwhile the family of Jack Whittingham had heard nothing from McClory since the mid-60s. He'd not even notified them about his intention to make *Never Say Never Again*. "I felt very cross about that," says Sylvan. "After all, it was a second film. Dad was contracted to make one film and Kevin had used his screenplay again. He might at least have had the courtesy to ask us." Jack Whittingham does receive a credit on the film for original story, but McClory manages to get his name put first. "I'm afraid Kevin has diluted dad's contribution all the way along," argues Sylvan.

Since the mid-60s, Sylvan's own life had taken some fascinating turns. Bored with secretarial work she'd read a horoscope that advised her to "follow every golden opportunity" that month. Sending off a demo disc of her singing and playing guitar to the Radio Luxembourg Talent Search, Sylvan surprised everyone by reaching the top six in the London finals having never sung in public before. Encouraged to take singing lessons to strengthen her untrained voice, it wasn't long before Sylvan was discovered and plucked from obscurity from Soho's coffee bars to write and record her first record, "We Don't Belong," released in August 1965, not long before the opening of *Thunderball*. The single caused some controversy due to its subject matter - that of a suicide pact between young lovers. Appearances followed on TV shows and Sylvan even promoted the single on Radio Caroline, the pioneer pirate ship. Saying hi to regular DJs Tony Blackburn and Dave Lee Travis, a storm sprang up out of nowhere and Sylvan was stranded on the floating station for two days.

Sylvan's second single, "When You Do What You're Doing" was penned and dueted with her future husband Barry Mason, with whom she went on to co-compose hits for Tom Jones, most famously "Delilah" and "Love Grows Where Rosemary Goes" for Edison Lighthouse. With the proceeds from "Delilah" Sylvan and Barry Mason bought Kinfauns, George Harrison's house in Esher. Kinfauns was where the Beatles gathered in May 1968 to record demos for The White Album and when Sylvan and Barry took it over, all the exterior walls were daubed with graffiti and art work perpetrated by the Beatles themselves and other 60s icons like Mick Jagger and Marianne Faithful.

Sylvan continued writing lyrics for artists as diverse as Englebert Humperdinck, Diana Dors and Demis Roussos through into the early 70s. Then a chance encounter with Ernie Wise on holiday in Malta resulted in Sylvan reworking an old folk song into "Following you Around" which became the signature tune for the 1972 Morecambe and Wise show.

In the mid-70s Sylvan moved into freelance photography, spending 23 years in the corporate village of the Wimbledon Tennis Championships, 15 of those exclusively for NBC Sports. Photography remains the career that she still excels at today.

When McClory contacted Sylvan out of the blue one day after decades of silence, it was to report that he was going into litigation again, having recently discovered that Richard Maibaum had seen Whittingham's *Thunderball* screenplay before embarking upon his own, and thus may have been influenced by it. "Kevin said he could prove all this," says Sylvan. "But he'd lost his papers from the 1963 trial." This was a remarkable admission to make; that he'd mislaid his own set of documents pertaining to a case that had had such a profound affect on his life and that could now help him win a vitally important suit involving huge sums of money. In truth he never had them to begin with. "What happened was that he hadn't paid a substantial amount of Peter Carter-Ruck's fees because he was still aggrieved with him about the settlement, and was accusing Peter of being in league with Saltzman and Broccolli," says Sylvan. "So he made another enemy there and couldn't get his papers back. Now he wanted me to go to Peter and get my father's court papers back. 'Don't tell him it's for me,' he said, he won't give them to you if he thinks they are for me.' 'Tell him it's for a journalist.' So I went to see Peter, who I hadn't seen since the *Thunderball* case. It was lovely meeting him again and I collected up my dad's papers."

Since the *Thunderball* case Peter Carter-Ruck had forged an even greater legal reputation. He'd taken over Oswald, Hickson, Collier & Co and built it up over the intervening 20 years into the biggest libel litigation firm in the country. Then when he was 67, his partners forced him into retirement. That weekend, feeling bitter and angry, Carter-Ruck returned to his office and removed

Chapter 39: McCLORY BOUNCES BACK

every single document from every case he'd personally brought to the company, which was practically all of them. Then he found out that the floor above Oswald, Hickson, Collier & Co's office was for rent and so he moved in the following week and set up as Peter Carter-Ruck & Partners. Next he took over the ground floor and had Collier & Co sandwiched in the middle. "And the partners took him to court to try and get these papers back," recalls Sylvan. "But the judge ruled that providing the clients whose papers these were agreed, Peter could keep them, and of course the clients all did. So he did it again - built up the Peter Carter-Ruck partnership which became one of the biggest in the country with 20 partners. And then it happened again to him when he was 82; he was persuaded to retire with a consultancy fee. He was very cross about that. A remarkable man. Tenacious is the word to describe Peter Carter-Ruck. A fighter's spirit, which he needed to win the *Thunderball* case."

Sylvan contacted McClory with the news that she'd retrieved her father's papers. McClory was most anxious to see them and also asked Sylvan about the possibility that her father may have made jottings or developed story ideas that weren't included in any of his *Thunderball* scripts. Having already remade *Thunderball* once, the story material at McClory's disposal for another prospective Bond film was thin at best. Just how often can you keep on remaking the same story? What McClory was looking for was simple. Say Whittingham had written down on a scrap of paper the idea that Largo steals the bomber but lands not in the Bahamas, but say in the deserts of Egypt and his base is inside a pyramid. This would open up a galaxy of new possibilities. Alas there was no fresh story material in amongst Jack Whittingham's papers.

But, said Sylvan, McClory was still more than welcome to look at her father's court papers, but on one very special condition. "By now my brother Jonathan had entered the scene and we're thinking, why should we help Kevin. Why *should* we do this man a favour after everything he's done to dad?" McClory at this time was also contemplating writing a book about his whole saga with Fleming,. "which would include," he wrote to Sylvan, "The now indisputable fact that Ian Fleming, prior to the 1963 trial, had purported to sell to Broccoli and Saltzman and/or their companies the film rights of *Thunderball*." This was done, despite Fleming knowing full well that he didn't actually own them. "At no time during the trial did Fleming or his trustees disclose this fact or the documents that would have proved it. I would not have agreed to the settlement with Fleming in 1963 had I been aware of this."

McClory now believed that Richard Maibaum's 1961 *Thunderball* screenplay played an important part in the Bond producers winning a deal with United Artists; a screenplay heavily based on his own ideas and Whittingham's script. When *Thunderball* was shelved and substituted by *Dr No*, followed by *From Russia with Love*, both penned by Maibaum, it was inevitable said McClory that substantial elements from *Thunderball* would appear in those screenplays, "As indeed they have," the use of SPECTRE, for example. McClory saw the whole thing as an ongoing cover up by Fleming, his trustees and Broccoli, and intended to make the whole intriguing story public, "to put the true facts of the literary evolution of the James Bond film series." Not least because of the generally held assumption that Jack Whittingham and himself were interlopers into the hugely successful Bond series (*Thunderball* being the fourth in the series had, in his view, made such a myth possible) "and not innovators as we undoubtedly were."

Besides the book idea, McClory also hoped to set up a case for damages, claiming he was owed money from the sale and leasing of Bond videos that infringed his *Thunderball* copyrights. If he were successful in this venture, no doubt helped by the use of the papers now in the possession of the Whittingham family, McClory would agree to discuss the tempting subject of compensation. "I feel that Jack's heirs should benefit not just by credit but in a monetary way," he wrote to Sylvan. Jonathan, Sylvan's brother, now took up the matter and wrote to McClory: "If that statement truly represents your feelings and beliefs, Kevin, then perhaps you will be kind enough to explain to Sylvan and myself, why arrangements for either royalties or payments were not made prior to the production of *Never Say Never Again*. The credits were clearly forthcoming. The money was not."

McClory's excuse was logical enough. Both *Thunderball* and *Never Say* were licensed by himself to the companies responsible for making them (Eon and Taliafilm respectively) and they were not legally bound to pay Whittingham anything further. In their eyes Whittingham was a writer 'for hire' and had already been paid, and in any case had assigned his copyright in the scripts away. McClory too was not legally bound to pay Whittingham anything further, but it seemed he was changing his tune. "I know the amount of time and effort Jack put into *Thunderball*," he wrote back, "and deploring the whole handling of the situation over the years, feel that his family from a moral view should benefit, if I am successful in my claims." Such compensation, McClory said, would depend on what use he made of their father's legal papers.

Numerous promises were made about payment to Whittingham's heirs, but in the end nothing was forthcoming, so McClory never got the papers. The last letter Jonathan Whittingham wrote to McClory read: "Kevin - the carrot you dangle is tantalising, but on closer inspection, it disappears." The one positive thing to come out of McClory's re-entry into Sylvan's life was that her father's papers came back into her possession. Previously it had never occurred to her to hunt them down and get them. Nor was it to be the end of her dealings with Kevin McClory.

CHAPTER 40
THE ADVENTURE OF A LIFETIME

In-between all these incidents a very strange thing happened indeed which shines some fascinating light on the personality of Kevin McClory. The year was 1987 and a young Irish actor, and huge Bond fan, Andrew Taylor, was in a bookshop in Dublin when he spied a familiar figure – McClory. He knew he couldn't let this opportunity pass by and so approached the producer who told him he was in the midst of writing his autobiography (which never saw print, indeed was it ever finished?) and compiling books for reference purposes. Taylor told McClory that he would happily loan him items from his own collection, and so the two men got talking and McClory ended up inviting the actor to his hotel, the Westbury, one of Dublin's finest, for drinks that evening. "I remember feeling like an idiot," Taylor recalls. "Because I don't drink but McClory was a major drinker - a bottle of Jack Daniels a day, and he was in the papers around that time having lost his driving licence for being caught so drunk, so many times. So I met him and gave him the books and it was slightly embarrassing because he asked if I wanted a drink and for some reason I said a martini and of course he then replied, 'oh, shaken not stirred.' I felt like a plonker. Needles to say I was half pissed on this one martini. But we got on great."

For hours, McClory regaled his guest with stories of his days in Hollywood, as the lover of sex queens like Elizabeth Taylor, about his parents and his own childhood, and being torpedoed in the war. "You got the impression that he warmed to you, but I think that was his technique, that was his way with people," says Taylor. "He was very enigmatic and drew you out; you felt that he was wonderful company. And he was a phenomenal raconteur, and the stutter added to it. On the one hand, Kevin was a rogue and yet he had a sort of vulnerable quality."

The two men stayed in contact over the course of the next few weeks, and then one day McClory rang with an unusual proposal. "I have a property in the Bahamas that I've had for a while but I haven't been living there, and word has come back from the people who look after it for me that it's been broken into, so I've decided to sell it. I can't go down there myself because I'm busy, but I need an agent down there to represent me and oversee the sale of the property. I will pay you expenses, and I will pay you for your time out of the sale of the property. Would you be interested?" Interested! Taylor was mentally packing as McClory was talking. It really was an offer too good to refuse.

By this time, McClory was staying in a different hotel in Dublin. "A significantly less salubrious hotel," recalls Taylor. McClory occupied two rooms there, complete with a trio of secretaries and an assistant. The return tickets to the Bahamas arrived and were valid for six weeks, the period of time McClory wanted Taylor to remain at his house overseeing matters. After explaining exactly what he wanted from the actor, McClory added, "By the way, you can use the facilities at my house. There's the outside Jacuzzi, the swimming pool, there's a Mercedes in the garage, you'll find there's a 4-wheel trike you can have, there's also another car in a garage in Nassau that somebody's looking after for me, they're at your disposal. All you have to do is do what you think is necessary, and liaise with me."

McClory also helpfully sketched out on a piece of paper directions on how to locate his house. The Bahamas is literally split in two; the main island and then a bridge that leads to a very small outcrop of land called Paradise Island, a tax free haven and holiday resort with plush hotels and a major casino. No wonder stars like Richard Harris and Connery made their homes there. "You go across the bridge," related McClory. "You turn left, you go up the long road that leads to the Holiday Inn and halfway up that road there's a turning in to the left that you can barely see. Go in through the bushes, and you will come across the gates. There's a gardener who lives on the property and there is a maid that comes in every other day. I will instruct the maid, or the gardener, to leave the keys under a coconut beside the gates. My dog lives there as well, so if you can feed the dog occasionally, great." That's all Andrew Taylor had in terms of information.

Then between that meeting and the date that Taylor was due to go, which was about a week, he never spoke to McClory. "I couldn't get hold of him, and he was going to give me some expenses, which obviously I needed. Right up to the wire I kept ringing and getting his secretary and leaving messages; no reply back, no sign of money and I was thinking, how can I go? How can I afford to arrive in the Bahamas without a bean in my pocket? I certainly wasn't going to use my own money; that would be madness."

It was now the evening before Taylor was due to leave for the Bahamas and he still hadn't got hold of McClory. In desperation he sat in the foyer of the hotel waiting for him to come home after being promised the cash would be forthcoming. At midnight, McClory arrived, slightly drunk, and handed over an envelope with a thousand dollars in it. The actor raced back home to pack in order to catch the early morning flight, little knowing just what was in store for him.

The plane touched down early evening and Taylor hailed a cab to take him more or less near where he knew McClory's place was. "It was now dusk and I was making my way through the trees thinking, where the hell am I? Is this the right place? God only knows. By now I was fairly sure that things weren't even half as McClory had suggested, and I was ready for significant disappointment in a number of areas. Even before I left Heathrow, there were serious warning bells at the back of my head, but weighing it up, you couldn't miss this opportunity for adventure. So, of course, the likelihood of keys being under coconuts… there were many coconuts, but none with keys under them. So there I was, standing on one side of a big fence and I had to get into the house because the Bahamas was plunging into darkness. I threw my bags over the lower part of the fence, climbed over and landed plonk in the dog's enclosure. Thankfully the dog turned out to be reasonably friendly, but there I was in this caged area with a bloody guard dog. I climbed over that and now faced the front of the house that I'd no keys to get into. I figured I had to find some other way in, I'd no choice. I had to get in."

Taylor spied an upstairs window, clambered onto the roof with his bags and climbed in. Once inside he discovered there was no light. The gardener who was supposed to live on the property was no where to be seen and the maid was long gone. Too tired to do anything about it that evening Taylor found a bedroom and crashed out.

In the cold light of the next morning, it transpired that the picture McClory had painted of his property bore little resemblance to actual reality. "The house hadn't been lived in for over two years, the electricity bill hadn't been paid so the electricity had been cut off, the phone bill hadn't been paid

Chapter 40: THE ADVENTURE OF A LIFETIME

so the phone had been cut off, there was no running water and the boiler had a hole through it. There was a generator with luckily enough oil in the bottom of the tanks to switch it on for an hour a day to get water running to flush the toilets but nothing else. I had to shower outside with a hose pipe attached to a tree. I also had to eat at the local Holiday Inn because there was no fridge or cooker. Once I did get some food in and left it in the kitchen area overnight and came down in the morning to find it crawling with cockroaches. There were cockroaches all over the house. I remember being woken up at night by one crawling over my face. I learnt the best sprays for killing them, but the death throes of cockroaches will keep you up all night as well."

The house itself was magnificent, built no doubt out of the proceeds from *Thunderball*. The main building comprised of five bedrooms, a study and various other rooms. It was filled with traces of fine living (a large television, a Steinway piano, an enormous satellite dish outside), and of happier times; the actor found a guest book where the last person to sign in had been the actress Brooke Shields. McClory's past also echoed round the empty place, not least in the lounge where a giant poster of *Thunderball* adorned one of the walls. There was also a significant collection of records and books; all just left, seemingly abandoned. A musty, damp smell pervaded the whole house. "I also later discovered," says Taylor, "near the gates, in the bushes, barely visible, the bomb sled submarine from *Thunderball*. This was the original that had been built for a significant amount of money; a major prop that could have toured endlessly, that should be in a museum somewhere, and there it was literally rotting away. The fibre glass body was collapsing on itself; it was in a really sorry state. I was amazed and horrified at the same time. It was deplorable that it had been allowed to get into that state. In the course of cleaning up, I also found the Vulcan bomber model in the garden shed. That was in perfect condition and I took a photograph of it and got McClory's dog to stand in for scale."

The grounds that surrounded the house, comprising something like six acres, were hugely overgrown. There was the obligatory swimming pool, a beautiful lagoon-like pool that had been designed by Larry Hagman's wife. It had featured at the end of *Never Say Never Again*; Rowan Atkinson was thrown into it. In fact that whole final scene, Connery relaxing in an outside Jacuzzi etc, was filmed on McClory's estate. In one shot you can clearly see the house in the background. "The pool, however, was black," says Taylor. "The result of two years of the filtration system not being switched on and vegetation falling in. The Jacuzzi, equally, looked like mushroom soup. Down at the end of the garden, a couple of football pitches down, there was a motor cruiser sitting, not on a trailer, but on the lawn. A crane had obviously lifted it and just plonked it on the grass. It was McClory's and I imagined instead of paying fees for keeping it moored somewhere, when he was leaving the Bahamas he just said, stick it at the end of the garden."

Looking round the house, Taylor found no sign of the break in that had supposedly taken place. "But it was quite scary living there because I had been told that this area was notorious for muggings and for murders. So I would sleep at night in this pitch black house, no lights on whatsoever. I had just a torch and a small hatchet that I'd come across that I'd thought would be wise to have as some sort of protection. But there would be noises during the night when I'd think, this is it, I'm for the high jump."

Undeterred, Taylor started to get things moving in the property, when suddenly one day the gardener turned up. "And for some reason this guy loved McClory, as did the maid. They loved McClory, but they hadn't been paid in a long, long time. The gardener was called Bamboo and was Haitian. He spoke almost no English. And they were willing to return to work if they were put back on the pay roll." Word must have got round about Taylor's presence at the house because he started meeting a lot of people who were owed money from McClory. It was then that all the bubbles started to burst. "The car that was in the garage, sure enough it was a beautiful 1960s convertible Mercedes, but the drive belt was gone, so that wasn't working. The four wheel trike never materialised; somebody had purloined that long before. There was a car in a garage up in Nassau, where it had remained since someone had written it off and the garage owner was more than delighted to hand it over as soon as the repair bills were paid."

A couple of weeks had now passed, and while Taylor was being confronted with all these problems he hadn't heard so much as a twitter from McClory. It had also been praying on his mind exactly why he'd been chosen for this task, a relative stranger that McClory had known for only a short period, as opposed to a trusted confidant or legal specialist. Thank god for the Holiday Inn, which the actor used as his base, ringing McClory's hotel in Ireland and talking to one of his secretaries, relaying information about what he'd been doing at the house, that in order to get the property to the point where it could be sold the electricity needed to be put back on, as did the water and the phones. "And in the course of doing all this stuff, getting people in, making payments, just existing, I started to spend the money quite quickly and soon was running out of it."

Still no word from McClory. When Taylor phoned, the secretaries would plead that they hadn't been able to contact their employer. "Eventually I started to use my credit card, my first ever credit card, and thank god I had it because I had no access to any other cash. I would have starved to death." Eventually McClory did send another $500. "But for me, by that stage, the writing was very much on the wall. It was impossible to speak to McClory; he was non-communicative."

Other things were rousing Taylor's suspicions. When an estate agent showed up at the property expressing interest, he naturally thought it would be fine to show him round the general grounds. When McClory heard about this he exploded in anger. Odd behaviour from someone hoping to sell his property. Now the light dawned about Kevin McClory and this whole bizarre business. This house had remained idle for two years. One could speculate that because he possibly owed a significant amount of money, McClory had just upped and left, and it wasn't a problem to him, he knew it was there; he knew he owned that property. What's the problem? Until somebody must have told him it had been broken into, and then he must have thought, "I must do something. I know, I'll send someone over there." "Now it became apparent to me why he would chose someone like me, and not a professional, just a dogsbody, somebody of no significance. That seemed to be the way his mind had worked. Problem; problem solved. And as long as he throws me a few bob every so often." Taylor later heard that McClory appeared quite content to keep him out at the house indefinitely, certainly way beyond the original six weeks, which were now almost up. Important acting jobs were also starting to come Taylor's way and that proved the clincher. "I'd really had enough anyway so I phoned the secretaries and said, look, I'm out of here."

Before leaving Taylor wanted to arrange for the gardener and maid to come back and look after the house. Since the gardener didn't speak English, Taylor organised McClory's secretaries to phone him the next morning at the Holiday Inn, where he'd be with a translator, and they could talk with the gardener and sort out any issues. "The next day I sat in the hotel and the phone didn't ring. We waited for an hour. I rang. I got the secretary and she said, 'why are you ringing?' I said, 'why am I ringing! Why aren't you ringing? I'm waiting here. This is the arrangement. I'm sitting here with the translator and the gardener who doesn't really know why the hell he's here trying one last ditch effort to do something along the lines that I've been asked to do.' Needless to say the electricity was never put on. The water was never put on. The phones – nothing happened except what I instigated. I said, 'right, that's it, you can tell Kevin I am out of here.'"

Incensed, Taylor returned to the house and shut and locked every door. He also arranged for a security company who carried out a local round to add McClory's property to their route. "What else could I do?"

Taylor used his return ticket to fly back to London and then on to Dublin at his own expense. "I was seething and I wanted to get hold of Kevin. I went to his hotel. He wasn't there – he'd checked out. 'Would you know where he's gone to?' I asked reception. The man looked up. 'No, but if you find out we'd be very interested in hearing because the cheque he gave us has bounced.' I also contacted the travel agent who supplied my air tickets and they said, 'would you know where Kevin is because the cheque he paid for the flights has bounced.' And I thought, I could have really been stuck. I could have gone to the Bahamas airport with a ticket that hadn't been paid for!"

Chapter 40: THE ADVENTURE OF A LIFETIME

McClory, Taylor discovered, had moved to Galway where he'd hired a particularly sharp lawyer. "I knew where Kevin was and should have gone straight to the house where he was staying, but it was now becoming confrontational. Instead I ended up talking to this lawyer on the phone and telling him. 'Look, as far as I'm concerned Kevin owes me money. I went down to do a job. I did it to the best of my ability. I got no support. But for six weeks of my time, I want to be paid.' All I'd had so far was expenses. I had all the bills and everything. I went on, 'also I've got a bunch of keys in my hand to every door in the house that's now locked so if Kevin wants access to his own home we'd better make a deal.' The lawyer went on the offensive; you have something belonging to us, we want it back and we'll sue you blah blah. He played hard ball. So I played hard ball back. I said, do your best."

When the lawyer rang back, the tact had changed. McClory had spoken to someone down in the Bahamas who'd seen the property and told him that it had been well maintained. McClory was now willing to discuss things, but first, as an act of faith, Taylor should hand over the keys. "So I met the lawyer and handed over the keys and it was – bye." Taylor never saw or heard from McClory again. "I should have known, but by this stage I was totally wrecked. But looking back I have to admit I had a phenomenal adventure."

Taylor later heard an amazing, but unconfirmed story that the house McClory moved into in Galway was a huge mansion owned by an American family who lived in the States, but their daughter resided there. She had the basement apartment and rented out it to McClory who moved in with his entourage and his dogs, which were Doberman Pinchers. According to the tale he had heard, unexpectedly one day an elderly American couple, who actually owned the house, arrived to begin their summer vacation in Galway. They got out of the taxi and were walking down the path when two Dobermans came out of nowhere and attacked them. The woman supposedly lost some fingers in the attack. "Who is this man living in our house?" they shrieked. They wanted him out. But McClory wouldn't go. Eviction proceedings got underway, along with god knows what kind of lawsuit for this woman allegedly losing fingers to McClory's dogs on their own property.

As for the house in the Bahamas, it was sold in the mid-90s to Club Med, a neighbouring resort complex who renovated the place completely. In the midst of all that, the *Thunderball* bomb sled vanished. Whether it was purloined or merely ended up as rusty compost, nobody knows. McClory's house also eventually bit the dust, bulldozed over a few years later to make way for new buildings. Another piece of Bond history gone.

A luxury motor boat abandoned in the garden of McClory's Bahamain home

CHAPTER 41
THE KIDNAPPING OF JAMES BOND

In 1992, newspapers reported McClory's proposed plan to bring Bond to TV in the form of 26 one-hour adventures to be shot in Britain and around Europe. Under consideration to play 007 were Lewis Collins, Liam Neeson and Pierce Brosnan. Like McClory's previous statements, the rhetoric hadn't changed, nor the tactics, nor indeed the end result as again the project never materialised. To the public in general, it must have seemed that the only people getting rich off McClory's feud with Eon were the lawyers.

Eon, under the auspice of their Swiss-based company Danjaq, reacted quickly to McClory's latest proposal by placing the following announcement in the world's two biggest cinema trade papers Screen International and Variety – "JAMES BOND 007 – NOTICE AND WARNING TO ALL INTERESTED PARTIES. No one other than Danjaq and United Artists Pictures, a division of MGM Pathe, jointly has a right to make James Bond 007 television films or series, or to use in such television films or series the James Bond name or character, the 007 mark, and any other characters or organisations appearing in the James Bond 007 films produced by Danjaq. Any such use not authorised by Danjaq and United Artists would be illegal, and is protected under the US copyright and trademark laws and other legal principles. Danjaq and United Artists will vigorously protect their rights."

This seemed to silence McClory, but not for long. No doubt influenced by the resurgence of interest in Bond after Pierce Brosnan's 1995 smash hit debut *GoldenEye*, McClory was back. Late in 1996 he trumpeted a new film, *Warhead 2000*, starring ironically enough Timothy Dalton, the man who Brosnan had replaced as Bond. Unlike previous announcements from McClory, which all seemed pie in the sky and were quickly snuffed out, this time he attracted the attention of Sony Pictures, the movie studio wing of Japanese electronics giant Sony. Executive Gareth Wigan, who knew McClory from the days of swinging 60s London, was intrigued enough to enter into negotiations with the Irishman. They were quickly joined by John Calley, the newly appointed boss of Sony Pictures. Calley had come from United Artists, where he oversaw the resurrection of Eon's 007 series with *GoldenEye*, and had also been an executive at Warners in the early 1980s during the time of *Never Say Never Again*.

Calley approved of the McClory negotiations, fitting as it did his commitment to bring big franchise films to Sony. In October 1997, Sony made the announcement that they were to team up with McClory and his company Spectre Associates Inc, convinced that this gave them a legal right to produce Bond movies. "We've done due diligence and there's no doubt Kevin McClory has the rights to make a series of James Bond films and he has licensed those rights to Sony Pictures." Said Peter Wilkes, a Sony spokesman. McClory told the press he was pleased with the deal and that Sony, with its experience, production facilities and global distribution abilities was the studio of choice to, "propel James Bond into the 21st century." First off was yet another *Thunderball* remake set for a 1999 release. By now though most people were thinking, just how many times can you make the same movie?

Though it was never made public, McClory is said to have received $2m for selling his rights to Sony, with a stipulation that he would get a huge fee when and if they made a Bond film from those rights.

MGM, who since their 1983 merger with United Artists acted as distributors of the Bond films, were not pleased by Sony's announcement, especially as it came on the eve of the studio putting themselves on the stock market in an initial public offering of $250 million of common stock. MGM executives had spent more than a year planning the move and courting Wall Street financiers, focusing most of the attention on the lucrative Bond franchise. MGM said it would do "whatever it took" to protect its property. "Any claim that Mr McClory can create a James Bond franchise is delusional," MGM chairman Frank Mancuso said in a terse statement. "We hope that Sony has not been duped by Mr McClory's deception. Today, more than ever, we will vigorously pursue all means to protect this valued franchise that United Artists and the Broccoli family have nurtured for more than three decades."

But Sony was unrepentant and intended pressing on. So, in mid November, not long before the release of Eon's 18th 007 epic *Tomorrow Never Dies*, MGM filed a $25m lawsuit in federal court against Sony Pictures for trademark infringement and unfair competition. Two of Hollywood's biggest studios were now at war over the lucrative James Bond movie series. Joining MGM in suit was Danjaq, now run by Albert R. Broccoli's daughter Barbara and stepson Michael G. Wilson after Cubby's death in 1996.

Once the king of movie studios, MGM was now floundering after a succession of box office flops. Bond was really the only jewel left in its rather battered crown and they intended holding on to it at any cost. The studio was also desperate for cash, thus the reason for its entry into the stock market, which it blamed Sony for disrupting by announcing its competing 007 film plans at the same time. "They calculated the timing to inflict maximum injury to MGM." Said attorney Pierce O'Donnell, hired by MGM to spearhead its legal battle. O'Donnell was a powerful Hollywood legal eagle who had successfully sued several studios several times over. Speaking to Variety, O'Donnell stopped short of saying that Sony's announcement of its rival Bond project did in fact cause MGM's poor showing on Wall Street, but didn't rule it out. "We are studying that. We may decide it's more than $25m."

The main thrust of MGM's suit was a full-on assault over McClory/Sony's claims of ownership of Bond properties stemming from *Thunderball*. "Although Fleming granted McClory his interest in the copyright in certain preliminary script materials, Fleming did not, and could not, grant McClory the

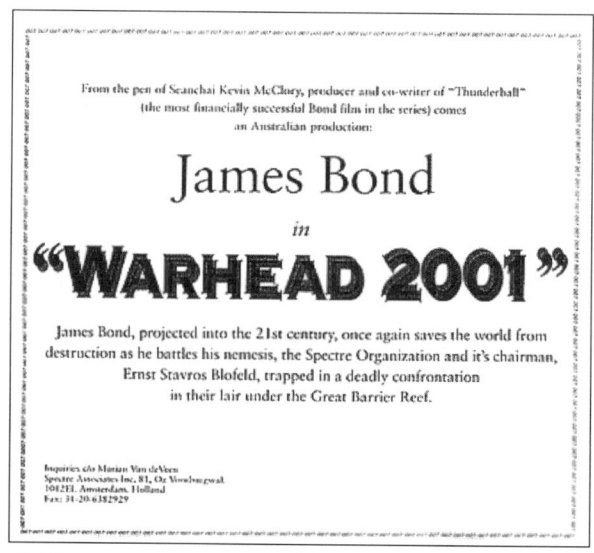

> From the pen of Seanchai Kevin McClory, producer and co-writer of "Thunderball" (the most financially successful Bond film in the series) comes an Australian production:
>
> # James Bond
> ## in
> # "WARHEAD 2001"
>
> James Bond, projected into the 21st century, once again saves the world from destruction as he battles his nemesis, the Spectre Organization and it's chairman, Ernst Stavros Blofeld, trapped in a deadly confrontation in their lair under the Great Barrier Reef.
>
> Inquiries c/o Marian Van deVeen
> Spectre Associates Inc, 81, Oz Voorburgwal.
> 1012EL Amsterdam, Holland
> Fax: 31-20-6382929

McClory announces one of his many thwarted attempts to re-make Thunderball (again!)

Chapter 41: THE KIDNAPPING OF JAMES BOND

right to use the character James Bond in non-*Thunderball* films." Said MGM. "They are out of the James Bond business," teased O'Donnell. "I don't think they can make a martini that's shaken, not stirred."

MGM however, levelled its more personal charges – theft of trade secrets and breach of contract - against Calley, who ran United Artists for several years under MGM's Frank Mancuso before jumping ship in 1996 to head up Sony Pictures. Indeed, Calley was intimately involved in *GoldenEye* and the reinvigoration of the Bond franchise. "During his tenure at UA, Calley acquired highly valuable proprietary information about the optimal ways to develop and exploit the franchise and bring it into the 21st century," claimed MGM. Sony induced Calley, the suit alleged "to misappropriate this highly confidential information, which they are now using to, and intend to continue to use, to compete unfairly with the James Bond motion picture franchise."

Some reports hinted that a personal vendetta was involved. According to a story in the Los Angeles Times, when billionaire investor Kirk Kerkorian and Australian media conglomerate Seven Network Ltd paid $1.3 billion to acquire MGM in 1996, Calley and other executives were purposely kept in the dark during negotiations,. At the time of the sale, went the story, Calley received only a small bonus for his work in helping revitalise MGM, compared to Mancuso's bonus of $14.5 million. But Calley was adamant. "There is nothing personal about this." He told reporters. But the timing, and the use of Bond, had Hollywood tongues wagging. One can't help but see a level of personal acrimony in part of the wording of MGM's lawyers' complaint. "This case is about the specious efforts of a global media empire and a disgruntled former executive of United Artists to lay claim to the most successful and enduring motion picture franchise in history."

In February 1998, the legal battle grew even more bitter when Sony countersued MGM claiming that McClory owned a chunk of the 007 pie because his *Thunderball* scripts modified and reinvented Fleming's Bond character specifically for the movies. McClory sought acknowledgement that this first Bond screenplay, devised by himself and written by Whittingham, was the source of the cinematic James Bond character as opposed to the Fleming version, which in many respects differed to that of his screen counterpart. "Although they try to depict us as interlopers, we were in fact innovators," McClory stated. "MGM's rights came after our rights. There is no doubt about this; we created our work with Fleming."

Sony's startling claim of ownership of the 007 franchise, through their association with McClory, was a high-risk strategy on the part of the studio. In essence it was a kidnap attempt to wrestle James Bond away from MGM. Sony claimed that Bond himself and the Bond series were. "All based on the sort of action originally written in the story line for *Thunderball*." As a result of McClory's contributions to that script, Sony argued, he was the co-creator and co-owner of "an original cinematic Bond character" with full legal rights to exploit such a character. Pierce O'Donnell wasn't impressed, calling Sony's assertions "preposterous" and likening McClory to the "Rip Van Winkle of copyright laws. He has been sleeping on his putative rights for over 20 years."

O'Donnell further disputed Sony's attempts to use 1965's *Thunderball* film as the source of McClory's ownership. The cinematic Bond had already been fully established before *Thunderball* was made, said O'Donnell. He then branded Sony's claim that someone who spent a few months working on an unsuccessful *Thunderball* script with the man who created Bond could somehow become the owner of the cinematic Bond as, "bizarre."

Sony's next demand was even more preposterous. Because McClory claimed part-ownership of the Bond film character, he was also owed a portion of the estimated $3 billion of profits the series had generated. MGM quickly moved to dismiss such an idea. They argued that McClory had never pursued a claim for profits before. Only after MGM sued Sony did the producer make the astonishing assertion that he was entitled to a slice of the Bond fortune.

However absurd the claims made by Sony, due law had to go through its motions and Hollywood waited with bated breath as the date of the trial loomed. If the wording in the agreement awarded to McClory in the 1963 court case was loosely constructed and open to interpretation, it was possible that Sony's attorneys would be able to create a scenario to suit themselves. Perhaps all the judge really needed to do was compare the substance of the CVs of the people in MGM's corner (Fleming, Broccoli, Saltzman) to that of Sony (Calley, McClory). No contest.

In a move no doubt prompted by the Sony lawsuit, and in a bid to control every Bond film ever made, even those outside Eon's fold, MGM acquired the world-wide distribution rights to *Never Say Never Again* from Taliafilm. "We have taken this definitive action to underscore the point that the Bond franchise has one home and only one home – with the collective family of United Artists, MGM and Danjaq," stated Lindsay Doran, UA's president. "We want to make it clear to any and all encroachers that MGM will do everything to protect what has been established over 35 years to be the most valuable film franchise in history."

Amid the legal wrangling Sony began pre-production on their rival Bond movie. Dean Devlin and Roland Emmerich, the director/producer team behind *Independence Day*, the box office hit of 1996, and 1998's big budget remake of *Godzilla*, were being wooed by Sony to handle their Bond series. Liam Neeson was approached to star as 007 and according to press reports was interested. The plot seemed a rehash of the Deighton/Connery Warhead script with Blofeld hi-jacking ships in the Bermuda Triangle, stealing nuclear weapons and threatening the world. Connery's name was even mentioned as a candidate to play Blofeld.

Rumours then circulated that Connery would return as Bond himself, despite his age of 68. A source said, "Sean Connery has been approached and he is very interested. It is a question of money – they have the money and they will get him." The news, however preposterous, got Hollywood talking. "I don't care how old Connery is," said esteemed screenwriter Robert Towne. "I'll guarantee you'll have a hit if you cast him again." Others were not so charitable. US television chat show host Jay Leno joked that any new Connery Bond film should be called 'Octo-prostate.'

When news reached MGM of Sony beginning preparatory work on their 007 film, they filed a preliminary injunction to cease all such activities. "We don't want them in the process of making movies while the suit is in litigation." MGM argued. In July, Federal Judge Edward Rafeedie ruled that Sony couldn't prepare a screenplay, hire talent or enter into any agreement to produce a 007 film. Production was stifled and essentially marked the beginning of the end for McClory's ill-fated second *Thunderball* remake. Many saw the injunction as a portent of what would happen in the trial, set for December, especially when Rafeedie ruled that MGM had, "demonstrated a likelihood of prevailing" in its suit.

In response to MGM's successful injunction to stop his Bond movies' progress, McClory filed his formal opposition to the studio's legal quest to quash Sony's efforts to develop a rival 007 franchise. The filing (on 14 July) had been delayed after the 74-year-old producer collapsed at his Washington residence a few months earlier. For some years McClory had been plagued with illness and although he maintained his health problems were now behind him he was presently undergoing minor exploratory surgery. In his declaration, McClory spelt out his ownership claims to 007 and also took issue with MGM's tactics to date. It read: "The level of stress I have suffered during this period has been exacerbated by an exorbitant number of internet death threats made against me personally, along with inquiries as to the whereabouts of my children and other family members." This McClory blamed on public statements regarding his character by spokesmen acting on behalf of MGM. Things were starting to get ugly and personal. "My concern has been the statements from Pierce O'Donnell," McClory told Variety. "I think people like O'Donnell should temper their rhetoric. He referred to me as Rip Van Winkle. He should remember that Rip Van Winkle woke up."

The insults continued to fly when MGM again disputed McClory's claims of ownership, revealing that a 28-year US copyright term on Fleming's work had expired and that a recent renewal of those rights brought all of Fleming's US copyrights, including *Thunderball*, under the MGM/Danjaq banner. "McClory is largely a fading footnote in this lawsuit. His declaration is supremely irrelevant," said O'Donnell.

Chapter 41: THE KIDNAPPING OF JAMES BOND

For MGM the stakes were enormous. With James Bond the ailing company's only consistent money-maker, it was unthinkable that the series would end up going to Sony; it might even mark the collapse of arguably Hollywood's most famous studio. And so it was to their enormous relief when in preliminary hearings US district court Judge Edward Rafeedie decided many of the pre-trial issues in MGM's favour. Refeedie ruled that the rights Sony purchased from McClory did not rise to the level under US copyright law of making McClory the joint owner of the Bond character, as Sony had argued. Ergo, his preliminary conclusion was that Sony couldn't create a Bond series to compete with MGM. "Based on today's ruling, it's clear that Sony's claim that they are building a new home for Bond is built on legal quicksand," triumphed O'Donnell outside the courthouse. "This has to be one of the darkest days in the history of Sony studios. Their attempt to kidnap James Bond has been foiled and once again 007 has prevailed." Sony were understandably disappointed, but took a small crumb of comfort from the fact that this wasn't the judge's final ruling on the matter. That would come later. But things weren't looking good.

In the months that followed, both sides went back and forth in legal argument and the original 15 December trial date was pushed back to April 1999. Alas, what many were predicting to be one of the biggest entertainment court cases of recent history never happened. With the new trial date looming the matter was settled out of court, decisively in the favour of MGM. Strengthened by the judge's favourable pre-trial statements, MGM's lawyers were able to avoid a trial and really put the squeeze on their rivals and Sony cracked. They agreed to cease all efforts to make Bond films either inside or outside the US. MGM had pressed for an international component to the deal because Sony could theoretically attempt to make a Bond film outside American territory. In addition the company agreed to fork out $5m damages to MGM. "Essentially," said Sony attorney David W. Steuber, "we have given up the universal right to make a James Bond picture."

For their part, MGM paid Sony $10m to acquire the film rights to *Casino Royale*, which Sony held due to its ownership of Columbia Pictures, the original copyright holders of Ian Fleming's first James Bond novel. This settlement was a complex conclusion to a complex case. What started out as a dispute over rights to *Thunderball* finished with MGM winning the rights to the one Fleming Bond novel that was never under Eon's control. The *Casino Royale* rights were a lucky ace in the hole for Sony, becoming very useful in the company's strategy to end the lawsuit. Their sale to MGM allowed Sony to profit from rights they would never have been able to use otherwise. *Casino Royale* was released in 2006 as Daniel Craig's 007 debut.

This deal did not, however, include the stubborn McClory who claimed that he would continue his lawsuit against MGM on his own. McClory also hinted that he was considering action against Sony for "settling the case out from under him." But after losing so heavily surely no major studio would ever want to touch McClory's rights again and without studio backing he faced near impossible odds financing a private action. Was this finally the end for McClory?

CHAPTER 42
DIE ANOTHER DAY

In the midst of the Sony lawsuit, McClory had once again contacted the Whittingham family asking for various documents. "We went through a two year correspondence with him," recalls Sylvan. "I met with Peter Carter-Ruck again, who was helping me to confront Kevin, and who was also hoping to reclaim the money McClory still owed him. Because there was still a deep wound about what he'd done to our father – a lot of resentment, I wrote and told McClory what I thought of him. It was very cathartic."

Part of the letter read: "Dad supported you during the trial at a time when he was suffering with acute angina pain. Even though it was against doctor's orders he would struggle up to London so that he did not let you down in court. Apart from his great affection for you, his motivation for supporting you was because he expected, indeed he was led to believe that he was joined with you in the *Thunderball*/Bond films venture. We realise that this promise became untenable due to your situation with Broccoli and Saltzman. However, Dad was very, very hurt at the way you appeared to dump him and ignore him when the case was over. We feel you should have at least paid his costs when Fleming died – thus nullifying dad's own case for damages."

As before, McClory made promise after promise to the Whittingham family that if they allowed him access to the court papers in their possession he would reimburse them. "It was one per cent of this and two per cent of that, which we knew we'd never get," says Sylvan. "So in the end we didn't part with anything and he lost the case. After that we had no contact whatsoever."

Incredibly, despite the collapse of his case with Sony, McClory was carrying on his action against Danjaq and MGM. Another court case was in prospect, this time McClory stood alone against Hollywood's big guns. It still remained his strongly held belief that because of his involvement in the *Thunderball* scripts he transformed Fleming's rather stuffy literary hero into the marketable and recognisable movie character of today and that he therefore had a stake in the series. Also, because Richard Maibaum had read Whittingham's *Thunderball* screenplay before commencing his own script elements of it naturally crept into *Dr No*, thus the style and format of all the subsequent Bond films were influenced by it. It became almost a blueprint of sorts. That was McClory's argument, and it had a sort of logic to it.

This was all disputed. Danjaq testified in court that Maibaum did not have access to the McClory/Whittingham scripts, although it was admitted that he saw the book. Danjaq also wanted it to be known that to their knowledge this was the first time McClory had ever made the claim that he, essentially, helped create the film James Bond. McClory even listed the Bond films that he alleged infringed his rights. They were *Dr. No, From Russia with Love, Goldfinger, Thunderball, You Only Live Twice, Diamonds are Forever, The Spy who Loved Me* and *The World is not Enough*. This also included "Any and all infringements in DVDs and any other new media."

With his case due to be heard, McClory asked for a delay so he could travel to England to oversee funeral arrangements for his sister-in-law. This was denied. McClory could attend the funeral and travel to LA in time for the trial, the court ruled. To the surprise of both sides, McClory failed to show up on the first day of the case, sending a letter stating that he could appear and testify two days later. Danjaq moved to dismiss the case due to McClory's no-show. This was overturned and their sole witness, company president Michael G. Wilson, took the stand.

Two days passed and McClory failed to show yet again. Neither the court nor his own attorney knew of his whereabouts. In any case, his attorney stated, McClory would "not contribute much more to what is in the record." With this representation the court proceeded with closing arguments. Eventually McClory sent word that he had had visa problems and been unable to re-enter the US. For a man who frequently travelled the world, was in and out of America often and had a house in Washington, that he should have visa problems on the day he was meant to be in court was, let's say suspicious to say the least.

Not surprisingly the judge took a dim view of McClory's absence from court, which hardly helped his case. But the Irishman was on a losing wicket from the start and few Hollywood observers were very much surprised when on 11 May 2001 the original 1999 finding that McClory was not entitled to a share of profits from the Bond series was upheld.

The overseeing and long suffering Judge Edward Rafeedie threw the case out of court stating that McClory had taken far too long in bringing his suit to bear. The judge pointed out that in the four decade history of this Bond litigation and in the three previous cases involving McClory and Bond rights (1961, 1963 and 1976), it wasn't until 1997 that he claimed that he was co-owner of the Bond character, despite numerous opportunities to do so. McClory contended that he did not know of the extent of the infringement until recently. But the court didn't buy that one. "This is not a case of secret computer code," scorned the judge. "But of 18 publicly released, widely distributed movies, beginning some 40 years ago. In short, McClory has offered no viable justification for the delay."

McClory, the court concluded, must have known of the alleged infringement since at least 1961. And why in 1963, following his just concluded struggles with Fleming over the *Thunderball* rights, did he not file suit against Danjaq for any purported infringement in *Dr. No* or *From Russia with Love*. They had, after all, being playing in cinemas. No, instead he went into business with them. In 1965 McClory and Danjaq negotiated a ten-year licence on *Thunderball* which, the court said, suggested an absence of bad faith on Danjaq's part. When McClory sued in 1976 alleging that *The Spy who Loved Me* infringed upon his rights in *Thunderball*, Danjaq responded by removing the allegedly infringing material. The suit was settled. And although Danjaq had released numerous other Bond films by that time, McClory never pursued a claim that Danjaq had pirated the Bond character. Even McClory's own correspondence and advertisements for his "Warhead" project merely rehashed past events and did not assert that he owned the entire cinematic Bond character. In other words, why had there been a delay of decades between McClory's knowledge of the potential claims and the initiation of litigation?

Judge Rafeedie went on to say that McClory's failure to bring the case to court at an earlier date had prejudiced MGM's defence because nearly all of the witnesses who could, "potentially help untangle McClory's web of allegations and intrigue are long dead." Namely, Fleming, Broccoli, Saltzman,

Young, Maibaum and Whittingham. One wonders what secrets and truths had gone to the grave with them. Michael G. Wilson also presented testimony that many of the relevant records were missing too, notably the original Maibaum scripts for *Thunderball* and all but the final draft of *Dr. No*'s shooting script.

McClory's delay, for whatever reason, innocent or otherwise, of bringing his claims of ownership to the Bond character had proved his undoing. "We are called upon to determine whether McClory waited too long to claim his piece of the pie – whatever that share might have been," the judge summed up. "We conclude that McClory's claims are barred in their entirety by the doctrine of latches and, on that basis, affirm the district court's dismissal of McClory's suit."

Latches is an equitable defence that prevents a plaintiff, who with full knowledge of the facts, acquiesces in a transaction and sleeps upon his rights. In other words, it was inequitable for the owner of a copyright, with full notice of an intended infringement, to stand inactive while the proposed infringer spends large sums of money in its exploitation and to intervene only when his speculation has proved a success. Delay under such circumstances allows the owner to speculate without risk with the other's money; he cannot possibly lose, and he may win. The court felt it unfair that after massive investment by Danjaq in Bond over four decades that McClory, after waiting 40 years, would then profit from the risk inherent in Danjaq's investment in the franchise.

In every respect, the district court's judgement played in Danjaq's favour, although Judge Rafeedie did mention that their conduct had not totally been beyond reproach. As already covered, McClory argued that certain elements first developed in the *Thunderball* script materials made their way into Maibaum's *Dr. No* screenplay and thus were passed on through the series. In particular the *Thunderball* script originated the cinematic Bond character, in that he was witty and dashing in counterpoint to his dour and introspective literary counterpart. "But even assuming this allegation to be true," said the court, "McClory could show at most only infringement, not *wilful* infringement. He has put forward no direct evidence of wilful infringement, nor does the circumstantial evidence support this claim." Indeed, the court made plain Danjaq's ignorance before the current litigation that McClory claimed a right in the supposed cinematic creation of Bond. After all, Bond had appeared in seven books before McClory came along. He was an already established figure. Even assuming, said the court, that McClory reinvented the Bond character in the *Thunderball* script materials, there was simply no way for Danjaq to know of his intention to lay claim to such a property. "Given that lack of notice, and the absence of evidence of willfulness, a jury could not find wilful infringement," was the court's decision. "We must affirm the district court's conclusion that McClory is unable as a matter of law to demonstrate deliberate infringement." The court dismissed McClory's case with prejudice. He'd lost and this time there was no going back.

In 2004 the "for sale" sign went up outside MGM. This once proud Hollywood institution had finally admitted defeat after years of churning out worthless product nobody wanted to see. Not even its cash cow, James Bond, could save it now. And in one of movie history's greatest ironies the studio who bought MGM was the very same studio who just a few years earlier was plotting to bring about its downfall and steal its number one asset in James Bond – Sony! The price they paid, just under $3 billion. Sony's take-over of MGM predictably raised rumours of McClory's resurrection. However, with Sony controlling MGM there seemed little point in creating a rival Bond film, seeing as they now owned the rights to the official series anyway. So after nearly 50 years the battle between McClory and the Bond franchise had finally come to an end.

Where did that leave McClory? All but a broken and dying man – a man whose vast fortune had been squandered chasing a quixotic dream. "He'd been involved in so many bloody court cases, which he was never going to win, and it cost him a fortune," says Jeremy Vaughan. "And the little information I received was that he became pretty well broke. Which was sad for a guy in his 80s. But provided he had got a roof over his head, it didn't do him any harm either."

The millions McClory earned from his participation in *Thunderball* could've set him up for life. He could have used that fortune to create his own production company with which to make any choice of film he wanted. Few, if any, filmmakers at the start of their careers have ever had the golden opportunity that McClory was given. But instead of using Bond as a fantastic platform from which to go on and do anything with his life, he threw it all away on an idiotic, solitary quest that ended in failure and which ostracised him from a film industry that could have given him so much more. "What went wrong?" concludes Vaughan. "God alone knows. He became obsessed more or less, and I think he thought that his rightful place in movie history had been stolen off him by others. The last time I saw him was years and years ago in Paris and he was not a happy man. I think he felt that the world had not treated him as he would have wanted it to."

Deep down, though, all McClory really ever wanted was some form of recognition for himself as having been an innovator of the 007 series, and not an interloper as he believed the Fleming trust, Broccoli and the Bond studio made him out to be to the public. "Kevin was bitter about Saltzman and Broccoli," says Sylvan. "He was bitter that he didn't get more recognition. They took off with his idea; that's how he sees it."

But bitterness remains in the Whittingham family too at the way McClory profited from their father's work without any extra financial contribution, either towards the costs he had to pay for his aborted case when Fleming died or towards the family, as had been promised several times in the past. Whittingham was paid just once for his *Thunderball* screenplay, but McClory made another film out of it (*Never Say*) without ever offering remuneration to his family over and above the original fee. This for a screenplay that McClory claimed in the 1990s the entire Bond film series had emanated from. Surely that was worth more than £5,000. There was bitterness too that it was their father's contribution and loyalty that enabled him to win his case against Fleming and to reap the huge financial rewards he had enjoyed these past four decades. "Kevin created a 40 plus year fantasy using my late father's talent and work for which he gave him scant credit," argues Sylvan.

Over the years, McClory has always cast himself as the key player in the *Thunderball* story. Of course his significance is beyond question, but he seemed to have forgotten that he was indebted, morally as well as financially, to many people. Chief among them was Jack Whittingham who at the peak of his career wrote a first class and ahead of its time script and who loyally supported him during the court proceedings. And Peter Carter-Ruck, the libel lawyer whose skillful and meticulously thorough research won the case for McClory. "But despite the fact that we had these resentments, you couldn't help but have affection for Kevin," says Sylvan. "Even now I'm amused by Kevin. I smile when I remember his antics. We were very angry with him and I think he was bloody selfish, but I never hated him. I think he was in another world, Kevin, really. He lived in the clouds. We have to come down and live on the ground don't we at some point."

Kevin McClory's final battle was played out on 20 November 2006. It wasn't with lawyers, avenging film producers or studios, but the sad inevitability of a diseased ravaged body. He died peacefully, it was reported, surrounded by his family in a nursing home in Ireland. "He will be remembered for his love and larger than life presence in the lives of his family and friends," ran a private statement. "As Ned Kelly always said, such is life."

The statement also announced that a cremation service had taken place privately. What wasn't divulged was the precise nature of the ceremony. McClory was in fact given a Viking funeral. Was this his own final dying wish - to leave this world in a way that he perhaps hoped he'd always lived it – in a blaze of glory? Or simply the final act of a man with a warped sense of grandeur and self-importance.

Closure for Sylvan in the whole *Thunderball* affair came when Peter Carter-Ruck contacted her again in August 2003 and asked for her support. In recent years, the life of this once great and feared lawyer had come to resemble a Shakespearean tragedy. Ann his wife of 62 years had just died and he found himself at the age of 89 years in litigation with his own daughter, Julie, a lawyer herself, who was suing him over her mother's will. On top of all that, he was diagnosed with lung cancer which carried a terminal prognosis of a few months. But Julie continued with the court case. Sadly, in spite of strenuous efforts of friends to reconcile father and daughter, their fight continued to the bitter end.

With loyal staff and Sylvan looking after him, Peter died on December 19th 2003. "I'm glad I had that time with him," says Sylvan. "It was a great privilege and a way of saying thank you and a closure on our long friendship. Our lives had crossed at the beginning of the Thunderball story, and we were together at the end. Full circle!"

Before he died Peter Carter-Ruck passed on to Sylvan a few personal items, but most importantly all of the remaining *Thunderball* court papers. Just in time too. He was hardly cold in his grave when his house was cleared and many of the meticulously kept files from his famous cases were shredded. A fascinating and revelatory part of Bond history might have been, and very nearly was, lost forever.

APPENDIX 1
THE CUNEO MEMO

In Ernest Cuneo's story, M informs Bond that mysterious radio signals have been picked up by a British submarine emanating from a plane full of British/American USO (United Service Organisation) performers on their way to entertain Allied forces on a US Arctic air base. Bond and his CIA buddy Felix Leiter are assigned to the case. M tells Bond to go undercover as a British entertainer. Influenced by the use of star cameos in *Around the World in 80 Days*, Cuneo has Bond going to seek the theatrical advice of Noel Coward (who coincidentally was a close friend and neighbour of Fleming). Bond and Coward watch performers such as John Gielgud, Margot Fonteyn and Robert Morley in the hope that some of their theatrical genius will rub off on him. "Bond's efforts to imitate until he finds his metier can be amusing," suggests Cuneo. Eventually Coward, now joined by no less a personage than Laurence Olivier, works out a suitable act for him.

Bond joins a combined British/American troupe for morale boosting shows around various NATO bases. "Todd-AO shots of great cities like Paris, Rome, Athens etc," writes Cuneo. He discovers that one of the baggage sergeants aboard the USO plane is a top enemy agent using a short-wave radio transmitter (hidden in a trunk) to communicate with enemy submarines. The enemy spy's diabolical plan, Bond reveals, is to detonate an atomic bomb on an American base. Distinct shades here of the plot of 1983s *Octopussy*, where a mad Russian general, under the cover of a circus troupe, plans to detonate an atomic device on a US air force base in Germany.

Bond reports his findings to M, who decides that the sergeant is not to be arrested but kept under surveillance so that the entire spy network might be crushed. When the bogus sergeant puts in for transfer to the Caribbean USO, and marks his base preference as Nassau, Bond follows, now as a civilian. He quickly discovers that a mysterious new company has ordered a fleet of fishing boats ("for Iron Curtain country" Cuneo emphasises), all of which come equipped with water tight underwater hulls – the forerunners of the Disco Volante. Atomic bombs are to be delivered to them by enemy submarines, with the whole transfer operation being conducted unseen beneath the waves. Bond reconnoitres amongst the Bahamian reefs and finds the foreign crews of the fishing trawlers are actually enemy frogmen rehearsing and drilling on the ocean floor, "right under our noses."

Cuneo's idea for the film's climax is unquestionably his most inspired contribution, and pretty ambitious and far-sighted for its time; that of a pitched underwater battle between the baddies and Bond's unit of scuba men. In Cuneo's story the underwater battle takes place during an evening of celebrations on the island with a huge USO show. We see the likes of Frank Sinatra and Milton Berle boarding a plane to take them to Nassau from Miami, while British/American frogmen dress for battle. Cuneo wanted the fun and gaiety of the concert to switch backwards and forwards with the death struggle happening underwater just yards away in Nassau harbour. He wrote, "Beautiful songs floating out near the water, lovers looking at the moon, while forces are engaged beneath the surface right at their feet, building up to a terrific finale." Cuneo's idea for an underwater battle was such a cracker that when *Thunderball* finally hit screens in 1965 no one could better it for an ending.

APPENDIX 2
IAN FLEMING'S FIRST SCRIPT TREATMENT

Fleming's script begins with all the cheap thrills of a paperback pulp novel. "A white head-and-shoulders cardboard target fills the centre of the screen against the wall of an underground shooting gallery. XANADU PRESENTS comes on the screen across the target; there is a roar of muffled automatic fire, which sprays bullets into the heart of the target."

The credits then roll in imaginative fashion, each title card emblazoned on screen as fresh targets are riddled with bullets before darting off sideways. When finished, the camera withdraws down the gallery and we see the sweating face of Bond firing an automatic pistol. Watching him is the armourer and the two engage in a factual conversation about weaponry. The armourer asks Bond what he's currently using. "Baretta .25. Eight rounds. Pretty good gun; hasn't let me down yet." The armourer smiles. "Bit of a ladies' gun, isn't it, sir?" Bond replies grimly, "Some people haven't thought so." This exchange is remarkably similar to the one in the film of *Dr No* when Bond is rebuked for his choice of Baretta as a weapon. The armourer then condemns it as being nice and light, in a ladies handbag. To which Bond reveals that he's never missed with it yet.

We follow Bond through various corridors until he arrives at the offices of the Double 0 section and is met by his secretary, Loelia Ponsonby (who occupies the same role in the books). Fleming describes her here as "motherly but authoritarian." After a bit of banter, Bond enters his own busy-looking office. On his desk are various personal mementos from his war service including the fuse cap from a shell and a large piece of shrapnel. He also uses a rusty commando dagger as a paper knife. Strolling over to a window, Bond stares vacantly out towards Regent's Park and begins one of those internal monologues so favoured by private eyes in Hollywood film noirs. It's a device that Fleming occasionally uses in this script when, as he put it, "complicated pictorial explanation would hold up the pace." Essentially, Bond is introducing himself to cinema audiences and explaining that his double 0 gives him a licence to kill. "That means that I get given the dirty jobs; the jobs you never read about in the newspapers; the ones even the government would rather know nothing about. I don't particularly like these sort of jobs but now it is months since

I've been able to get out of this damned office and all this paper work, and it's Monday and Mondays are hell anyway."

But things are about to change when he's summoned to M's office. Already there is Sir Ronald Vallance, head of CID (a semi-regular character in the novels) who asks Bond what he knows about the Mafia. "More or less what everybody knows. They're a sort of Sicilian Trades Union in crime." Vallance explains that one of the top Mafiosi, a huge bear of a man named Henrico Largo, has come to Britain and opened a night-club called The Spangled Room outside Epping Forest. Telephone tapping has revealed that following a meeting there of the eight top Mafia men in the world, Largo is assembling a gang of professional gunmen to accompany him on a huge raid. Not a bank robbery, but a particular thing. "What sort of a thing?" asks Bond. "A thing the Mafia needed," says Vallance mysteriously. "A thing that would increase their power a millionfold." The rendezvous is at Shoeburyness at the mouth of the Thames at midnight tomorrow. "Shoeburyness?" says an incredulous Bond. "But that's the back of beyond. There's nothing there but marsh and sand." Not quite, as M informs Bond that it's the location of a new atomic rocket site. "And, as it happens, the first one that's been fully stocked with A-bombs."

The magnitude of the situation is beginning to dawn on Bond, but why would the Mafia want a nuclear weapon? Again Vallance supplies the answer. Their protection rackets don't work anymore thanks to organised trade unions and the police are cracking down on the drug trade. "So they looked around for something progressive, up-to-date, and they got on to the thing that's been in all our minds, that some small country or organisation gets hold of an atomic bomb and holds up the world to ransom." M cuts in saying the whole thing is ridiculous, but if it turned out to be true they wouldn't be able to do much about it. You can't keep London permanently evacuated and if news leaked out there'd be mass hysteria. To make things even more difficult the Mafia could always give a choice of targets, New York, Paris etc. "Think of the damage that could be done from an ordinary delivery van parked outside Rockefeller Centre, or a bogus police car," says M. "There are dozens of ways of getting the bomb to the right place. No, I'm afraid it would work if the right people were behind it."

Bond advocates rounding up Largo and his gang and shooting them, but Vallance has to remind him that this is England and not Russia or Red China. Besides, all they've got to go on is a few phone calls and the midnight rendezvous. All the rest is a hunch. Vallance makes reassurances that a battalion of the Royal Air Force regiment, plus a complement of commandos guard the rocket site. Even M can't see the Mafia gunmen winning against that lot. Bond has been called in purely as a precaution just in case anything goes wrong and an A-bomb gets smuggled abroad. "Then you've got to get after it and find out where it is."

Bond leaves the office, and in his four and a half litre Bentley with the Amherst-Villiers super-charger makes his way to The Spangled Room to investigate Largo. Fleming subjects Bond (and us) to another interior monologue while tearing up the countryside roads, this one making him sound even more like a gumshoe detective. "I'd spent the afternoon at Scotland Yard going through the files and I must say I was getting interested. Somehow there was a smell of trouble in the air." But Bond just can't make himself believe that Largo's Mafia gang would think of taking on a well-guarded rocket site, deducing that their ruse was probably "robbing a bank in Southend or something of that sort."

In order to check out Largo's night-club, Bond is wearing a disguise. His hair is parted in the middle, his cheeks are fuller thanks to rubber cheek pads and he has a prominent gold tooth. Inside the club is loaded with, "rather well-dressed Spivish characters." Bond orders Bourbon and soda and a glass of iced water and scans the room for his contact, a member of Scotland Yard's Ghost Squad who is working there incognito as a cigarette girl. Her name is Dominique Smith, known to her friends simply as Domino. When the iced water arrives Bond takes out the carnation he's been wearing and puts it in the glass, the recognition signal Vallance has fixed with his girl. As the cabaret begins the cigarette-girl returns and passes Bond a message written on a box of matches. It reads: "Watch out, they're nervous tonight."

Appendix 2: IAN FLEMING'S FIRST SCRIPT TREATMENT

Bond returns to his car where he dresses in overalls and takes out a small tool bag with PHANTOM BURGLAR ALARMS written on it. He goes up a ladder to a skylight on the roof and sees an unoccupied bedroom. Opening the skylight he drops softly inside. Walking along a passage, past a throng of chorus girls, Bond sees a door marked "private", boldly enters and encounters a hulking guard. Bond makes up a story about a reported fault in the alarm system. "These are Mr Largo's private quarters. There's no alarm here. It's outside. Le'mme see your pass." Bond puts his hand inside his pocket and whips out a cosh and cracks it across the man's head.

While hiding the body, Bond hears voices coming from a nearby room. He sneaks a peek. Inside are three men playing poker, dressed in American air force uniforms. Bond creeps across the passage and we hear the sound of an organ being played. It's coming from behind the end door. Bond eases it open and enters what is Largo's rich looking office. Largo himself, in a velvet dinner jacket, is sitting in an alcove playing the organ, a bored henchman is lounging against the wall. Largo turns and sees Bond but doesn't buy his burglar alarm repairman story and when the coshed guard is discovered all hell breaks loose. In the ensuing fight Bond is knocked out. "Put him in the boiler room." Says Largo. "That will soften him up. He'll be either melted or stifled by the time we're gone."

In a nod to female emancipation, it's Domino that rescues Bond from the boiler room. She tells him Largo and the men have left and together they urgently drive back to London to alert Vallance. By the time Bond gets to Scotland Yard it's too late, a message arrives with news that an American colonel and two sergeants, with correct passes, entered the Shoeburyness rocket base half an hour ago. They claimed to be from another base with a warning that some of the newly arrived warheads were believed to be leaking Strontium 90. Shown to the storeroom the men used Geiger equipment to detect the offending bomb, which was carefully carried out. "Tell your men to keep clear. We're all wearing protective material under these suits." The bomb was then loaded onto an amphibious helicopter, which took off over the English Channel.

Largo's escape route is also a convoluted one. From helicopter the bomb is transported to a rusty, old tramp steamer anchored in the Channel's busy shipping lane. Largo then uses a sub-machine gun to riddle the hull of the helicopter, which sinks out of sight. Finally the steamer passes the bomb on to a Sunderland flying boat that heads across the Atlantic to the Bahamas, its final destination.

At M's office, Bond and Vallance are kept up with news of the search for the missing bomb conducted by the Air Ministry and the Admiralty. Cut next to Bond in a speeding Motor Torpedo Boat. The tramp steamer has been spotted and Bond and armed seamen climb aboard. It's deserted. One of the sailors is about to push open the captain's cabin door when Bond spies a flash of thin wire. "Look out, it's booby trapped!" Back on board the MTB Bond fires its Bofor gun and the steamer disintegrates into the water.

Fade to London Airport. Bond meets Vallance who tells him the Sunderland boat has been spotted in Nassau. Local immigration has also revealed that 15 men came ashore leaving a crew of seven aboard, all Italians. They've booked in at a hotel for a textile convention. Another 20 guests for the same convention are arriving shortly. Vallance guesses they're the Mafia big shots from the States. Everyone's behaving respectably, and customs have been over the plane with a Geiger counter hidden in a briefcase and turned up nothing. "I simply don't get the picture," says Bond. "Even if they have managed to hide the bomb somewhere what the hell are they going to do next. There's no target in Nassau except the airport and a handful of ageing millionaires. It seems to me that there's nothing to do but wait until they make the next move." Vallance tells Bond the Mafia have already made it, a letter addressed to the Prime Minister signed CAPO MAFIOSI, the head of the Mafia. It says that within 14 days the bomb will be used to destroy a vital defence installation of the Western Allies. The alternative is the payment of £100 million in gold, to be co-ordinated in a series of night drops over a broad area of Sicily. Once all the gold is recovered instructions will be sent as to where the bomb is to be found.

Bond is ordered to Nassau to begin investigations. The US President is sending his own man to team up with 007, Felix Leiter of the CIA. Domino also goes along for the ride, ostensibly to help identify the Mafia gang but more than likely to provide Bond with a bit of nooky in-between bouts of action. She also hasn't been told about the stolen bomb. Disguised as a BOAC stewardess on Bond's flight Domino comes down the aisle offering a basket of sweets to passengers. She offers one to Bond and their eyes meet. "Anything written on the inside of the wrapping this time?" "No, sir," replies the demure Domino.

Fade to Nassau hotel and Largo greeting Impellitini, head of the New York Mafia who has just arrived with his men in a 500-ton yacht called The Virginia. Like everyone else he's dressed in slacks and a vivid tropical shirt. He complains about "some damned Limey" called Bond taking up the best room in the hotel, the one directly above Largos. They also reassure each other that their men have had intensive underwater training.

Bond and Domino lie together on the beach observing the behaviour of some Mafia men as they frolic with beach girls. Bond has heard that Largo is holding a big party this evening at the casino and wants Domino to attend. He himself then leaves to meet up with Felix Leiter. Despite having a long relationship in the books Fleming stresses that in the film the two should never have met before. M then calls to inform Bond that he and his Chiefs of Staff believe the probable target is the new Anglo-American rocket site on the Grand Bahamas just north of Nassau. Bond's mission is to find out how the Mafia intends to get their bomb to the site. Bond and Felix agree to keep The Virginia under surveillance and request a submarine from the US navy.

Using the cover of darkness Bond makes an underwater survey of the Mafia yacht and is disturbed by a frogman sentry. In a violent fight Bond kills him and sharks dispose of the body. Back at the hotel Bond uses a rope ladder to climb down into Largo's room where he installs a listening device.

At the party, Largo is suspicious of seeing Domino, his former employee from the night club, here in Nassau and is unconvinced by her cover story that she worked there only while waiting for her BOAC appointment to come through. Invited back to Largo's suite, Domino is caught rifling through some desk drawers and is accused of being a spy. A struggle ensues. Bond, listening to all this upstairs, swings down onto the balcony and enters the room unobserved. He moves swiftly forward and taps Largo on the shoulder saying. "If you must murder your wife, I wish you'd make less noise about it. I sleep just above you and I simply can't get to sleep. Couldn't you wait and kill her in the morning." An astonished Largo backs off while Domino, pretending not to know Bond, pleads to be taken to her room. "Would you like me to hit him, just once?" Bond offers. Largo backs away, gun in hand. "Just you try, mister. You move a step and I'll shoot you and say it was self protection." Bond and Domino leave. No doubt beholden to Bond for rescuing her from being pulverised, Domino submits that evening to his carnal desires.

The following day, the yacht sails with all the Mafia gang aboard. Fleming writes, "The men in their black rubber suits go below decks to a pressure chamber and thence through a concealed hatch in the ship's side into the water where they practice underwater drills after being cautioned about sharks." A Mafia leader announces, "One of them got Phillipo when he was on guard last night." A lengthy sequence follows with, says Fleming, "plenty of underwater photography; the men practising with CO_2 guns against fish, lobsters etc." A huge light in the water flashes rapidly recalling the men into the ship. An approaching speedboat has been sighted. Bond is water-skiing behind it and Leiter is at the wheel with a bevy of beautiful girls who wave and call to the yacht. "Wave, you bastards, wave!" orders Largo to his men lining the rail. "Don't stand there looking like a lot of dummies." The gangsters wave feebly with fixed grins. The speedboat circles the yacht with Bond displaying admirable water-skiing skills and through the clear water sees the last of the frogmen entering the underwater hatch in the ship's hull. He makes a thumbs-up sign to Leiter and they head back for shore.

Largo calls a meeting in the yacht's stateroom where he reveals that they are on their way to pick up the bomb which the Sunderland plane dropped with a marker buoy on its approach to Nassau. Then tonight they sail for the Grand Bahamas where at dawn an underwater team will place the bomb, with a time clock device, up against the harbour of the rocket site. The bomb is safely collected and the yacht returns to Nassau where it is observed by a US submarine containing Bond and Leiter. Reporting to M, Bond has guessed Largo's plan and proposes to shadow the yacht and then fight it out with the underwater Mafia gang using picked men from the submarine crew. Bond suggests that they should have large white numbers painted on their backs to distinguish them from the gangster frogmen. Bond is naturally number one.

Outside the hotel, Largo greets Domino and apologises for his earlier crude behaviour and invites her to an evening cocktail party aboard the yacht. She accepts. On the beach, Domino meets Bond and tells him of Largo's invitation. Having discovered that the yacht intends to sail that night, Bond lets Domino into the secret of the stolen bomb and asks her to take a Geiger counter on board. He explains how it works, showing that it ticks when held over the luminous dial of his watch. Domino puts it into a shoulder bag. If she gets a reaction anywhere in the ship she's to get ashore as fast as possible and report, then the ship and its crew will be arrested. Bond tells her to watch her step.

At the party, Domino cleverly feigns drunkenness so she has an excuse to go below decks. But Largo, who obviously lusts after her, is still suspicious and alerts two of his men to follow her. Domino nears the hold when suddenly her Geiger counter begins to tick loudly. She stands transfixed and is about to make her exit when the two men attack. Taken to Largo's cabin she's tied to the bed. Informed of developments, Largo breaks up the party and orders the crew to set sail immediately. He then goes below to deal with Domino, submitting her to a bout of aggressive questioning, this time with a kinky twist when a Mafia strongman produces a lighted cigarette. This idea ultimately developed into the cigar butt and ice cube torture scene in both the novel and film versions of *Thunderball*. Gamely, Domino sticks to a rehearsed cover story that she was paid by customs to search the ship for a big haul of stolen Swiss watches and that the Geiger counter would reveal their presence. Largo appears to believe her but now realises it's too late to put her ashore and so she has to come on the trip with them. Releasing her from her bonds, Largo locks the cabin door to prevent any further prying.

When a dinner tray is taken to Domino, she hides one of the knives and then uses it to break her way out of her prison. As dawn rises and the shoreline of the rocket site approaches, Domino takes a wet suit, aqua lung and CO_2 spear gun and dives into the sea. She waits under cover of the ship's hull until the gangster frogmen team have left through the false hatch and swum on ahead. She follows.

Meanwhile the US submarine has been trailing the yacht all the way, and its underwater team now emerges and proceeds in formation to cut off Largo's men. The thrilling and now famous underwater battle climax is here described by Fleming for the first time: "We alternatively follow the gangster team with its heavy burden swung from webbing between four of the men and the shadowy, pursuing figure of Domino Smith and, converging upon them, Bond's underwater army. A great pitched battle then ensues with CO_2 guns and knives, culminating in a life and death struggle between Bond and Largo. Bond is about to get the worse of it and Largo's knife is raised when Domino shoots Largo with her CO_2 gun." The concept of Domino saving Bond's life would pop up later in the novel, the movie and its remake *Never Say Never Again*.

The guards at the rocket base have seen the commotion in the water, dead bodies etc, and a naval patrol boat is launched. The submarine then surfaces and fires a shot across the bow of the yacht. Finally the US frogmen rescue the bomb and make it safe. The battle won Bond and Domino swim alone to a shallow alcove. Taking off his mask and then hers Bond kisses Domino strongly on the mouth. The credits roll.

APPENDIX 3
IAN FLEMING'S SECOND SCRIPT TREATMENT

In his second treatment, Fleming adopted Whittingham's new opening sequence of the Mafia informant being killed and fed to the sharks word for word, but changed Sophia back to Domino. He then races straight into Petachi hi-jacking the bomber and crash landing it near Largo's yacht. Inside an expertly outfitted radio cabin Largo contacts his masters. Cut to a street in Palermo, Sicily, and a big office building. "Inside, in a long room, ten men, the heads of the Mafia, are sitting in silence," writes Fleming. As one of their number manipulates a short-wave radio set, "we get a close-up of all their strained, sweating faces, one by one, and particularly of the Capo Mafiosi, a quiet, formidable man."

When contact is made with Largo, the men round the table become jubilant. The chief then stands up, commanding immediate silence. "This letter (he holds it up) goes off at once to the Prime Minister of England. You will proceed this evening to the rendezvous and then to the target area." He warns them not to let slip their cover of being members of the Italian/American Garment Federation on their way to a convention in Nassau.

Again, Bond is introduced at the shooting gallery, but Fleming cuts the scene in his office and instead has him seeing M straight away. We follow Bond down a corridor and are afforded a glimpse into the daily life of the secret service. Sounds bombard us, from zings of radios to telephones ringing, while secretaries and clerks dash about with armfuls of papers and worried expressions. Reaching an end door, Bond walks through into M's staff office and greets Moneypenny. "Know what it's all about?" he asks. Before she can answer, the Chief of Staff enters, who smiles when he sees Bond and says, "There's quite a swerve on this one, James. Better fasten your seat belt."

There is a buzz on the intercom and Moneypenny tells Bond he can go in to see M. Sitting down, M looks coldly at Bond across the desk. "What do you know about the Mafia?" 007's reply is as before, the Sicilian Trades Union of crime jibe, followed by a lengthy summation of their activities. M then asks for Bond's knowledge about atomic bombs and what stocks England has and where. Bond doesn't know, but is aware that the American Air Force has plenty in the country and is carrying out training flights with them. "That's right," says M. "And that Valiant bomber that's been missing for 48 hours was carrying one." M shows Bond a copy of the Mafia blackmail letter. It confirms that the Mafia is in possession of atomic warhead number BC 4503. "That's the number of the one the Valiant was carrying," says M. "That rules out bluff." The Mafia's threat and demands are as Fleming laid out in his first treatment, except that he's cut the original 14-day deadline to a more nerve tingling seven days.

M tells Bond that the PM has spoken to the US President and that if the bomb isn't recovered within six days they've no alternative but to pay. "What's the last radar trace of the Valiant?" asks Bond. The Air Ministry say it left their outer defence system heading for the western Atlantic. The Americans then picked up an unidentified plane 100 miles out from the Bahamas but lost it. M assumes it must have come down somewhere in the Bahamas group. "That would make sense." He says. "There's Cape Canaveral, the American rocket base, not far off and there's our own on Grand Bahama Island. They would fit in with the size of target the Mafia are talking about." Bond ponders a while and then says, "All right, sir. What do you want me to do?" M orders 007 catch that evening's flight to Nassau where he'll meet someone from the CIA. "You and this American can call on London or Washington for anything you need." M reassures. "But you've got to find this bomb."

Cut to a beach hotel in Nassau. The Mafia men we saw in Palermo, all wearing bright rosettes that proclaim them to be members of the Italo-American Garment Workers' Federation, are filing into a conference room. After security precautions, Largo holds a brief conference in which the bomb operation is discussed. At Government House, Felix Leiter is grilling the Chief of Police about ships and aircraft that have entered Nassau in the past 48 hours. He asks in detail about Largo's yacht and it's revealed that 20 American visitors and 20 from Italy arrived the day before for the garment convention. It's decided that all ships in the harbour must be searched with Geiger counters. The authorities haven't been told about the bomb, instead a cover story that a valuable radio-active capsule has been stolen. Just then Bond arrives and meets Felix for the first time.

Both men decide to accompany the police's Geiger search of Largo's yacht. They go swiftly from cabin to cabin, entering at one point the private bedroom of Domino, who is scantily clad at the dressing table and resents the intrusion. In the end, the search proves negative and they leave. Bond and Felix next charter a small plane and fly a circular course round the islands. The shape of the Valiant is spotted below the water, surrounded by sharks, but instead of exploring their discovery it's decided governmental clearance is needed and they request a submarine. Upon arrival, Bond joins a team of US frogmen in the water. Fleming writes: "At the wreck there is a massacre of the sharks with CO_2 guns and Bond then penetrates into the cabin while the submarine team searches for the bomb under the plane. Bond finds the corpses of the crew and, later, the body of Petachi." Back on board the sub Bond alerts his chief that the bomb is missing. Vitally Fleming doesn't include Whittingham's idea of having Bond find the important evidence of Largo's treachery (Petachi's watch or ring) which he can use to more effectively confront Domino.

At Government House, Bond tells Leiter that his suspicions are focused on Largo's yacht. "These garment people look innocent enough, but they are, after all, Italians," writes Fleming. Bond attends a party held at the local casino and meets Domino at a black jack table. "He apologises for his intrusion into her cabin that afternoon and, reluctantly, she melts," writes Fleming. She tells Bond that her name is Domino Pelagra and talks of her fondness for England because her boyfriend works there for the American Air Force, Guiseppe Petachi. Bond realises this is the man whose body he found only a few hours before.

Bond next has a rendezvous with Felix by the docks and changes into his scuba gear to carry out an underwater search of Largo's yacht. He cautiously swims along the hull and notices the trap door to the underwater chamber. One of the Mafia men is doing underwater sentry duty and notices Bond. "The sentry raises his CO_2 gun and fires," Fleming writes. "The spear clangs on the side of the ship a foot away from Bond's body. Bond turns, reaching for his knife. There is an underwater battle. Bond kills the sentry. He is dragging him back towards the shore but the blood attracts the sharks. They attack the dead sentry and tear him to bits while Bond is lucky enough to get away with his life."

Back on shore, Bond tells Leiter about a ship off Gibraltar during the war that had just such an underwater trap door through which sabotage operations were carried out. Plus, no innocent yacht would have an underwater sentry. Obviously, says Bond, the garment workers are Mafia and the yacht is for transporting the bomb, which presumably is planted somewhere out at sea. But they can't lock up 40 apparently innocent men without hard evidence, so it's decided to wait until the yacht picks up the bomb and then follow it. It's now that Bond decides to us the Petachi connection in order to penetrate the gang through Domino. They only have 24 hours left.

Bond returns to the casino and persuades Domino to meet him for a swim the next day. Domino tells him that Largo has ordered her to stay ashore tomorrow as he's taking the whole party on a long cruise. Bond concludes from this that Domino knows nothing of the Mafia plot. Suddenly Largo appears and removes Domino from Bond, to whom he gives a hard, suspicious look. Bond seeks out Leiter and tells him to shadow the yacht tomorrow while he continues working on Domino.

Fade to yacht steaming out to sea. Largo is scanning the horizon through binoculars and picks up a small marker buoy. The yacht comes alongside and the underwater drill for recovery of the bomb is put into action. "We see the frogmen lifting the heavy tarpaulin-wrapped object from amongst the coral." Just then, a speedboat approaches with Leiter on water skis behind, "acting the cheerful playboy." He waves at the yacht while at the same time observing the activities underwater. Taking no chances Largo orders his men to open fire with machine guns on the boat, killing the driver and Leiter. One wonders why Fleming decided to kill off a character that had become such a popular foil for Bond in his books, particularly when it was hoped that a series of Bond films might follow this one. At least the writer gives him a chilling send-off. "Largo issues another order and a boat puts off from the yacht to the up-ended water skis still attached to Leiter's feet. They wrench them off and we briefly see the white soles of Leiter's feet before he sinks."

Fade to a lonely beach with Bond and Domino walking out of the water. Stripping off their scuba equipment they lie together on the hot sand. Bond stares out to sea and Domino asks why he's being so quiet. Bond says he can't tell her. Domino presses him, and Bond divulges the whole plot, including the death of her boyfriend. Anxious for revenge, Domino asks what she can do. Bond says he thinks Largo has put out to sea to recover the bomb and will she take a Geiger counter back with her. "If, in her cabin, it clicks, it will mean that the bomb is on board," writes Fleming. "It will be nightfall and he will be watching the yacht. She must signal him with a torch from her porthole and he will do the rest. She agrees."

Dissolve to the yacht back in harbour. Domino climbs aboard and is greeted by Largo. She cannot conceal her hatred for him, which he thinks is due to her feelings for Bond. In her cabin the Geiger counter starts clicking. She goes to the porthole and flashes the signal, receiving an answering gleam from the shore. Above on deck, the watchman has spotted the stabs of light and reports to Largo. Going downstairs he breaks into Domino's cabin as she quickly drops the Geiger counter and torch through the porthole. Largo confronts her but she stubbornly denies everything. He doesn't believe her and has her locked up. The yacht sails to plant the bomb.

At Government House, Bond argues with the Governor and Chief of Police that the yacht and its crew must be arrested immediately. He's also aware that Leiter is two hours overdue and coldly deduces that he must be dead. Wasting no more time, Bond races to the harbour and out to the submarine. But the sub is late in getting underway and the yacht has a good head start. The radar operator picks up the yacht on screen as being 50 miles ahead and making 15 knots. The captain tells Bond the sub's top speed is 20 knots, so it's going to be a close call who gets to the Grand Bahamas first.

The chase goes on through the night and, as dawn breaks, the sub sights the yacht and creeps up until she is parallel. In the distance, the great rocket installation glitters in the early morning sun. As before, a detachment of US frogmen, white numbers painted on their backs, exit the sub in arrowhead formation, led by Bond. The Mafia underwater team leaves through the false hatch carrying the bomb.

Domino also dives into the sea from her porthole and follows. This time, Fleming is much more descriptive about the climactic sequence. It almost reads like the finished film version: "A great pitched battle ensues with CO_2 guns and knives. There are many individual fights. In one, an oxygen pipe is cut; in another a glass mask is shattered; in another a man rips a small octopus off a coral-head and slams it across the neck and mask of his opponent. Everywhere there is foam and blood, flying harpoons and glittering knives. The surface of the sea is a turmoil amidst which bodies float head downwards."

Domino again saves Bond's life by killing Largo with a harpoon and the sub crew rescues the bomb. Aboard the yacht the radio operator is talking hysterically with Palermo HQ when a blast from the submarine shatters the bridge and the radio room. We cut to the Capo Mafiosi sitting beside the radio set as it goes silent. "For a moment he sits looking at it," writes Fleming. "Then slowly he opens a drawer in the desk, takes out a heavy revolver, opens his mouth wide and inserts the muzzle of the gun. Fade at the same time as the explosion of the gun."

Fleming again ends the script with Bond and Domino kissing after wearily pulling themselves ashore.

APPENDIX 4
JACK WHITTINGHAM'S FIRST SCREENPLAY

The now well-established opening of the Mafia informant's death, the hi-jacking and scuttling of the plane in the sea, plus the Air Ministry reaction to the missing bomber remains unaltered. But this time, Petachi isn't shot while making his way to the yacht. Whittingham has two divers swim to the submerged cockpit where they cut the pilot's air intake tube and he drowns.

We then fade to a house (Xanadu) on a deserted shore, protected by mangrove swamps, where Largo radios in to Sicily. There follows establishing shots of Palermo. Focus in on a building and sign advertising OLIVE OIL EXPORT CO. The Mafia leaders assemble inside and we learn about their ransom demands etc. Whittingham makes the point that wherever possible the camera should play on the Capo Mafiosi's back, so we don't see his face. One wonders if this is where the idea came from not to reveal Blofeld's identity in the official series until much later on?

Whittingham also ups the stakes in the Mafia's demands. The money's the same, the deadline is now ten days, but the group threatens that failure to pay will result in the first bomb being exploded in an area of strategic importance, serving as proof that they mean business. If the ransom is still not paid, the second bomb will be detonated in a major city with the inevitable loss of millions of lives. Cut to familiar target range scene and audience's first glimpse of Bond. Holding a score card, the armourer is rating Bond's shooting. Looking at an empty space next to 008 the armourer asks after the agent, only to be told he's been killed. "You'll have to scrub him," Bond says, rather coldly. The armourer takes a pencil and draws a line slowly through the horizontal 008 column. Bond is told by M that agents are covering a wide area in the search for the bomber and he's been given the Bahamas, where he will liaise with old friend Felix Leiter. Ironically, Bond arrives in Nassau on the same flight as a certain Dr Grundisch, a German atom scientist and recent Russian defector, hired by the Mafia to detonate the bombs.

Largo and the Mafia experts conduct their clandestine meetings under the guise of a business convention; not garment this time, but garbage hauling! At the same hotel, Bond meets Domino at the bar and she starts chatting to him about Largo, his yacht and Petachi (no longer her boyfriend but her brother). Bond recognises the name as one of the missing bomber crew, but reasons there must be hundreds of Petachis. Largo spots the two together and grows suspicious. At Government House, Bond wants to know all about Largo and this convention attended by so many Americans of Italian extract. Both appear to be bona fide and Largo's yacht was big game fishing at the time the plane disappeared. The police are taking the precaution of secretly photographing (with a lapel-camera) all new arrivals on the island. But the Governor is of the opinion that the Bahamas would be a most unlikely area to try and conceal a giant bomber, there being no landing strips suitable. Besides, an aerial search of the islands has turned up nothing. Bond and Leiter might just as well relax and enjoy the amenities.

Cut to a night club under the stars. Bond orders a special dinner "with characteristic Bond fastidiousness," for himself and Felix. Largo and some of his goons (Ferrari and Albertini) enter. Leiter recognises him not as Largo but as one Spider Spinelli, a Brooklyn racketeer with a bulging FBI file. His presence in Nassau is too much of a coincidence so Bond decides to pursue his acquaintance with Domino. There follows a series of short scenes of the pair swimming, dancing, water-skiing, etc. Meanwhile Leiter has identified, from police airport photographs, Dr. Grundisch and two Italians decorated for their midget submarine activities during the war: Inconclusive facts maybe, but enough to give Bond and Leiter second thoughts about Largo.

Bond and Leiter charter a plane and fly over Xanadu and the waters where the yacht was fishing the day the bomber vanished. Nothing is found and they decide to head back when Bond sees some sharks thrashing about near a dark, rather shapeless rock. Bond says that sharks don't get excited by lumps of rock and wants a closer look. Under a huge tarpaulin Bond spies the bomber and they request a naval gunboat and divers. Bond finds the body of Petachi, with his air intake pipe severed. The navy divers discover that both bombs have been removed. M tells Bond that under the cover story of a missing consignment of heroin they are to check Largo's yacht. Policemen arrive aboard that evening with hidden Geiger counters and disturb Largo in his private cabin. Suddenly the concealed Geiger starts clicking. The police halt and stare at Largo who rises as if to challenge them. The Chief of Police's hand goes to his gun. Then Largo breaks out into a smile and from his desk picks up a piece of radioactive metal used as a paperweight. "I never knew that heroine was radioactive," says Largo. As the door closes behind the retreating police Largo's smile is replaced by a look of extreme worry.

There are now only three days left and Bond is convinced the bombs are hidden somewhere on the island, but where? Looking at aerial photographs of Xanadu Bond notices suspicious tracks leading from the sea and across the sand to a boat house. That night at the casino, Bond observes Largo and guests arriving, including Domino. Walking up to her Bond says they must talk, alone. She follows him to his car and they speed away. But an angry Largo has seen them leave. At a remote beach, Bond breaks the news that her brother is dead, using as proof the identity disc he took from his corpse. Bond tells Domino the whole story and "her Sicilian blood boils for revenge." But Bond persuades her to control her feelings and carry on with Largo as before. If she wants to avenge her brother's death, she can best do it by helping him.

Back on his yacht Largo is a worried man. Why did the police bring Geiger counters on board? They must know something. And who is this man Bond? Domino arrives and goes below to her cabin. Largo enters and violently interrogates her about Bond. One of his blows sends her reeling across the bunk. "She lies there staring at him. The strain of withholding what she would like to say to him is almost unbearable." Largo leaves and Domino breaks down in tears. The next morning Domino sees Bond in his hotel room and agrees to help Leiter get into Xanadu. Knowing Domino has gone to meet Bond Largo orders for the pair to be shadowed and if the occasion presents itself to have Bond liquidated.

Domino shows Leiter a secret way into Xanadu through the mangrove swamp, but they have been followed by some of Largo's men and are ambushed. Both Leiter and Domino are thrown into the dangerous part of the swamp. "Leiter sinks rapidly until his head disappears. Domino, who is sinking more slowly, screams with terror." Largo arrives and wants the man's body exhumed and identified. His thugs pull at the arms until the head shows. Largo can see that this is not Bond but Leiter, who is quite obviously dead. Then, as Domino is sinking up to her mouth, he orders them to yank her out. She might still be useful to him. Carried to the house and then threatened with being thrown back in the swamp, Domino makes a fake phone call to Bond asking him to come to Xanadu because Leiter is hurt. Bond smells a trap.

On the yacht that night, Largo is greeted by the recently arrived Capo Mafiosi, here called Cuneo, who orders him to pick up the bombs and upon Bond's death to sail to the target area. The divers get ready but the underwater doors jam and fail to open. Suspicious of Domino's phone call, Bond has requested a police launch to take him close to the yacht and hears the sound of hammering coming out of the water. Slipping into scuba gear he investigates. Aboard the yacht Largo and Cuneo spot air bubbles breaking the surface and send a diver down to check it out. Cuneo also spots the dim outline of the police launch and orders divers over there too. Under the hull, Bond has discovered the underwater hatch and is attacked by a frogman. Bond disposes of him with a knife. Exhausted after the fight, Bond clings to the hull to rest just as the compartment doors open. A dozen frogmen swim out, some manning underwater sleds. Bond observes them and then makes his way back to shore.

Largo and Cuneo stare down at the water. A body slowly surfaces. Is it Bond? The body slowly rolls over, face up. They see it's their diver. Cuneo sees Bond's air bubbles rising 40 feet from the yacht. Largo hurls a hand grenade which explodes in the water. Waiting to see Bond's dead body float up, Largo and Cuneo are disappointed when only a dozen dead fish appear. Cuneo gives orders to signal Xanadu that Bond is heading for shore. Half-stunned by the explosion and exhausted from his fight, Bond tries to find strength enough to keep going. He also has to manoeuvre his way past a dangerous shoal of barracuda and a shark. Meanwhile, the police launch is attacked by Largo's divers and the occupants killed. Bond staggers ashore in a state of collapse and is at once seized by Mafia thugs, knocked over the head and thrown into the swamp near Leiter's body.

With Bond safely out of the way, Largo orders his divers to pick up the bombs, sealed in watertight rubber coverings and lying on the sea bed, and bring them back to the yacht which sails to its target, the rocket base on Grand Bahamas. Meanwhile a search party has failed to locate either Bond or Leiter, and M, conscious that the situation is now critical, demands Largo's yacht is seized. To his horror he learns that it has already sailed.

Back at the swamp, bubbles break the surface of the muddy water, then an arm emerges, then a head. Bond is alive. He has the breathing tube of his aqualung still in his mouth. With great effort he drags himself free. Then he sees Leiter, but hasn't the strength left to pull him out. Noticing that the yacht has sailed and the Xanadu house looks deserted, he staggers forward and trips into the road from sheer weakness. He gets up and lurches forward again, reeling along the middle of the road like a drunkard before collapsing once more. "He does not see them, but the headlights of a car driven at high speed are closing in on him," writes Whittingham. "At the last minute, the driver sees his body. There is a squealing of tyres and the car shudders to a halt half an inch from Bond's body." Mumbling about "Government House," Bond is driven back to Nassau and informs the Governor that Largo has the bombs and the yacht must be located at once. If it's far enough out at sea, so as not to cause danger to civilian life, she must be destroyed along with its deadly cargo. "Bond himself will be on board the naval bomber for the kill."

Half a mile out from the shore of the rocket site, the yacht weighs anchor. The underwater hatch opens and a dozen black skin divers, Albertini at the head, emerge with an underwater sled containing the bomb. Watching from the deck is Cuneo, Largo and Grundisch. Suddenly they hear the sound of a plane. It's heading straight for them, as if on a bombing run. Largo grabs a machine gun. Aboard the naval bomber, Bond has seen that the underwater sled holding the atomic device and the yacht are too near the rocket site to risk bombing it. "Again the bomber dives. But now we see, one after another, 12 parachutists jumping from the bomber. Camera holds their drop until just as they are about to touch down on the sea, they slash their parachutes free and submerge. They are in skin diving suits with numbers on their backs."

Bond, leading the navy divers engages in a pitched battle with Largo's men and the atom bomb is recovered. This time, however, the underwater duel is between Bond and Albertini, with 007 obviously emerging victorious. Meanwhile Domino has escaped from her room and set the second atom bomb to explode in three minutes. Largo and Cuneo reason that they are safe so long as they are in control of bomb number two. No one dare attack them for fear of detonating it. They will hug the shore, making for the Hudson River, and plant themselves in the heart of New York. Then Domino enters. "She accuses Largo of the murder of her brother. She hopes he will rot in hell. Largo laughs in her face; then he draws a gun. She does not care. She is smiling. She laughs – she is beyond any further hurt." Boom - the screen is enveloped in a mushroom cloud. The end. It's a great climax, the kind of Bond girl self-sacrifice that May Day later executed in *A View to a Kill*. And, with the possible exception of Bond's dead wife over the rolling credits of *On Her Majesty's Secret Service*, would have been the most downbeat ending to any 007 film.

APPENDIX 5
JACK WHITTINGHAM'S SECOND SCREENPLAY

Before the main action, Whittingham includes a bizarre short prologue that takes place in 1945. We see the White House in Washington and then former US President Harry Truman sitting at his desk in the oval office warning the audience about the nuclear peril. "The future may see a time when such a weapon may be used suddenly with devastating power by a wilful nation or group against an unsuspecting nation. With its aid, even a very powerful nation might be conquered within a very few days by a much smaller one. The world would be eventually at the mercy of such a weapon. In other words, civilisation might be completely destroyed." It was actually hoped that Harry Truman himself could be persuaded to record the scene. It was an apt choice for such an anti-nuclear statement, Truman having been the President who ordered the use of nuclear weapons against Japan at the end of World War II.

The credits roll over a montage of old maps of the Caribbean and touristy shots of waves breaking ashore, all to the accompaniment of calypso music. Then the action begins with Mafia informant Martelli flying from the wintry fog and snow of London and New York to the sunny paradise of Nassau, no doubt influenced by Whittingham's own recent journey. Upon arriving, Martelli meets with Largo (here called Joe, short for Giovanni). Impressed after his visit to Bryce's home Xanadu and its lush surrounding grounds, Whittingham changed Martelli from landing on Largo's yacht to him arriving by boat outside Xanadu and being led up to the house and inside. There, after $20,000 payment, he tells them that NATO pilot Antonio Petachi is their obedient servant, after threats to his family. "He has been made aware of the consequences of not co-operating." Says Martelli. Then, after inquiring over the health of Martelli's children, Largo, putting a friendly arm round his shoulder, asks, "One last question, my friend, before you relax in the warm blue water. You're absolutely certain that you covered your tracks?" Martelli is positive. Janni, a sinister henchman, shoots Martelli in the back of the neck. Another goon, Albertini, retrieves the wad of dollars. "See that he gets his swim while he's still bleeding," says Largo, casually. "Then clean up the mess."

One new and drastic change is the heroine. Whittingham never liked the name Domino, so here she's called Gaby, and although she operates the same role, her personality is totally different. Without question, one of the most disagreeable of all the Bond women, Gaby is out to get what she can, no matter the consequences to others. Her personality is revealed early on during a game of chemin-de-fer with Largo when she wins a hand and demands payment. "You'd sell your mother," he says, ruefully. After the death of Martelli, Largo, in the mood for sex, returns to Gaby who is sunning herself on the terrace. "Not now," she says. "Yes, now," he orders. But she wriggles free of his advances. "I could kill you. It would be so easy," Largo announces, his hands on her throat. "But you won't." She counters, pushing him away.

Martelli's body has been stripped and thrown into the sea. Largo and Gaby are playing Chemin-de-fer again for high cash stakes. He spots a fin cutting through the water towards Martelli's body and stares in macabre fascination. Taking the "saved" $20,000, Largo throws it on the table amongst the kitty. "We don't *have* to play again – not if you want to be *sure* of winning." Gaby gets his meaning. "She hesitates for a moment, her eyes holding his, then she scoops the money up and puts it into a bag, then lies back on the mattress. His body goes down on hers, his mouth seeks hers. Camera pans slowly off." This scene has an underlying perversion about it; that the sight of Martelli's body being ripped apart by sharks should turn Largo on.

Cut to documentary type scene of the bomber taking off. Instead of shooting the crew during the hi-jack, Whittingham this time has Petachi using a cyanide gas cylinder. The scene plays identical to the finished film. "Petachi removes his own mask and puts on a private oxygen re-breather, so that he is independent of the central oxygen supply. Now he pushes the nozzle of the cylinder into a rubber pipe in the central oxygen supply system and releases the poisonous gas. One by one the crew reacts, then slumps unconscious." As the pilot dies, the plane is thrown into a deadly tailspin. Petachi clambers to the controls and manages to right the aircraft and then change course. Again the bomber's rendezvous with Largo's yacht plays very similar to the film version. "Petachi puts on underwater breathing apparatus. Then he switches off the engines. The eerie hissing sound of air on wings. He starts circling around the yacht, losing height. From Petachi's eye line in the cockpit, the yacht's searchlights have been turned on. From Largo's eye line, the aircraft circling lower and lower, then straightening up into the beam from the searchlight and pancaking on the sea 100 yards from the yacht. It starts to sink."

For his troubles, Petachi is again murdered by having his air intake tube cut, by Janni. "Water rushes into his mask. He struggles desperately, but is forced back down into the cockpit, and in a moment he has drowned." This is a fate which greets Petachi in the film, but not the novel, where he's gruesomely dispatched above the waves with a stiletto in the throat. Back on Xanadu, Largo enters a large sitting room. Janni slides back the wooden panels to reveal a bank of transmitters and short wave receivers. The mission-accomplished signal is sent out to Palermo. At Mafia headquarters Bastico, the Capo Mafiosi, reads the message. "Stage one of the operation has now been completed, gentlemen," he informs a meeting of six Mafia leaders. "As a brotherhood we are now more powerful than any nation, for we can attack, but we cannot be attacked." Whittingham brilliantly suggests overlapping the section of Bastico's speech where he threatens that the second bomb will be exploded in a capital city with shots of Waterloo Bridge at rush hour, covered in traffic and thousands of commuting workers. The power of such a scene is undeniable.

On a commuter train various headlines in the evening papers scream out at the screen. "Atom Bomber Vanishes." "Search for A-Bomber Continues." "Sabotage Not Ruled Out." Cut to a conference attended by Air Ministry bigwigs where news on the search for the bomber is discussed and the fact that even if the nuclear bombs are lost no one but an expert can explode them. "But what if one fell into the hands of an expert?" asks a Minister. Laughing, the Air Marshal replies, "Come, come now. You've been reading too much science fiction."

Finally and almost a quarter of the way into the script, Bond makes his first appearance at the shooting gallery. The armourer again dismisses his Baretta as a ladies gun, but this time suggests he swap it for a Smith and Wesson or a Walter P.P.K. "Those are real stopping guns." Going in to see M, Bond learns that it has been established that the aircraft was hi-jacked by the Mafia. Whittingham includes a brief scene in which Whitehall people are shown a New York Police Department film on the history of the Mafia, which puts the audience in the picture. They've eight days to pay the $100 million ransom. Bond is sent to the Bahamas, where M has an inkling the bomb may be. "Dozens of islands and cays, where a bomb could be hidden away," he says. "And within easy reach of America – if that's where the target is," says Bond. His cover story is that he's made a killing on the stock market and on a well-earned holiday. "But watch out," warns M. "Don't overdo the holiday."

Again, Bond arrives by plane into Nassau on the same flight as the nuclear scientist hired by Largo. The scientist has had plastic surgery to disguise his features and changed his name from Dr. Carlo Volpe to Galante. Next there's some nice sparring between Largo and Gaby who wants to stay and skin dive not sail back to Nassau for the fake convention. "I got business to do," says Largo. "I got to earn my living, so you don't have to earn yours." Gaby smiles. "You think I don't?" Largo then asks her to "get yourself looking respectable" for his guests. "You want me respectable? Well, well. You had too much sun?"

Bond enters his hotel just as Largo's fake garment workers convention is getting underway. Walking to the outside terrace, packed with tourists, Bond sits at the bar two seats away from Gaby. "She looks him up and down, quite unashamedly, and appears to like what she sees." Bond orders a Planter's punch and gets chatting with Gaby who allows him to buy her a vodka martini. Playing the tourist, Bond asks if she will show him the sights. "You know your way around?" Gaby smiles at the question. "I should do. I've *been* around – quite a time." Holding her look, Bond says, "It's my first visit and I'm very eager to learn." Gaby answers. "What would it be that you're so eager to learn?" After agreeing to become Bond's guide Gaby is asked about the convention and specifically the man looking at them - Largo. "He's the boss," she says. "That's his little dinghy lying out in the harbour." Bond follows her look and spies the yacht. "Expensive little dingy." "But kind of comfortable – if you like to be comfortable." Bond smiles. "Which I gather you do." "You gather right Mr...?" "Bond."

The convention meeting concludes and Largo approaches the bar where Gaby introduces him to Bond. Largo orders Gaby to look after his guests and ushers her away. "Be seeing you, Mr Bond." Largo looks angry. "That's a binding contract," says Bond. Meeting Felix Leiter, Bond tells of his suspicions about Largo's yacht, The Sorrento, and the convention delegation. It's too much of a coincidence that 20 Italians have suddenly turned up on the island. That night, both agents visit the Junkanoo night club. After ordering dinner, Bond spies Largo entering with Gaby. Leiter is sure he's seen a picture of Largo's face. "And it wouldn't have been in the society glossies!" He decides to have the Italian's photograph sent to Washington. Meanwhile, Bond writes Gaby a note to meet him tomorrow ("What about that contract. It's binding – don't forget."), and asks a waiter to make sure she gets it. Reading the note she smiles briefly across at Bond, then nods.

While Largo and his delegates indulge in typical touristy activity, tailed by Leiter, Bond and Gaby enjoy the day together, deep-sea fishing, water-skiing etc. Bond tries to press her about Largo but it's clear she knows nothing. During their conversations we learn that Gaby can't have children. She also tries to teach Bond Italian. "How do you say, I go for you, Gaby," Bond says. "I could eat you." She comes close to him. "That you don't *say* in Italian." They kiss hungrily. That evening, Gaby returns to the yacht during a party and firework display taking place aboard. "Not unnaturally in this male company she is the focal point of attraction. Completely outdoing the fireworks." In her cabin, Largo demands to know where she's been all day and is jealous when he learns it was with Bond. "He's dated you for the last time."

Later that night, Bond receives a note asking him to meet Gaby at a secluded road at nine. When he gets there, Bond watches as the lights of a car flash on and off, like a signal. He steps into the road to show himself and the car manoeuvres forward. When it is within twenty feet it suddenly accelerates. Bond jumps back but the left wing catches him and hurls him into a ditch. Sitting in the car is Albertini and Janni who double back to finish off Bond. Just then the windscreen shatters. Bond is ready for them, gun in hand. The thugs flee.

At police HQ, Leiter informs Bond that Washington has identified Largo as one Antonio DeSuca, a high ranking Mafia man. "Hell! This is interesting," says Bond. Police undercover photos of new arrivals in Nassau also reveal the true identity of Galante as a missing scientist called Volpe. On this new information, Bond and Leiter carry out an aerial search of Xanadu and around the area where Largo's yacht was seen on the night the bomber vanished. As in Whittingham's previous draft, Bond is about to give up when his attention focuses on a group of excited sharks around a mass of rock which turns out to be tarpaulin camouflaged as coral out of which a wing-tip is visible. "The sharks have patently been tearing at the tarpaulin to get at the decomposing bodies of the crew." Bond and naval divers hack away with knifes at the ropes securing the tarpaulin to metal hooks driven into the seabed. Bond sees the bombs have been removed and investigates inside. 'We see the corpses of the crew, swollen and bizarre.'

On being informed of the plane's discovery, M orders a Geiger search of Largo's yacht under the missing heroin cover story. Customs officials board The Sorrento while a party is in full swing. "A Bahamian dancer is doing a fire dance as part of the fun, or a striptease, if we can get away with it," writes Whittingham hopefully. When the search proves fruitless M phones Bond from England at an ungodly hour of the morning. This would have resulted in a quite unique sight – M in pyjamas! Adamant that the bombs must be somewhere else in the area, M tells Bond he has just 48 hours left to find them or Operation Zebra would have to take effect, the complete evacuation of the islands by air and sea.

That night, Largo is enjoying a healthy run at the casino in the company of Gaby. Playing baccarat and as banker, he deals the cards. When the bank is at $8,000 his opponent cuts his losses and leaves. "Largo looks round the table. No one seems willing to play against him." Just then we hear Bond's voice: "Banco." All eyes turn in the direction of the voice. Bond takes a seat opposite Largo and slips a packet of dollar notes on to the table. Largo deals the cards and Bond wins. He looks up at Gaby who smiles across at him. Largo sees this exchange between them. Incensed he raises the bank to $50,000. Now, from other tables, people have crossed to watch this game. There is a tense, excited silence. Largo deals and after a stand off of bluff and counter bluff Bond reveals his winning hand. Largo smiles. "Congratulations. I can't go on. You've cleaned me out."

Bond and Gaby leave the casino together in a car. Largo and Janni follow them. "We're going to do the job efficiently this time," says Largo. "But if Gaby gets hurt, it'll be your last ride too, Janni." Bond stops the car and he and Gaby walk to a beach. Taking out a sniper's rifle, Janni fires just as Bond's foot slips on some loose stones and the bullet misses by an inch and ricochets off a rock. Instinctively Bond pulls Gaby down and drags her behind the shelter of the rocks. Janni fires again, this time the bullet skims over their heads, almost killing Gaby. "You bastard!" yells an outraged Largo. "You nearly killed her. We've got to get closer." Bond and Gaby run into a nearby cave as Largo and Janni head after them. Luckily two motorcycle cops appear and ask Largo to move his car as it's blocking the road. Bond and Gaby can finally relax. "Why did they want to kill us?" she asks, not unreasonably. "Because Largo's a killer," says Bond, who proceeds to relate the whole story about the missing bombs, Largo's Mafia connection and that if the West don't pay a major city will be blown up. "Do you remember what happened at Hiroshima?" asks Bond. "Out of a population of 250,000, 78,000 were killed. Your home town is Jacksonville, isn't it? Well, just imagine one of those bombs falling on your own family, utterly obliterating everyone you know there." Bond wants Gaby's help, but she's frightened to go back to Largo. Bond tries one last time. "A town teeming with people, women and children, could be devastated in a few days from now. A town like Jacksonville." Gaby looks up; there are tears in her eyes.

Though Bond's winning over of Gaby is effectively done in this scene, with Whittingham's removal of the Petachi blood connection, the pilot is now no longer either her brother or lover, removing much of the emotional punch. Nor does Bond give Gaby a Geiger counter to take on the yacht, instead he asks her to merely look out for anything suspicious or the hope that Largo might give himself away.

Appendix 5: Jack Whittingham's Second Screenplay

Largo hears Gaby return to her cabin on the yacht and confronts her. His hands go round her throat. "I'll kill you for this. Kill you." As he looks down at her, with her life in his big hands, the strength in his massive body suddenly seems to ebb away. "You see, you can't kill me," says Gaby, no doubt relieved. But then she confesses about Bond being an agent and that he suspects Largo is involved with the missing bomber. Largo dismisses Bond as mad and leaves. But outside his face is one of worry and concern.

At his hotel, Bond tells Leiter that Gaby now knows the whole story. "I wanted to stir things up. Force them into action. Panic them." Bond also confesses he told Gaby how to render an atom bomb from "safe" to "live" and back again. "But that's secret information," blasts Leiter. "You could get yourself busted for that." Just then a policeman arrives with the aerial photographs taken over Xanadu. They spy deep tracks leading from the sea to a small beach hut. Both suspect they were made by something that was dragging the heavy bombs. Leiter decides to take a look, but the house is surrounded by swamp and it won't be easy.

Just then the phone rings. It's Gaby speaking quietly in case she's overheard. She's been doing some snooping around on her own. "They're picking something up tonight, then sailing... no, I don't know where." Bond persuades Gaby to rendezvous with Leiter near Xanadu and show him safe passage through the swamp. This she does. Alone, Leiter enters the hut and to his disappointment sees that what must have made the tracks is a small boat. Just then Albertini enters with a gun and takes Leiter prisoner aboard the yacht. Back at Government House, Bond is worried that Leiter isn't back. The Governor suggests taking a gunboat and stopping the yacht, but Bond isn't sure the bombs are onboard yet. Bond goes to investigate in a police launch and Whittingham uses the same device as before - that the yacht's hatch has jammed and the noise of its repair alerts 007's suspicion and underwater he locates the hidden compartment. Again, Bond kills the frogman sentry, watches as divers and an underwater chariot emerge from the open hatch, and has a grenade thrown after him by Largo as he returns ashore. There, bleeding from his fight, and half-stunned, two thugs seize him, knock him out and throw him in the swamp.

Largo's divers approach an undersea cave and pick up the two hidden bombs and return to the yacht through the underwater compartment. A naval gunboat nearby is spotted on radar and Largo orders a diver to place a limpet mine on its hull. The yacht begins to sail for its target area, Miami. Whittingham decided to substitute Miami for the missile base due to the logistical problems of replicating a large rocket installation in the Nassau area. The gunboat follows. In Largo's cabin, Gaby is enjoying supper. "Bond's dead, isn't he?" Largo fills her brandy glass. "Sure." She continues. "Why don't you be content with that?" Largo is puzzled. "Bond told me. You're going to blow up a city. You've got the atom bomb. Do you want to become a mass murderer – a monster?" Largo laughs. "A mass murderer! You're nuts, Gaby. I'm going to be a multi- millionaire." Gaby isn't convinced. "But what good's all that money going to do you? You'll be on the run." Largo smiles. "Yes – with the other bomb. They won't touch me. They daren't." Gaby looks at Largo in a new way, impressed. "What's my share?" she asks. Largo, sensing her mercenary streak, agrees to keep her on side. "We're in this together."

Bond summons the energy to pull himself out of the swamp, escaping the predatory gaze of hundreds of migratory crabs encircling him. Nearly hit by a car, Bond is raced to Government House. He tells the Governor that the bombs are aboard and the trailing gunboat should attack The Sorrento now and blow it out of the water. As the gunboat begins to open fire the limpet mine goes off and the craft is destroyed. Unhindered the yacht closes in on Miami and anchors half a mile from shore. As the anchor chain reels out, Leiter, tied up in the anchor room, holds the wire binding his wrists against the out-reeling anchor-chain. The chain cuts through the wire. Meanwhile Galante has activated the bomb and Janni, Albertini and six divers, with the chariot, submerge and swim off in the direction of the Miami sea front. There is the distant sound of an aircraft. Bond is aboard, in the co-pilot's seat, and sees the activity in the sea. Eight Royal Marine divers including Bond, jump out of the plane and land in the water, ready for battle. On the yacht, a panic-stricken Largo orders the crew to get his private plane ready and to load the second bomb aboard it.

Largo's divers enter the wreck of a tanker to plant the bomb, closely followed by Bond's scuba army. Cue underwater fight. Largo's divers are armed with CO_2 guns. Bond's men only have knives but are faster and more agile in the water. "The individual combats should go on through funnels, in the wheelhouse, along gangways, in the holds, anywhere the wreck can provide. An oxygen pipe is cut, a mask is smashed, a harpoon in someone's back, a knife in another's etc. The highlight should be the individual encounter between Bond and Janni, and Janni's death.'

On board The Sorrento, Largo promises Galante $20 million if he'll come with him and threatens. "Next time it will be New York." Their conversation is overheard by Leiter, and also by Gaby who slips into the back of the plane and hides next to the bomb. Bond and his divers surface victorious with the chariot and bomb and are picked up by a naval gunboat. Largo and Galante have seen what's happened. "We better get going – now," says Largo. Just then Leiter attacks them. A fight ensues in which Galante is knocked into the sea and Leiter is shot. On the gunboat Bond defuses the bomb and then hears the sound of an engine revving hard. He watches as a catapult mechanism releases Largo's plane into the air. "Shoot her down!" yells Bond. But it's soon out of range.

The gunboat comes alongside the yacht and Bond jumps on board finding the injured Leiter. "Other bomb, in plane, with Largo," he says. "Girl's with him, too. Warn New York. That's the next place." Bond looks into the sky, the plane is no more than a speck now. Suddenly there is a blinding flash. "She's done it. She had the guts to do it," Bond says to himself. "The sky, and the screen, is completely filled with a great, boiling, surging cloud of many colours, mushrooming upwards. The roar of the deafening blast echoes and rumbles away in the distance." Fade Out.

Granddaughter Aimi visits Jack Whittingham's grave in Malta.

INDEX

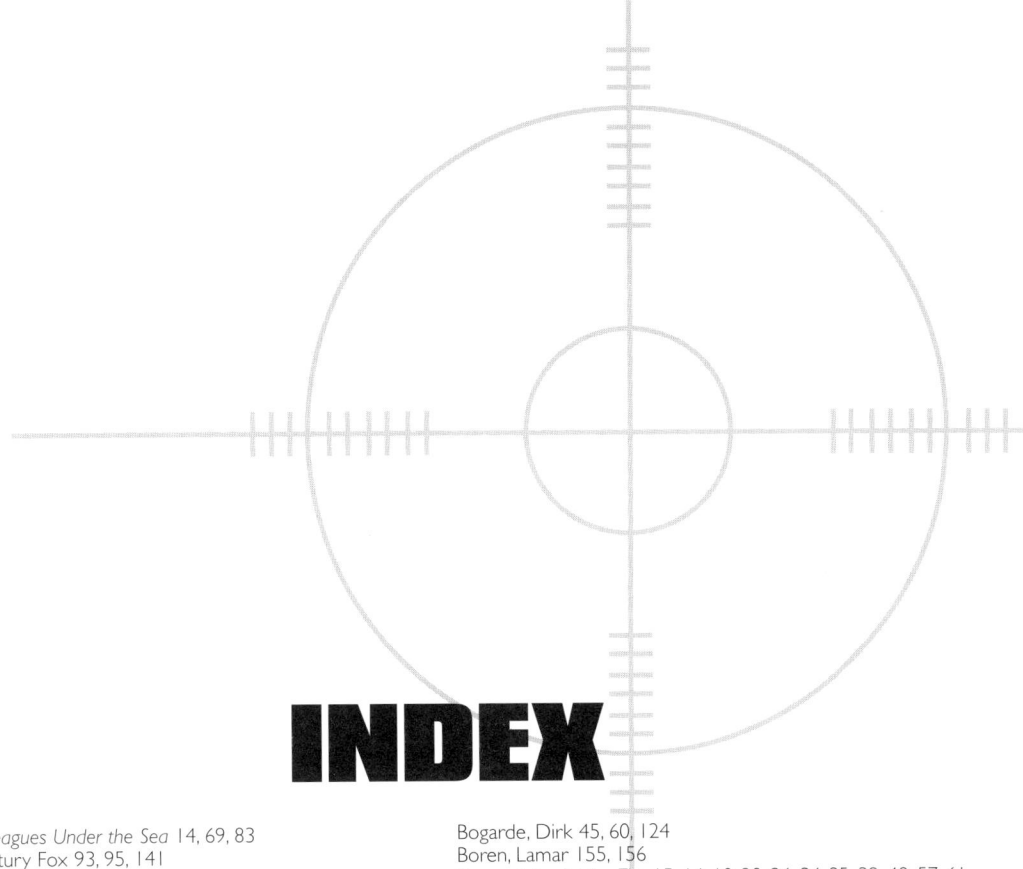

20,000 Leagues Under the Sea 14, 69, 83
20th Century Fox 93, 95, 141

Adam, Ken 135, 137, 139, 143, 145, 147, 151-153, 155, 158, 160, 161, 167
African Queen, The 13, 16, 135
Aman, Leigh X, 16, 36, 39, 40, 43, 45, 60, 61, 66, 88, 114, 115, 119
Ambler, Eric 43, 115
Amis, Kingsley 24
Andress, Ursula 172, 192
Anna Karenina 13
Armstrong, Vic 199, 201, 207, 208
Armstrong, Wendy 207
Around the World in 80 Days 12-15, 20, 22, 145
Asquith, Anthony 33, 34
Atkinson, Rowan 206, 221
Attenborough, Richard 35, 186
Auger, Claudine 141, 142, 145, 150, 172, 176

Baker, George 59
Baker, Stanley 59, 149
Balcon, Sir Michael 61, 127
Bardot, Brigitte 88
Barry, John 135, 171
Basinger, Kim 192, 198, 200, 201, 206
Bassey, Shirley 171
Beaverbrook, Lord 12, 15
Bellan, Ferdinand 167
Beswick, Martine 149, 176, 178
Betjeman, John 122
Bianchi, Daniela 172
Binder, Maurice 171, 172, 191
Black, Don 171
Blackman, Honor 123, 124, 176
Blackwell, Blanche 120

Bogarde, Dirk 45, 60, 124
Boren, Lamar 155, 156
Boy and the Bridge, The 15, 16, 18, 20, 26, 34, 35, 39, 40, 57, 61, 64, 69, 70, 78, 82, 87, 94, 114, 115, 119
Boyd, Stephen 83
Branwell 123
Brandauer, Klaus Maria 192, 193, 198, 199, 206
Bricusse, Leslie 171
Bridge on the River Kwai, The 47, 57
British Lion Films 37, 96
Brittan, Leon 182
Broccoli, Albert R. (Cubby) VII, VIII, 13, 40, 48, 62, 106, 107, 109, 110, 119, 121, 123-125, 129, 133, 135, 139, 141, 142, 145-148, 150, 151, 155, 159, 160, 163-165, 172, 175-177, 187-191, 211, 215, 228, 231, 232, 234
Broccoli, Barbara 208, 226
Broccoli, Dana 164
Broome, Patrick 80
Brosnan, John 140
Brosnan, Pierce 225
Brown, Courtney 157, 158
Browning, Ricou 156, 157, 175, 207
Bruyere, Jean de la 35, 43, 55, 56, 61, 63
Bryce, Ivar V, VIII, IX, 11, 12, 15, 16, 18, 20, 22, 24-29, 33-36, 38-43, 45-48, 51-66, 69-72, 77-90, 93-100, 102, 103, 107, 111-115, 117-122, 182
Buccella, Maria Grazia 141
Burton, Richard 59, 61, 124, 125, 149

Caine, Michael 137, 146, 147, 168, 182
Call Me Bwana 164
Calley, John 225-228
Cameron, Earl 145, 147, 164, 178
Carrera, Barbara 23, 192, 194, 198, 199, 205, 206, 208
Carter-Ruck, Peter VIII, IX, 14, 109-111, 119, 120, 121, 131, 216, 217, 231, 234, 235

INDEX

Casey, Bernie 194
Casino Royale 11, 12, 18, 32, 90, 93-95, 106, 118, 125, 133, 172, 229
CBS 11, 53
Celi, Adolfo 142, 143, 172, 176, 177
Charteris, Ann 12
Chitty Chitty Bang Bang 105
Christie, Julie 141
Christopher Mann Ltd 61
Cilento, Diane 145, 146, 164
Clapton, Eric 181
Clark, Sir Andrew 82, 112
Clement, Dick 197, 198, 200-203, 205, 206, 209, 212, 213
Cleopatra 59, 88
Clift, Montgomery 59
Cockleshell Heroes 13
Colditz Story, The 40
Collins, Lewis 225
Columbia Pictures 37, 56, 57, 62, 69, 88, 96, 229
Connery, Jason 145
Connery, Micheline 186, 190, 192
Connery, Sean VII, VIII, 40, 60, 88, 124, 125, 134, 137, 139-151, 156, 158-161, 163-165, 168, 172, 176-179, 181, 183, 185-194, 197, 199-203, 205-207, 209, 211-213, 215, 220, 221, 228
Coppola, Francis Ford 189, 198
Cousins, Frank 156, 158
Cousteau, Jacques 20, 183
Coward, Noel 21
Craig, Daniel 229
Craig, Michael 59
Crawford, Joan 175
Creature from the Black Lagoon, The 156
Crichton, Charles 61
Cummings, Bill 161
Cuneo, Ernest V, VI, IX, 19-22, 24, 29, 43, 49, 53, 61, 62, 66, 70, 71, 75, 77-79, 94-97, 113, 114, 118-120, 129
Cushing, Peter 59

Daily Express 12, 46
Daily Mail 164
Dalton, Timothy 225
Danger Man 129
Davis, Edwin 95, 96, 100, 102
Dawson, Anthony 164
Dearden, Basil 61
Dehn, Paul 33, 35, 59
Deighton, Len 182, 183, 187, 189, 228
Devlin, Dean 228
Diamonds Are Forever 18, 20, 24, 40, 121, 135, 149, 165, 183, 191, 194, 232
Die Another Day 139
Disney, Walt 61, 69, 129
Divided Heart, The 45
Doctor Zhivago 141
Doleman, Guy 164, 176
Donovan, General William 19
Dr. No VII, VIII, 11, 40, 70, 74, 75, 107, 134, 139, 153, 164, 165, 171-173, 191, 217, 231-233
Dunaway, Faye 142

Ealing Studios 45, 46, 127
Ekberg, Anita 164
Elstree Studios 197, 208
Emmerich, Roland 228
Empire Strikes Back, The 190, 203, 204
Eon Productions VI, 106, 107, 139, 142, 146, 152, 159, 164, 183, 187-189, 191, 211, 212, 215, 218, 225, 226, 228, 229
Evans, Laurence X, 25-27, 34, 51, 58, 60, 85-87

Fairchild, William 35, 36, 39, 45

Fantastic Voyage 142
Feldman, Charles 133
Fenn, Robert 86, 96, 97, 100, 103, 113, 114
Finch, Peter 59, 83, 93
First Great Train Robbery, The 194
Fleming, Ann 57, 58, 119, 122, 131
Fleming, Casper 58
Fleming, Ian VI, VII, VIII, IX, X, 11, 12, 14, 17-27, 29-43, 45-66, 68-75, 77-91, 93-107, 110-122, 124, 127-129, 131, 134, 135, 142, 143, 148, 151, 177, 179, 182, 187, 189, 191, 194, 211, 217, 228, 229, 231-234
Flipper 153
Flowers for Mrs Harris 16
Flynn, Errol 14
For Your Eyes Only 18, 73, 74, 91, 187
Foreman, Carl 46, 47, 48, 88
Fox, Edward 194
Frankovich, Mike 37, 88, 93
Frend, Charles 60
Frobe, Gert 172
From a View To a Kill 74
From Russia with Love 24-26, 59, 107, 109, 110, 122, 134, 137, 149, 153, 157, 164, 172, 173, 191, 217, 232

Gallico, Paul 16
Garner, James 59
Gee, Prunella 208
Geeson, Judy 181
Glidrose Productions Limited 115
GoldenEye 225, 227
Goldfinger V, 33, 40, 48, 73, 111, 123, 125, 133-135, 137, 139, 146, 147, 149, 151, 152, 157, 165, 167, 171-173, 176, 177, 187, 194, 232
Goldwyn Jr., Samuel 87, 88, 93
Gray, Charles 194
Green, Janet 33
Grimes, Stephen 35
Guinness, Alec 25, 35
Guns of Navarone, The 47, 88

Hama, Mie 172
Hamilton, Guy 40, 88, 135
Harbottle, Laurence 86, 95, 96, 99, 100, 102
Harris, Richard 60, 127, 220
Harrison, George 216
Hartford, Huntingdon 145
Hartford, Marie-Josephine 15
Harvey, Laurence 123, 124
Help! 158
Hildyard, Jack 88
Hill, The 137
Hitchcock, Alfred VII, 34, 39, 41, 43, 45, 48, 51, 55, 56, 58, 62, 88, 115
Holden, William 59
Hoover, J. Edgar 16
Hopkins, John 129, 133
Howard, George Wren 100, 103
Howard, Michael 74, 90, 91
Howard, Trevor 14, 35, 59, 60, 115, 127, 186
Hunt, Peter 135, 157, 159, 173
Hunted 45
Huston, John 13, 16, 35, 55, 88, 94, 96, 123, 127, 181

Incredible World of James Bond, The 175
Ives, Burl 84

Janson-Smith, Peter 100
Jenkins, Richard 146, 147, 150, 159, 162, 168, 177, 179
Johannsen, Ingemar 60
Jonathan Cape (Publishers) 74, 90, 98, 100, 102, 103, 120

INDEX

Jones, Tom 171, 176
Kelly, Charles Joseph 64
Kerkorian, Kirk 227
Kershner, Irvin 190-193, 195, 197-199, 201-207, 209, 212
Klein, Jordan 153-158, 160, 161
Korda, Sir Alexander 11, 16, 45, 46
Koscina, Sylva 123, 124, 125

La Frenais, Ian 197, 198, 200, 201, 209
Lamb, James 86, 87
Lamont, Peter 153, 158
Lazenby, George 88, 165, 199
Lean, David 11, 88, 125
Lee, Bernard 35, 164, 194
Lee, Christopher 59
Leech, George 147, 165, 168, 169, 207
Legrand, Michel 212
Leigh, Suzanna 143
Live and Let Die 11, 18, 40, 48, 53, 187, 194, 199
Llewelyn, Desmond 146, 153, 163, 164, 194
London Films 45
Lorimar Pictures 189, 191
Losey, Joe 61
Lumet, Sidney 137
Luxford, Bert 139, 168

MacKendrick, Alexander 88
MacLaine, Shirley 12, 61, 181
Maibaum, Richard 33, 48, 106, 107, 129, 133, 134, 139, 148, 151, 155, 164, 167, 168, 216, 217, 231-233
Mallet, Tania 176
Man With the Golden Gun, The 40, 187
Mancuso, Frank 226, 227
Mandy 45
Mankowitz, Wolf 106
Mann, Christopher 87, 125
Margaret, Princess 16
Mars-Jones, William 111, 112, 115, 120
Mason, Barry 216
Mason, James 59
Mason, Sylvan Whittingham VIII, X, 14, 48, 72, 75, 102, 103, 109, 110, 115, 117, 121, 128-131, 182, 216, 217, 231, 234, 235
Maxwell, Lois 164, 194
MCA 25, 26, 48, 80-88, 90, 93, 96, 100, 103, 113, 115, 117
McClory, Bobo 14, 119, 123, 124, 181
McClory, Branwell 123
McClory, Desmond 14, 16
McClory, Kevin V-VIII, IX, X, 12-24, 26, 29, 33-37, 39-41, 43, 45-48, 50, 53-61, 63, 64, 66, 69-75, 81-90, 93-103, 105-107, 109-115, 117, 118, 119-121, 123-125, 127-129, 131, 133-135, 143, 145, 146, 155, 156, 159, 160, 161, 175, 176, 179, 181-183, 186-190, 212, 215-223, 225-229, 231-234
McCowen, Alec 194
McGoohan, Patrick 59
McNair, Philip 86, 96, 100
Mengel, Philip 189
Mephisto 192
Meredith, Burgess 181
MGM VI, 69, 211, 225-229, 231-233
Middlemas, David 143, 153, 154, 157
Moby Dick 13
Monlaur, Yvonne 141
Moonraker 11, 18, 93, 197
Moore, Roger 40, 187, 190, 199, 212
Moore, Ted 135, 158
Moulin Rouge 13
Murton, Peter 153

NBC 11, 175
Neame, Ronald 61

Neeson, Liam 225, 228
Nelson, Barry 11
Netter, Douglas 88, 93, 96, 115, 119
Never Say Never Again VI, VIII, 23, 35, 66, 172, 190-192, 194, 195, 199, 201, 203-209, 211-213, 215-217, 221, 225, 228, 234
New Yorker, The 48
Next Man, The 143
Niven, David 59, 77, 83, 84
Norman, Barry 124
North by Northwest 39, 58, 62, 71
Nutter, Rik Van 164

O'Brien, Vincent 181
O'Donnell, Pierce 226, 227, 228, 229
O'Donovan, Desmond 115, 119
O'Toole, Peter 59, 121, 124
Octopussy 192, 211, 212
Offence, The 134
Offield, Betty 46
Olivier, Laurence 21
On Her Majesty's Secret Service 64, 88, 133, 153, 165, 173, 183, 199
Orme, Geoffrey 16
Outland 143

Paluzzi, Luciana 142, 146, 148-150, 159, 161, 165, 168, 172, 176, 178
Paramount 69, 186, 188
Paul, Gloria 141
Peake, Sir Francis 35, 42, 43
Peters, Mollie 143, 147, 149, 168, 176, 178, 208
Pinewood 139, 142, 143, 147, 148, 153, 163, 164, 167, 172
Pleasance, Donald 194
Plomer, William 73, 90, 111
Plowden, Julian 191
Pohlmann, Eric 164
Powell, Dilys 177
Prince and the Pauper, The 129
Psycho 62

Rafeedie, Judge Edward 228, 232, 233
Raft, George 32
Rank 11, 84, 149
Ratoff, Gregory 93, 94, 118
Reed, Sir Carol 11, 88
Rietty, Robert 172
RKO 45, 69
Robinson, Hubbell 25, 26
Roosevelt, Franklin D. IX, 19
Rosser-James, William 87, 94, 97, 114, 119
Rubin, Steven Jay 213
Russhon, General Charles 152-154

Salem, Pamela 194
Saltzman, Harry VII, 40, 48, 62, 106, 107, 109, 110, 119, 121, 123, 125, 129, 133, 135, 139, 141, 143, 145-147, 150, 151, 154, 159, 164, 165, 172, 175-177, 187, 188, 228, 231, 232, 234
Savalas, Telly 194
Schlesinger, John 14, 110
Schwartzman, Jack 189, 190, 191, 197, 198, 203-206, 209, 211, 212, 215
Sellers, Peter 125
Semple Jr, Lorenzo 191, 193, 198, 201, 202, 206
Shepperton Studios 13, 26, 37, 145
Shire, Talia 189
Sigrist, Bobo 110
Silent Enemy, The 35, 36, 39, 48
Simmons, Bob 139, 147, 165, 168, 169, 172
Sinatra, Frank 21, 143
Sinden, Donald 59

Skone-James 102, 103, 111
Slocombe, Douglas 203
Solomon, Michael 178
Sony 231, 233
Sony Pictures 225, 226, 227, 228, 229
Sopel, Stanley 139
Spy Who Loved Me, The 165, 187, 232
Star Wars 139
Stears, John 135, 152, 158, 161, 168
Stein, Jules 80, 81, 82, 84, 85
Steinbeck, John 14, 15
Stephenson, Sir William 19, 20
Stewart, James 51, 55, 61
Suitor, Bill 139
Sullivan, Nicholas 160
Sunday Times 12, 58, 105, 112
Sydow, Max von 194, 195

Taliafilm 189, 218, 228
Taylor, Andrew 219, 221-223
Taylor, Elizabeth 12, 219
Taylor, Rod 123, 124
Thunderball (Novel) V, 24, 32, 73-75, 90, 95, 97-100, 102, 103, 105, 106, 110, 112, 114, 117, 120, 127, 143
Times, The 105
Todd, Michael (Mike) 12, 13, 14, 15, 20, 87, 145
Todd, Richard 59
Tomblin, David 199, 203, 205
Tomorrow Never Dies 149, 226
Tors, Ivan 153, 154, 156, 160, 161, 177

Udell, Ronnie 153
United Artists 106, 107, 139, 171, 187, 188, 191, 211, 217, 225-227

Vaughan, Jeremy 14, 40, 57, 107, 129, 176, 181, 233, 234
View to a Kill, A 64
Von Ryan's Express 143

Wacker III, Charles 35, 42
Walker, Alexander 177
Ware, Leon 15
Warhead 183, 184, 187, 189, 228
Warner Brothers 83, 190, 225
Warwick, Dionne 171
Waugh, Evelyn 122
We Don't Belong 216
Welch, Raquel 141, 172
Welles, Orson 186
West of Zanzibar 45
Whitford, John 111
Whittingham, Derek 46
Whittingham, Jack VI, VII, VIII, IX, X, 14, 45, 46, 48-54, 57, 58, 61-66, 68-79, 81-85, 87-90, 95-97, 100-103, 106, 109, 110, 112-120, 127-129, 131, 148, 182, 216-218, 227, 231-234
Whittingham, Jonathan 72, 120, 217
Whittingham, Margot 129, 130
Whittingham, Neville 46
Whittingham, Sylvan (see Mason, Sylvan Whittingham)
Wigan, Gareth 225
Wilberforce, Justice 102, 103
Wilson, Michael G. 208, 226, 232, 233
Wood, Christopher 187
World is not Enough, The 232

Xanadu Productions IX, 15, 16, 18, 20, 21, 24-27, 34, 35, 38, 39, 41-43, 47, 55, 56-58, 60-66, 68, 70-72, 77, 78, 80, 82, 83, 85-87, 89, 90, 94-97, 102, 107, 113-115, 118-120

You Only Live Once: Memories of Ian Fleming 121, 182
You Only Live Twice 58, 88, 149, 153, 156, 165, 172, 179, 183, 190, 199, 201, 232
Young, Freddie 88
Young, Terence 40, 107, 129, 134, 135, 137, 141, 143, 144, 146, 148-152, 155-157, 159-161, 163, 168, 169, 172, 173, 177-179, 190, 233

Zanuck, Richard 142
Zyl, Nikki van der 172